The Britannia Diaries
1863–1875

Selections from the Diaries of
Frederick C. Wilton

Edited by

JIM DAVIS

From the original manuscript in the
Mitchell Library,
State Library of New South Wales

SOCIETY FOR THEATRE RESEARCH

First published in 1992
by The Society for Theatre Research
c/o The Theatre Museum, 1E Tavistock Street
Covent Garden, London WC2E 7PA

© 1992 The Society for Theatre Research
ISBN 0 85430 052 X

Printed in Great Britain
at the Alden Press, Oxford

Contents

Acknowledgements

The discovery of Wilton's Diaries in the Mitchell Collection of the State Library of New South Wales was something of an accident. I was checking through the catalogue of the Mitchell Collection for quite other reasons when I came across a reference to the Britannia Theatre. I made a mental note to have a look at the material listed at some future date and, a couple of months later, ordered the Wilton manuscripts, not expecting to find much more than a few receipts and lots of blank pages. However, once I began to read the first closely packed volume of Wilton's diaries, it soon became clear that here was a unique and detailed account of $12\frac{1}{2}$ years in the life of one of East London's leading theatres during the Victorian period. I found Wilton a curiously empathetic figure: like him, I was born in Bristol, England; like him, I lived in east London (even performing once or twice at Hoxton Hall, just across the road from the Britannia's site), in the early 1970s; and eventually I too migrated to Australia. Yet it was on account of the value of the material in his diaries rather than any personal affinity that it seemed imperative than the theatrical contents of the diaries should be published.

My first debts of gratitude, therefore, are to the State Library of New South Wales for granting me permission to publish selections from the Wilton manuscripts and to the Society for Theatre Research for taking up my suggestion of an edition of selections from Wilton's diaries, thus providing me with the incentive to prepare this book. In particular, I am very grateful to George Speaight, whose enthusiasm for this project and editorial skills have provided enormous support. He has contributed much to the identification of (and footnotes on) performers mentioned in the diaries, as well as providing help and advice in the selection of illustrations. He has coped with the problem of communicating between continents and has been tireless in his efforts on behalf of this book.

Inevitably, in the course of researching this edition, I have been greatly aided both by individuals and institutions. In particular, I would like to thank Clive Barker, the late Kathleen Barker (even generous with her time and interest), Tracy C.Davis, John Golder, Kevin Long, Bill Manley, David Mayer and Jack Reading for help in various ways. I am also grateful to David Mander and his staff at the Hackney Archives; Stephen Holland of the Library of the University of Kent at Canterbury; the Theatre Museum; the Greater London Record Office; the Public Record Office; the British Library (Reading Room, Manuscripts and Newspaper Division); the Guildhall Library; Exeter Public Library; and Somerset County Records Office.

Research support and study leave from the University of New South Wales are also gratefully acknowledged. I should like to thank the following for hospitality and support during my visits to England: Bill and Laurette Bray, Michael Collins, Ches Coyne, Andrew Davies, Martin Priestman, Pat Roach, Bill, Anne and Michael Rogers and Queenie Saoul.

JIM DAVIS

Illustrations

The Britannia Theatre Managerial Tree on page 240 is reproduced by permission of *Theatre Survey*, the Journal of the American Society for Theatre Research.

Introduction

The Origins of the Britannia Theatre

The origins of the Britannia Theatre are intricately bound up with the fortunes of Samuel Lane, a Devonshire man who trained as a carpenter and served in the navy before coming to London[1]. In the 1830s he and his first wife, Mary, had been landlord and landlady of the Union Tavern in Shoreditch High Street. Attached to the tavern was a saloon, in which two performances an evening were given. According to J.A.Cave:

> Here the best talent was to be found, for the proprietor was a man of spirit and enterprise, and very soon made his theatre one of the most popular in the metropolis. The programme usually comprised a drama, and a variety of singing and dancing[2].

Lane held (or had applied for) a Music and Dancing License from the Middlesex magistracy, but this did not officially entitle him to present spoken drama. Under the new Metropolitan Police Act, brought in by the Whig government in 1839, greater powers were given to the police to put a stop to performances contravening licensing regulations, in order to safeguard the interests of those already holding licenses. It seems possible that the Union Saloon was selected in advance for a police raid as a means of testing the new act. One Monday evening, early in September 1839, a large body of constables was taken to the Union Saloon, where Inspector Robinson, giving evidence, said he:

> found Mrs Lane acting as a check-taker at the inner door, and on entering the room he perceived two men and a woman dressed in character upon the stage, all of whom on seeing his party immediately made their exit. He pursued them into a small room under the stage, where he found several performers . . . . The saloon was in the meantime the scene of the wildest confusion from the efforts on the part of the company to escape, many of whom made their way up to the roof, and fled over the adjoining house-tops, dislodging tiles and demolishing glass in every direction. The other prisoners were selected out of the audience and conveyed to the station-house. He saw on the stage a regular scene, capable of being shifted and rolled up[3].

There was an audience of about 900 present, in a room about 60 feet long, at the end of which was a stage about 7 feet high and 17 feet wide, fronted by 19 gas lights, assembled to witness *The History of Lumpkin's Journey* and *The Three Lovers' Plot and Counterplot*. Many criticised the police action, some of the local magistracy disassociating themselves from the prosecution, and there were complaints that the police had used unnecessary harshness:

> It happened that three gallons of beer were accidentally capsized in the rush

made by the panic-stricken assemblage, and the defendant's wife, who was unfortunately standing under it, received the whole of the 'heavy' cascade upon her person, which was drenched from head to foot, notwithstanding which the police refused to allow her to retire and change her apparel, although earnestly urged to do so[4].

The *Weekly Dispatch* commented:

> We have received several letters . . . from which it appears (the police) acted with unnecessary violence when they made the capture. The fellows rushed about more like madmen than conservators of the peace and destroyed many articles of value[5].

The police had refused bail for many of the audience taken into custody (about 70 in number), including three servants of a Mr Pearce, an ex-church warden.

The police case included evidence that amongst the audience in custody were several associates of thieves, one convicted smasher and a common prostitute[6]. However, the majority proved to be respectable local citizens: their fines were paid by members of the local authorities to ensure that none of them remained in prison. Officially, the penalties were a fine of £20 or two month's imprisonment with hard labour for procuring such an entertainment; one month's imprisonment with hard labour or a fine of 40s for being present. In this instance Mrs Lane was fined 40s or fourteen days' imprisonment and all other prisoners either 5s or 1s each. Samuel Lane was summonsed separately and appeared at Worship Street charged 'with unlawfully keeping a house for the performance of stage plays and dramatic entertainments, the same not being a licensed theatre, whereby he had incurred a penalty of £20 or two months' imprisonment, under the New Police Act'. However, the magistrate, Mr Grove, dismissed the case, on the grounds that the evidence was insubstantial and that, since he was dealing with a highly penal statute, he could not convict without the clearest evidence. Moreover, even if stage plays had been performed, he considered the fine exacted against Lane's wife was sufficient penalty[7].

In consequence of the prosecution Lane closed the Royal Union Saloon and next materialised as landlord of the Britannia Tavern, which he took over from John Noah Crowder, in whose name a Music and Dancing License had already been granted[8]. Situated in Hoxton the Britannia Tavern, in its earliest days, as suggested by John Hollingshead, might have been a tea-gardens[9]. It certainly existed in 1792, in which year the Britannia Public House and Gardens were advertised for auction[10]. In 1839 there is a press report of a fatal fight outside the Britannia Public House[11]. According to Hollingshead, Hoxton, at the time Lane moved there:

> retained some of its old rural characteristics. It was still celebrated . . . as the home of madhouses and meeting houses. If on one side of the old winding 'High Street' you saw a 'tabernacle', on the other side you were sure to see the barrel windows of a private asylum. The psalm-singer and the howling maniac had a large share in the town, as the nursery gardener had in the surrounding country. Business people who lived over their shops, warehouses or offices in the city of London looked upon an evening drive to Hoxton as a country trip

in the days before railways and steam boats . . . . In the fullness of time these gardens were claimed by the speculative builder . . . and a jungle of not very sightly brick work grew up and smothered the flowers[12].

On assuming his tenancy of the Britannia Tavern, Lane immediately erected a theatre in the tavern gardens, which opened on Easter Monday, 1841, with entertainments under the direction of Henry Howard (of the City of London Theatre). A company of about 50 performers was employed, including Miss Pearce (later a popular music hall vocalist at the Oxford and Canterbury halls) from the nearby Grecian Saloon and a Miss Bloomfield from the Italian Opera. John Douglass, second only to T.P.Cooke in nautical roles and later to be manager of the Standard Theatre, was also in the company, as was J.A.Cave, both as an actor and, with Richard Flexmore, as part of a black-face entertainment. Cave recalls how:

> The first part of the sports consisted of an excellent concert given by some of the most popular vocalists of the day . . . . The concert was followed by an entirely new melodrama . . . entitled *The Red Lance, or The Merrie Men of Hoxton* (E.Lancaster) . . . . The piece was interspersed with songs and choruses; one, I remember, was from Weber's *Der Freischutz*, 'Why, good people, are you gazing?' The production was marked by the closest attention to every detail, and in the matters of scenery, costumes, and properties could not have been better presented at any West-End theatre of the day . . . . The drama was followed by an Intermezzo, in the course of which I and Flexmore 'brought down the house' with 'Jim along Josey' and the 'Squash Hollow Hornpipe'. The performance terminated with the farce of *The Tailor of Tamworth* . . .[13].

As well as farces, domestic dramas and spectacles, dancing, rope-dancing, singing, gymnastics and even a balloon ascent from the grounds of the theatre featured amongst the entertainments. An early review of the Royal Britannia Saloon commented that Lane:

> evinces considerable taste in his selection of *artistes*; and the flattering success that he meets with shews that his labours do not go unrewarded. Lancaster's beautiful spectacle of *Warwick the Kingmaker, or the White and Red Roses*, written especially for this establishment, has met with great success, having been performed nearly 50 nights. In addition to the above, the vaudevilles are highly amusing, and the dancing and singing excellent[14].

Such success was short-lived, for in October 1841, when Lane applied for a Music and Dancing License in his own name for the Britannia, his application was refused. It was to be two years before he could open the Saloon again for regular dramatic entertainments, as a result of the Theatre Regulations Act of 1843, which took away the licensing of metro-politan theatres and saloons from the local magistracy and invested it in the Lord Chamberlain's Office.

The history of the Britannia from 1841–1843 is best reported in Lane's own words (or more probably those of his lawyer) in a memorandum submitted to the Lord Chamberlain in 1843:

> In or about the month of December 1840 I became the purchaser of a Mr

Crowder's interest in the Britannia Tavern, which was then licensed for Music and Dancing . . . . At the period of my so becoming the purchaser the Room in which the stage representations took place was not larger than 33 feet by 18 feet and the stage occupied a large portion of such room. Conceiving that so long as the performances were conducted with decorum and propriety that the license would be granted as heretofore, and at the request and solicitation of many of the frequenters of the tavern, I discontinued the performances in the small room and at an outlay of between £2000 and £3000 built a theatre capable of accommodating about 150 in the boxes and 850 persons in the pit, and gave a performance there which immediately raised the character of the property under my direction from continual loss to a source of great emolument. Commencing such performances about the Easter Monday of the year 1841 and continuing until the Quarter Sessions of the month of October of the same year . . . . I then made an application for the first time in my own name to the magistrates for a license believing that I had entitled myself thereto from having afforded greater accommodation to the public by the Building I had erected and also from the great improvement I had effected in the style of entertainment given . . . . I was however unfortunate in such application . . . . Of course the magistracy did not give any decided reason for their refusal, but I gleaned . . . that it was in consequence of my having built the Theatre and discontinued the Room to which I have before alluded. In the hope of a more favourable result if I were enabled to resume my application in the ensuing year and with a view also of not offending the authorities by whom such License was to be granted I refrained from continuing the performances and immediately discharged the company there under my management – The failure to obtain a License led to other misfortunes and I became a Bankrupt, but am proud to say that the Brewers Messrs Elliot, who were my largest creditors, retained me in the House. I passed my last examination and obtained the allowances of my certificate with as little delay as the forms of law would permit. In the month of October 1842, on the annual licensing day, I again applied and was again unsuccessful, although my application was seconded by the Officers of the Parish and most of the respectable inhabitants, the same reason being urged against the granting of the license as before . . . but I cannot disguise . . . that much stress was laid upon the fact of my having failed, although such failure was entirely owing to my being deprived of my license in the year 1841 after I had expended my means in the erection of the theatre . . . . Since that period I have kept open the Theatre by merely having a Pianoforte and engaging vocalists to sing, without giving any Theatre or stage representation – While I kept open the theatre in 1841 under Mr Crowder's license the character of the entertainment was melodrama and farce . . . . The price of admission to the Theatre was one shilling to the Boxes and sixpence to the Pit; the performers engaged by me amounted in number generally to about 35; and persons altogether about the establishment to about 50. The theatre when licensed was open all the year except the nights expressly forbidden. The class of persons engaged by me were those holding respectable situations in other minor theatres and my weekly expenses amounted to about £80 or £90[15].

Lane also drew attention to the serious loss already sustained, after expending the savings of many years, through the refusal to grant him a license. A note on the bottom of the memorandum stated that Lane's actors were paid 2/6 per night and that his profits were about £25 per week.

Lane's request for a license from the Lord Chamberlain was supported by his brewery and also by local inhabitants of Hoxton. Trustees, overseers and church wardens of the parish all signed a testimonial on his behalf, as well as many local tradesmen (shoemakers, cheesemongers, drapers, dyers, coal and timber merchants, cabmen, auctioneers and pocket book makers amongst them). One of the reasons given for licensing the Britannia was the need for a neighbourhood theatre, since previously local inhabitants had been compelled to walk or incur the expense of riding a considerable distance to a theatre, there not being one nearer than the City of London Theatre at Bishopsgate, which was most inconvenient to get to in the winter season. The Britannia was granted a license along with the Eagle (or Grecian) Saloon, the Albert, the Earl of Effingham, the Apollo and the Albion. All these theatres were designated saloons since access was only possible to the theatre buildings through the taverns to which they were attached. This distinguished them from those buildings licensed as theatres, where access was independent of any other building. Drinking and smoking were prohibited in the saloons themselves, thus differentiating them from those establishments which were to develop into music halls[16].

Lane's troubles were still not over. Raided by the police in 1839, refused Music and Dancing Licenses in 1841 and 1842, he seems to have been a marked man. In 1844 a number of police reports spoke of the Britannia in most favourable terms. The first – dated 22 July – stated that the Albert and Britannia Saloons were resorted to 'by the lowest class – prostitutes and thieves – old and young – who are admitted nightly for 6d at the Albert and 3d each at the Britannia'[17]. On 20 September another report on the Britannia stated that:

> This place is (resorted to) by the very lowest grade of both sexes viz. Watercress girls, Hearth stone and match boys and girls from about 10 to 16 years of age. There can be no doubt that this place is calculated to corrupt the morals of the growing youth in that low and thickly populated neighbourhood to a great extent[18].

Lane was summoned to the Lord Chamberlain's Office, where the police report was read to him. Lane maintained that no-one under age was admitted to the saloon and suggested that the police report had been concocted to benefit another saloon and injure him. On 27 September Lane wrote to the Lord Chamberlain denying the charges made against the Britannia relative to admission charges and audience composition. He pointed out that there had been no complaints made to the Police Court in the district arising from any disturbances in the saloon and that the loss of his license would endanger the livelihood of about 100 people as well as spelling utter ruin for him. He added:

> The only reason I can assign for the complaint is that about a week since about 40 or 50 boys congregated outside the Saloon and I was compelled to

seek the assistance of the Police to remove them, but my impression was that such boys were sent there for the purpose of creating a disturbance and to bring me into disrepute[19].

The following day Lane sent to the Lord Chamberlain a certificate of his having conducted the saloon in 'a proper and decorous manner', signed by Church Wardens, Trustees of the Poor, Trustees of the Parish, and many of the most respectable inhabitants living contiguous to the saloon. A further memorial from 104 local inhabitants also arrived, stating that they had been in the habit of visiting the Britannia regularly during the previous year, that the audience had been 'quiet and respectable' and that they were entirely satisfied with Lane's conduct of his establishment.

Lane was summoned again to visit the Lord Chamberlain's Office on 30 September, along with Brading of the Albert Saloon and Allen of the Apollo, and told that the saloons would be permitted to open, so as not to injure those employed by them, but that renewal of their licenses would depend on their merits. On 3 October a further police report was sent to the Lord Chamberlain, showing that the police had not forgotten Lane's former history. He was erroneously described as the former Proprietor of the Standard Theatre, Shoreditch, and it was stated that the licensing magistrates of Clerkenwell Court had discontinued his license 'in consequence of the improper manner in which he conducted' the Standard. The report added that Lane had been refused a license for the Britannia in 1842 by the Bench who remarked that he 'was not a fit or proper person to grant (a) Music License to'. As for his management of the Britannia Theatre since 1843:

> Since he obtained his present license, the Establishment has been resorted to by the lowest class of Prostitutes and Juvenile Thieves who are supposed to form one half of the audience – There are also a number of Blackguard Boys – who assemble outside during the performance obstructing the thoroughfare, insulting the passengers and annoying the inhabitants by their noise and foul language and some of them have thrown water (brought from an adjacent pump) over respectable persons as they passed and on the Police attempting to take them into custody they took shelter in the Saloon. From 26th April last there have been 7 persons charged before the magistrates from this place, 5 of them for disorderly conduct and 2 for assault . . . . The inhabitants of the neighbourhood have repeatedly complained to the police of this Saloon being a perfect nuisance.
> It has frequently occupied the time of 2 or 3 PCs to maintain order and keep the thoroughfare clear in front of the house[20].

As a result of this report the Britannia was described as 'an unmitigated nuisance' and since 'the neighbourhood is altogether bad . . . the recommendation of the inhabitants rather tells *against* the Saloon than for it'[21]. Nevertheless, the commissioner of police, Mr (later Sir Richard) Mayne, advised that Lane should have his license renewed, on the express understanding that it would be cancelled if the unfavourable reports continued – consequently, the license was only provisionally renewed for 2 months. Lane was again summoned to the Lord Chamberlain's Office on 10 October.

What especially wrankled was Lane's alleged effrontery in denying the truth of the police reports, which had been drawn up by two Inspectors and 11 constables. Two points were emphasised in the meeting with Lane:

> 1st the great nuisance caused to the neighbourhood by the numbers of blackguard boys who crowded about the front of the saloon, for the purpose of selling Tickets of Admission to the Passers by – insulting those who would not be purchasers – using obscene language and being otherwise most disorderly. 2nd the fact that great numbers of the lowest sort of prostitutes and other characters resorted to his saloon, who from their conversation and behaviour would make it impossible for any respectable people to avail themselves of the Britannia[22].

Lane felt the report was highly coloured, but conceded that some boys did occasionally cause an obstruction in the street opposite his saloon – some of these might be present in the hope of securing checks from those leaving the theatre early, either to resell or to gain admission themselves; others were occupied in selling fruit. He flatly denied the presence of prostitutes in the audience, claiming that 'his house was resorted to by respectable working people and Tradespeople and their families'. However, he agreed to co-operate – he had no other option – and to assist in any future prosecution of boys who were creating a public nuisance outside the establishment. The license was renewed and a police report of 24/3/1845 stated that the Britannia was now conducted in an orderly and proper manner and that there had not been any complaints of any sort[23].

The Britannia Saloon: 1843–1858

When the Britannia Saloon re-opened in October, 1843, its new company included E.Edwards, 'one of the best melodrama actors of the 30s and 40s'[24] as stage manager, vocalists such as Jo Plumpton and Richard Starmer, and a Miss Wilton (actually Sarah Borrow, the future Sarah Lane). Many new plays were added to the repertoire and some, such as *Warwick the Kingmaker*, were once again revived. In December 1843 Frederick Wilton joined the company for the first time as stage manager and staged the first Britannia pantomime, *The Giant Frost, or Harlequin Robin and the Fairy of the Rose*. In January 1844 he staged *The Drunkard's Doom*, another play by Edward Lancaster, who seems to have been the theatre's first house dramatist. Wilton departed in 1844, to return two years later, but in the meantime George Dibdin Pitt took on the function of house dramatist and acting manager. From 1845–1846 the celebrated melodramatic actor, N.T.Hicks, was employed as stage manager, a period recalled by P.Hanley:

> Hicks opened as Rolla on December 26th 1845 and shortly afterwards appeared in a drama entitled *The Wizard of the North, or The Ship of the Avenger*. He played the dual characters of a pirate captain and the commander of an English frigate, characters which he had represented most successfully at other theatres. Then came several new pieces from the pen of

the veteran author and actor Mr Dibdin Pitt. The leading actor at the time Hicks appeared was Mr H.Dudley, who was exceedingly popular, so that there was a strong professional rivalry between the two actors, and as the author generally wrote two good parts in each piece their chances were pretty equal[25].

The Britannia Saloon established a strong repertory, an excellent company and an ever increasing reputation during the late 1840s and 1850s. Dibdin Pitt provided a constant succession of Gothic and domestic melodramas, including the first ever Sweeney Todd play, *The String of Pearls*, adapted from a serial in *Lloyd's People's Periodical* and first performed in February 1846. He was capable of writing a new drama almost every fortnight, including such plays as *Varley the Vulture*, versions of George Cruikshank's *The Bottle* and *The Drunkard's Progress*, and *Lady Hatton*, which Dickens described when he visited the Saloon in 1850. Demons, apparitions of the skeleton monk and the King of Terrors, 'a grand and awful view of Pandemonium, and Lake of Transparent Rolling Fire', were amongst the memorable features of the last-named play. The quality of presentation enhanced the appeal of such dramas: 'At no minor Theatre in London', commented the *Theatrical Times* (17/3/1849), 'do we find more attention paid to the "getting up" of pieces'. Without an appropriate repertoire of plays, however, it is unlikely that the theatre would have succeeded on staging alone. According to one account:

> One peculiarity of the Britannia, and one to which its long and prosperous career may be largely due, is its always employing its own stock dramatists. They were not Shakespeares . . . but they were as a rule men with a wide knowledge of stage effect and a complete knowledge of the audience they catered for. Everything that had once tickled and pleased a Britannia audience was more or less thinly disguised in all the plays that succeeded, they were all cast in the true Britannia mould, and there was never the least doubt about their success in a greater or smaller degree. Failures were almost unknown[26].

The formulaic quality of Britannia plays was to continue in the work of future house dramatists like William Seaman, who followed Pitt, and the prolific Colin Hazlewood. The formula was, of course, quite straightforward:

> Strange adventures by sea and land occupy the stage of 'The Britannia' and the incidents are frequently such as to keep crowded audiences in a state of breathless suspense. They follow the fortunes of some domestic heroine who is possibly, for a time, in the power of a villain; and the thwarting of his nefarious schemes, and the ultimate triumph of persecuted beauty and innocence, eventually bring down the curtain amidst tremendous cheering[27].

The most popular melodramas were revived again and again over the years; yet the Britannia did not rely on revivals, for it submitted on average more new plays for licensing each year than any other theatre in London[28]. Melodrama was the mainstay of the theatre's repertory, but the longest running production each year was the pantomime, eventually considered to be one of the best in London, and by the end of the century one of the last to retain the traditional pattern of an 'Opening' followed by a Harlequinade. Farce was only occasionally played, although burlesque was a little more frequent from the late 1850s. From its beginnings the theatre maintained a policy of employing 'extras' – gymnasts, vocalists such as W.G.Ross and Charles Woodman, trapezists, clog dancers and others – to appear between the plays.

A strong, loyal and long-serving company was gradually assembled by Samuel Lane. His first wife, Mary, died in childbirth, probably between 1841 and 1843, and he married Sarah Borrow around 1846–1847. Sarah Lane, as she now became, combined the vocal skills of Nelly Power with the acting ability of the veteran Mrs Keeley. She performed at the Britannia for almost 56 years, her presence in the cast of any play guaranteeing an additional attraction. Those who remained with the company for around thirty years or more included Frederick Wilton, Cecil Pitt (the prompter), Robert Rowe (master carpenter since 1841), Joseph Reynolds (leading actor), and G.B.Bigwood (who became the theatre's low comedian in 1862). The Borrow family also became increasingly involved in the theatre: Sarah Lane's father, William Borrow, became the theatre's treasurer in 1844 and two of her sisters, Charlotte and Polly, made their debuts as actresses at the Britannia. Charlotte married a Britannia actor, W.R. Crauford, formerly of the Bower Saloon and particularly strong in dialect parts – in 1858 he also became landlord of the Britannia Tavern. Polly married William Robinson, who became acting manager of the theatre in the 1870s, whilst Sarah's brother, William, married Celeste Stephan, the theatre's premiere danseuse from 1850. An uncle of Sarah Lane's, a Mr Fowles, acted as surety for the theatre in the 1850s and early 60s, while a cousin of hers, named Gregory, was employed as a super. Among the actors who joined the Britannia company in the 1850s and provided long service were John Parry (who played the 'heavies'), W.Newham (pantaloon and low comedian) and his wife, C.J.Bird and Emma Yarnold. Of all the actors employed as regular members of the stock company Joseph Reynold and, latterly, G.B.Bigwood, were perhaps the most celebrated. Reynolds:

> was strikingly like Phelps in appearance, both as regards his figure and his remarkably mobile face. Without being as great as that master of tragedy and comedy, Joe Reynolds was very impressive and had a strong vein of pathos[29].

The long service of actors such as Reynolds and Bigwood undoubtedly contributed to the appeal and popularity of the Britannia's offerings, just as the Borrow dynasty provided a secure framework through which the theatre could operate.

As well as its own company the Britannia also employed actors in starring engagements. In 1852 and 1857 the negro tragedian Ira Aldridge was at the Britannia, where he played Othello (Reynolds was Iago) and Aaron the Moor in *Titus Andronicus* (Shakespeare's play transformed into a run-of-the-mill melodrama for the occasion). In 1851 the tragedian James Anderson opened at the Britannia for a three week engagement, at a salary variously given as £100 and £120 per week. He played his first role, Coriolanus, to:

> a house crammed and jammed from floor to ceiling with an enthusiastic crew. I played the tragedy four times in the first week. *Macbeth, Hamlet, Othello, The Robbers, Richard III* and *William Tell* drew tremendous houses in the following weeks. Between Easter and Whit-Monday is a trying time for the folks at Hoxton. However, the manager neither grumbled nor complained, but always continued courteous and cordial throughout the many engagements I have played with him. Mr and Mrs Lane were very jolly people, and most kind and hospitable[30].

Although Anderson writes with a certain degree of hyperbole about his popularity at the Britannia Theatre, he was to return there several times over the next twenty years. Another tragedian, who enjoyed an even longer association with the Britannia, was J.B.Howe. He first played at the theatre for W.Newham's benefit, probably in 1852. The following day he was offered a 12 month engagement, at a salary of £2 per week, with half a clear benefit. However, on reading his contract, he found that although he was engaged for a share of the leading business, it was not for the 'lion's share'. The fact that he could play a leading role one night, but sink to the role of ostler in *Dick Turpin* the next, determined him to break his contract and try his luck in America. Consequently, despite a rise in salary to £3 per week, he left the theatre surreptitiously after his benefit night. On returning to England Howe was again engaged at the Britannia, sometimes as a stock actor and sometimes as a star[31]. Other starring engagements included that of Lysander Thomson, a provincial actor who specialised in Yorkshire characters, in 1849.

Lane was enterprising in his choice of personnel, be they dramatists, actors, visiting stars or speciality acts. Among others who became closely associated with the Britannia and contributed to its reputation in their different ways, were Samuel May (costumier), W.Clarkson (wig-maker), W.Paine (pyrotechnist and founder of the famous fireworks dynasty), H.Morgan (limelight man) and William Batey (caterer, who went on to found a lemonade and ginger beer factory locally). By 1849 it was clear that the saloon was too small for the audiences it was drawing and the standards it emulated; if John Hollingshead is to be believed, the theatre had been so constructed that, 'to get to the stage boxes, you had to go on the stage and ascend a ladder at the side amongst the ropes, at the imminent risk of ringing the curtain bell and bringing down the curtain'[32], although the plan of the theatre submitted to the Lord Chamberlain in 1843 fails to clarify whether this was so[33]. Whether or not the accommodation was as cramped as this, Lane certainly succeeded in rebuilding and enlarging the theatre without closing it down for a single night. The *Theatrical Journal* (28 June, 1849) commented on the gorgeous decoration of the theatre and the fact it had been 'fitted up with all the latest mechanical improvements'; so concerned had Lane been for the safety and comfort of the public that the commissioners appointed under the building act to inspect the reconstructed premises hinted that he had been rather too lavish in his expenditure.

A police report of 1847 showed that Lane's enterprise was also attracting a more acceptable audience:

> a great many respectable Tradesmen and Mechanics, with their wives and children, generally frequented the Boxes there, the Galleries being frequented by the lower classes of both sexes from the age of 12 years and upwards. Children under the age of 12 years are generally accompanied by their parents or friends . . . . Smoking is strictly prohibited in the Saloon, and any parties misconducting themselves are immediately expelled by the officers belonging to the establishment . . . . Mr Lane has conducted it (the Saloon) much better for the last 2 years than when it was first opened[34].

In 1850 Dickens visited the Saloon and his account provides an even fuller testimony as to the nature of the theatre and its audience:

> The place was crammed to excess, in all parts. Among the audience were a large number of boys and youths, and a great many very young girls grown into bold women before they had well ceased to be children. These last were the worst features of the whole crowd, and were more prominent there than in any other sort of public assembly that we know of, except at a public execution. There was no drink supplied, beyond the contents of the porter-can (magnified in its dimensions, perhaps), which may be usually seen traversing the galleries of the largest Theatres as well as the least, and which was seen here everywhere. Huge ham sandwiches, piled on trays like deals in a timber-yard, were handed about for sale to the hungry; and there was no stint of oranges, cakes, brandy-balls, or other similar refreshments. The Theatre was capacious, with a very large, capable stage, well lighted, well appointed, and managed in a business-like, orderly manner in all respects . . .[35].

Dickens noticed that one advantage of this theatre was that proper provision was made for the audience to see and hear, instead of their being packed away in a dark gap in the roof, as they were at Drury Lane or Covent Garden. As a result:

> The audience, being able to see and hear, were very attentive. They were so closely packed that they took a little time in settling down after any pause; but otherwise the general disposition was to lose nothing, and to check (in no choice language) any disturber of the business of the scene[36].

Dickens' comments support the view that the Britannia's reputation was on the ascent; placed beside the earlier police reports, a definite improvement seems to have taken place.

The relationship with the Lord Chamberlain's Office also improved after its uneasy beginnings. Occasionally plays were submitted late for licensing, allegedly because the copyist 'had been extremely ill'[37] or because of 'the circumstance of the stage manager being nearly at the point of death, which has caused the greatest confusion in the Theatre'[38] – both 1845. Lane was eager to assure the Examiner of Plays, John Mitchell Kemble, that one of these plays, Dibdin Pitt's *Tally Ho*, was 'a moral lesson and of an exemplary Domestic nature . . . . There is no allusion to either Church, Highway or Politics', while *The Primrose of Ireland* (also

1845) was described as 'of a simple and unobjectionable nature'[39]. Plays were occasionally refused a license: *Terry Tyrone (the Irish Tam O'Shanter); or, the Red Beggar of Ballingford* (G.D.Pitt) was not allowed in 1847, because it took the Irish rebel Robert Emmet as its hero. Another play by Pitt, *The Revolution of Paris; or, The Patriot Deputy*, was refused a license in 1848, because it related too closely to contemporary events in France. Lane, who wrote to say that it would be 'improper' to stage it at the present time, was actually thanked by the Lord Chamberlain for his 'good discretion and rightmindedness' in withdrawing this particular play from examination[40]. In 1853 yet another play of Pitt's, *Wrath's Whirlwind; or the Neglected Child, the Vicious Youth and the Degraded Man* was refused a license. A member of the Lord Chamberlain's staff wrote, in regard to this play, that 'it is highly desirable to elevate the tone of the drama and it is especially necessary in the case of the Saloons to prevent as much as possible the representation of any pieces which have a tendency to lower the morals and excite the passions of the classes who frequent those places of resort'[41]. In 1854 and 1855 the management was warned that, in the case of *Eliza Fenning* and *Lynch Law, or, the Warden of Galway* respectively, no representation of an execution, if such was intended, could be allowed upon the stage[42]. Yet, by 1862, W.B.Donne (then the examiner of plays) was amicably prepared to go over the manuscript of *George Barrington, or, A Hundred Years Ago* with Frederick Wilton and 'by a very few cuttings rendered it unobjectionable'[43] and, when a questionable exchange of dialogue in *The Borderer's Son* was excised in 1874, Donne wrote that 'this slight excision is almost the one exception that proves the rule of the faultless characters of the Dramas licensed for that house'[44]. The improved relationship may have been partly due to Lane's increasingly co-operative attitude towards the Lord Chamberlain's Office; it also seems to date from W.B. Donne's full-time appointment as Examiner of Plays in 1857.

In 1856 Lane decided to pull down the old Britannia Theatre and build a new theatre on the same site. He employed as architects Finch, Hill and Paraire, submitting their plans to the Lord Chamberlain's Office and adopting all the recommendations made by Mr Fincham, the architect who accompanied Donne and Spencer Ponsonby when they inspected the theatres. On 12 May 1858 Lane visited Donne and laid before him plans for the proposed alterations to the Saloon. These had now been under consideration for two years and would involve alterations to the tavern and refreshment rooms, separate entrances to the Box and Pit, the whole interior would rest on solid bricks from 10–24 inches thick, the stage would be enlarged, as would the boxes and the gallery. At the request of Donne a new water tank with pumps and hoses attached would be supplied and the ventilation of the theatre improved. It was agreed that the theatre would be inspected before it again opened to the public[45].

The Britannia Saloon closed in July 1858 and rebuilding commenced. In October, as the theatre was nearing completion, Lane approached the Lord Chamberlain for permission to call the Britannia a Theatre instead of a Saloon. He had once before applied, unsuccessfully, in 1848 for this change in nomenclature, when he had argued that he had endeavoured to give support to 'the legitimate English drama' by engaging at heavy expense D.W.Obaldistone, J.R.Scott, J.H.Kirby, E.Saville, N.T.Hicks and many others. He added that he had experienced great difficulty in persuading several of these performers to accept engagements, on the grounds that accepting an engagement at a Saloon would lessen their character and position in public esteem[46]. Now he argued the need for the change on account of the extra accommodation provided, the need to improve the character of the dramatic performances, and because there was no longer any communication between the Theatre and Hotel. This last factor was the decisive one in determining the status of a theatre as opposed to a saloon and Donne argued within the Lord Chamberlain's Office that the Britannia should be granted full status as a theatre. Firstly, Donne described how the Theatre and Hotel were separated:

> in so far as no one can pass from one to the other without going round by the street, or without passing through different barriers where the check takers and servants of the Lessee are stationed. The respective bars of the Hotel and Theatre are, in the proposed arrangement, kept apart by an inner parlour, appropriated to the waiters, and by a wooden partition running from end to end. The upper panels of the partition will be of glass, but it will be ground or figured glass, so that the customers at either bar will be invisible to each other, besides being some yards apart[47].

Since the theatrical and hotel customers would be henceforth separated from each other and since both establishments were under Lane's control, who would thus have a vested interest in maintaining orderly conduct within the hotel, Donne was convinced that the situation at the theatre would be much improved. Donne also spoke highly of Lane's intentions:

> Mr Lane himself is not only a highly respectable man, but desirous also to raise the dramatic character of his house, and first and last has expended, I am informed, many thousands of pounds upon it . . . . I think, too, though he has not directly mentioned the subject to me, that he would gladly, and advantageously to himself and the public, accept your kind offer to entitle his establishment *Theatre* and not *Saloon*. The latter word has ugly associations connected with it, and moreover is in itself a bar to the performances being advertised in the *Times*, and other respectable journals[48].

Donne considered that, provided the Saloons 'raised the character of their performances', all would benefit and an empty distinction done away with.

The New Britannia Theatre 1858

Despite a builders' strike, work on the new Britannia Theatre was still completed on schedule. The overriding criterion in the design of the new theatre was to provide a close and adequate view of the stage from all parts of the theatre. To this end an elliptical form, rather than the more usual semi-circular or horseshoe shape, was chosen for the auditorium. A description of the new building appeared in *The Builder* (25/9/1858):

> The site of the Hoxton Theatre may be described as two parallelograms of ground, whereof one, next High Street, 36 feet by 52 feet, is appropriated to a tavern and two entrance-ways, – and the other, at the back, 150 feet by 110 feet, is occupied by the theatre and its accessories – as promenades, scene-painters' rooms, and carpenters' shop. Between the two main buildings is a corridor, to be covered with glass. Into this, both the entrances lead; and it is united by wide archways to a similar space in the theatre building, at the back of the pit, the whole together forming a promenade of 50 feet by 30 feet, from which access is gained to the pit, and by the staircases to the other parts of the house; but in the centre, the space corresponding in height with the two upper tiers is occupied by one large gallery, which extends to the full limit of the building, or over the saloon, which itself corresponds with that part of the promenade which is immediately attached to the pit. The pit extends under the lower tier of boxes. It measures 76 feet in width, and is 58 feet from the back wall to the orchestra front. The stage is the same width – 76 feet; and it measures 60 feet from the footlights to the back wall. The curtain opening in the proscenium is 35 feet across and 36 feet in height. A portion of the pit is arranged as stalls. The accommodation in that floor is estimated at 1,200 persons seated (1,000 in the general area and 200 in the stalls); but bringing into consideration the standing room in the promenade and at the back of the pit, it is thought that the total number will be 1,500 persons . . . . The seats in the lower tier of boxes . . . will give 600 sittings; but it is thought that standing-places in the refreshment room adjoining will raise the number to 650 persons. The side boxes in the upper tiers . . . and the great gallery . . . will altogether hold 1,250 persons; whilst the sum of accommodation in all parts of the house at 1 foot 6 inches to each sitter, will be 3,250 persons.

Plenty of egress had been provided in event of fire. The two entrances in High Street were each 14 feet wide and there were five staircases in the theatre, only one of which merely provided communication between different parts of the house. The roof of the theatre would be used neither for a property-room nor carpenters' shop nor for storage, since Lane felt that the roof was often the source from which fires commenced in theatres; more pragmatically, he also acknowledged that it was harder to supervise work carried out in so inaccessible a venue.

The decor within the new theatre was ornate, even slightly vulgar. The prevailing colour throughout the house was pale salmon, the enrichments being white, fawn and gold, relieved occasionally by vermillion and blue. The auditorium was lit by 16 small cut-glass chandeliers suspended from the pit ceiling, the work of Messrs De Fries and Son of Houndsditch. The *Building News* (12/11/1858) commented that the 'gods', when sitting on the upper seats of the gallery in a number of theatres, had frequently complained that their view of the stage was much impeded by the large chandelier used to light the auditorium; the Britannia's provision of smaller chandeliers was thus designed to counter such a problem. Equally, the ornamental portions of the ceiling had a function beyond mere decor: louvred openings, communicating with the internal area of the roof and with the open air, had been included to enable better ventilation. The proscenium was also profusely embellished:

> On each side are two twisted columns of peculiar design, finished in white and gold, and over them a highly-enriched entablature. The act-drop has been painted by Mr William Beverley, the eminent scene painter, and is a highly meritorious production. It is an original composition, having the ruins of a Roman temple in the foreground, with a group of figures, among which are recognised Apollo, as the principal, playing on the lyre. In the background is mountainous scenery, admirably painted[49].

The brick work was exceptionally fine; indeed, Lane was said to be so proud of it that it was deliberately left uncovered. The seats had not been painted, but the plain wood of the backs and rests had been varnished. The pit, which was separated from the stalls by wooden frames with open work panels of iron, had an unusual incline for that time – as much as 1 in 12, which enhanced considerably the view of the stage from that level.

Equally noteworthy were both the backstage and the refreshment facilities. Of the former the *Builder* (20/11/1858) stated:

> The stage floor inclines 1 inch in five feet; and it contains twelve of the 'slides' (formed by pieces of battens on canvas, and moveable by means of windlasses), required to be removed for the passage of a scene through the stage. For these purposes the space below the stage descends at the back to a depth of 18 feet. The height of the 'mezzanine', or floor where the traps are worked, is 6 feet. There are nine spaces left for traps, small and large . . . . The dressing-rooms are partly below, and for the ladies are at the side. The painting-room is to the north, external to the general plan. Also external are refreshment rooms, one on each side.

The range and spaciousness of the refreshment rooms were much commented upon. A writer in the *Illustrated Times* (11/12/1858) was particularly impressed by this aspect of the newly constructed theatre:

> There are three distinct refreshment rooms, upon the railway model, divided into first, second and third class – gallery, pit and boxes. Though the tavern part of the establishment is now completely divided from the theatre, it still exerts its beneficial influence upon the character of the refreshments . . . there is plenty of good, wholesome beer and ale, joints of meat and loaves of bread, and sandwiches piled up like mahogany planks at a timber wharf. The spirits you get *are* spirits; the wine *is* wine. Bottled beer is confined to the first-class refreshment room, and draught beer to the second and third.

The plain brick walls, broad passages and lofty arches of the new theatre reminded the writer of the terminus of the Great Northern Railway. The *Sunday Times* was also reminded of a large railway station in the provision of water closets, refreshment rooms and other conveniences at the theatre[50].

The cost of rebuilding the theatre and tavern was estimated at £15,000, allowing for refurnishing and re-equipping the premises, as well as clearing the site and rebuilding[51]. Wilton, however, gives a figure of £22,000. On 4 November, 1858, the new theatre was inspected, W.B.Donne noting that it had now been 'rendered one of the most spacious and commodious theatres in the metropolis'. All the suggestions made by the Lord Chamberlain's Office had been incorporated and Donne found it only necessary to state generally that:

1. The precautions against Fire are quite sufficient.
2. The ventilation is excellent in all parts of the Theatre.
3. The Exits and Entrances are numerous and of good width.
4. The doors, without exception, swing both ways.
5. The accommodation afforded to the public is very good especially in those parts of the House which are likely to be the most frequently visited viz. the pit and the gallery[52].

On 8 November the theatre re-opened with a programme which included a specially written piece by William Seaman, *Old Friends in New Frames*, in which a number of Britannia stalwarts gather on a seaside railway station, en route for the new Britannia. They fall asleep and are brought to wakefulness again by Sarah Lane, in the guise of Britannia, to whom they recount their experiences of the past few months – equestrian and provincial engagements in some instances, engagements at the Bower and City of London theatres in others. Although a strong emphasis was placed on welcoming back the old Britannia audience, the theatre now had aspirations to be more than just a 'People's Theatre', a designation that disappears from 1858 onwards. Playbills for the new theatre state that no persons will be admitted to the stalls or boxes unless suitably attired and emphasise that these can now be reached by separate entrances[53]. Such developments were likely to attract a more socially diverse audience and foster the improvements that both Donne and Lane desired[54].

The New Britannia Theatre – Post 1858

The new Britannia Theatre won golden opinions all round. One of the best designed and most capacious theatres in London, it particularly drew the praises of W.B.Donne, who wrote in his annual report on the London theatres in 1859 that:

> It would be very ungracious to Mr S.Lane . . . merely to record 'no defects'. For, in every respect, solidity of structure, commodious interior, number and facility of exits, precautions against casualties of every kind, uniformly good ventilation, and in everything conducing to the security and comfort of the Public, this Theatre, since its re-erection, stands pre-eminent[55].

He gave the Britannia an equally good report in 1860, adding as an appendix an article, written by Charles Dickens, which had appeared in *All the Year Round* (25/2/1860). Dickens was particularly impressed by the ventilation of the new theatre and by the scale on which it had been constructed:

> Magnificently lighted by a firmament of sparkling chandeliers, the building was ventilated to perfection. My sense of smell, without being particularly delicate, has been so offended in some of the commoner places of public

resort, that I have been obliged to leave them. The air of this Theatre was fresh, cool and wholesome. To help towards this end, very sensible precautions had been used, ingeniously combining the experience of hospitals and railway stations. Asphalte pavements substituted for wooden floors, honest bare walls of glazed brick and tile – even at the back of the boxes – for plaster and paper, no benches stuffed, and no carpeting of baize used: a cool material with a light glazed surface, being the covering of the seats. . . . It has been constructed from the ground to the roof, with a careful reference to sight and sound in every corner; the result is, that its form is beautiful, and that the appearance of the audience, as seen from the proscenium – with every face in it commanding the stage, and the whole so admirably raked and turned to that centre, that a hand can scarcely move in that great assemblage, without the movement being seen from thence – is highly remarkable in its union of vastness with compactness. The stage itself, and all its appurtenances of machinery, cellarage, height, and breadth, are on a scale more like the Scala at Milan, or the San Carlo at Naples, or the Grand Opera at Paris . . . .

Dickens stated that his objective in visiting the Britannia was to examine its spectators and he provides an impressionistic description of the pantomime audience in 1860:

We were a motley assemblage of people, and we had a good many boys and young men among us; we had also many girls and young women. To represent, however, that we did not include a very great number, and a very fair proportion of family groups, would be to make a gross misstatement. Such groups were to be seen in all parts of the house; in the boxes and stalls particularly, they were composed of persons of very decent appearance, who had many children with them. Among our dresses there were most kinds of shabby and greasy wear, and much fustian and corduroy that was neither sound nor fragrant. Besides prowlers and idlers, we were mechanics, dock-labourers, costermongers, petty tradesmen, small clerks, milliners, stay-makers, shoe-binders, slop workers, poor workers in a hundred highways and byeways. Many of us – on the whole, the majority – were not at all clean and not at all choice in our lives or conversation.

An equally impressionistic view of the audience around this period is provided by Thomas Erle, the usefulness of whose reports is marred by their sacrifice of authenticity to facetiousness. He refers to the fact that babes in arms are admitted to the theatre and describes the youths in the gallery:

who are gifted with a flow of exuberant animal spirits which find a safety valve in shrill whistlings . . . . Since the temperature up in their sixpenny heaven is so high . . . they find it 'cool and convenient' to sit without their coats. They evince, too, a noble independence of bearing and sentiment towards the swells in the body of the house (who are in this case the counter-skippers of Kingsland and Dalston) by turning their backs to the chandelier, and sitting along the gallery rail like a row of sparrows at a telegraph wire. In this position they confront their friends in the back settlements, and exchange with them a light fusillade of bandinage . . . which is sustained with much animation during the time that the curtain is down between the pieces[56].

Such accounts, although lacking in empirical weight, suggest that the

Britannia audience retained its popular and local characteristics, despite the changes of 1858.

Further light on audience composition and behaviour at the Britannia is shed by an account published in *L'International* (11 & 12/5/1870), a French journal based in London. The author of this had been attracted to a benefit performance at the Britannia by a large red poster he had seen stuck to a public house door in Hoxton. He arrived at 9.o'clock, after the first piece was over, and after noticing the smell of gas from the crowded Britannia Tavern, entered the theatre and purchased a ticket for the stalls. He first visited the refreshment room common to the boxes and stalls; the bloated faces and bulbous noses he observed on entering reminded him of the average bar room in an ordinary public house. Two fish wives, drinking gin, their elbows resting on the bar counter, were pitying the misfortunes of the heroine in the previous play; two young men in their Sunday best were talking animatedly to two female labourers; others were sitting alone, looking sadly at their drinks. As soon as someone called out the next play was about to start, the bar emptied in seconds. On entering the auditorium the writer was struck by three features in particular: the ornateness, equal in appearance to any West End theatre; the strong 'smell of poverty'; and the 'sea of moving heads' in the gallery, receding into darkness. He noticed that, even though they were in their shirt sleeves, sweat still streamed down the gallery occupants' faces and made their clothes stick to their skin. In the stalls and pit he noticed many young female workers from the neighbourhood, accompanied by their sweethearts; many children; but few older people. He was also struck by the fact that no-one seemed to remove the hats they were wearing. The noise was tremendous, particularly from the gallery, where the occupants were passed back to their places over the heads of the spectators already seated. When the curtain at last rose, cries of Order, Order went on for so long that much of the first scene was lost. Throughout the action the audience kept up a running commentary; if it became too noisy there were further cries of 'Order!', although these might only provoke further outbursts. Meanwhile the actors, evidently accustomed to the din, continued to play as if nothing had happened. At the end of the play the audience again went wild; their cries, however, were overwhelmed by shrill and piercing whistles, which seemed to be the normal mode of applause at the Britannia. The heroine, when called back on the stage, was showered with orange peel. Then there was an interval before the last piece; this time the writer traversed the brick corridors and colonnades of cement known as the 'Catacombs' to the pit bar; this was packed with drinkers who, if not very genteel in appearance, provided the most picturesque of sights.

The only dissatisfied customer, in the aftermath of all the improvements at the Britannia, seems to have been a J.Brooks, who wrote to the Lord Chamberlain complaining that he had not been allowed egress from the theatre to obtain refreshment in 1864, unless he paid admission again for re-entry. He claimed that this was a source of constant complaint amongst the visitors to the theatre, since it restricted them to drinking the 'abominable' concoctions sold at the theatre at 15–25% more than could be obtained elsewhere in the neighbourhood. Another problem was the constant passage of 'the Proprietor's servants with long cans of porter . . . which are not only knocked wrecklessly against the audience, but frequently some of the contents are spilt over them'; if anyone complained, they were abused. The letter, with name and address deleted, was forwarded to Lane, who replied angrily that he didn't give return checks as the practice had led in the past to an assemblage of disreputable persons annoying the audiences as they left the theatre and obstructing passers by, and that anyone who wished to leave the theatre and return was free to do so, if he informed the check taker. Apart from feeling that the writer of the letter should be 'criminally indicted' Lane vouched for the quality and low prices of his refreshments, a factor which tended to encourage the majority of his audiences to remain within the theatre:

> The articles all sold here are positively as good as can be bought – I have never heard of any complaints respecting the persons who take in the refreshments – The Ginger Beer is sold at 1d the Bottle – Porter 1d the Half Pint – sandwiches of Ham and Beef 1d each – Bread $\frac{1}{2}$d a slice – Pastry, Fruit &c &c all equally cheap and decidely cheaper than in the neighbourhood. Spirits are never taken into the theatre for sale . . . .

W.B.Donne noted, at the bottom of Lane's letter:

> I am inclined to believe all Mr Lane's statements. On one or two occasions I have been to various parts of the Britannia . . . and observed nothing to lead me to infer discontent or disorder of any kind[57].

Problems of a different sort beset Lane as authors began to be more protective of their copyright. In 1860 he agreed to withdraw *Eily O'Connor*, under threat of an injunction from Boucicault, on the grounds that the action of Hazlewood's new play was based on *The Colleen Bawn*. Once Boucicault's rights were conceded, permission was granted for the Britannia play to continue[58]. Subsequently he even offered the Britannia's Eily, Charlotte Crauford, an engagement to play Eily in the touring production of *The Colleen Bawn*, an offer she was unable to accept[59]. A year later another Hazlewood adaptation was placed in jeopardy when the proprietor of *All the Year Round* issued a notice threatening to serve an injunction if Dickens' tale *A Message from the Sea* were to be performed. On the night advertised as its first performance Frederick Wilton appeared on the stage to ask the audience's indulgence and said that the play of *Charley Wagg* would be substituted. Dickens wrote to *The Times* (8/1/1861) stating that he and Wilkie Collins had been unwilling to assert the principle of copyright against the proprietor of the Britannia Theatre. He praised the frank and honest way in which the proprietor had instantly withdrawn the piece, on the night it was announced for performance, and when the audience was assembled. He regretted that he had been unable to give Lane earlier notice and thereby inconvenienced a gentleman for whom he had a great respect. The difficulties were soon resolved, for the play subsequently figured in the Britannia's repertory[60].

By the early 1860s the Britannia had firmly consolidated its position in the east end of London, a position it was to maintain until the end of the century. A definite yearly cycle had also evolved. The season began annually on Boxing Day with the Britannia pantomime, which usually ran for about twelve weeks. A second piece, usually performed for the first time on the last night of the old season for Sarah Lane's benefit, followed it – invariably a melodrama of some sort. At Easter and Whitsun new pieces were produced for the holiday audiences – sometimes a spectacular melodrama, sometimes a burlesque. During the summer months, when the actors took their benefits, and a range of visiting artists was engaged, Sam and Sarah Lane were absent from the theatre. Lane was an ardent yachtsman, owning two yachts, the *Wanderer* and the *Phantom*; a member of the Royal Thames Yacht Club, he had won over 50 trophies. He once told James Anderson that the two pit stands for selling apples, oranges and ginger beer paid all the expenses for keeping his two yachts throughout the year[61], although a supernumerary named Milton claimed that he paid for them out of the supers' fines levied at the theatre each year[62]. Sarah Lane made her reappearance in October in a new piece brought out for her sister, Charlotte's and, latterly, W.R.Crauford's, benefit. This was always a melodrama. In early November the annual production of *Guy Fawkes* with fireworks drew crowded houses and in mid-December Sarah Lane took her benefit on the last night of the season. This occasion always included the unique and celebrated 'Britannia Festival', which commenced when the green-baize curtain (known locally as the 'cabbage leaf') rose to reveal the Britannia company, seated in a semi-circle around the stage, each individual dressed as his or her most popular role from the preceding season. The proceedings were initiated by Frederick Wilton, in his everyday role as stage manager, then each performer came down to the footlights in turn and spoke a few rhyming couplets alluding to the character impersonated. Later accounts suggest that gifts were showered upon the performers by the audience[63], whilst Sarah Lane, at the centre of the festivities, was regaled with floral tributes, an otherwise rare offering in the east end[64]. Crauford states that the Festival commenced on the night the old theatre closed in 1858, but extant playbills show that it was in existence earlier than this, for in 1855 the 'Festival' proved so popular that an extra performance of Sarah Lane's benefit programme had to be given.

The annual Britannia pantomime was usually based on a nursery tale, except for a period of French influence in the 1870s. Although *Entr'acte* (9/12/1871) scathingly called the Britannia pantomime 'a melodrama played in large masks' and attacked it for its lack of humour, other reports were more favourable. The pantomime usually began with an overture of popular airs, such as 'Pretty Polly Perkins of Paddington Green' and other music hall favourites, accompanied and often drowned by the hands and feet of the gallery inhabitants. The music hall influence continued through the 'Opening': in 1870 20 to 30 music hall songs were allegedly included, whilst in 1866 Esther Jacobs had introduced the popular 'Champagne Charlie'; as might be expected, the audience usually joined in the choruses.

The regular Britannia company, particularly Sarah Lane and the low comedians, Bigwood and Elton, were a feature of these 'Openings', as were specially engaged burlesque artists like Esther Jacobs and, from the late 1860s, music hall stars, including Fred Foster, Patti Goddard and G.H.MacDermott. The 'Opening' always contained many topical allusions: banking swindles, Fenianism, the suppression of skittle playing, income tax grievances, the privileges of the rich, poor law overseers and guardians, ministers of state were among the subjects targeted. Sometimes topical figures appeared thinly disguised, as in the case of Sir Roger De Wrenne in the 1871 pantomime, whose make-up approximated to the appearance of the Tichborne claimant[65]. The 'Opening' moved inevitably into a gorgeous transformation scene, always a highpoint of the Britannia pantomime. Then followed the 'Comic Scenes' or Harlequinade, in which the antics of Harlequin, Columbine, Clown and Pantaloon were interspersed with the activities of the 'sprites', usually embodied by a troupe of acrobats. The satire of the 'Comic Scenes' was usually less specific, although anti-authoritarian in spirit. Jean Louis, for many years the Britannia Clown, showed the usual disrespect for other people's property and W.H.Newham proved 'as ancient and helpless a Pantaloon as could be wished'[66]. Most memorable of all was the audience assembled on Boxing Day for the pantomime's first performance. Consisting largely of boys, who beguiled the time before the pantomime began by flicking orange peel at each other, it was so noisy that the pantomime could hardly be heard above the uproar[67].

The melodramas of the 1860s and 70s tended to take the side of the underdog, a number of them supporting the victims of poverty and a fair proportion revealing a strong sympathy with the plight of the Irish. Spectacle and good acting roles were often the major determinants in a melodrama's popularity, however, and the Britannia's ghost effects and sensation scenes invariably drew crowded houses. Among the most frequently revived melodramas at this theatre was *Lady Audley's Secret*, mainly on the strength of the scope it offered for bravura performances by leading actresses. Hazlewood, the author of this particular play, was the most prolific contributor of plays to the Britannia during this period and his sources ranged from recently published novels and serialisations in such journals as the *Family Herald* and *Bow Bells* to juvenile literature, popular paintings and newspaper reports. The drawing power of melodrama was enhanced through the 1860s and onwards by an escalation in the number of music hall acts engaged, a factor that led H.Chance Newton to describe the Britannia as the most prolific of all London theatres in its provision of regular engagements to music hall artists[68].

Hazlewood wrote at least 125 new pantomimes, burlesques and melodramas for the Britannia Theatre during the $12\frac{1}{2}$ years covered by Wilton's diaries. This represents about $\frac{2}{3}$ of the new plays presented at the Britannia during this period. After Hazlewood the most prolific authors of new works over these years were Dibdin Pitt's two sons, Cecil and W.H.Pitt, with just under 20 new plays, and Frederick Marchant with 12. The most regularly performed dramatist after Hazlewood was Dibdin Pitt, about 30 of whose dramas were revived for longer than 'one-off' benefit performances between 1863 and 1875. Plays written by Hazlewood prior to 1863 were also revived during this time. However, Hazlewood is never officially referred to as house dramatist and, throughout his association with the Britannia, wrote frequently for other theatres as well. Sometimes the Britannia commissioned a new play from him, sometimes he offered the theatre a new piece, but he does not seem to have been paid a regular salary. He does not appear on the 1862 list of salaried staff presented to the Lord Chamberlain, which is printed below. Surviving letters of Hazlewood written to the publisher Thomas Lacy, between 1869–1871, suggest frequent impecuniosity. Although this need not imply the lack of a regular salary, the letters, which are preserved in the Hackney Archives, suggest that he depended on the outright sale of his plays to theatre or publisher to secure his livelihood. Indeed, it may have suited both the Britannia management and Hazlewood to operate within a free market economy as far as the sale and purchase of plays was concerned. Despite H.Chance Newton's claim (*Referee*, 27 January, 1924) that Hazlewood was actually employed at the Britannia as a resident dramatist and that his job was to 'furnish forth a new drama, about every fortnight or so, at a salary varying from £3 to £5 per week', no other evidence authenticates this statement.

Such, then, was the routine and programme of the Britannia during the years covered by Wilton's Diaries. By a fortunate co-incidence it is also possible to provide full details of the Britannia's company just prior to the Diaries' commencement. In 1862 the Lord Chamberlain agreed for the first time that the theatres might open during Passion Week. This alleviated great hardship, since normally theatre companies lost a week's salary as a result of this enforced closure. A number of theatres sent petitions to the Lord Chamberlain thanking him for lifting the ban. Included amongst these was a petition from the Britannia Theatre, neatly compiled in Frederick Wilton's handwriting, listing every member of the company and their function. Exceptionally, the Britannia also sent a second list, with number of dependants enumerated against each name, to show how large a number had benefited from the new edict[69]. (See list on pages 24 and 25.)

The Later History of the Britannia Theatre

The period of 1863–1875 is fully documented in Wilton's *Diaries*, which may be allowed to speak for themselves. Perhaps the most significant event in this period was the death of Samuel Lane, late in 1871, as a result of which Sarah Lane became manageress of the theatre. In 1872 the death of her father, William Borrow, who had been acting manager of the theatre, led to the engagement of sister Polly's husband, William Robinson, in his place. A.L.Crauford writes of this period that:

> The reputation and prosperity of the theatre for a few years was fairly well
> maintained, but gradually a decline began to show itself, the cause of which

was as follows. There was no longer a manager with the flair for the selection of attractions. An outside sinister influence took a hand in choosing the plays and this soon made itself felt.

This was Johnny Gideon, who began to send plays over from Paris:

> Dolores . . . being a great romantic play, was a considerable success. On the strength of this, Gideon bombarded Sallie (Sarah Lane) with French plays. But they were not *Patries* (Sardou's original from which *Dolores* was adapted): they were utterly over the heads of the Hoxtonians and consequently quite unsuitable. Yet Sallie considered Gideon was infallible and unwisely tried to force indigestible food upon her patrons.

Although she was an outstanding performer, Sarah Lane, in the opinion of her nephew, Crauford, was not a good manageress and needed someone to rely on. William Robinson, however:

> was not particularly adapted for the part; he was a very good square peg, but in a round hole! After all one cannot be *facile princeps* in all things. He was, however, too much of a businessman not to see that the Britannia was going downhill and with growing acceleration. He ventured to protest strongly against these French importations. Sallie resented his interference. Quarrels arose. Business became worse and worse[70].

Since Crauford replaced Robinson as acting manager in 1881, his account may be slightly one-sided. It is worth noting, as Clive Barker has pointed out, that throughout this time the Britannia also retained much of its more traditional repertoire[71].

After a brief incursion into French influences the Britannia pantomime returned to its unique form. Authors were encouraged to use original stories, rather than the fairy tales used in modern pantomime, with plenty of scope for trap-work, spectacle and the traditional Harlequinade. During the 1880s Tom Lovell became a regular fixture as the Britannia Clown; at the end of the decades the Lupinos (briefly at the Britannia in the mid-70s) returned and played there throughout the 1890s. The engagement of music hall stars continued: Marie Lloyd, Charles Coburn, C.H.Chirgwin (the 'White-eyed Kafir') and Topsy Sinden were amongst the artists employed. These later pantomimes were invariably written for the Britannia by J.Addison. Yet, despite the traditional form of the pantomime, a major shift of policy did occur at the Britannia in the 1880s, when far more West End successes were imported into Hoxton. These were always played by the stock Britannia company rather than by a touring company and old Britannia favourites also remained in the repertory. George R.Sims' *Romany Rye*, produced at the Princess's Theatre by Wilson Barrett and first performed at the Britannia in 1882, is

The Britannia Company 1862

Actors	Supernumeraries constantly employed in the theatre	Ladies of the Ballet constantly employed at the theatre
J.Reynolds		
W.R.Crauford		
T.G.Drummond	J.Aldridge	E.Green
J.Parry	C.Brown	Beaver
J.Holloway	W.Milton	E.Westbrook
G.Harding	H.Fisher	K.Scott
C.Pitt (Prompter)	Medcalf	Melrose
F.Marchant	Dixon	Rogers
E.Elton	Davison	Geary
G.Blythe	Oakes	Sylvester
W.Newham	J.C.Abbott	Pearson
J.Plumpton	Taylor	Westbrook
J.Marshall	Rodway	Groves
F.Wilton (Stage	Manning	Claremont
Manager)	Luff*	Mrs Bailey*
G.B.Bigwood	E.Chamberlain*	Mrs Maynard*
		Miss Rodway*
Actresses	Money-Takers	E.Giles*
Mrs Sarah Lane	B.Bridgins	
Mrs E.Yarnold	Walter Farmer	Check-takers
Mrs Atkinson	W.Borrow	J.Carter
Mrs W.Crauford	J.Palmer	J.Wall
Mrs W.Newham		T.Swain
Miss A.Downing	Stage door-keepers	D.Jacobs
Miss Elton	F.Buck	W.Huntley
Mdlle C.Stephan	T.Swaine	A.Andrews
Miss E.Clayton		E.Elliot
		J.Thorne
Treasurer		J.Perkins
W.Borrow		A.Matthews

Orchestra
W.H.Brinkworth
  (Leader)
E.Craven (2nd
  Violin)
G.Acraman
  (Violincello)
H.Geneiver (Flute)
T.Mason (Cornet)
E.Perry (Drummer)
G.Burford
  (Repetiteur)
E.Furber (Tenor)
H.Betts (Bass)
T.Riddle (Cornet)
G.Rogers
  (Trombone)

Scene painters
John Gray
H.Muir

*Assistant scene painter
constantly engaged*
F.Matthews

*Property men
constantly engaged*
W.Hart
J.Short

*Carpenters and scene
shifters constantly
engaged*
R.Rowe (Master
  Carpenter)
Elijah Pryce
Robert Kell
C.Wallace
E.Maynard
T.Bruce
J.Kirck
R.McMillan
T.Sampson
Kendrick
T.Attwood
J.Jones
D.Monks
W.Jefferies

Pyrotechnics
Wm.Pain
H. Morgan

Bill deliverers
C.Chapman
T.Raynor
T.Davey
J.Grey**
H.Summers**
T.Rainbird**

Saloon-keepers
W.Batey
W.Morgan
W.Ellis
Henry Fowles
J.Plumridge
J.Light
R.Bradley
W.Dorman
Alfred Cowell
W.Clarke
W.Rugg
J.Long
W.Strange
H.Cunningham

*Saloon-keepers'
assistants*
W.Brown
J.Loveridge
R.Simons
W.Hall

Wardrobe
S.May

Cleaners
Mrs Ellen Bayliss
Mrs Matthews
Mrs Clements
Mr J.Matthews

*Entered on second list – may not have been constantly employed.
**Also employed as Saloon Assistants.

one of the first examples of this trend. By 1887 the transfer of West End plays had become a regular policy: Sims' *Lights O'London*; Henry Arthur Jones's *The Silver King* and *The Noble Vagabond*; Adelphi melodramas such as *Harbour Lights*, *In the Ranks* (Sims and Pettit) and *Shall He Forgive Her*; Drury Lane melodramas, including *The Duchess of Coolgardie* and Raleigh and Hamilton's *White Heather* (both 1898); all of these figured among the West End melodramas also to be seen in Hoxton. Irish plays, particularly Boucicault's *Aarah Na Pogue* and *The Shaughran*, were also presented during these years, although the most popular genre was undoubtedly military melodrama. Sarah Lane herself spoke of these changes in an interview given not long before her death:

> . . . she remarked on the change that had come over the audience. *The Middleman* had just been performed there with great success. 'I can remember the time, many years ago', she said, 'when *The Middleman* wouldn't have drawn at all after the first night. In those days we used to put on such awful rigmaroles as *Sweeney Todd, the Barber of Fleet Street*, who used to murder the people who came to be shaved, cut them up, and sell them to Mrs Lovat, a pastry cook, to make pies of them. But', she added, 'the play must have a good moral, whatever it is; our people wouldn't care for anything that hadn't a moral'[72].

An account of Sarah Lane in a series entitled *Women of the World*, published in 1890, described how she would 'have nothing said or done upon the stage that shall tend to debase the minds of those who give her their support'[73]. This was borne out by her response to a complaint made about a W.Parker who was engaged at the theatre in November 1875. According to the *Weekly Independent*:

> a most indecent suggestive song is sung between the pieces by a person who comes upon the stage with his face blackened. These doggerel verses have the refrain of 'cover it up' and they cause many an artisan's wife and daughter to hang her head in shame.

A copy of the review was sent to J.Ponsonby Fane at the Lord Chamberlain's Office, who wrote to Sarah Lane, drawing her attention to the problem. She immediately wrote in reply that she was sorry that they should have been troubled to write to her about the song, which was 'of the ordinary style of music hall singing':

> I told him on Saturday night not to sing it as there was an objection to it – he replied 'tis one of my best songs and I am singing it nightly at two other houses. He left my theatre then and will not sing in it again . . .[74].

In returning the 1877–78 pantomime *Rominagrobis* to the Britannia, with a list of omissions, the Lord Chamberlain's Office commented:

> the introduction of notoriously objectionable songs from the Music Halls before audiences largely composed of women and children will doubtless be prevented by the manager of this well-conducted theatre[75].

Indeed, the only black spot in later dealings with the Lord Chamberlain's Office was a request that in *Called to the Front* (1885) the playbills should omit describing the villain, Captain Frazer, as 'of the Guards':

By the unnecessary identification of the villain of the piece, the writer commits an unwarrantable libel on the British army, and by such an offence to the public and patriotic feeling, abuses and depraves the privilege of the stage[76].

Overall, the Britannia continued to maintain its good relationship with the authorities, at least until the London County Council took over some of the Lord Chamberlain's functions.

Sarah Lane seems to have been held in high regard by her employees. 'An autocrat in matters of organisation and discipline', she:

was a true democrat in spirit. To a great extent she gave back with one hand what she received with the other. She not only allowed those who worked for her 'a living wage', but when bad times came upon them she provided for their needs[77].

That Sarah Lane was clear-headed and quick to make decisions is indicated in many of her pencilled notes to Wilton concerning stage business and lines to be cut on surviving Britannia prompt copies[78]. Her selection of personnel was, despite Crauford's claims, as astute as her husband's had been in many cases and many still served the theatre for long periods. Bigwood, who ceased drinking heavily and became a teatotaller, was appointed stage manager by the 1890s; he later retired to Southend where, the longest surviving member of the Britannia company, he ran a tobacconist's shop. After the retirement of Joseph Reynolds the theatre's leading man was a Devonian, Algernon Syms, who commanded great popularity. J.B.Howe, who was determined to die in harness, re-engaged with the company, as did his wife, a former Britannia actress of chambermaids, Julia Summers. Indeed, in October 1901, Howe celebrated his diamond jubilee benefit on the boards of the Britannia Theatre, playing *Richard III*. Howe's contract with the management of the Britannia when he rejoined the company in 1888 still survives. He was engaged at £1 per night for the period from the termination of the pantomime through to Sarah Lane's benefit, with half a clear benefit after expenses. He had to agree to play whatever cast: a refusal would render him liable to a fine of £15 plus one week's salary or to the cancellation of his engagement. If he was ill for a period in excess of six weeks his engagement would cease; needless to say, no salary would be paid for any night he was absent due to illness. He was not allowed to play at any other theatre, without prior permission of the management, and was liable again to a fine of £15 for each breach of contract[79]. Such provisions suggest that the longevity of the Lanes' association with the Britannia was due as much to good business sense as to a pastoral regard for their employees.

If the repertoire and performers at the Britannia gradually changed, so arguably did the audiences. By the end of the century Hoxton had become a much poorer neighbourhood and the audience, once again, was an increasingly local one. Even in 1885 John Hollingshead wrote that the Britannia's audience was essentially a local one. He claimed that it drew none of its audience from the western districts and that audiences, actors and pieces were more or less of native growth[80]. This is not altogether true, in so far as a number of actors, however long their period with the theatre, were not necessarily natives of East London; moreover, the trend towards presenting West End pieces had already commenced. In 1896 Crauford told a reporter from the *Sketch* (24/6/1896) that the audience was a local one for everything but the pantomime. The audience was a poor one, particularly in the gallery:

> Coats were scanty, waistcoats few and far between, collars and neckties practically unknown . . . . There was a pathetic interest in the presence of hard-worked, anaemic-looking young boys and girls, who, after the hard week's labour in the factories, were enjoying their evening together.

Less than ten years later, according to John M.East, 'poverty, squalour and depression were to be seen everywhere (in the neighbourhood of Hoxton); indeed many families housed in nearby tenements were on the verge of starvation'[81]. A vivid description of the audience in the post-Wilton years is given in the *Illustrated London News*:

> The large and somewhat sombre auditorium, crammed to the uttermost limit of its capacity, the huge rake of the pit, extending far back into a vast and gloomy cavern under the balcony; and the enormous gallery, piled tier above tier to upper darkness with faces, seemingly packed one on top of the other, like sloping stacks of oranges in a fruiterer's, are most impressive. There are some white ties in the stalls, but these take the shape of those immense cotton bolsters wherewith gentlemen of the costermongering fraternity delight to encircle their throats. The stalls flank the orchestra on either side, and curly-headed children are to be seen seated on the knees of their parents in the front row. Children, indeed, abound; nor are baskets lacking. The Hoxtonians combine business with pleasure and, on Saturday especially, vary their marketing with a visit to the Britannia, bringing with them a store of perishable commodities[82].

Despite changes in the nature of the audience, the provision of food continued unabated. The *Sketch* critic described how 'strong men without coats, and with huge baskets on each arm, came among the audience, and dispensed sandwiches, saveloys, bread, pasties, ginger-beer and oranges'. Another visitor to the theatre in the 1890s, H.G.Hibbert, recalled that:

> Few restaurants got rid of so much solid food as the Britannia audience would consume during five or six hours dramatic debauch. Men walked to and fro incessantly with trays groaning beneath the weight of pies in infinite variety, thick slices of bread plastered with jam, chunks of cheese, slabby sandwiches, fried fish, jellied eels. Gallons of ale washed down mountains of food[83].

Under new management in the early years of the twentieth century the Britannia continued to live up to the reputation for refreshment achieved under the Lane management:

> The prevailing smell suggested a subtle blending of orange-peel, human perspiration, greasepaint, dust and pregnant women. The refreshments on sale included coram populo, thick boiled-beef sandwiches, tail and middle fish, hot saveloys and hot pies and peas. The provisions were handed around by shouting attendants staggering under the weight of their huge trays. The

hot pies and peas were contained in an iron canister about the size of an ordinary mop-bucket, beneath which was a lighted spirit lamp, to keep the contents hot. Two women followed at a discreet distance. Their function was to carry a small vat of gravy. When anybody purchased a twopenny pie and proceeded to bite a piece out of it, the gravy-vendor stepped forward briskly, and poured some gravy into the cavity left by the consumer.

Liquid refreshment was equally well organised. Draught beer was pumped up by strong-armed barmen at long pewter-covered counters. All round the auditorium were short-sleeved beer-bearers. Some carried the precious fluid in pewter pots, but that was a refinement reserved for the stall patrons. The pit and gallery folk were content with the use of cans. Other vendors wore zinc belts round their waist, and these were divided into porter and ale compartments. Each division was provided with a tap, from which the beer-bearer drew off a mug to measure. Not that the temperance playgoer was neglected. Special bars judiciously blended ginger-beer and lemonade[84].

Most of the practices described here derive from the Lane management: the many testimonies to the quality of the Britannia's catering suggest that this was, in fact, a key factor in the theatre's long-lived popularity.

Among those who described the Britannia towards the end of Sarah Lane's regime was George Bernard Shaw. Although his praises of the theatre stemmed partly from a desire to attack West End theatre practices, he provided a vivid impression of a visit to the pantomime in 1898. Having described the difficultly with which one turned to the stage, since the auditorium and composition of the audience were so fascinating in themselves, he referred to Sarah Lane as a manager who 'thrives on enterprise, and success, and is capable, self-contained, practical, vigilant, everything that a good general should be'[85]. The quality of staff employed at her theatre also impressed him: Bigwood, for instance, was 'a real stage-manager, to whom one can talk in unembarrassed terms as one capable man to another'. The quality of the pantomime, both in terms of presentation and performance, impressed Shaw, who noted also the pleasure caused by a rather Rabelaisian depiction of sea-sickness in one of the scenes. Despite the rather excessive length of the pantomime, Shaw was struck by the audience's response:

The enthusiasm of the pit on the last night . . . was frantic. There was a great flowing of flowers and confectionary on the stage . . . The atmosphere was altogether more bracing than at the other end of town.

Shaw recommended his readers to sample the Britannia pantomime in future years if they wished for a respite from the boredom and dreariness of the fare offered them in the West End.

The year in which Shaw visited the Britannia Theatre was also to be the last year in which Sarah Lane appeared in a Britannia Festival. On this occasion *Pure as the Driven Snow* was revived and Sarah Lane appeared in her role as Duchess of Coolgardie during the Festival part of the proceedings: those present on stage also included J.B.Howe and Algernon Syms. In 1899 she was compelled to give up the active part she still played in the Britannia's management, despite an apoplectic stroke some years previously. She died in the summer of that year, the funeral taking place on 22 August, when her body was brought from her residence in St. John's Wood to the Britannia, prior to her burial in Kensal Green Cemetery. The crowds that turned out were so immense that Hoxton Street was almost impassable. The cortege, which was preceded by mounted police, included a six-horse, glass-panelled carriage with plumes, a four-horsed floral carriage, and six mourning-coaches, each with four horses. Henry Irving was unable to attend, but sent his carriage and a wreath. Sarah Lane's estate had a net value of £122,320[86].

The ostentation of Sarah Lane's funeral and the almost legendary reputation enjoyed by the theatre concealed a number of problems that had been fermenting behind the scenes for some time. The building was old and unsafe; ever since the London County Council had taken over the Lord Chamberlain's function of inspecting the metropolitan theatres in 1889, the Britannia had been under increasing pressure. Not long before Sarah Lane's death the L.C.C. had ordered a full inspection of the theatre, a fact that both A.L.Crauford and his brother were aware of when they announced their intention of continuing in management and maintaining the old traditions. When the L.C.C. subsequently submitted a list of requisitions, including the demolition of adjacent properties, structural changes and various sanitary improvements, in all estimated to cost £8,000, as a condition of renewing the license, the Craufords changed their minds[87]. They cannot have been altogether surprised, since there had been difficulties throughout the 1890s. In 1891 when the theatre was asked to remove flap seats in the pit and gallery as a safety precaution, A.L.Crauford considered the request, together with a requirement for other structural alterations, was unreasonable, since he had already spent £3,000 over the last seven years in improving exits and staircases as a precaution against fire. The dispute was resolved in 1892, but only after Crauford had threatened to take the matter to arbitration[88]. The theatre was now subject to surprise inspections, such as that carried out on 5/2/1894, which led to the following report:

> This theatre was visited during the performance on Saturday night . . . . On that occasion one pair of the gallery entrance doors were bolted twenty minutes after the performance had commenced, all the barriers were fastened across the various entrances with bolt and stay bars: the lever handle bolts to the exits were fastened with string. There were three loose ladders against the wall in the gallery entrance.
>
> Behind the barriers the check takers were stationed with loose check box and chairs or stools. The house was crowded in every part; not only was every seat occupied, but every gangway was literally packed with people standing from the back or side of the seats to the walls. Although the house was so full people continued to be admitted and at 8.20 a fresh crowd entered for half price. This state of affairs was immediately pointed out to Mr Crauford the manager. He had the gallery doors unbolted and some of the barriers thrown back, but others remained fastened till 8.40. Mr Crauford estimated that there were over 3,500 in the house.
>
> To clear the pit exit the check taker would have had to take up his stool and

check box, and unfasten three separate barriers. It would have been perfectly impossible to do this if at any time a rush had occurred. The other entrances were similarly obstructed . . . . Mr Crauford stated that during the 11 years he had been manager of this theatre there had been two panics and no one had been hurt[89].

The report recommended that all these defects be immediately attended to and the theatre was visited again on the following Monday to check that they had been carried out. Just over a week later another visit was made: this time the gas lights on the stage were found to be defective, a number lacking wire guards to protect them; hydrants in the flies and on the stage were unconnected; and a gas stove in the caretaker's office and a coke stove in the painter's room were deemed too dangerous to remain[90]. In future years complaints were made about the amount of lumber stored in the flies, cellar and on stage (due partly to frequent changes of programme and consequently the need for accessible scenery); a small canvas enclosure on the stage, which was used as a dressing room; a carpenter's bench under the stage; insufficiently safe provision of limelight; the use of gas rings for heating size in the paint dock; lack of sufficient fire-proofing between the dressing rooms, workshops and property rooms on the south side of the theatre; broken lamps; and dirty and illegible exit notices[91]. By May 1899 the L.C.C.'s superintending architect had decided the time had come for a full-scale inspection of the Britannia Theatre. Over the next seven months the theatre was inspected not only by the architect, but also by the Metropolitan Fire Brigade, the Engineer's Department and the Public Health Authority.

The potential dangers of the Britannia Theatre had been identified as far back as 1887, when the *Saturday Review* published a series of articles on 'The State of the London Theatres'. The safety provision at the Britannia was deemed insufficient: a lack of exits, too many barriers, too many doors bolted, a labyrinth of passages, a man asleep across the gallery stairs, inadequate lighting were all criticised, foreshadowing some of the L.C.C.'s complaints[92]. Safety Regulations certainly became far more stringent under the L.C.C., but it is possible that the management, under Crauford, had grown rather slipshod in these areas. The reports that now materialised in 1899 and 1900 showed how impossible the situation had become. The Fire Brigade considered the theatre would have to be virtually reconstructed to reduce fire risks: better ventilation; new floors, walls and doors; repairs to the roof; the closure of the upper slips; and wider exits (with consequent loss of revenue) were all recommended. The Engineers' Department noted that there were no heating appliances in the public part of the theatre, but were mainly concerned with the dangers of 'a small portable steam boiler used for stage effects – heated by gas'. The architect observed that the theatre would fail to comply with L.C.C. regulations unless it occupied more land, but commented that a suitable supply of land was limited. Finally, the Public Health Committee criticised inadequate lavatory provision, poor ventilation, poor dressing room facilities and poor drainage[93].

With the departure of the Craufords the theatre's fortunes declined. The
new lessees lost the support both of local playgoers and also of the stage
staff, who went on strike and issued leaflets in Hoxton High Street urging
the public not to support the new management. Eventually Tom Barrasford took over the lease of the theatre, carrying out a number of renova-
tions and instituting a programme of twice-nightly variety. This was no
more successful and in 1904 Sidney Hyam and John East leased the theatre.
East, whose first precaution was to purchase a revolver, 'for rumour had
it that more criminals lived in the square mile surrounding the Britannia
Theatre, Hoxton, than in any comparable area in Great Britain'[94], retained
the majority of the resident stage staff, amongst whom was Monks, a
bill-poster, who had been employed at the Britannia for 55 years. His
opening attraction was *The Flood Tide* by Cecil Raleigh, the latest Drury
Lane success. Other revivals followed, including Charles Reade's *It's
Never Too Late to Mend*, but receipts began to fall off. Even such attractions as a weekday matinee, known locally as the 'Tit's Matinee', on account
of the breast-feeding mothers who attended it, failed to improve the
situation and in 1905 Hyam and East left the theatre with a month still to
run on their original lease. In March 1909 Barrasford gave up the theatre's
license to present stage plays and the theatre was used as a venue for
boxing matches[95]. An attempt by George Conquest to revive the Britannia
as a melodrama house from 1910–1911 failed and from 1913 onwards it
functioned almost exclusively as a cinema. In the Blitz of 1941 it was
totally destroyed by enemy action.

Frederick Wilton: Early Career

Frederick Charles Wilton was born in Bristol in the early years of the
nineteenth century. According to the census returns of 1861 and 1871 he
must have been born in 1803 or 1804, whilst an announcement of his death
in the *Era Almanack* for 1890 suggests that he must have been born in
1802. In a memo in his diaries he states that he was 45 when he joined the
Royal General Theatrical Fund in 1846, which suggests 1801 or 1802. His
date of birth was December 3rd, but Bristol records for the early nineteenth century are insufficient to confirm the year. The only information
concerning his family background that has come to light is that his father
was drowned together with an uncle surnamed James (according to the
diaries) and that he had a brother, James George Wilton, who died in
Bristol on 20 October, 1830[96].

Both Frederick and James became actors, which creates another conun-
drum, since they were actually in the same companies for some of the time.
A further complication ensues from the fact that Marie Wilton's father,
born about the same time as the Wilton brothers and hailing from nearby
Gloucestershire, was also a provincial actor, although not related. In
tracing Wilton's provincial career it has therefore been necessary to
separate these different Wiltons from each other. Frederick Wilton is not

connected with John Wilton of Wilton's Music Hall in any way and the anomaly that the actress Sarah Borrow (the future Sarah Lane) commenced her career under the pseudonym of Sarah Wilton is a further coincidence.

Wilton states in his diaries that he made his debut in James Dawson's and David Obaldistone's company at Devonport and travelled with them for five years, which means that his stage career must have commenced in 1821. Dawson's company played at Penzance, Redruth, Truro, Bodmin, Falmouth, Liskeard, Devonport and Dartmouth. The problem with tracing Wilton's activities in this company is that his brother seems to have belonged to it as well. A fellow actor was Robert Dyer, who recorded his experiences there in *Nine Years of an Actor's Life* in 1833. Dyer had joined the company in 1822. He refers to 'poor James Wilton, "who sleeps the sleep of those that dream not" . . . . Wilton was a hard, but sensible actor; in some things truly excellent and in all things good. But his littleness unaccountably made against him. There are many much less in stature than he, who yet appeared giants by his side; and while he strengthened the general axiom that "Mind gives dignity to the man" – for he had a six-foot intellect – yet he always appeared *under* a five-foot figure'[97]. This must be a reference to Wilton's brother, yet the slightness of stature and intellectual prowess would apply equally to Wilton himself. Equally, the numerous references to a Wilton in reviews of the Dawson company printed in *The Drama* (1821–1825) probably refer to James. Both Dyer and James Wilton eventually left Dawson to join Richard Brunton's company, which was playing the Exeter and Plymouth circuit, whilst in 1826 Frederick Wilton headed for an engagement in Scotland. Accompanying him was his wife, Amelia, whom he must have met during his time with Dawson. A native of Devonport she was two years younger than Wilton, according to the diaries, and seems to have appeared as a dancer and in minor roles, when not rearing her family[98].

Wilton's name appears on Edinburgh playbills from March 1826: he played small roles such as Corin in *As You Like It*, Gonzalo in *The Tempest* and Duncan in *Macbeth*, specialising in old men. He performed with such visiting stars as Charles Kemble, Charles Young and Edmund Kean. His wife was also occasionally billed in small parts. At Edinburgh he would have met James Dewar, musical arranger and leader of the orchestra at the theatre – the Dewar family, particularly James Dewar's son Fred and his daughter Rose, were to become firm friends of the Wiltons later in the century. In the summer of 1826 Wilton appeared at the Theatre Royal Perth, where his roles included Old Norval in *Douglas*, and he was there again in 1827 (as well as at Montrose), playing Iago for his benefit on 29 September. A youthful James Anderson, who had just joined the company, was later to recall how a small portion of the Edinburgh company played at Perth during the summer season under the leadership of Montague Smythson. 'During this season', he says, 'we had some clever, gentlemanly young fellows in the company', amongst whom he includes Frederick Wilton[99]. After the 1827 summer season at Perth

Wilton's name does not appear on playbills for the 1827–1828 season at Edinburgh[100].

Wilton's next traceable engagement was at the Birmingham Theatre, under Brunton's management, where his brother was already a member of the company. When the theatre opened on 26 May, 1828, he was announced as Mr F.Wilton from the Theatre Royal Perth and billed to play Duncan to Macready's *Macbeth* (a role he had played to Kean's *Macbeth* in Edinburgh). Wilton's wife occasionally appeared and visiting stars included John Liston, Charles Kean, T.P.Cooke and Madam Catalani. On 20 October, 1828, for the benefit of Messrs (J.) Wilton and Stuart, *The Comedy of Errors* was played, with the two Wiltons as the two Dromios[101]. The season closed on 15 December, 1828; a month later Brunton had moved his company back to Plymouth, where they had previously been based, and from 13 January 1829 both Wiltons feature on the Plymouth playbills. James Wilton soon disappeared from the bills (perhaps on account of ill health), but Wilton remained with Brunton, playing not only at Plymouth, but also at Bristol and Swansea for the next two years, until Brunton's bankruptcy in July 1831.

Wilton continued to specialise in playing old men, winning mixed notices for his performances. 'A Lover of the Drama' wrote to the *Bristol Gazette* (3/9/1829) that in *The Wood Demon* 'Mr F.Wilton was very diverting as Guelpho'. *Felix Farley's Bristol Journal* (16/1/1830) commended his Andrew in *The Vampire*. But, when he played with Macready, he drew less favourable comment, as in the premiere of *Werner*, when the critic of the *Bristol Gazette* (28/1/1830) said of Wilton's Stralaheim he could 'not speak in any terms of commendation: if anything would license the guilt of Ulric's crime, it was that his victim was already murdered'. And again, of his Appius Claudius to Macready's Virginius: 'If it was part of the author's plan to render the Decemviri unpalatable to the Romans, he could not have succeeded better: Mr Wilton's assumption of supreme power rendered it ridiculous: his declaration of passion for Virginia was merely disgusting. When he choked "no man cried, God bless him!" and the only effective hit he made was in setting off Mr Macready's attitude over his dead body'. (18/2/1830)

After Brunton's bankruptcy it is likely that Wilton remained connected with the Plymouth Theatre, for although there are no bills surviving in the collection at the British Library for 1831 and most of 1832, Wilton's name appears on a bill for 20 December, 1832. A number of names which recur in the diaries also appear on the bills at this time, including Vivash, Kimber and Davis. Wilton remained with the Plymouth company until May, 1836; then, from July of the same year, his name appears on playbills for the Devonport Theatre, once more under Dawson's management. On 17 October of that year he announced himself as stage manager of the Devonport Theatre:

Mr F.WILTON
in assuming the duties of the Stage Management, respectfully begs to state

that the most unremitting energy, regularity, and precision shall characterise the department over which he will have the honour to preside – The Curtain will rise every night *precisely* at the appointed hour. – The shortest possible time will be allowed to elapse between each Act, and 15 minutes only between each piece. He further promises that his time, his personal efforts, and his whole mind shall be incessantly employed in endeavouring to make the stage Arrangements worthy of the approbation of the Patrons of the Theatre Royal Devonport[102].

Wilton's efforts as stage manager bore fruit in the instructive paragraphs that often appeared under the titles of plays to be produced on the bills and he also continued to play his usual range of parts.

Wilton had a benefit at the Devonport Theatre in July 1836, patronised by many distinguished members of the community, including Admiral the Right Honourable Lord Amelius Beauclerk, commander in chief of the port. He was praised for his performance as Abou Hassan and as Clerimont in *The Old Maid* he "was about the most romantic, love-stricken hero we have seen – his admiration was perfectly enthusiastic – and did lovers generally follow his example, success would be certain nine times out of ten'[103]. The address on his benefit bill was no. 7 Gloucester Place, Plymouth, where his wife was earning a living as a Teacher of Dancing and Callisthenics[104]. His assumption of his duties as stage manager was so effective that the *Devonport Independent* (15/10/1836) was drawn to comment on the fact that the programme had been completed by 11 o'clock. On the occasion of his benefit early in 1837 the *Independent* commented:

> Monday next is set apart for the benefit of a very old favourite, Mr F. Wilton. Whether we speak of him as a useful actor – as an indefatigable stage manager – or as a member of society endowed with an intellect far above mediocrity – we at all events will treat him as he deserves and recommend him strongly to the lovers of the drama as every way deserving their patronage and support. (25/2/1837)

He apparently secured the best house of the season at his benefit, but his labours did not cease here. When the Devonport season ended he undertook the management of the Victoria Theatre (formerly the Pantheon) in Vauxhill Street, Plymouth, which opened for a short summer season on 10 May, 1837. He was praised for rendering the theatre comfortable, but no other details are recorded[105]. The death of William IV on 20 June, 1837, may in fact have led to the premature close of the theatre.

From July 1837 Wilton returned to Hay's Exeter company (he had also been there from January–March 1836, when he had played Catesby to Kean's Richard III). Samuel Phelps was also a member of the Exeter company: Wilton played Rawbold to Phelps' Sir Edward Mortimer in *The Iron Chest* and was given equal billing with Phelps when he played Ulric in *Werner*. Macready visited Exeter in 1836[106]. Many years later Wilton recalled in one of his diaries:

> It was from this theatre Macready engaged Phelps. Phelps showed me the letter of engagement in the dressing room one night when we were playing *Werner*.

Wilton remained in Exeter, playing also at other theatres in the circuit such as Torquay (where he supported the negro impersonator, T.D.Rice, on a short starring engagement), until July 1840. His wife also played in the company as did (occasionally) his daughter Lizzie and his son Ned[107].

When not playing in the Exeter circuit Wilton performed at smaller West Country theatres, such as Yeovil and Honiton. For such visits he formed sharing schemes with other actors and took partial responsibility for the company's organisation. Surviving playbills for the Honiton Theatre, situated behind the Fountain Inn, for December 1838–January 1839, reveal Wilton, his wife, Lizzie, Ned and another son, George, as performers. Wilton played such roles as Captain Absolute in *The Rivals* and organised the sale of tickets, which were available from him at the King's Arms[108].

In the autumn of 1840 it is possible that the Wiltons travelled to London to make their first appearance at the City of London Theatre. From the fragmentary evidence surviving it seems that they were a part of the company for the 1840–1841 season[109]. Obaldistone, whom Wilton knew from his earlier engagement in Dawson's company, was there, and the presence of Henry Howard who, as leading actor at the Britannia, was first to introduce Wilton to Sam Lane, also supports the supposition that the Mr and Mrs Wilton engaged must have been Frederick Wilton and his wife[110]. After March 1841 Wilton's movements are again a mystery, until he resurfaces on 26 September, 1843, the date on which he made his first appearance at the Theatre Royal, Gravesend, then leased by J.L.Thornton. Announced as from the Theatre Royal, Drury Lane (although no Drury Lane playbills from 1841–1843 name him in any capacity) he took over the stage management of the Gravesend Theatre from a Mr Fenton[111]. The principal artist there was C.J.Hawthorn, later employed at the Britannia and later still at Philadelphia; Wilton remained in contact with him, through correspondence, for the rest of his life. Wilton performed a range of roles in the Gravesend company and also provided a translation from the French of *Marie; or, The Pearl of Savoy*. At the conclusion of the season, in December 1843, Wilton returned to London, joining the Britannia Saloon as stage manager. He left the following year, after a dispute with Sam Lane, returning to the Gravesend company, where Fenton had now resumed his duties as stage manager. He remained at Gravesend from August 1844 until the season ended early in 1845. After this his movements are again uncertain until, in January 1846, he returned to the Britannia as stage manager, remaining there for 29 years.

Life in London

Wilton was a sociable, yet efficient, stage-manager, whose presence at the Britannia did a lot to enhance the quality of its presentations. In 1843–44 he staged the first in a long line of Britannia pantomimes and the upward spiral in the Britannia's fortunes during the '40s and '50s must have been due, in part, to his influence. In A.L.Crauford's history of the Lanes, *Sam and Sallie*, no mention is made of Wilton, the stage management allegedly being in the hands of Bill Browne, an ex-criminal, who is eventually packed off to Australia at the Lanes' expense on account of ill health[112]. James Anderson and J.B.Howe, on the other hand, both recall Wilton's period at the Britannia in their memoirs, Howe describing him as 'one of the best practical stage managers' he had ever seen[113]. An anonymous writer, discussing the Britannia, recalls how: 'Above all do I remember one of my first friends, dear old Mr F.Wilton, most scholarly, clever, gentlemanly of stage managers'[114]. Wilton was at the Britannia continuously for 29 years and, although his diaries only recall the last $12\frac{1}{2}$ years of his engagement, he was active throughout his time there. Both the playbills that survive for the period and the prompt copies, marked in his handwriting in the Pettingell Collection, bear testimony to his endeavours.

Wilton's functions as stage manager were many and various. He was responsible for what happened on stage during performance; for marking up the scripts of new melodramas and pantomimes and ensuring that the carpenters, scene painters and property men created the effects required; and for rehearsing the play. He had to cut plays which were over-long; distribute roles to be played; and arrange for substitute performers in the event of absence or illness. Another task was the drawing up of the weekly playbills and newspaper advertisements, as well as correcting the proofs once the playbill was printed. Just before the Christmas pantomime commenced he also had to compose and copy out pre-performance puffs for distribution to the newspapers. He had to prepare changes of programme and mark up scripts for benefit performances. Whilst new actors and actresses were hired by the management, Wilton sometimes took responsibility for hiring speciality acts and extras, including soldiers for military spectacles. He also had to tell performers when their engagements had expired or were to be discharged ('one of my most disagreeable duties as stage manager'); he also had to dismiss female performers when their confinements seemed imminent.

Wilton was sometimes required to act on behalf of the Britannia's management, as when the theatre's license became due for renewal. He usually accompanied the Examiner of Plays and his colleagues from the Lord Chamberlain's Office on their annual tour of inspection of the theatre and often had to take responsibility for implementing their suggestions. If problems concerning safety or the licensing of specific plays arose, then Wilton was often sent on the theatre's behalf to sort them out with the Lord Chamberlain's Office. He was also used to resolve disputes with other theatres over ownership of plays performed at the Britannia. His one perk, apart from his salary of £2 per week, was a free dinner at Simpson's (or an equivalent venue) once a year, when in company with the theatre's sureties he visited the Lord Chamberlain's Office to pay the annual licensing fee and collect the theatre's license. Immediately after Samuel Lane's death in 1871 Wilton helped to sort out some of the more pressing financial and legal problems this had caused, including the transfer of the theatre's license to Sarah Lane. From the Spring of 1872 he also became responsible for assisting the Treasury in paying out salaries to many of the 'extra' performers engaged at the theatre. In the 12 years documented in the diaries he was never once absent from the theatre. He also continued acting, playing small roles in many of the plays presented.

Many prompt copies marked in Wilton's handwriting survive. These reveal just how concerned he was with every aspect of performance. Timing was particularly important, especially if the scene changes were taking too long. Lighting and sound cues are clearly set out, plus information on the staging of particular scenes. At the end of Act III of *The Angel of Peace and Pardon* he notes 'No "pepper" used in this act'; at the end of Act II he writes: 'Ghost Effect required; READY LIGHTS & STORM & READY GHOST EFFECT'. His script for *The Casual Ward* contains a diagram revealing the disposition of the supers and ballet girls who are playing the inmates of the casual ward as they lie on the straw mattresses scattered throughout the ward. In *Wildfire Ned* Wilton has added a note to the script concerning both lighting effects and safety precautions:

> [Blue Fire for Ghost & but little Red Fire behind . . . L.H. to avoid its killing the Blue. A Tin Bucket brought on stage by Property Man the instant the Act is down for the Supers to quench torches in].

Sometimes the scripts also contain Sarah Lane's requests to Wilton, either for cuts or for changes in staging to facilitate back stage manoeuvres or even concerning the content of the playbill for the play in question. The prompt copy of *Left-Handed Liberty*, which commences with a paragraph describing morganatic marriage, includes a note to Wilton from Sarah Lane stating, 'Mr Wilton, please put this in the bill'. On the script of *The Volcano of Italy* Wilton notes of Act II, Scene 2, set in a ballroom:

> For the first month the supers and the ladies of the Ballet all came on here to begin this scene and continued promenading about the Ball-Room & sometimes in the garden &c until the Countess entered . . . . But at the end of the 4th week Mrs S L, considering that the promenades distracted the attention of the audience, cut them.

Scripts involving battle scenes, such as *Napoleon, or The Story of a Flag*, or supernatural effects, such as *Left-Handed Liberty*, are particularly indicative of Wilton's task. Towards the end of the latter script Wilton's notes fully reveal the complexity of operations under his control. After a scene in which a German Baron and the figure of Retribution see Time on a Globe and Death on a square tombstone rise before them, not to mention the appearance of an Angel, a Dragon and a Ghost, the location changes to a Fiery Region in which Fiends with flashing torches are discovered. As Retribution waves his sword, the clouds on which he and the Baron have been standing change to a fiery volcano and they sink through it as the act drop falls. Here are Wilton's comments:

> Ring Down when shower of fire out.

Screams & yells & all sorts of noises. Coloured fires burning.
Braces falling on sheet iron.
Squids emitting sparks from Dragon Mouth.
. . . Red Lights full up.
No supers can be used to assist in this last change of scene as all are on stage.
MEM.
On the 1st production of the piece there were no *screams or yells*, no *noises*
except the crash worked in the prompt entrance, no falling Braces or sheets
of iron — all the supers and everybody else in the Theatre being busily
engaged on other matters, working the scene.

Many further examples of Wilton's work can be seen in the Britannia
manuscripts now housed in the Frank Pettingell Collection at the University of Kent, Canterbury.

There is little information available about Wilton's domestic life prior
to 1863. He cites 3 Walbrook Place as one of his addresses, whilst working
at the Britannia, but in 1863 he was resident at 115 Houndsditch, where
he and Amelia supplemented their incomes by running a grocery business.
(Wilton gives Comedian and Grocer as his occupation on the 1861
Census). He was astute at supplementing his income in other ways, collect-
ing rent for the Rochester Theatre and, in the 1860s and 1870s, acting as
a go-between for Holloway's pills and the Australian newspapers edited by
his sons and son-in-law in which the pills were advertised, for which he
earned a commission. Four of his children had emigrated to Australia:
Edward and Tom left in April 1853 and his daughter Lizzie, married to a
John Byron, departed in May 1857. George also left in 1857, returned to
England the following year, then went back to Australia in 1860. Two
further daughters, Harriet and Jessie, remained in England.

Appropriately the year in which Wilton's surviving diaries commence
was the year in which he and his family moved to the last address at which
they were to live while he was still stage manager of the Britannia Theatre.
In 1863 Amelia was eligible to collect her pension from the Royal General
Theatrical Fund, so that she and her husband decided to sell their business
and leave the lodgings in Houndsditch which they had shared with the
Isaacs family. They found a house to rent at 91 Nichol's Square, just a few
minutes walk from the theatre and sandwiched between Hackney Road
and Kingsland Road. Built about 1840 on land where the house of
Hogarth's former editor, John Nichols, had stood, the square retained
Georgian and regency influences, whilst its architecture also anticipated
the coming Victorian phase of building. Here Wilton was able to indulge
his taste for gardening and there was also space to rent out the front room
to a lodger. The household consisted of Wilton and his wife; their youngest
daughter, Jessie, who in 1863 was working from home braiding dresses;
Milly, their grand-daughter, whose father, George, was estranged from his
wife and then living in Australia; a domestic servant; and Garibaldi the
cat. For much of the year Milly was boarded out at a school in Victoria
Park, Hackney, run by a Miss Fitch. The move took place on 17 June.
'This house is too comfortable to last – it suits me too well to last, – it

won't last!' wrote Wilton, but the twelve years that followed proved him wrong.

There were inevitably problems in running the household. Servants often proved unreliable or dishonest; more than one was dismissed for pilfering. Lodgers could be equally troublesome, as in the case of the man who brought his father along to share the front room with him and then intended adding his brother to the room's occupants. He received notice to quit, as did a Mr Benjamin, whose reluctance to get up and go out each day was matched only by his reluctance to pay his rent. Sometimes, however, lodgers became firm family friends, as was the case with a Mr Drielsma and with the Browne family from Aberdeen. Less problematic was the garden, in which Wilton invested much time, energy and money (£2.10.4½ in 1863). He was planting seeds in the 'stony-hearted, hungry soil' of the garden even before he had signed the agreement to take the house. Initially, he scoured Shoreditch and Hackney for plants and seeds, drawing on the assistance of other theatre personnel, including John Martin, the gasman, and William Batey, one of the caterers; he also purchased several books on gardening from a local book-stall in the month he moved into the house. Apart from occasional annoyances, such as the theft of wall-flowers or damage caused by workmen when the house was being redecorated, the garden was to be a source of great pleasure over the coming years.

Wilton's passion for fishing, however, superceded even that for gardening: his diary entries for his fishing trips are often more detailed and vivid than the theatrical entries. On the majority of Sundays from the spring through to the autumn, as well as on public holidays such as Good Friday, he would usually set out for a day's fishing. His companions might include his son-in-law, Fred Rountree, or fellow workers at the Britannia, such as the door-keeper, George Taylor, or the scenic artist, Thomas Rogers. Alf and Harry Beckett, sons of the Britannia's printer, and Alfred Davis, a provincial manager and son of Wilton's old friend E.D.Davis, are also among those with whom Wilton enjoyed a day's fishing. A typical fishing trip is described in a diary entry for 14 August, 1864:

> To Higham Lake, Woodford, with F.Rountree on card . . . borrowed for me by Mr Superintendent Mott . . . . Day hot, bright and scorching. Didn't expect a *single* fish. Caught only 1 Dozen very small perch between us and one small Eel . . . . Told by a labouring man who knew the lake well that there were Perch, Eels, Roach, Tench and Jack in it, – and that only three months ago two gentlemen came down from London and caught a Jack 10 or 12 lbs weight there. He also said that some years back he had several times assisted to net the lake & they used to take great quantities of fish out by that means, but not many Jack. For fishing this lake a punt, or boat, is necessary to reach the middle – fishing at the sides is of little use.

Interestingly, Superintendent Mott, who was in charge of London's N Division of Police, was a frequent visitor to the Britannia and on good terms with Wilton, often securing him passes for fishing. At night they would occasionally discuss fishing at the theatre; once Mott told Wilton that he had just caught 24 lb of roach after fishing for two hours in the Ordinance Waters at Waltham. On another occasion Wilton noticed him among the crowds when the Siamese Twins were engaged at the Britannia and was able to thank him for a fishing ticket to Ponders End that he had supplied. Once he even sent a small fishing bag to Mott as a present – in such manner were relations between police and theatre maintained in the 1860s and 1870s.

Apart from gardening, fishing, chess (another enthusiasm) or merely smoking his meerschaum pipe, Wilton also found other ways to relax. He was an avid reader and his diaries are peppered with quotations. 'Books', he wrote down in 1863, 'are masters who instruct us without rods or wrath'. Poetry exercised a particular appeal – he possessed copies of the works of Milton, Pope, Cowper, Crabbe, Samuel Butler, Burns and many others. New poems by Matthew Arnold, Tennyson, Browning and Swinburne are often copied, in part, into the diaries. Wilton was also familiar with the work of Lamb, Hazlitt and Leigh Hunt and with more contemporary essayists such as Carlyle. He spent the last day of 1865 reading *Our Mutual Friend*, although this was partly for professional reasons. He read *The Times* regularly, noting down anything in its pages that caught his interest. During his time at Nichol's Square he learnt how to bind books and periodicals: the *Nation*, *Round Table* and *Routledge's Shakespeare* are amongst the volumes he records binding. Wilton had a rudimentary grasp of French and a little Latin; he was certainly *au fait* with some of the classical texts, noting with interest the appearance of a new translation of the *Aeneid* in 1866. Every year he would also renew his ticket to the Reading room of the British Museum: his visits there were infrequent, but he would occasionally go to chase up a quotation or copy a page from a volume which was missing in his own library. As stage manager of the Britannia he also accumulated a large number of play texts, most of which he disposed of when he emigrated to Australia. A few of these, usually prompt copies and gifts given by actors arranging benefit performances, are now held in the Pettingell Collection. Typical is a copy of *Catherine Howard*, which is inscribed 'F.Wylton/hys propertye/and/Pryvate Prompte/Boke/Ye gyfte of Mistress/M.A.Bellair/June 16th 1874'.

In his diaries Wilton reveals a keen interest in the world around him, a curiosity about the changes then occurring and an acute observation of detail. Natural phenomena always intrigued him: on 14 November, 1867, at 1 a.m. in the morning, he observed great numbers of shooting stars coming from the North East, in many instances right overhead. 'They seemed', he noted, 'like the blue stars shot out of rockets, leaving long trails of light behind them, of very brief duration'. In July 1870, coming home from the theatre one night, he noticed an eclipse of the moon, 'the portion eclipsed about 11.45 p.m.' appearing of a 'swarthy, copper colour'. Going to the theatre at about 6 p.m. one evening in 1867 he observed a beautiful 'Mackerel' sky and commented on its recurrence two days later. The weather was a constant source of interest, wet or dry, cold or hot; in the icey January of 1867 Wilton noted that:

Last Tuesday the customers at the 'American Stores' Oxford Street, where Harriet Rountree was, *skated* into the bar – right up to the counter. She repeatedly heard shouts of people in the streets at others falling down, and stock exclamations as 'How's her dress?' One gentleman and his wife stood a long time in the passage of her house, or one adjoining, waiting for a cab. They had been to the Princess's Theatre (only doors off) – and when a cab was got, the driver demanded £1.10.0 to take them home – only a short distance – & the gentleman was obliged to give that sum, the lady being dressed in Opera Cloak &c.

A year later Wilton recalled the 'memorable slippery night' of 1867. Equally vivid were thunderstorms, such as one in June 1871, when the first half-a-dozen claps of thunder were 'singularly short ones like a volley of big guns – afterwards each clap lengthening, with sharp, fierce flashes of lightning forked and most vivid – evidently close over head'.

Wilton was equally impressed by the new scientific developments taking place in the Victorian age and by the new buildings constantly being erected in London. He followed eagerly the progress of the Atlantic Cable between Great Britain and America, when it was being laid by the *Great Eastern* in 1865. The year before he had travelled down the Thames with Fred Rountree to look at the new bridges under construction and to compare Battersea Park with Victoria Park. (Battersea he found much inferior.) In 1867 he records a visit to see the new lions in Trafalgar Square and he is continually sampling the new metropolitan railway lines as they open. In 1863 he travelled on the newly opened line between Farringdon Street and Paddington; in 1865, when the North London extension opened (passing the end of Nichol's Square), Wilton was able to take the train from Shoreditch to Broad Street. The previous year he and Amelia had travelled for the first time on the Chatham and Dover Railway between London Bridge and Charing Cross. The current affairs and events of the day were equally noteworthy: in 1863 the marriage of the Princess of Wales, the procession and the illuminations in celebration of the event (not to mention the deaths and injuries occasioned by the crush) are all recorded. The assassination of Abraham Lincoln, the Reform meetings of 1867, the Fenian explosions at Clerkenwell Prison, the Abyssinian War, the opening of the Suez Canal, the Franco-Prussian War, the Tichborne case are just a few of the many events to which Wilton refers. As with most of his entries Wilton merely states what he knows or has observed: he rarely comes out with any strong opinions.

Wilton's social and domestic life is also well documented. His physical health and any night-time disturbances are regularly described:

Woke out of sleep in middle of night by a strange sensation like drowning – lasted 3 quarters of an hour.

or:

Fell asleep by the fireside at 7 minutes to one o'clock (midnight) and fancied Lizzy was calling to me repeatedly, 'Father! Father!'

Several times, in reading the diaries, one feels that Wilton may have stage-managed one too many a melodrama for his own good. Sometimes, however, the cause of disturbance is rather mundane, as in November 1867:

> Seized with giddiness about midnight, on rising to go to bed – staggered about – could neither sit, stand nor lie, unable to get up stairs, lay on the first step for some time, stomach working all the while – relieved by one slight vomit of some thin liquid. Had taken nothing for supper but coffee and bread and butter (& two pills as usual). Had had a glass of stout, last thing before leaving Theatre.

One Sunday, after eating baked hare, beautifully stuffed, followed by plum pudding, the entire family was taken ill with diarrhoea, whilst Wilton had 'a violent attack of bile, vomiting for two hours'. 'So much for baked hare and rich veal stuffing!' he wrote. Sometimes domestic incidents had less painful consequences, as when the chimney caught fire:

> This afternoon threw a handful of green branches of the Laburnum Tree (cut down last Monday) on the kitchen fire, & to my surprise an hour after, while working in the garden, saw thick black smoke coming from the chimney. Shut and locked all the doors. A mob assembled outside and a fireman came. Refused to let him in. He fetched a policeman. Went out to hide in the garden. He demanded name and number of house. Gave them. Fireman said he should take out a summons – and went away. Mob then dispersed. Saw Mr Superintendent Mott. Told him of it. He called Sergeant Ruff and told him to go down to the Fire Brigade's Office in the morning and soften them up as much as he could. There were 3 sweeps with the fireman, indignant at not being let in.

Life was not always so turbulent, although it was certainly full. A constant stream of visitors passed through the Wilton household, including another married daughter, Harriet, and her husband, Fred Rountree; Fred Dewar, the actor, and his sister Rose Wilton; the Newcastle manager E.D.Davis; Richard James, a cousin of Wilton's, and his family; the Browne family from Aberdeen; and many, many more. Sundays, in particular, were busy, but there were frequent visitors throughout the week. There were family outings as well, such as one to Shooter's Hill in June 1865 to gather strawberries, which were scarce that year. After a dinner of sandwiches in a copse at the bottom of the hill, Wilton wrote, 'A beautiful day, fine and bright, with a gentle breeze tempering the heat! – long streaking clouds indicating wind'. In September, on an outing to Chingford, where they dined and teaed al-fresco, the family were photographed by Alf and Harry Beckett, who earlier in the year had taken photographs of the Wilton family and home to send to Australia. In 1867 the family visited Abbey Wood, in a wagonette lent by W.Crauford of the Britannia, pulled by a horse borrowed from W.Batey. The horse proved very 'sweet-tempered' and tractable, although he was much worried by flies whilst grazing in an orchard where they had stopped – 'and to see him kick out and run round the orchard at times, when their attentions became too pointed, was a caution!'

Wilton's daughter Harriet, who had formerly assisted with the grocery business, had only just married Fred Rountree when the diaries commence. Fred's widowed mother kept a public house, the Red Lion, in Rosoman Street, Clerkenwell, whilst Fred and his wife kept the bottle shop beneath it. Business was slack and, in the public house itself, Mrs Rountree was running up an enormous debt, £600 by October 1863. Mrs Rountree was something of a harridan; only grudgingly did she allow Fred access to property left him in his father's will and she and Harriet had at least one major altercation. Fred eventually left the shop, sold a pub called the Grimaldi, left to him by his father, and took over the White Swan in Chandos Street, Covent Garden. Subsequently, Fred was summonsed for being open after hours and, although the summons was unsuccessful, the licensing magistrates refused to grant him a license the following January, with the result that he had to leave the Swan. Before January ended Fred's mother had committed suicide by taking Prussic Acid and he found himself saddled, at the age of 22, with bankruptcy, accentuated by his mother's debts and the fact that his father's estate was still undischarged. After travelling for a tobacconist and selling biscuits on commission, with little success, Fred applied for a clerkship with the Railway Clearing House. After sitting a series of examinations he secured a post, commencing employment on 30 December, 1864. His new career proved a great success and he was still in the same employment when Wilton left for Australia twelve years later.

One of Wilton's sons, George, returned from Australia in 1868, showing 'no signs of age – none whatever thank God! he has a large beard – his hair is all perfectly brown, not one grey hair'. In Australia he had dug for quartz and gold, run a shop and later was to set up in trade as a coal merchant. Whilst in England he was urged by his father to take a greengrocer's shop up for sale in the Kingsland Road, but he returned to Australia early in 1869, working his passage as a ship's cook. George's daughter, Milly, remained with her grandparents, but, whilst in England, George arranged an apprenticeship for her with Mr Evans, a linen draper, in City Road. Milly completed her three year apprenticeship rather listlessly – lodging away from the excitement of the Wilton household proved extremely dull. Her mother, from whom George was estranged, is referred to mysteriously in the diaries as 'that woman'. On 25 January, 1863, Wilton noted that Harriet saw '*that* woman in Hoxton, very shabbily dressed' and then lost her; he himself records a sighting in March, 1864. A year after George returned to Australia a Camberwell tailor named Vincent Roda called at Wilton's house to enquire if George had been legally married to the woman in question, as she was now his wife, but he wished to divorce her (after 5 years of marriage) on account of her horrible temper. Milly was occasionally accosted by her mother; in 1863 she stopped her and gave her sixpence; ten years later she unexpectedly called at the shop at which Milly was engaged, subsequently writing to say that George had revived his intimacy with her when he was last in England and threatening to disgrace all the family. A few days later Milly received a second letter from her mother, if possible, noted Wilton, 'more disgraceful than the first'. When George returned to Australia in 1869 Wilton went down to the East India Docks to see him off, only to find the boat had already gone 'and George gone! "Gone! Gone!" This word kept booming, booming in my mind till I got back to the railway station'.

By far the greatest domestic upheaval to Wilton's life was caused by the death of his wife, Amelia, in May 1873. One senses that he was rather bereft without her, even though he survived her by sixteen years. Regular visits to Highgate Cemetery are a feature of Wilton's activity after her death and great care is taken in organising an appropriate headstone for the grave and in planting flowers beside it. Wilton now lived with his youngest daughter, Jessie, but a rift occurred between them after the arrival of his son-in-law, John Byron, from Australia in 1874. Jessie's activities had included not only braiding, but an attempt to become an actress (prematurely halted by the intervention of Samuel Lane), adaptations and translations of plays (some of which were staged at the Britannia) and for four years a regular supply of 'Gossips' on events in London, syndicated to Australian newspapers through family connections. Within a short time from John Byron's arrival she had fallen out with the entire family and had been barred by Wilton from re-entering the house. Whether the cause was jealousy of her two sisters, both successfully married and under no compunction to earn a livelihood or whether the matter went deeper, it is impossible to say. She quarrelled bitterly with her father and alienated John Byron, who was less patiently disposed. From 1874 onwards the diaries record angry interviews, begging letters and recriminations, which were, if anything, accentuated after Wilton had secured her an engagement with Chute, manager of the Bristol Theatre, for the 1874–75 pantomime. The rift with Jessie certainly clouded Wilton's final years at the Britannia (which is why the entries towards the end of his period there are much less informative on theatrical affairs) and they had not made their peace with each other when Wilton sailed for Australia in 1876.

The problems with Jessie may have helped Wilton in his resolve to leave the Britannia Theatre and to emigrate to Australia. Not long after John Byron's arrival, his wife Lizzie and their adopted daughter, Milly (in actual fact a daughter of Ned Wilton), arrived in London. Much of Wilton's spare time and social life now centered around the Byron family and, on leaving the Britannia Theatre in July 1875, he moved with them into 2, Penshurst Road, South Hackney. Once Byron had completed his business (establishing a telegram link between England and Australia for Gresham's, which he co-owned with Tom Wilton), he and his family returned to Australia. With them, leaving on the *Northam* in November 1876, went Frederick Wilton and George's daughter, Milly.

Australia 1877–1889

Wilton kept a detailed log of his voyage to Australia, recording the sunsets he observed; his first sighting of the Southern Cross; flying fish and porpoises seen from the deck; his teaching of the ship's captain to play chess; and the problems of deep-sea fishing, when sharks deprived one of one's bait. On the 8 January, 1877, at 1.30 p.m., he 'saw the Land of Promise, 1st time, very misty, over the lee bow'. The following day, at 4.30 p.m., he landed in Sydney at Circular Quay and was reunited with his sons Tom, Ned and George; he also saw Tom's daughter, Amy, for the first time. He was soon out exploring Sydney, visiting George's coal merchant's business and travelling inland to Lithgow, where Tom was a shareholder in a coal mine. Observing a 'Bush Ball' at Lithgow he was amazed to see the orchestra smoking cigars and meerschaums, whilst playing, and dogs wandering around the Assembly room. Back in Sydney he went sailing and fishing in the harbour, as well as visiting Manly, Watson's Bay and the Botanical Gardens. In March he left Sydney for Melbourne, where he was to reside with John Byron (returning to run the Melbourne office of Gresham's), Lizzie and Milly Byron. Milly Wilton remained in Sydney, with her father George.

The Byron family resided at 10 Greville Street, Prahran, within easy access of the city of Melbourne. From Prahran Wilton also visited a station in the outback, where he describes efforts to hunt koalas, possums and even a platypus, as well as fishing in the Yarra. He became fully engaged in the social life of the Byrons, as well as playing frequent games of chess, reading widely and continuing his regular fishing expeditions. His visits to the theatre were now rare – on one occasion when he did attend a performance, he complained that he could not hear clearly. Nevertheless, he kept in touch with English theatrical news through regular correspondence and was frequently mailed copies of the *Era*, *Entr'acte* and other theatrical journals. On one occasion he noticed in the *Era* that in a production of *Michael Strogoff* at Booth's Theatre in New York, the grandest tableau of the evening had not been saved up as the climax to the last scene, which was played in a pair of chamber flats. 'They would not have done this at the Britannia', he noted at the bottom of the entry. His interest in things theatrical was also revived when figures from the past visited Australia: Professor Pepper, who visited in 1879, was actually managed by an acquaintance of the Byrons; J.B.Howe visited in 1882. Australian theatrical news also intrigued him: the controversy over the staging of *The Happy Land* in Melbourne was commented on. Another theatrical link was maintained through the wigs that he had shipped out from Clarkson's, the London theatrical wig-makers.

Wilton was soon fully absorbed in the life of Australia. His diaries detail not only domestic events such as picnics, but also the landscape; bush fires; the Melbourne Cup (Australia's premiere horse race); the vexatious effects of mosquitoes; and the latest exploits of bushrangers such as Captain Moonlight. Nevertheless, his focus is invariably the family, as in this description of a Christmas dinner at the Byrons in the hot Australian summer:

Dinner, a fine Turkey . . . , suet dumplings, Ham, Green Peas, French Beans,

Potatoes, Plum Pudding with Brandy, Strawberries & clotted cream with powdered lump sugar, Almonds & Raisins, Cherries, Plums, Oranges & Pine Apple. Brandy & Tahbilk wine afterwards. All splendid. Never had a better dinner – may we never have a worse. (1879)

This was the last Christmas in Melbourne, for in January 1880 Wilton returned to Sydney, shortly to be followed by John Byron, who was disposing of his share of the telegram business. Back in Sydney Tom was still based at Gresham's Telegram Office; Ned had returned after some unsuccessful newspaper ventures in Dubbo and Newcastle; George remained in his coal business. Wilton resided with George at 201 Cleveland Street, sometimes accompanying him on the waggon to collect bills or visiting Paddy's Market, 'the rendezvous of a Saturday night of all the larrikins and scum of Sydney'. From George's he could walk to Moore Park in search of wild flowers, on one occasion losing his way and having to scale a five foot fence as a result. Another time he observed, on Flagstaff Hill, 'a majestic lady in black, with a long train and parasol, walking there – Never saw so stately a form before – Thought she was attitudinising to attract observation'.

A good reason for returning to Sydney in 1880 was the International Exhibition, which Wilton visited several times. On his second visit he saw:

a party of Chinese Ladies there in Chinese costume painted up to the eyes and all round the eyes with Chinese (sic) and their eyebrows painted black and lips crimson, the latter apparently laid on with gum. The two principal ladies with very small feet, supported by nurses on each side, arm in arm; two little boys with the party having shaved heads and pig-tails; & one infant in arms who, strange to say, cried exactly as any other child would do! The ladies chatted and laughed incessantly.

Through Tom, Wilton was introduced to Julian Thomas, a well-known Sydney journalist writing under the pseudonym of 'The Vagabond'. Thomas was amongst those who helped Wilton trace, through newspaper files, the movements of an actor, W.C.Dillon, who had purchased the Australian rights to some of Sarah Lane's pieces. In 1879 Dillon wrote to Wilton, informing him that Sarah Lane had instructed he be forwarded bills of the performances. He also requested clarification of the stage business necessary for *Dolores*, since it was not clearly marked on the manuscript.

In July 1880 John Byron was appointed to the chief compilership of the Census in Sydney, a three year appointment, at £500 per annum. Not long after this he and Lizzie took a house in Glebe, at 9 Derwent Street, close to Sydney University, and Wilton moved in with them. George and Milly soon became neighbours, moving into number 15, and Ned took a cottage in the same road. Tom, the most affluent member of the family, lived several miles away in Ocean Street, Woollahra, on the eastern side of the city. In 1881 Milly Wilton became engaged to a Mr Dobson, formerly the manager of a station and now speculating in real estate, and Milly Byron became engaged to a Mr Long (a printer). Both girls married the following year, but Dobson died of cancer and left Milly a widow. Milly Long

produced a number of children, descendants of whom are still living in
Sydney today. Two of Ned's children – Charlie and Fanny (Hilsinger) –
also produced families. Back in England Jessie had married a Mr Drury
and given birth to two children, one of whom died from burns after
an accident at Aldershot in 1882. Although Wilton remained estranged
from her, his Australian diaries are full of references to her doings and
whereabouts.

Wilton lost none of his sense of humour, even if he was sometimes
anxious about the estranged Jessie. On 15 November, 1881, he wrote:

> Look out! *THE END OF THE WORLD*, according to Mother Shipton's
> Prophecy, to take place today.
> *Au contraire* – The day was a remarkably quiet one – dull, cloudy and close,
> almost suffocating all the morning. After Noon, a spitting of rain, & ultimately
> a slight shower occurred.

Now approaching 80 his faculties were still intact and he was physically
fit, apart from a slight deafness and the occasional attack of lumbago. By
1886, however, he was suffering throughout the winter from what he called
'Senile Bronchitis' and smoking a daily pipe of tobacco which, in his
opinion, helped to alleviate the symptoms. Three years later, on 9 September
1889, Wilton finally expired at the house of one of his grand-daughters in
Darlington Road, not far from the old Derwent Street address.

Notes

1.   *Hackney Gazette*, 14 March, 1873. This information is derived from a probate
case which occurred when Samuel Lane's will was contested. A.L.Crauford's
account of Lane's origins in his semi-fictional *Sam and Sallie* (London, 1933) is
impossible to verify. In general I have drawn on Crauford as little as possible for
primary evidence.

2.   *A Jubilee of Dramatic Life* (London, 1894), p.35.

3.   Clipping, 15 September, 1839, Britannia Cuttings, Hackney Archives, Rose
Lipman library.

4.   *Weekly Dispatch*, 22 September, 1839.

5.   *Ibid.*

6.   *Ibid.*, 15 September, 1839.

7.   *Ibid.*, 22 September, 1839.

8.   Middlesex Licensed Victuallers' Records, MR/LMD/2, Petition dated
October, 1840, Greater London Record Office (GLRO).

9.   'Rule Britannia', *Entr'acte Annual* (1885), p.4.

10.   Clipping, undated, Britannia Cuttings, Hackney Archives, Rose Lipman
Library.

11.   *Ibid.*

12.   'Rule Britannia', p.4.

13.　*A Jubilee of Dramatic Life*, pp.38–39.

14.　*Weekly Dispatch*, 1 August, 1843.

15.　*Lord Chamberlain's Papers* (*LCP*), LC7/5, Public Record Office (PRO).

16.　However, in 1844, Lane was allowed to provide refreshments in the saloon, in the intervals between performances, provided that all stands for bottles and glasses were removed. Letter, dated 31 July, 1844 & Memorandum, dated 5 August, 1844, *LCP*, LC7/5, PRO.

17.　*Ibid.*, LC7/6.

18.　*Ibid.*

19.　*Ibid.*

20.　*Ibid.*

21.　*Ibid.*

22.　*Ibid.* Memorandum, 10 October, 1844.

23.　*Ibid.*

24.　John Hollingshead, *My Lifetime* (London, 1895), I, 25.

25.　*Random Recollections of the Stage by an Old Playgoer* (London, 1883), pp. 25–26.

26.　Clipping, undated, Britannia Cuttings, Theatre Museum.

27.　Quoted in *Dramatic Notes* (London, n.d.), pp.74–75.

28.　Each year, from 1858 onwards, W.B.Donne listed the number of plays submitted for licensing by each London theatre. The Britannia was usually at (or near) the top of the list, although it was sometimes beaten by the large number of French plays licensed for the St. James's Theatre. *LCP*, LC1/70 et seq., PRO.

29.　H.Chance Newton, *Cues and Curtain Calls* (London, 1927), pp.209–210. Lane Crauford (A.L.Crauford's son) describes Reynolds as 'a very fine all-round actor', who 'could play anything well; equally good as Iago, MacDuff, the Ghost in *Hamlet* or in parts such as the flamboyant parts of popular melodrama'. *Acting Its Theory and Practice* (London, 1930), p.133.

30.　James Anderson, *An Actor's Life* (London, 1902), pp.208–209.

31.　J.B.Howe, *A Cosmopolitan Actor* (London, 1888), pp.59–62.

32.　*My Lifetime*, I, 33.

33.　*LCP*, LC7/5, PRO.

34.　Police Report, 12 July, 1847, *LCP*, LC7/7, PRO.

35.　*Household Words*, 13 April, 1850.

36.　*Ibid.*

37.　Letter, 25 April, 1845, Add. MSS. 42,984, British Library.

38.　Letter, 30 August, 1845, Add. MSS. 42,987, British Library.

39.　Letter, 11 September, 1845. Add. MSS. 42,987, British Library.

40.　Letter, 18 March, 1848, *LCP*, L1/49, PRO. The *Theatrical Journal*, 27

February, 1851, refers to *The Prodigal Son*, which was banned by the Lord Chamberlain in that year, on account of its biblical subject. Lane had apparently gone to great expense in securing an artist especially to paint new scenery and in scouring the country for animals belonging to Egypt.

41. Add. MSS. 53,703, British Library.

42. *Ibid.*

43. *Ibid.*

44. Add. MSS. 57,305, British Library.

45. Memorandum, 12 May, 1858, *LCP*, LC1/58, PRO.

46. Petition, 7 June, 1848, *LCP*, LC7/7, PRO.

47. Letter, 12 October, 1858, *LCP*, LC1/58, PRO.

48. *Ibid.*

49. Clipping, undated, Britannia Cuttings, Hackney Archives, Rose Lipman Library.

50. 14 November, 1858.

51. *The Builder*, 20 November, 1858.

52. Report, 14 November, 1858, *LCP*, LC1/58, PRO.

53. Britannia Playbills, Theatre Museum.

54. For a discussion of the Britannia audience, with reference to these developments, see Clive Barker, 'The Audiences of the Britannia Theatre, Hoxton' *Theatre Quarterly*, IX, no 34, Summer 1970, pp.27–41. Barker (p.35) also compares the changes in prices over the years: in 1847 these are – Boxes and Pit 6d, Upper Stalls 4d, Gallery 3d; in 1849 (after rebuilding) – Boxes 1s, Box Slips and Lower Stalls, 4d, Gallery 3d; in 1855 Private Boxes, Boxes and Stalls 1s, Pit 6d, Back Pit 3d and Gallery 4d; in 1858 (after the second rebuilding) – Private Boxes a guinea, seats in Private Boxes 2s & 1s, Boxes 1s, Orchestra Stalls 1s, Box Slips & Pit 6d, Lower Gallery 4d, Upper Gallery 3d. (Half Price restricted to Boxes and Stalls.)

55. Report, *LCP*, LC1/70, PRO.

56. *Letters from a Theatrical Scene Painter* (London, 1880), p.81.

57. Letter, 29 April, 1864, *LCP*, LC1/141, PRO.

58. Britannia Playbills, Theatre Museum. Boucicault stated, in his evidence to the Parliamentary Select Committee of 1866 on theatre licences and regulations, that he allowed such performances to continue as 'the theatre was so far off it could not interfere with the attraction of the piece at the Adelphi'. Q.4422. *Report from the Select Committee on Theatrical Licences and Regulations* . . . British Sessional Papers (1866), XVI, 156.

59. *The Players*, 13 July, 1861.

60. Malcolm Morley, 'All the Year Round Plays I', *Dickensian* LII – Part 3, No 319, 1956, pp.128–130. Further background is provided by K.J.Fielding, 'Charles Reade and Dickens – A Fight against Piracy', *Theatre Notebook* 10, no 4, July–Sept 1956, pp.106–110. Collins and Dickens had decided to write, register and print a dramatic version of their own to foil piracy. When the adaptation was

announced at the Britannia, Dickens instructed his solicitors to proceed against Lane, even though he privately referred to him, in a letter to his sister-in-law, as 'a very good man, whom I really respect'. Dickens wrote to Reade about the matter; Reade suggested to Dickens that he sold the right to perform this adaptation to one particular theatre and insist that the manager join him in any action against persons producing an unauthorised version.

61. *An Actor's Life*, p.209.

62. Crauford, *Sam and Sallie*, p.340.

63. H.G.Hibbert, *Fifty Years of a Londoner's Life* (London, 1916), p.65.

64. *Era*, 26 December, 1869.

65. *Ibid.*, 24 December, 1871.

66. *Ibid.*, 3 January, 1864.

67. *Ibid.*

68. *Idols of the Halls* (London, 1928), p.46.

69. *LCP*, LC1/113, PRO. See also Jim Davis and Tracy C.Davis, 'The People of the "People's Theatre". The Social Demography of the Britannia Theatre (Hoxton)', *Theatre Survey*, ASTR, vol.32 no.2, 1991.

70. *Sam and Sallie*, pp.316–318.

71. 'The Audiences of the Britannia Theatre, Hoxton', p.30.

72. H.Barton Baker, *A History of the London Stage* (1904), p.380.

73. Clipping, 31 May, 1890, Britannia Cuttings, Hackney Archives, Rose Lipman Library.

74. Letter, 22 November, 1875, *LCP*, LC1/298, PRO.

75. Add. MSS. 53,706, British Library.

76. *Ibid.*

77. *Era*, 19 August, 1899.

78. Frank Pettingell Collection of Manuscript Plays, University of Kent at Canterbury.

79. Britannia Cuttings, Theatre Museum.

80. 'Rule Britannia', p.4.

81. *'Neath the Mask* (London, 1967), p.204.

82. Clipping, undated, Britannia Cuttings, Hackney Archives, Rose Lipman Library.

83. *Fifty Years of a Londoner's Life*, pp.63–64.

84. East, *'Neath the Mask*, pp.210–211. East draws heavily for this account on H.Chance Newton, 'Tales of the Old Brit', *Referee*, 27 January, 1924.

85. *Our Theatre in the Nineties* (London, 1932), III, 351–355.

86. Clipping, undated, Britannia Cuttings, Hackney Archives, Rose Lipman Library.

87. East, *'Neath the Mask*, p.203.

88. Theatres and Music Halls Committee of the London County Council (THMHC/LCC), *Presented Papers*, Britannia Theatre, Hoxton, 1888–1909, GLRO.

89. *Ibid.*

90. *Ibid.*, 15/2/1894.

91. *Ibid.*, 2/1895; 18/6/1896; 5/1899.

92. 30 July, 1887.

93. THMHC/LCC, *Presented Papers*, Britannia Theatre Hoxton, 1888–1909, 31/7/1899; 6/9/1899; 18/1/1900; 24/1/1900, GLRO. Of particular interest in these reports are details of the lavatory provision at the Britannia. Assuming a house of 1,450 males and 1,450 females there was 1 WC to every 362 females, 1 WC to every 290 males and 1 urinal stall to every 56 males. This suggests either a predominantly male audience or an almost total disregard for the comfort of female patrons.

94. East, *'Neath the Mask*, p.204.

95. THMHC/LCC, *Presented Papers*, Britannia Theatre, Hoxton, 1888–1909, 17/3/1909.

96. *Bristol Gazette*, 27 October, 1830.

97. p.56.

98. Amelia's stated age is two years less than Wilton's on both the 1861 and 1871 Censuses. They had 3 sons: Ned, George and Tom; and 3 daughters: Lizzie, Harriet and Jessie. They may have had a fourth son, Charlie; certainly Wilton records a number of visits to the grave of a Charlie Wilton at Highgate Cemetery, but never indicates his precise family relationship.

99. Anderson, p.24.

100. Edinburgh Playbills, British Library.

101. Birmingham Playbills, British Library.

102. Devonport Playbills, British Library.

103. *Devonport Independent*, 9 July, 1836.

104. Devonport Playbills, British Library.

105. *Devonport Independent*, 13 May, 1837.

106. William Toynbee (ed.), *Diaries of William Charles Macready 1833–1851* (London, 1912), I, 289.

107. Exeter & Torquay Playbills, British Library and Exeter Public Library.

108. Honiton Playbills, British Library. One of the actors in the company was Frimbley, to whom Wilton refers in his diaries as an actor involved in 'sharing schemes'. It seems likely that this arrangement applied at Honiton. Wilton also refers to acting at Yeovil in his diaries.

109. City of London Playbills, Hackney Archives, Rose Lipman Library.

110. Wilton states in his diaries that he was introduced to Lane when Henry Howard was stage manager of the Britannia Theatre; Howard moved to the

Britannia from the City of London in 1841, remaining there until Lane was refused his license later the same year. Jemmy Howard and his wife, both of whom were known to Wilton, were also members of the City of London company at this time.

111. Gravesend Playbills, British Library.

112. pp.283–284.

113. *A Cosmopolitan Actor*, p.99. See also Anderson, *An Actor's Life*, p.302.

114. Clipping, undated, Theatre Museum.

The Diaries

A Note on the Text

The original manuscripts of the Wilton Diaries, which are held in the Mitchell Library of New South Wales, Australia, are in an excellent state of preservation. They consist of 14 volumes covering Wilton's last years in England from 1863–1876 and 8 volumes covering his retirement in Australia (1877–1882 and 1885–1886). It is clear from entries in the surviving diaries that Wilton kept a diary prior to 1863, but no volumes appear to have survived. In 1863 Wilton moved from Houndsditch to Nichol's Square; perhaps the earlier diaries were lost during the move.

The English diaries contain not only theatrical material, but much of a more general and domestic nature. Theatrical matters account for well under 50% of the entries during these years. Theatrical events or reminiscences form about 1% of the material in the Australian diaries. The diaries as a whole, however, provide much of interest to the social historian and offer a fascinating vista of day to day life in England and Australia in the latter half of the nineteenth century.

In editing Wilton's diaries for publication I have transcribed only material relating to his work at the Britannia Theatre. This has meant excluding occasional details concerning his connection with the Rochester Theatre; references to family visits to other theatres or to theatrical friends like Fred Dewar and his family; his daughter, Jessie's, experiences as a provincial actress (an account of which appears in *Theatre History Studies*, USA 1992); and general comments on other theatres or theatre-related news items. However, even with these excisions, the original transcription of the diaries proved too long to facilitate an economically viable publication. Consequently, further cuts had to be made. Most significant are the cuts made from 1872 onwards. For the last $3\frac{1}{2}$ years of Wilton's period at the Britannia only major entries are retained and weekly details of plays performed and artists engaged are dispensed with. All theatrical entries after Wilton's retirement are also omitted. Two frequent diary entries have been excluded in order to save space. Sometimes, on a Monday, Wilton gives 'Same Performances as last week' or merely lists the same performances as the previous week. On a Wednesday night, the regular date for benefit performances at the Britannia Theatre, Wilton often writes, 'No Benefit, thank heaven!' In the absence of an entry for Monday night, the reader should assume that the theatre's programme was the same as the previous week's; if no reference to a benefit performance is made on a Wednesday, then the reader should assume that there was no benefit (thank heaven!). Entries which are merely repetitive have also been omitted.

A microfilm of the Diaries is held by the Rose Lipman Library (Hackney Archives Dept.), De Bouvoir Street, London N.1.

Days on which no theatrical entries of note occur are not included in the text. When non-theatrical entries intervene between the theatrical entries on the same day, their existence is indicated by dotted lines (. . .). Changes of line within a day's entry, often used by Wilton to indicate a change of topic, are also indicated by dotted lines, in order to economise on space. Single theatrical entries for a specific date are given without dotted lines before or after, even when domestic entries occur before and/or after the theatrical matter transcribed.

Transcription of the diaries has been greatly facilitated by the legibility of Wilton's handwriting. There are two distinct modes of handwriting, suggesting that Wilton may have been ambidextrous. Wilton's original spelling and punctuation have usually been retained, unless alterations were necessary for the sake of clarity. Similarly, I have retained capitals, although erratically used, unless clarity of meaning has been impeded. Wilton is often inconsistent in spelling proper names, largely because he is relying on sound rather than sighting. As far as possible I have attempted to standardise or correct these spellings. Underlinings, plus all titles of plays and most sums of money, are represented in the printed text by italics. Where an underlining in the original manuscript appears to be arbitrary rather than emphatic, it has been removed.

Occasionally, within the main text of the diary, I have integrated additional material from the appendices of the volumes, where these refer to events on a specific date. I have also transferred entries made on the wrong date to the correct date. (Wilton will often enter a comment on, say, a Thursday, because he forgot to enter it or had run out of space for the correct day of that week on which it should have been entered.) My main purpose in editing the manuscript has been to provide a readable and accurate text, faithful to Wilton's original, whilst clarifying any ambiguities that might merely confuse the reader.

Notes identifying names referred to in the text are usually printed at the bottom of the page on which the name first occurs. If Wilton's own identification is sufficient or if the name has proven unidentifiable, then no note appears. Longer notes and those on more general issues are printed at the end of the text.

The Diaries

1863

JAN 1 Thurs   Paid *£13.7.6* subscribed at the Britannia Theatre in aid of the Lancashire Distress Fund, to Mr Ledger, editor of the *Era*, to be inserted in the *Era* of January 4th[1].

2 Fri   Wrote to J.Kimber* hoping he would not forget his debt to Mr Lane for the masks sent to him 6th November last.

5 Mon   Pantomime *Abou Hassan* introducing Tom Sayers* & Signori Angelici and Arena, the Neopolitan Minstrels. *Some Bells that Rang.* Immense House.

6 Tues   J.C.Heenan, 'the Benicia Boy' (Tom Sayers's antagonist in the late fight for the championship) in the manager's Box this evening, – recognised by the audience, called on the stage and shook hands with Sayers – seemed much younger than him (10 years it has been said) and at least half a head taller – had jet black hair and wore large moustachios.

13 Tues   Ned Edgar* at Theatre, left M.S.S. to read.

22 Thurs   Letter from John Kimber (in reply to mine of last week) apologising for not being yet able to pay for the masks and saying that what he wanted was '*a silent financial friend*'.

26 Mon   1st change of piece at the Britannia since Xmas. *Mary Edmonstone.* Pantomime &c as before.

28 Wed   Mrs Casse, Clara* and Miss Reed* here to tea. With Harriet,* Amelia,* Mrs Casse and Clara afterwards to the Britannia. Mrs Borrow* told Amelia that the receipts at the Britannia have been £40 per night more this season since Xmas than they were at the same season last year, & on some nights fully double as much, all owing to Tom Sayers.

*John Kimber, whom Wilton first met in the Plymouth Company in the 1830s, had been stage manager for Newcombe, the Plymouth manager, and at North Shields. He had been prompter at the Lyceum for Charles Mathews the younger, conducted front of house for Selby at the New Royalty Theatre and toured his own company (or circus) in the provinces.

*Tom Sayers, the pugilist, had been engaged especially for the 1862–63 pantomime. He had won his first championship belt in 1857; on 17/4/1860 he and J.C.Heenan (an American) had fought for the championship of all England at a venue near Farnborough, a fight which ended in a draw. Sayers retired from the championship on 28/5/1860.

*E.F.Edgar was an actor, who from 1875–79 became secretary of the Royal General Theatrical Fund. In the 1850s he had acted at the Marylebone Theatre, where he briefly became involved in management. In the early 1860s he was engaged at the Standard Theatre in the East End.

*Clara St. Casse, singer and burlesque actress, had occasionally undertaken starring engagements at the Britannia since 1856. **Miss Reed** is not identified. **Harriet Rountree** was a married daughter of F.C.Wilton. **Amelia Wilton** was F.C.Wilton's wife. **Mrs Borrow** was Sarah Lane's mother; she also acted as her dresser.

30 Fri   Business apparently beginning to fall off at Theatre.

FEB 3 Tues   Last subscription to Fund (General Theatrical) paid today –
18/8 to Mr Cullenford* at Lyceum Theatre.

5 Thurs   Miss Sophie Miles's* 1st Rehearsal at the Britannia (To make her 1st
appearance next Monday).

6 Fri   Young 'Wyndham'* (*mad* Wyndham, *Railway Guard* Wyndham) in the
Boxes (P.S.) of the Britannia, this evening. Nothing *fast* in his appearance
(manner or dress) and certainly no *madness* in his eyes. The same with a lot
of fighting men – Jem Mace,* Nat Langham* &c &c.

9 Mon   Performances same as last week with addition of new piece, *Circlet
of Gold.* 1st Appearance of Miss Sophie Miles.

11 Wed   Business falling off at the Britannia.

23 Mon   *Woman's Devotion* 1st time (Faucquez's* piece). Pantomime.

MAR 2 Mon   Mrs Atkinson* refused the part of Mrs Polonaise in *Ellen and
Susan* and was told she must take a week's notice from tonight.

6 Fri   Mr Lane received Notice that his terms for opening the theatre free
next Tuesday are accepted[2].

7 Sat   Mrs Atkinson's last night at Britannia.

9 Mon   *Ellen and Susan.* Pantomime.

10 Tues   Performances same as Monday night. Did not begin till 6.15, over
about 10 m. p. 11. New song by Plumpton* 'God bless Prince of Wales'. 'God
Save the Queen' (2 verses) sung on the stage by all the Company in full dress.
Marriage of the Prince of Wales and Princess Alexandra of Denmark. All the
London Theatres open free . . . After the performances at the Britannia went
up to Fred's* and brought Amelia home, taking the Bank, Mansion House
and Exchange in our way – no crowding anywhere at that late hour. Too late
to see the Bank Illumination which was extinguished.

11 Wed   Tom Sayers's Benefit at Britannia. J.C.Heenan appeared on the

---

*William Cullenford, formerly of the Adelphi Theatre, was the secretary of the Royal General Theatrical
Fund, of which he was one of the founding members.

*Sophie Miles was engaged as a leading actress. She had previously been appearing at the City of London
Theatre. Her husband, George Fisher, was low comedian at the Standard Theatre. She was 'one of earth's
most gorgeous creatures!' according to John Coleman.

*W.F.Wyndham, Jem Mace, and Nat Langham were all well-known pugilists. Langham was the only
pugilist ever to beat Tom Sayers. Mace had recently sold his circus and stud of horses, with which he had
been travelling. The 'notorious' Wyndham was a friend and patron of Mace's.

*Adolf Faucquez was a French Royalist emigré, who not only wrote plays, but gained his chief livelihood
by giving French lessons in the New North Road, close to the Britannia.

*Mrs Catherine Atkinson had been an actress at the Britannia since 1848. An actress of the name
subsequently appeared at the Grecian Theatre.

*Jo Plumpton, singer and actor, who partially modelled himself on Sims Reeves, had a long association
with the Britannia, dating back to at least 1843. He also performed in music halls. Fred was Fred Rountree,
Wilton's son-in-law, married to his daughter, Harriet.

1. Exterior of the Britannia Theatre, 1858.

2.   Samuel Lane.

3. Sara Lane.

4. Interior of the Britannia, from the auditorium, 1858.

5. Scene from a pantomime, 1864.

6. Interior of the Britannia, from the stage. 1858.

1866.

2nd *Month.*

FEBRUARY.

4 SUNDAY.

35 (*Sexagesima.*)

5 MONDAY. Perform^ces same as last week.

1st ^36 Appearance of John King, boatswain of the boat
(& of 3 other) seamen (one being Carpenter's mate)
saved from the "London". Mr Drummond says that
he engaged John King (who is to have £10 for the week), and the Carpenter's mate £4 per week; Another of the seamen, A.B. £2 per
week and the third, an Ordinary seaman, £1.10.0 for the week.
That Mr Lane had promised to give him (Drummond) £5 for his
trouble — and that to-night, when John King was saying that he did
not know that he had as much as he ought to have for going on the Stage
since, all day long, gentlemen were giving him sovereigns, Mr Lane
put his hand up his waistcoat pocket & saying "Well, & I can give you sove-
raigns too" — gave him one!

Sent Mrs B. Ware, 18 Postage Stamps by Post. 1 7

6 TUESDAY.

37 Wrote to Secretary of "Union Savings Bank" Devonport
(yesterday) 1st letter, requesting Transfer of Milly's
Deposit to Moorfields Savings Bank."

Mr J. Drummond told me tonight that John King
is to have £30 for appearing next week.

Johnny Day & his father both recognised
the best Champion Walker, 9¾ years of age..
the Photographic Portraits of Edward & his son, Charley.

7 WEDNESDAY. Speaking of the demerits of the
38 present Britannia Pantomime, M^r C.
Beckett, (Printer) informed me to-day, that an
acquaintance of his took his Children to
see it a few evenings since — and that the
Children cried "to go home" before the Pantomime was over' — which he (C. Beckett) considered decisive as to its merits.

8. Nichol's Square, Hackney, where Wilton lived.

stage, in the Transformation Scene. Shook hands with Sayers, bowed to the audience and then returned to the Box where he had previously been sitting. Mrs S.Lane having said previously 'These are *England's* wonders of world wide renown, And in our 3rd Comic Scene *Mr Sayers* will appear as Clown'. In the 3rd comic scene however the audience roared so tumultously for a *Set To* that Heenan finally yielded and a short *Set To* with gloves took place.

12 Thurs   Very bad house tonight – the natural result of the two preceding houses.

16 Mon   Spectre of the Sea. Jeannie Deans (Burlesque, 1st time). *Ellen and Susan.* Wrote to J.Kimber about masks (not yet paid for).

17 Tues   Bad Houses at Britannia.

19 Thurs   Very cold, fine and dry . . . Letter from John Kimber detailing particulars of his desperate position. Showed it to Mrs S.Lane. She said, very kindly, she was sure it was of no use urging such a poor devil and added 'Write and tell him not to grieve about it – but to wait till he was able, and then send the money', (£3) due for masks sent to him *before* Xmas. Very bad business at Theatre all the week.

23 Mon   Return of the Wanderer. Jeannie Deans. Spectre of the Sea.

30 Mon   Courier of Lyons. Jeannie Deans. Return of the Wanderer. Sent letter to Mr Cullenford, making Amelia's claim on Theatrical Fund.

APRIL 1 Wed   Mr Bigwood's* Benefit. *Hookheim* (*Scarlet Mantle*). *Volunteers* (*Mayor of Garratt*). *Return of Wanderer.* Bad House, not £25 in the House. *Mr Pepper's* 1st Rehearsal of his *Spectral Illusion* for Easter, with real skeleton[3].

2 Thurs   2nd Rehearsal of Mr Pepper's *Spectral Illusion.*

3 Fri   Another Rehearsal of Pepper's *Spectral Illusion* at the Britannia from 2 to 5, (Good Friday!) A slight Fire at the Britannia this morning, about 11 a.m., in one of the Ladies' Dressing Rooms, owing to Mrs Clements, one of the cleaners, having a lighted candle near the door on which Miss S.Miles's dresses were hanging. These dresses caught alight from the candle on the cleaner's opening and shutting the door to go out (unperceived by her). The workmen being in the theatre soon became alarmed by the volume of smoke, and with some effort extinguished the fire.

4 Sat   Night Rehearsal of Machinic Effect (*Flight of Angels*, for Easter piece) after performance. Tom King,* the pugilist, presented with a belt on the stage by some of his friends, Mr T.Drummond* making the speech necessary to deliver it. *Good*, but not *great*, House.

*George B.Bigwood** had been first low comedian at the Britannia Theatre since 1862. He had previously appeared at the Marylebone Theatre, where he had been involved briefly in management, and at the Standard. He was to be one of the theatre's longest-serving performers, eventually becoming stage manager. He retired to Southend, where he opened a tobacconist's shop.

*Tom King** had recently announced his intention of fighting J.C.Heenan later in the year. **Thomas G.Drummond** had been the Britannia's leading 'Heavy' or actor of villains since 1860. He had previously performed at the Grecian.

6 Mon Faith, Hope and Charity (1st time) with Professor Pepper's 'Spectral Illusion'. *Jeannie Deans. Circlet of Gold.* (First piece played 4 hours all but 2 minutes – 31 minutes wait between the 2nd and 3rd acts, preparing the 'Illusion' – 18 minutes between the 3rd & 4th Acts). Capital House. *1st Night of the Ghost.*

7 Tues 43 minutes saved and cut from the new Piece tonight.

8 Wed Received letter from Mr Cullenford as follows:

T.R.Haymarket . . . April 7th, 1863
Dear Madam / I have this day laid your claim before the Directors and have the pleasure of stating that you have been placed upon the list of Annuitants. The Annuities are paid quarterly viz. in the first week of Feb, May, Aug & Nov. I shall therefore be prepared to pay you one month's amount on the Friday in the first week in May, between 2 & 3 o'clock at the Committee Room, Lyceum Theatre.
Mrs Amelia Wilton   Yours faithfully, Wm Cullenford (Secretary)

17 Fri Mr E.L.Blanchard* & Mr Kingsbury* on stage after 1st Piece.

20 Mon Widows and Orphans (*Faith, Hope and Charity*, newly named). *Aurora Floyd*, (1st time). Capital House – Pepper's 'Ghost Effect' attractive.

25 Sat Good House at Brit.

27 Mon Capital House.

29 Wed A Society's Benefit.* No change of Pieces (Thank Heaven!) Good House.

30 Thurs Benefit of Messrs Jacobs, Thorne & Carter.* *Widows and Orphans. Hand of Cards. Doomed City.* Good House. £78.

MAY 2 Sat Fine day, but cold at night. Wind E. Immense House at Britannia.

4 Mon Performances same as last week. Very good House. A fine, warm, summer's day. (The Ghost Effect attractive still).

7 Thurs Good House (Ballet Girls' Ticket Night).

18 Mon Performances same as last week – excellent house.

23 Sat Received 12 more scarlet geraniums & 6 fuschias from Bethnal Green Road (thro' 'Monk',* scene shifter at Theatre).

25 Mon Whit-Monday. No change of performances! Extraordinary! To the Grecian to see their 1st piece by desire of Mr and Mrs S.Lane. Found no

---

*E.L.Blanchard was a well-known author of West End pantomimes and contributor to *Punch*. F.Kingsbury was a musical conductor.

*Philanthropical Societies regularly hired the Britannia for benefits.

*Darve Jacobs, John Thorne and J.Carter were all Britannia check-takers. Jacobs later became Bill Inspector and Theatre Messenger.

*D.Monk(s) was still employed at the Britannia Theatre in 1904, as a Bill-poster.

resemblance between their Phantom Effect and ours. (Name of their Piece, *The Bridal Phantom* in 4 acts – one of the Dream Pieces) – a crammed house and a terrible squeeze in the pit.

28 Thurs   Mrs Crauford* confined – daughter. (She played last night!)

31 Sun   Home all day, reading 2 Pieces for Faucquez' Benefit (July 8th).

JUNE 1 Mon   Widows and Orphans. The Maladetta (1st night). Indifferent House.

2 Tues   Wrote to Jas Robertson Esq., superintendent of Great Eastern Railway, soliciting Pass for 'self & son' to Chelmsford and back, next Sunday, in return for our case and exhibition of June bills & Boards of Great Eastern Railway* . . .

3 Wed   Mr Browning* called on Tuesday May 2nd, said he was painting silk Banners for the Foresters, and lives in the City Road (Chart Street). His brother, Frank, is keeping a Baker's shop in Treville Street, Plymouth, his wife attending to it, while he paints scenery for Newcombe of the Plymouth Theatre . . . John Kimber, he has been told, is now Prompter at the St. James's Theatre, London, and Newcombe has the Devonport Theatre . . . - Frank was at the Lyceum Theatre, London, for a week, last Xmas, assisting to paint the Theatre for *The Duke's Motto* . . . 'House' very bad tonight at Theatre (People got no money – spent all, doubtless, last week, Whitsun Holidays).

4 Thurs   Bad House at Theatre tonight.

8 Mon   Performances at Britannia same as last week, with addition of the Conrad Brothers* between Pieces.

9 Tues   Shy House at Britannia.

10 Wed   Shy House again at the Britannia.

11 Thurs   Mr Lane's yacht, *Phantom*, won another Prize today.*

15 Mon   Widows and Orphans. Brothers Conrad, Woodman* & *Daughter of Night.*

22 Mon   Wishing Glen (with 'Ghost Effect'). C.Woodman. Brothers Conrad. *Daughter of Night.*

*Charlotte Crauford, a younger sister of Sarah Lane, was married to William Crauford, another Britannia actor and Landlord of the Britannia Tavern. Born in 1837 she had commenced her career on the Britannia stage playing boys' roles. She also played heroines in melodrama and Harlequina (and other roles) in pantomime, being an excellent dancer.

*Wilton does not clarify if the bills were displayed at his grocery shop or at the Britannia.

*Mr Browning must have been known to Wilton when he was a member of the Plymouth company.

*The Conrad Brothers were Americans who appeared at the Alhambra and, in 1875, at Hengler's Circus.

*Samuel Lane, manager of the Britannia Theatre, was a member of the Royal Thames Yacht Club. His yacht won the second class race and Lane was awarded with the 50th piece of silver he had received for his prowess at sailing.

*Charles Woodman was a very unusual double-voiced singer and instrumentalist, who was said to play the smallest violin in the world.

24 Wed   No Benefit since April 1st – Thank Heaven. Mrs Atkinson called.

29 Mon   The Wishing Glen (2nd week). Les Frères Conrad (on the Tight Rope). C.Woodman. *Paved with Gold.* Good House.

JULY 2 Thurs   Miss Elton* here to get papers signed for joining the 'Gen Theatrical Fund'.

4 Sat   A Gold Whistle[4] subscribed for by the Company of the Britannia presented to Cecil Pitt,* the Prompter.

6 Mon   Performances same as last week. Randall* (Comic Singer) engaged in addition (his 1st week). Cecil donned his Gold Whistle – His 1st day of wearing it. Miss Burdett-Coutts* and party at the Britannia, occupied Box over Mr Lane's. Had the *Ghost* business explained to them and exhibited again after curtain fell, Miss B.C. and party being on the stage at the time . . . Mr Crauford* attending them.

8 Wed   M.Faucquez' Benefit. *Willow Marsh* (1st time) Ghost Effect (one scene only). Les Freres Conrad (Tight Rope), W.Randall, C.Woodman. *Sacred Trust.* Capital House, notwithstanding the heat of the weather.

9 Thurs   After performances tried experiment to produce a new *Ghost Effect*, a distant, upright figure advancing – failed.

13 Mon   Wishing Glen with Ghost Effect. Woodman & Randall. *Ocean Monarch.*

15 Wed   Mr Crauford's Benefit. 1st act of *Wishing Glen* (Ghost Effect). W.Randall & C.Woodman. *Hive of Life, Its Drones & its Workers* (Calvert's* Piece) 1st time – and *Mary Dudley* (Marchant's*Piece) 1st Night with Horse & Ass. – Intensely hot day. – Immense Posters (6 sheeters) & lots of Woodcuts. House not so great at first as expected, but filled up afterwards, and became crowded with £60.1.0.

17 Fri   Received negative from T.Taylor* about *Ticket of Leave Man.*

*Miss Elton was a ballet girl at the Britannia Theatre from 1859–1869. She may have been related to Edward Elton, the Britannia's second low comedian.

*Cecil Pitt was the son of George Dibdin Pitt, who had been house dramatist at the Britannia Theatre in the 1840s and 1850s. Cecil Pitt, who wrote plays himself, was extremely tall, and had a very loud voice and specialised in villainous roles. He had previously played at the City of London Theatre, before joining the Britannia company in 1845.

*William Randall was a comic singer of domestic songs, such as 'Jones's Sister' and 'The Charming Young Lady I Met in the Train'. Angela Georgina Burdett-Coutts was a well-known philanphropist. William Samuel Crauford, born 1829, had joined the Britannia from the Bower Saloon in 1853. He married Charlotte Borrow in 1855 and had recently taken over from Samuel Lane as Host of the Britannia Tavern. He was particularly skilled in rustic characters and as an actor of 'breezy bucolic and Irish characters'.

*Charles Calvert wrote several dramas for provincial and south London theatres between the 1850s and 1870s. Frederick Marchant was engaged as an actor at the Britannia from 1858–1862, playing Juvenile Leads. He was also engaged at the Victoria with J.A.Cave and at a number of East End theatres. He sometimes played the melodramatic hero or lover in his own plays, such as *Forsaken*, in which he was almost sawn in half in a sensational saw-mill scene.

*Tom Taylor's play *The Ticket of Leave Man* had just proved a great success at the Olympic Theatre with Henry Neville in the leading role.

19 Sun Home all day partly engaged on new Piece for Miss Downing's*
Benefit.

20 Mon   Willow Marsh. Ghost Scene from *Wishing Glen.* W.Randall,
C.Woodman. *Hive of Life. Ship on Fire* (i.e. *Ocean Monarch*) . . . Capital
House.

22 Wed   Messrs C.Pitt, Swaine* & Brinkworth's* Benefits. *Avarice* (calling it
The Miser's Daughter). Ghost Scene. C.Woodman, W.Randall. *Crime &
Remorse.* Great House (£75.0.0) Cash about £43, Tickets £32. Much rain
yesterday and this morning, clearing up about noon . . . The Beneficiares
tonight cleared about £8.10.0 each by their Benefit.

23 Thurs   Wrote and gave *Notices of Discharge* to Messrs Plumpton &
C.J.Bird,* the former to terminate on the 9th Sept and the latter on the 6th
Oct.

27 Mon   Avarice, or *The Miser's Daughter.* Ghost Scene. W.Randall,
C.Woodman. *Hive of Life. Curse of Disobedience* . . . Mrs Fowles (sister-in-
law of Mrs Borrow) died this morning, after being raving mad all yesterday
– her husband left with nine children!

29 Wed   Miss Downing's Benefit. *Fitz-Alwyn, 1st Lord Mayor of London*
(new Piece written by Mr Hazlewood for Mr Drummond). W.Randall,
C.Woodman, Ghost Scene. *Guilty Mother.* Good House – Hot Day.

30 Thurs   Mr Frederick Peel* & a large Party at the Theatre tonight. In hopes
to see Ghost Scene, then round on to stage to see how Ghost managed, then
into Manager's Box to see *Hive of Life* . . . Mr Hazlewood* at Theatre,
consented to allow me to play his piece *The Detective* for my Benefit 19th
August.

31 Fri Went to Victoria Theatre, to get M.S.S. of *Detective.* Frampton*
would not lend M.S.S. while piece playing there, but consented to let their
copyist make a Transcript. Agreed with copyist for 10/0 to be brought
Tuesday night or Wednesday morning next.

AUG 2 Sun   Home all day making Bill of *Angel of Peace and Pardon.*

---

*Adelaide Downing** had been playing soubrette roles and chambermaids at the Britannia since 1861. She
later married the actor and comic vocalist, George Lewis.

*T.Swain(e)** was a check-taker at the Britannia. **W.H.Brinkworth** was Leader of the Britannia's Orchestra.

*Charles James Bird** had acted at the Britannia since 1849, but had moved to the Effingham Theatre for
a while after the Britannia Theatre closed for rebuilding. According to the *Players* (18/5/1861), 'his style
is gentlemanly, refined and finished, with an entire absence of all coarseness and vulgarity, and a far less
desire to pander to the feelings of an audience than to represent correctly the character he assumes'.

*Frederick Peel**, chief Railway Commisioner, was the second son of Sir Robert Peel. **Colin Hazlewood**,
a prolific author, particularly of melodramas, wrote regularly for the Britannia from the mid-1850s to the
mid 1870s. He also wrote for other East End theatres, as well as for the Victoria and the Marylebone. He
even found time to act; his line being low comedy.

*Frederick Frampton** was lessee of the Victoria Theatre where Hazlewood's play, derived from the same
source as Taylor's *Ticket of Leave Man*, was currently in the repertoire.

3 Mon   Blue Beard. Messrs W.Randall & C.Woodman. Ghost Effect scene
from *Wishing Glen. Miser's Daughter. Hive of Life.*

4 Tues   Received M.S.S. of *Detective* . . . Paid 10/0

5 Wed   J.Reynolds's* Benefit. Guessed about £65. Ghost Scene (to begin
with) from *Wishing Glen. The Rough Road tries the Mettle* (Woodcut).
W.Randall, C.Woodman. *Handsome Jack* (Woodcuts, J.B.Howe's* piece).

7 Fri   Amelia to English Opera House and received Quarter's annuity –
£7.10.0. Mem. We paid £1.14.5 p Quarter for 16 years preceding last
November (£6.17.8 per annum) besides Entrance fees.

9 Sun   Home all day making out Bill for Benefit, especially for *Ticket of
Leave.*

10 Mon   Angel of Peace (1st night). W.Randall, C.Woodman. *Ding Dong
Will. Blue Beard.* To Ransom & Warren's to ask loan of woodcut for *Ticket
of Leave* (my Benefit piece for next Wednesday week). Saw Mr Warren, who
was pleased with the idea and brought Mr Ransom to Theatre at night, when
both gave their promise. Afterwards to G.W.M.Reynolds's Publishing Office
for *Reynolds' Miscellany* to ask Mr Dicks the Printer to lend 1st Woodcut in
a work he is printing founded on Tom Taylor's drama of *The Ticket of Leave*[5].
Mr Dicks in country – saw foreman, Mr Jehring, who was with our son Ned,*
when a boy, at Mr Toms's, Warwick Square. To write letter to Mr Dicks for
Wednesday next.

12 Wed   J.Parry's* Benefit. *White Phantom.* W.Randall, C.Woodman, Ghost
Scene. *Soldier's Progress.* Very hot day – but good House, guessed £50
odd, proved only £47. To Mr Dicks's Publishing Office, 313 Strand, to get
woodcut from *Reynolds's Miscellany* for *Ticket of Leave* – lent grudgingly.
Also to Ransom & Warren's, 3 Bouverie Street, Fleet Street to get woodcuts
from their *Confessions of a Ticket of Leave* – great difficulty to find Mr
Ransom, who when found freely gave note to Printer for it. Block gone from
Printers to Engravers – & Mr R brought it himself to Theatre at night.

---

*Joseph Reynolds was a leading actor at the Britannia, which he had joined in 1851. One of the most
popular of East End actors, his acting was 'remarkable for its quiet gentlemanly tone. He is effective, even
melodramatic, without ranting'. (*Players*, 10/11/1860) **J.B.Howe** (actually 'Tommy' Burdett Howe) was
more noted as a leading melodramatic actor and tragedian than as a dramatist. He had joined the
Britannia from the Bower Saloon in the 1850s, had appeared at other East End theatres and in America,
and was to maintain a connection with the Britannia, through occasional engagements, into the 1900s. See
J.B.Howe, *A Cosmopolitan Actor*, 1888.

*Ned Wilton was now resident in Australia.

*John Parry had joined the Britannia, where he specialised in 'Heavy' roles, in 1856. His brother, Sefton
Parry, was a successful actor and manager. He himself had appeared extensively in the provinces and in
London at the Victoria, the Standard, the City of London and the Queen's, Tottenham Court Road, where
he had been stage manager.

13 Thurs Yesterday a note from Mr Lane to Mr Borrow,* saying he 'would let Alfred Davis* have *Faith, Hope and Charity* (M.S.S.) in preference to Mr Mortimer Murdoch* who had written for it – for *£6.0.0.*

14 Fri Billy N_____m's self-absorption!*

15 Sat Agreed with Mr Young, the copyist, that Mr S.Lane should pay him *6s.0d* for a copy of *Faith, Hope and Charity*, Mr S.Lane finding Ciphering books to write the piece up for Alfred Davis.

16 Sun Home all day – Plots for *Ticket of Leave.*

17 Mon *Angel of Peace.* W.Randall, Orville Parker* (Nigger Singer & Dancer). *Crime and Remorse.* Returned woodcuts to Ransom & Warren and Mr Dicks . . . Went up to Polytechnic to see Mr Pepper F.C.S.A. about 'Ghost Effect' for Alfred Davis – found Mr P was gone to Manchester. Letter from Mr Lane scouting Alfred Davis's offer of £6 for *Faith, Hope and Charity* in all theatres he and his father may possess.

19 Wed Own Benefit.* *Ticket of Leave.* W.Randall, Orville Parker. *Old Booty.* Total *£48.17.6.* Cash *£46.15.0.* Tickets *£2.2.6.* Weather rainy and cool yesterday. Gloomy morning, with some rain – cleared up at 3.p.m. – but a shower about past 5 to 6. Altogether glorious weather . . . Letter from Alfred Davis, reiterating his offer – will give no other terms. – Wrote Mr Lane to that effect.

24 Mon *Angel of Peace and Pardon.* Orville Parker. Charles Sloman* (Sloman's 1st night). *Ticket of Leave.* Good 'House' drawn by my piece, *Ticket of Leave.*

25 Tues Thunder-storm. Violent wind & heavy rain. Decent 'House' drawn by my *Ticket of Leave.*

26 Wed Benefit. Miss S.Miles. *Lady Audley's Secret.* Orville Parker, Charles Sloman (Improvisatore). *Pauline.* Heavy rain all day, till late at night . . . House expected to be a dead failure, but, in spite of rain, proved good. (Guessed at above *£50* – turned out better still).

---

*William Borrow, a former cab proprietor and father of Sarah Lane, was acting manager and treasurer of the Britannia Theatre. **Alfred Davis**, theatre manager and actor, was the son of **Edward Dean Davis**, manager of the Theatre Royal, Newcastle. E.D.Davis had previously managed a small-town country circuit in the West Country, which is where Wilton must have first met him. **Mortimer Murdoch** was a provincial tragedian, particularly well known in Glasgow and Liverpool. He had also played at the Marylebone Theatre.

*W.H.Newham had joined the Britannia as third low comedian and Pantaloon in 1856. His wife was also an actress in the company and many of his children appeared in roles in pantomime and melodrama. He had at one time been manager of the Woolwich Theatre. Wilton's entry, which probably refers to Newham's son, may be a discreet reference to masturbation.

*Orville Parker, an American, was billed as the 'Great New York Squash Swamp Dancer'.

*Wilton's Benefit Expenses are listed in Appendix A.

*Charles Sloman had gained a reputation in the Song and Supper Rooms for improvising songs on any person present or any subject proposed to him.

27 Thurs   Mr Donne,* Examiner of Plays, came to inspect the Britannia Theatre, this day, 12 o'clock[6]. W.Crauford and Mr Beckett* returned from their tour in Scotland.

28 Fri   Posted M.S.S. of *Faith, Hope and Charity* to Alfred Davis.

31 Mon   Angel of Peace and Pardon. The Boss Orville Parker. *Verdant Giles. Ticket of Leave.* Capital House, drawn by my piece (*The Ticket of Leave*) to which, on its first night, my Benefit, I had a shy House!

SEPT 2 Wed   C.J.Bird's Farewell Benefit. *Stolen Sheep.* The Boss Orville Parker. Ghost Scene from *Angel of Peace and Pardon. Will and the Way.* Good House, notwithstanding heavy showers at intervals all day and night. – Guessed between £50 & £60.

5 Sat   Private subscription among a few members of the Company, at the Theatre, to assist Mr G.Blythe* to bury his child, amounted to £1.10 . . . Paper sent in soliciting subscriptions for the widow of the late W.Rogers, low comedian, to assist her in Funeral Expenses, *unfavourably received by the Company* – partly because W.Rogers* had invariably, while alive, refused to subscribe to similar appeals, and partly because demanded rather than prayed.

6 Sun   Home all day (Plots of *Fan Fan* for Mrs S.Lane's return).

7 Mon   Lady Audley's Secret. The Boss, 'Orville' . . . Ghost Scene from *Angel of Peace. Ticket of Leave.* Capital House.

9 Wed   Mr J.Plumpton's Benefit & Last Night. *Lady Audley's Secret.* The Boss, Orville Parker. Madame Pleon (Swiss vocalist).* *Devil's Bridge. Skeleton Witness* (called in bills *Old Mordecai*) – Weather threatening, but otherwise favourable. Guessed over £70 & proved £75.

10 Thurs   Paid Young the copyist 10/0 for writing M.S.S. of *Faith, Hope and Charity* for Mr E.D.Davis, including two ciphering books in which the piece was written.

11 Fri   Sent off M.S.S. of *Faith, Hope and Charity* . . . to Mr E.D.Davis.

14 Mon   Lady Audley's Secret. W.Randall. The Boss, Orville Parker. Ghost Scene from *Angel of Peace and Pardon.* Madame Pleon (Swiss vocalist). *Ticket of Leave.* – Excellent House again.

15 Tues   Gave out Scene, Property and Music Plots of *Fanfan the Tulip* last night & Wardrobe Plot this evening.

16 Wed   Benefit of Perry (Drummer) and Wade (Band-master). *Dead Men*

---

*William Bodham Donne (1807–1882) had officially been Examiner of Plays since 1857; unofficially, he had been deputising for John Mitchell Kemble since 1849. Charles Beckett was Printer to the Britannia Theatre.

*George Blythe and occasionally his wife, Mary, had acted at the Britannia since late in 1859. William Rogers, low comedian and dramatist, had acted at the Britannia in the late 1840s and from 1856–1860.

*Madame Pleon's repertoire consisted of Swiss and German songs.

Tell No Tales. W.Randall. The Boss, Parker. Madame Pleon (the Swiss vocalist – who is a veritable Cockney). The Fireman's Band (at least 90 Performers) Master Rogers* (on the trombone) Master Simmons (a Jew-Boy, on the Side Drum). *The White Phantom* (C.Pitt's piece) preceded by the 'Ghost Effect'. Upwards of *£90* in the 'House'!

21 Mon   Lady Audley's Secret. W.Randall The Boss, Parker. Mme Pleon. Ghost Scene from *Angel of Peace. Green Lanes and Blue Waters.* Capital House owing, no doubt, to bad weather yesterday and today . . . Gave the M.S.S. of *Faith, Hope and Charity* to Mr Chart,* in Prompt Entrance, by desire of Mr Crauford and in his presence.

22 Tues   Went to Pavilion Theatre to see *Lady Hatton* by direction of Mr Borrow. Found the Plot, Characters and Language all different from our piece as well as Situations and Incidents, except that the Demon first appeared to Lady Hatton at the *Suicide's Tree* & took her thence to the ruined monastery of St. Martin's to sign the Compact with her own blood; that the Compact appeared on the Altar as ours did; that when she signed it Ghosts appeared from the Tombs as they did with us; and that afterwards, in the next act, the Demon showed her Pandemonium, where Ixion appeared bound to a Wheel as with us, – and there was the Vulture of Prometheus hovering above.

23 Wed   Mrs E.Yarnold's* Benefit (sold to some of the Check-takers &c in the front). *Phoebe Hessel.* Ghost Scene (from *Angel of Peace*). W.Randall. Orville Parker. *Momentous Question* & *Lady Audley's Secret.* Lowering, cold, showery day – upwards of *£104* in the house & upwards of *£60* cash!

28 Mon   Phoebe Hessel. Ghost Scene from *Angel of Peace and Pardon.* W.Randall. The Boss, Orville Parker, ill, unable to appear (Duet sung instead by Mr E.Elton* and Miss A.Downing). *Lady Audley's Secret.* Immense House . . . Went with Mr Beckett (Printer)* & Mr Fowles* (Mrs Borrow's brother) to the Lord Chamberlain's Office, St James's Palace, & obtained License for the Britannia Theatre for next year. Paid *£4.14.0* for it. Saw Mr Ponsonby* who alluded to the request made by Mr Donne (Licenser of Plays) Aug 27th that the doors in the Pit Lobby might be altered. Went afterwards to see House of Commons, Westminster Abbey and Bridge. Dined at Simpson's Hotel in the Strand . . . saw Mr Douglass,* Lessee of the Standard Theatre, & Mr Edgar,* now Lessee of Sadler's Wells, at Simpson's Hotel.

*Master Rogers was probably Harry Rogers, son of Jonathan Rogers, the Britannia's trombonist.

*H.Nye Chart was manager of the Brighton Theatre.

*Emma Yarnold joined the Britannia company as an actress in 1856. After gaining a reputation as a child actress and then in the West End, she moved to the Pavilion Theatre, Whitechapel, which her husband managed. On his death she took over the management, but then withdrew from the stage until offered an engagement at the Britannia. She was considered out of her element in the East End, more suited for the line of refined and idealised characters associated with Helen Faucit. (*Players*, 1/9/1860).

*Edward Elton was the theatre's second low comedian. Apparently a more finished comedian than Bigwood, he was a son of the tragedian E.W.Elton, who had been drowned at sea. Beckett's premises were in Kingsland Rd; Robert Fowles was a fishmonger and poulterer of 411 City Road. The Hon. Spencer Brabazon Ponsonby was Comptroller of the Lord Chamberlain's Office from 1857–1901. John Douglass, a member of the original Britannia company, had become lessee of the Standard Theatre in 1849. Robert Edgar, manager of Sadler's Wells Theatre from 1863–1871, was married to the popular tragedian, Miss Marriot. He had previously been acting manager at the Standard Theatre.

29 Tues   Sent M.S.S. of *Faith, Hope & Charity* to Mr Newcombe, T.R. Plymouth, asking for a P.O. Order for £5 (the sum agreed on).

30 Wed   Benefit of Messrs Summers* & Light.* *Tower of Nesle.* Ghost Effect (played first). W.Randall. Boss Parker (ill, did not come, either tonight, or any evening of this week). *Raby Rattler.* Tremendous House – very fine day – Receipts *£100.0.6.*

OCT 1 Thurs   Went to the Tower to enquire about soldiers for Mrs Crauford's Benefit. Found there were no Grenadiers there, the garrison being the 60th Rifles – Colonel Bingham (Sergeant Major Powley). Told by Mr Borrow, at night, not to engage any till he had written to Mr Lane and received his answer.

5 Mon   Mr & Mrs Lane returned.

6 Tues   Went to the Tower (2nd time) about getting soldiers for new piece (*Days of Louis XV*). Saw Sergt-Major Powley – told to come tomorrow at a $\frac{1}{4}$ to 12 to see the Adjutant.

7 Wed   Mr Bridgins'* Benefit. *Ida Lee*, 1st time (Large woodcuts). *Lady Audley's Secret.* Ghost Effect. W.Randall. Orville Parker. Madme. Pleon. *3 Fingered Jack.* Shameful heavy work for the Company . . . Went to the Tower again & obtained Permission of Colonel Bingham for 40 men, a Sergeant, Drummer and Bugler, to come to the Britannia to support the new Drama (*The Days of Louis XV*).

10 Sat   C.J.Bird died this day. Miss S.Miles taken ill – unable to play tonight. Obliged to go over to Manor Place, Walworth Road and fetch Miss Julia Seaman* to play *Lady Audley*, which she did – Told her only to ask a night's salary & cab fare home. She had never played the part, but managed to get wonderfully perfect. Saw Mrs Seaman, her mother, at her house in Bronte Place, East Lane. Learnt that Mr Seaman* had been arrested a day or two previous for the costs in his suit against Boucicault, for infringing his right in the Drama of *Jessie Browne.* Mr S. had been taken to Horsemonger Lane Jail!!!7

12 Mon   *Belinda Seagrave.* W.Randall. Sam Collins.* Mme Pleon. Ghost scene from *Angel of Peace.* *Lady Audley's Secret* (Lady Audley – Julia Seaman) . . . Dr Forshall says 'C.J.Bird might have lived years longer had his complaint been properly understood. He died of disease of the kidneys & the Doctors had put poultices on his breast for inflammation on the chest!!!'

---

*H.Summers** was a Bill Deliverer and Saloon Assistant; **J.Light** was a Saloon Keeper.

*B.Bridgins** was a money-taker at the theatre.

*Julia Seaman** was an actress, who had appeared at the Pavilion and Victoria Theatres. **William Seaman** had regularly supplied the Britannia with plays for a short time in the 1850s.

*Sam Collins**, popular singer of Irish songs, was to open Collins's Music Hall in Islington on November 4th this year.

13 Tues   Rehearsed soldiers (60th Rifles) 1st time in *The Days of Louis XV*.

14 Wed   Mrs Crauford's Benefit. Ghost Scene from *Faith, Hope & Charity*. W.Randall. S.Collins. Mme Pleon. Master Rogers on the Trombone. Master Shapcott (a very small 'master') on the Side Drum. *Days of Louis XV* (1st night with Mrs S.Lane's 1st appearance this season). New Scenery, Dresses and Decorations. *Eily O'Connor & Rendezvous*. Tremendous House (almost full before doors opened). Performance very long – *not over till a Quarter before One*!

16 Fri   Received tonight 2 Comic Scenes and a portion of the Opening of Pantomime from Mr S.Lane – being the first instalment for the Season. Read – wrote out & gave to carpenter Scene Plot of one of the Scenes.

17 Sat   Gave out Property Plots of the above two Comic Scenes & Carpenter's Plot of 2nd Ditto, and received remainder of the 'Opening'.

18 Sun   All day long engaged making out Plots of Opening of Pantomime.

19 Mon   *Days of Louis XV (Fanfan the Tulip)*. W.Randall. Sam Collins. Mme Pleon. *Eily O'Connor* . . . C.J.Bird buried today in Abney Park Cemetery.

23 Fri   Gave out Plots of Opening (Property, Wardrobe & Masks).

26 Mon   *Days of Louis XV* . . . Ghost Scene from *Faith, Hope & Charity*. Mme Pleon. W.Randall. *Pride & Passion, or Honour of the Family*.

27 Tues   Gave out last scene & Property Plots of Comic Scenes.

30 Fri   Began Bill of Pantomime (Comic Scenes first) . . . Mr C.J.Bird's wardrobe (Theatrical) sold at the Theatre (by Messrs Reynolds & C.Pitt) – fetched £30. A young man of the name of Sinclair, formerly a super at the Britannia (now manager, *not* Proprietor, of a Circus in the Southern States of America) buying £25 worth, the remainder bought by Messrs C.Pitt, J.Reynolds & W.Crauford.

31 Sat   Went to the Tower & obtained permission of Colonel Bingham through Adjutant Kelly for the 40 soldiers now nightly engaged in *The Days of Louis XV* to attend the week after next in the same drama, when played as a last Piece.

NOV 1 Sun   Stormy Day – Began Pantomime Bill.

2 Mon   '31st Week of the Great Ghost Effect!' *Days of Louis XV*. W.Randall, Mme Pleon & Deulin* (Nigger). *Pride and Passion*. Good but not great house. A rumour that S.Sawford Comedian died last Friday in a hospital – not true. Gave out Wardrobe Plots of Pantomime Opening & Comic Scenes.

9 Mon   '32nd Week of Great Ghost Effect'. *Days of Louis XV*. W.Randall (obliged to sing before the piece). Mme Pleon. Paul Deulin. *Jewess of the Temple* – very imperfect (1st night) – called tomorrow.

---

*Paul Deulin was billed as the 'Champion negro Spade Dancer', performing his 'Rocky Mountain Breakdown'.

11 Wed Benefit of a Confectioners' Club. Performances as above, only changing last piece to *Lady Audley's Secret*. No great things of a House . . . This week made a *subscription* for *T.Attwood* (scene shifter at Theatre) who is left by the death of his wife, a widower with 5 children – On Saturday, Nov 14th, this subscription amounted to £6.3.6 (beside 1/0 promised by Mr G.Cooke, actor).* Collected the £6.3.6 and paid to T.Attwood on Saturday Nov 14th.

13 Fri Mrs S.Lane taken ill – with 'Quinsy' in throat. Miss A.Downing played her part.

15 Sun Home all day about Bill of Pantomime.

16 Mon Mrs S.Lane still bad – Quinsy in throat. Miss A.Downing played her part again.

18 Wed W.Newham's Benefit. Performances as above, changing only last piece to *Woman's Worth*. Day fine – House middling (afterwards heard it reached £67).

20 Fri Mrs S.Lane ill all this week with Quinsy, Miss A.Downing playing her part.

22 Sun Home all day – about Bill of Pantomime – & Gardening.

23 Mon Mrs S.Lane not playing this week – ill of Quinsy.

29 Sun Wrote 16 long Puffs for newspapers.

30 Mon *Bottle*, 3 nights, Mme Pleon. J.Taylor.* Deulin (Nigger). *Fanfan* (3 nights). *Jewess of Temple*. Mr Graham* in Theatre tonight, – Clara willing to play for Mrs S.Lane's Benefit, – Mrs S.Lane wishing her to play the *Corporal's Daughter*.

DEC 6 Sun Home all day making out Mrs S.Lane's Benefit bill – very heavy work.

7 Mon '36th Week of the Great Ghost Effect!' *The Chimes* (dramatised by Hazlewood, from the serial called *Bow Bells*)[8]. Paul Deulin, Mme Pleon. Mr J.Taylor. *The Jewess of the Temple*.

8 Tues 1st Rehearsal of words of Opening of Pantomime . . . Mrs S.Lane's Benefit Bill printed – *jubilate*!

9 Wed T.Drummond's Benefit. *Lady of Lyons*. Mme Pleon. J.Taylor. Paul Deulin. *Adventures of a Ticket of Leave*. Rainy Day (House upwards of £90).

11 Fri Yesterday, the day of the *Great Fight* between *King & Heenan* for £1,000, when King beat Heenan.

---

*George Cooke** was engaged at the Britannia to play Juvenile Leads. He had previously performed at the Marylebone Theatre.

*James Taylor** was billed as the 'Funny Little Man – The Comic Star of the East'. He won a prize of £100 in a 'Champion Comic Singer Contest' at Weston's Music Hall the following year. **Mr Graham** was Clara St. Casse's husband.

12 Sat   First Rehearsal yesterday of Supers & Children for Opening of Pantomime. Saturday: Clown, Harlequin & Pantaloon's 1st Rehearsal. Madme Celeste Stephan* & Miss Newham* arrived at ½ past 9 p.m. from France.

13 Sun   Home all day making clear copy of Pantomime Bill & enclosing Puffs for Newspapers for which Jessy* wrote notes to Editors.

14 Mon   *Bottle*. Mme Pleon. J.Taylor. Ghost Scene from *Jewess of Temple*. Tom King (the Pugilist) his 1st appearance (after his great battle with Heenan for £2000) with his second, Bos Tyler, Mr Drummond speaking an Address to introduce them.* – concluding with *The Chimes*.

17 Thurs   Tom King (Pugilist) at Britannia every night this week.

19 Sat   Mrs Casse on stage this morning with Clara's baby.

21 Mon   Mrs S. Lane's Benefit & Last Night of the Season. Ghost Effect (*Jewess*) – *Corporal's Daughter* (Clara Casse). Arthur & Bertrand (soi-disant French Clowns). Mdlle Celeste Stephan 1st appearance: 'Marvels of Peru' (sprites for Pantomime). – 'Fairy Fountain'. New Britannia Festival. Mme Pleon. *Gorilla Hunt* (new Drama).

22 Tues   Rehearsal of Pantomime. Opening & Comic Scenes lasted from *11 o'clock a.m.* till *5 p.m.* – !!!

23 Wed   Rehearsal lasted yesterday from 11 till ½ past 5. Then commenced for scenery again at 7 & lasted till ½ past 12 midnight, and during the interval between ½ past 5 & 7 had to compose and write 10 short puffs for newspapers, after production.

26 Sat   Boxing Day. Morning Performance (12 o'clock). Ghost Scene from *Jewess*. Pantomime *Hickory, Dickory, Dock!* including sprites 'The Marvels of Peru' (being the Brother Ridgway)* – The 2 French Clowns (Arthur & Bertrand, Gymnasts or Posturers) – & 'The Fairy Fountain'* – (concluding at night with *The Gorilla Hunt*). – Unable to begin in the morning till 40 minutes past time; great confusion – immense houses.

28 Mon   Morning Performances at 12 o'clock. Pantomime *Hickory, Dickory, Dock*, preceded by Ghost Scene from *Jewess of Temple*, & including 'Marvels of Peru' (i.e. the Brothers Ridgway), the 2 French Clowns, Arthur & Bertrand, & Professor Wheeler's 'Fairy Fountain'. At night concluding with *The Gorilla Hunt*.

---

*Celeste Stephan** had been the theatre's premiere danseuse and regular Columbine since 1850. She was married to Sarah Lane's brother, William, who was a cab driver. **Miss Newham**, a daughter of W.Newham, later gained notoriety as Madame Colonna, leader of a troupe of cancan dancers.

*Jessie Wilton** was Wilton's youngest daughter, still resident at home.

*Tom King** was also appearing at Weston's Music Hall with Bos (i.e. John) Tyler.

*The Brothers Ridgway** were acrobats. In about 1873 one of them was seriously injured whilst practising at the Canterbury. **The Fairy Fountain** sent forth 'numerous jets of real water, to which all the hues of the rainbow are given'. (*Era*, 3/1/1864).

1864

JAN 11 Mon   A woman knocked at door late at night & saying she was the wife of Mr Hughes* of the City Theatre, insisted that a Miss Moore* lodged here, and with much abuse, demanded that Miss Moore should come out & she would tear her to pieces! Who the devil is Miss Moore?

13 Wed   Crauford's supper at the Britannia, tonight.

FEB 2 Tues   Sent off M.S.S. of *Man of Red Mansion* to C.Rice,* T.R.White-haven, & in afternoon received from him P.O. Order for 11/0 – Paid to Mrs Lane half a sovereign, the price agreed on for copying.

8 Mon   Pantomime. *Hickory Dickory Dock*, 2 French 'clowns' (Arthur & Bertrand); 'Fairy Fountain'. *My Lord Welcome* (1st time). No sprites (called 'the Marvels of Peru') one of them having hurt his hand on Saturday night – therefore none of the four would play.

9 Tues   No sprites in the pantomime again tonight – and Louis* drunk! hurt his arm in leaping . . . Wrote C.Rice (by desire of Mrs S.Lane) explaining difficulty of his using Ghost Effect at Surrey in *Stricken Oak*.

20 Sat   Last night of the Ghost Effect after a run of 46 weeks!

22 Mon   *Outcasts* (founded on new novel by Miss Braddon)* 1st night. Pantomime. No Ghost Effect . . . 5 Men executed this day at Newgate, for Murder & Piracy on board the ship *Flowery Land* 1. Capital 'House' at the Britannia Theatre tonight – supposed to have been caused by many thousands having made holiday on account of the execution!

24 Wed   Louis' Benefit. *Seven Sisters*. Forest Scene from *Valentine and Orson*. Pantomime. *Hickory, Dickory, Dock*. 2 Great French Clowns (i.e. contortionists or acrobats) & in last Comic Scene – Pantaloon – Louis, Clown – Firth,* Harlequin – W.Newham, Columbine – G.Bigwood. Very good House.

28 Sun   Home all day writing plots of new piece for tomorrow week.

MAR 4 Fri   Very great 'House' at Britannia tonight.

5 Sat   Last Night of Pantomime *Hickory, Dickory, Dock*. 10th week of its 'Run'. An immense House. No sprites have played in it these 4 weeks.

6 Sun   Home all day making bill for Easter Piece.

---

*Beaumont Hughes played Juvenile Leads at the City of London Theatre. Miss Moore has not been traced; there is no one of that name listed on City of London playbills during this period.

*Charles Rice had been an actor at the Britannia from 1856–1860. His managerial activities subsequently encompassed both the Bradford and Covent Garden theatres. His play, *The Man of Red Mansion*, had first been performed at the Britannia in 1851.

*Jean Louis had annually appeared as Clown in the Britannia pantomime since 1856. Short in stature, he was a great favourite with audiences and funny without being vulgar.

*Mary Elizabeth Braddon (1837–1915), a popular novelist, wrote several works which were adapted into Britannia melodramas, including *Aurora Floyd* and *Lady Audley's Secret*.

*C.Firth was an 'agile' Harlequin in the annual pantomime. It was customary for the Harlequinade characters to exchange roles for Louis the clown's benefit.

7 Mon Evil Hands and Honest Hearts (1st week). *Outcasts*. Mistake in Bills, Date wrong, February printed instead of March.

8 Tues Wretched House at Brit to-night.

9 Wed Bigwood's Benefit. *Evil Hands & Honest Hearts. The Fly & All About it* (New Farce said by Bigwood to have been written by himself. Founded on the old farce called *Bathing*). 2 Acts of *My Poll & My Partner Joe*. £57 in the House – a wonderful 'House', considering the weather. Heavy rain all last night and Sharp Rain mixed with thick snow all this morning – only partially ceasing in the afternoon . . . streets sloppy.

13 Sun Home all day, making out bill for Easter Piece.

14 Mon Evil Hands & Honest Hearts. George Barrington. Shy houses all last week and tonight – Everybody saying the Pantomime was withdrawn a week too soon.

16 Wed Benefit of Friendly Association. *Guilty Mother* (instead of *Barrington*) J.G.Forde.* *Evil Hands* first.

17 Thurs (MAR) – 16 Sat (APRIL) – Intermittent.
Anecdotes of the Britannia
Perhaps when these things happened it would have been considered ridiculous to expect anybody out of the actual Corps Dramatique and Employees of the Saloon to be interested in anything that occurred in so insignificant a place, but now that the Saloon has become a great Theatre, a huge wealthy metropolitan fact, a few matters tending to illustrate the peculiarities of the Management and establishment in its small beginning and during its rise from obscurity, may not be altogether unamusing even to strangers.

In those days (1843 and thereabouts) it was considered necessary for the safe evasion of the law against unlicensed theatres, to announce the Concert in the bills, and make the theatrical performances appear only a subordinate part of the Entertainment, – But at this date the Concert had dwindled down to a mere Chorus and a Song or two, and soon fell off to a chorus only, and finally even the chorus was dispensed with and the bills boldly assumed the same aspect as the bills of the Minor Theatres, though the place was still called, like others of the same class, a 'saloon'. I remember when in 1846 I joined the company for the second time, asking if the management didn't think half past six too early to begin the Performance, and if, as the class who chiefly supported the Saloon were working people, it would not be advantageous to begin a little later, 7 o'clock, for instance – but Mr Borrow (Mrs S.Lane's father) replied, 'Oh, no! – we nearly always fill directly the doors are opened'.

When I first saw Mr S.Lane, it was soon after he had taken the house and fitted it up for Theatrical performances (during the life of his first wife). His then Stage Manager, Henry Howard, took me one morning to see the Saloon.

---

*J.G.Forde, a patter vocalist, had been chief comic singer at Wilton's Music Hall in Wellclose Square in 1857–58. He 'wore a large frock coat, a heavy black moustache, a little dab of red on his nose, and a mop of black hair (his own)'. He could reduce audiences to helpless laughter by his comments on topics such as marriage.

Mr S.Lane was standing on one of the Pit benches, and was already making some alterations. I was struck with a certain rough independence about him and the clear and determined manner in which he gave his orders to the Carpenters. H.Howard introduced me as a friend of his who had been a country manager. He honoured me with only a slight, quick nod of indifference, and went on with his business, forgetting apparently in an instant that either of us was present. I had expected some diffidence in a man quite unacquainted with theatricals and, just venturing to open a theatre, an evident leaning on his Stage Manager for advice. On the contrary I perceived he was self-reliant and perfectly master of the position. He paid no attention to us, and was soon in another part of the theatre, absorbed in his alterations.

When in 1843 I first joined him as Stage Manager the lowest price of admission was 3d and the business had become very bad. The price paid for the House by Beneficiaries was only £8, for which Mr Lane found Bills and tickets! The business still falling off he asked my advice about lowering the price of admission to 2d and he gave me three days to consider it. Meantime he seemed to have forgotten the matter, while I thought he was anxiously expecting my opinion. At the end of the 3 days I went to him and said I had come to the conclusion that it would not do. I thought the reduction of a penny would be no attraction (although he might, as he said he would, keep up and even increase the goodness of the entertainment), while, if the experiment failed, the prices could not again be raised. To my surprise he answered that he had also come to a conclusion, and that was to make the reduction. Shortly after, on account of a slight quarrel, we parted. He reduced the price to 2d and from that time the business rose rapidly. The house was filled nightly to suffocation and the receipts never seriously again went down; although after a time the prices were again raised, and ultimately to a higher scale than ever[2].

20 Sun   Passion Week. Wrote 13 Puffs for Newspapers.

21 Mon   *Evil Hands*. J.G.Forde. Mr Geo. Clair & sister,* Mr J.Warde & sister (Comic Singers).* M.Sextillion (Posturer).* Pio Wautkini (juggler).* Mr Albert Steele (Comic Singer).* Harriet Coveney* (Comic Singer). *Sham Captain*. Very bad House.

22 Tues   Very bad House again.

25 Fri   Night Rehearsal of Scenery. Began *8 o'clock*, over *12.25*.

---

*Geo Clair & Sister: an actor named George Clair had performed at the Britannia in 1855 and at the Marylebone Theatre in 1858. **John and Emma Ward(e)**, duettists, were very vigorous performers, who emphasised dancing rather than singing. Eventually John married Emma D'Auban and his sister married John D'Auban, another brother and sister team of duettists, and formed a very successful quartet. **Sextillion** could strike a succession of bodily attitudes while balancing a score of glass tumblers in an inverted pyramid on his forehead. He was also noted for his backward somersaults. **The Watkini** (sic) Japanese Jugglers were on the bill at Wilton's in 1870. **Albert Steele** was apparently noted for an absence of the vulgarity often to be found in the comic singers of the day. **Harriet Coveney** was a popular comic vocalist. Her sister, Jane, was later to join the Britannia company as an actress.

28 Mon   Left Handed Marriage. Four Mowbrays (Master Percy Roselle).*
Sham Captain.

29 Tues   Horribly cold still. Wind N. Got Influenza & Chapped Hands. Everybody with a cold. Ill all day of *Indigestion*, caused by eating a hard boiled egg for breakfast. Could eat nothing all day after . . . Sick about midnight. Had to play two long parts at Theatre and work *Spectacle*. Slept soundly all night. Better in the morning.

30 Wed   Mr Lane ill, confined to his bed (sluggish liver).

APRIL 6 Wed   No Benefit, except a Society, thank Heaven! Consulting with Mr Borrow this morning about engaging Clara Casse for a fortnight to play in a new burlesque called *Deboleah*.* He searched his Account Books & found that Clara's salary when she played for a fortnight in 1862 was *£9.10.0* per week *without a benefit*; and for *one* week only in *1858*, without a Benefit, was *£10*. Engaged Clara Casse. Went up to Clara's lodgings at about $\frac{1}{2}$p.6. and engaged her to play in the new burlesque at £5 per week & $\frac{1}{2}$ a clear Benefit., for a month, to commence next Monday week. Clara to play next Wednesday for Mr Crauford's Benefit, & to receive a night's salary for that evening – Her month's engagement to commence on Monday the 18th and if the Piece should run a few nights longer, Clara to play those few nights receiving the same amount of salary.

8 Fri   Mr G.F.Cooke unaccountably absent from the Theatre all night – had to 'go on' for his part in the *Left-handed Marriage* at a moment's notice – Mr G.Blythe playing his (Mr Cooke's) part in *The Sham Captain*.

9 Sat   No certain news yet of Mr Cooke . . . Played his part again in the *Left-Handed Marriage*, – & played also in the other two pieces – harassed to death!

10 Sun   Home all day, studying & making out Plot for *Paul the Showman*.

11 Mon   *Left-Handed Marriage*. (1st night of Mr Bell,* actor from Standard Theatre). *Spoiled Child* (Master Percy Roselle). *Charlotte Corday*.

13 Wed   Crauford's Benefit. *Left-Handed Marriage*. New Burlesque, *Deboleah* Clara Casse, Miss Scott* (1st night of each). *Paul the Showman*, Mr B.G.Ellis* (1st night), Mrs Dyas* (1st night). Not a great house – (People are thinking of nothing but Garibaldi).

---

*Percy Roselle was a child actor. According to the *Illustrated Sporting and Theatrical News* (21/11/1868) he made his professional debut in Bristol at the age of 5 in 1859. He played both serious roles and in burlesques which were specially written for him. H.Chance Newton (*Referee*, 3/2/1924) suggests that he was substantially older than this when he appeared at the Britannia.

*Debo-Lear is subsequently given by the playbills.

*Robert Bell, although later engaged at the Victoria, was to enjoy a long association with the Britannia.

*Miss Emily Scott played particularly in burlesque and pantomime. B.G.Ellis may have been Brandon Ellis, whom H.Chance Newton describes as 'a very handsome man and one of the best and blood-thirstiest villains seen on any stage'. *Cues and Curtain Calls* (p.1) Ada Dyas first appeared on the London stage at the City of London Theatre in 1861. She was later engaged in the West End, before moving to America, where she enjoyed a considerable success.

17 Sun   Home all day, arranging Tableaux for the Shakespeare Tercentenary.*

18 Mon   Left-Handed Marriage. Deboleah; and the 5th Act of *Jane Shore*. Clara Casse commenced her month's engagement.

23 Sat   Obliged to play the Burlesque as a 1st piece tonight in consequence of Percy Roselle having to act at Drury Lane, for the Shakespeare Tercentenary Performance, in their last piece (i.e. the Drury Lane last piece).

Sun 24   Home all day making Plots of *Kate Kearney* for Wednesday night next.

27 Wed   Benefit of Jacobs, Carter, Thorne. *Left-Handed Marriage*. Ghost Effect (51st week). *Deboleah*. Clara Casse, Percy Roselle. *Kate Kearney* (1st time). Capital House, perhaps over £80, though queer, at first.

28 Thurs   Britannia *Shakesperian Tableaux* (performance in aid of Shakespearen Monument Fund), played instead of 5th Act of *Jane Shore*, consisting of Scenes or portions of Scenes from *Hamlet, Macbeth, Othello, King John, Merchant of Venice, Merry Wives of Windsor, Romeo & Juliet, Tempest & Richard 3rd*. A thin audience at first, but a Capital House at half Price – £46.0.0 – and *Tableaux* went off extremely well.

29 Fri   Clara Casse (or rather her husband for her) declined to renew her engagement for another burlesque to be brought out at Whitsuntide, Mr Graham saying the £5 per week offered her without another 'half-clear Benefit', was too '*ridiculously*' low a salary!

MAY 1 Mon   308th & following nights of the 'Great Ghost Effect'. *Left-Handed Marriage. Shakespearian Tableaux* as done on the 'Monument Fund' night (last Thursday) omitting 2 on account of length of performances (i.e. *Merchant of Venice & Tempest*). Concluding with *Deboleah*. (3rd week of Clara Casse at £5 per week and half a clear benefit, & 6th week of Percy Roselle). 52nd week of the Great Ghost Effect.

4 Wed   Benefit of a Widow (named Mrs Harris). *Left-Handed Marriage. Rough Diamond. Deboleah*. Rainy day & indifferent 'House' at night. Expenses not in.

9 Mon   Performances same as last week, only playing Tableaux last & substituting the Murder Scene in *Macbeth* for the 'Meeting of the Witches'.

11 Wed   Clara Casse's Benefit. *Left-Handed Marriage* (2 Acts only). *Daughter of Regiment*. 5th Act of *Macbeth* (Percy Roselle playing Macbeth & his sister,* Macduff.) *Pet of the Public*. Bad House, only £38.11.6.

---

*The Shakespeare Tercentenary celebrations at the Britannia had no official status within the official programme of events. For an account of the tercentenary itself see Richard Foulkes, *The Shakespeare Tercentenary of 1864*, 1984.

*Amy Roselle was born in 1854. She appeared with her brother as a child (towering above him even then), before developing her own career. Her marriage to actor Arthur Dacre was to end in a joint suicide whilst on tour in Australia.

16 Mon Whit-Monday. *Lashed to the Helm* (1st night). *Deboleah*. First 2 Acts of *The Left-Handed Marriage*.

18 Wed Benefit of John Reeves,* mutilated by Lions at the 'Agricultural Hall', Islington. *Lashed to the Helm. Deboleah*. Sketch from *Tom & Jerry*, written by Mr Mackay. Tom Sayers, J.C.Heenan, Jem Ward, Nat Langham, the two *Brooms*, J.Shaw & other Pugilistic Celebrities announced to appear, & First two Acts of *The Left-Handed Marriage*. Perhaps from £70–£75 in the House. A very hot day. J.C.Heenan did not appear. Turned out to be £59.

23 Mon *Lashed to the Helm. Rob Roy* (a new Burlesque) 1st night. 2 Acts of *The Left-Handed Marriage*. Shy 'House'.

24 Tues Very shy 'House' again, the brilliant weather, doubtless . . . It changed to cold this evening.

25 Wed 'Derby Day'. Benefit of 'The Sons of Labour'. Only change, *Barrington*, instead of *Left-Handed Marriage*, – leaving out of the night's Performances Messrs. J.Reynolds, W.Crauford, Ellis, Mesdames S.Lane, Crauford, Yarnold.

26 Thurs Miss A.Downing absent from Theatre, her parts played by Mrs Newham* & Miss E.Scott.

28 Sat Mr & Mrs Lane went away for their usual summer holiday.

30 Mon *Hogarth's Apprentices. Rob Roy* (burlesqued). Clara Casse. Percy Roselle. *Lashed to the Helm*. First Night of Mrs S.Lane's being away. Capital House. Miss Downing's name out of the bill. Mr Crauford away to see yacht race, his part played by Mr Bigwood.

Mem. Miss Downing out of the bill all this week – illness. On dit que '*Delerium Tremens*'.

JUNE 5 Sun   *Master Newham*
Painful discovery made in the Theatre, yesterday, Saturday. For some time past, money has been lost by various members of the Company, from their dressing rooms, out of their pockets, off their dressing-places &c. Miss Clara Casse having lost several odd shillings and her mother her purse from my Dressing Room. At last circumstances caused suspicion to fall on Master Newham (the son of one of the actors) who had been seen by Mr Ellis taking money out of the pockets of Mr Bell – Mr Ellis going suddenly into the Dressing Room when the other actors were out of it. The boy, being asked by Mr Ellis what he was doing, said he had been sent by Mr Bell to get him a pint of beer, and he was going to take twopence out of his pocket to pay for it. This, on enquiry of Mr Bell, turned out to be false. Mr Bell had neither given him permission to go to his pockets, nor desired him to fetch beer. The boy (who is about 11 years of age) being spoken to by Mr Bell some time after, denied

*John Reeves was a newly appointed assistant keeper at the Agricultural Hall Circus. He lost his hand in the accident, which took place on 28 January. (*Evening Standard*, 2/2/1864).

*Mrs Newham, wife of W.H.Newham, specialised in eccentric roles, maiden aunts etc. She remained at the Britannia well into the 1880s.

having said so to Mr Ellis, and asserted that Mr Ellis had not seen him with Mr Bell's trousers. Not a shadow of a doubt rests however in the minds of any members of the company. Too many circumstances have occurred to fix suspicion on the boy. One of the actors (Mr T.Drummond) undertook to give the culprit a severe lecture; it was hoped that to spare the feelings of his father and mother, the matter might be kept a secret from them and from the management. This however soon became impossible. The affair became talked of all over the theatre and reached the ears of the parents and of Mr Borrow (the manager, in Mr Lane's absence). The parents were greatly distressed and Mr Borrow on Tuesday had the boy turned out of the theatre. One of the most singular cases of abstraction that has occurred was the loss of a sovereign by Madmlle C.Stephan. The sovereign was taken out of her purse and 15/6 put back in its place!!!

6 Mon   *Hogarth's Apprentices. Rob Roy.* Clara Casse, Percy Roselle. *Lashed to the Helm.* (Same as last week). Clara Casse informed by Miss A.Downing that Mr T.Drummond was her (Miss A.D's) husband!

11 Sat   Two Ladies of Ballet Discharged – Last Saturday (Miss Scott, Miss E.Westbrook) – Two more to be discharged this night week (Mrs Chinn & Miss Groves). 3 *Supers* also to be discharged this night week. These supers, and the last two *'ladies'* mentioned above, to have notice tonight. Messrs. Murphy, Couriol (G.Taylor's* son-in-law) & 'Slopkins' (ie. Seymour).

13 Mon   *Message from the Sea. Rob Roy*, burlesque. Clara Casse. Percy Roselle. *Hogarth's Apprentices.*

16 Thurs   Told Clara Casse & Percy Roselle's father (by desire by Mr Borrow) that their engagements would terminate next Saturday week.

19 Sun   Home all day, making Plots of *Sowing the Whirlwind.*

20 Mon   *Frank the Ploughman.* Burlesque *Rob Roy. Hogarth's Apprentices.* News of the sinking of *The Alabama* arrived.

21 Tues   Christy's Coloured Minstrels* performed for an Engagement.

22 Wed   Percy Roselle's Benefit. 3rd Act of *Hamlet* (Hamlet, P.Roselle; Ophelia, Amy Roselle). *Beggar's Opera* (Clara Casse, Polly – Miss Scott, Macheath). *Irish Tutor* (O'Toole, P.Roselle). *Hogarth's Apprentices.* Indifferent House.

27 Mon   *Frank the Ploughman.* Christy's Coloured Comedians ('Niggers'). Mesdames Losebini and Constance (Singers).* *Downfall of Pride*, 1st Night.

29 Wed   Drummond's Benefit. *Romeo & Juliet* (done in 3 acts). Christy's

---

*George Taylor was the stage-door keeper at the Britannia and one of Wilton's regular companions on his Sunday fishing trips. He had formerly been employed at the Grecian.

*Christy's Coloured Comedians may have been an imitation of the original Minstrels which were introduced to London by Edwin P.Christy in 1857 at the St. James's Hall, and which were widely imitated.

*Madame Losebini and Constance Losebini were two separate singers, described as 'Sentimental Vocalists'. They were mother and daughter, soprano and contralto. Constance was to be remembered in *The Green Room Book* as 'one of the good old Gaiety brigade'.

Col'd Comedians (7 Niggers). *Scamps of London*. £86 in the House. Rain fell as the doors opened.

JULY 4 Mon *Abel Flint* (1st time). Christy's 'Coloured Comedians'. *Downfall of Pride*. Mesdames Losebini & Constance (Vocalists).

5 Tues This evening seven survivors of the Crew of the '*Alabama*' (Confederate Cruiser sunk in action off Cherbourg by the Federal Man of War, '*The Kearsage*') visited the Britannia, & were introduced by Mr W.Crauford, on the stage. The audience rose, '*en masse*', men cheering & females waving handkerchiefs. They were afterwards engaged by the Management to visit the Theatre every evening next week, and to begin on Saturday next[3].

6 Wed Miss A.Downing's Benefit. *Old House in West Street* (called *The Cheats of Chick Lane*). 'Christy's Col'd Comedians'. Losebini & Constance (Vocalists). *Downfall of Pride*. Indifferent House.

9 Sat First Piece changed tonight to *The Farm Servant* (now called *The Dying Flower*). Miss A.Downing's Last Night at the Britannia. Left because a reduction of Salary was offered to her, Miss A.D. having demanded and received a rise of salary last Xmas & ever since. 12 of the *Alabama's* Crew appeared tonight on the stage, not being announced in the bills as 'engaged' – but as 'visiting the Theatre'.

11 Mon *The Dying Flower* . . . 'Christy's Coloured Comedians' . . . *Downfall of Pride*. (Changed to this bill on Saturday). Survivors of Crew of *Alabama* & Mesdames Losebini & Constance.

13 Wed J.Reynold's Benefit. *The Tallyman*. 'Christy's Coloured Comedians'. Mesdames Losebini & Constance. Survivors of *Alabama's* crew. *Tower of Nesle*. (About £77 in the House).

18 Mon *Dying Flower*. 'Christy's Coloured Comedians'. Mesdames Losebini & Constance. *Downfall of Pride*. (A change on Wednesday & Thursday – & Saturday.) Charlotte (Mrs Crauford) came home.

20 Wed Benefit of C.Pitt, Harding* & J.Swaine (Stage Door Keeper). *Pawnbroker*. 'Christy's Coloured Comedians'. *Dead Men Tell No Tales*. House barely turned £50. Hot, sultry day.

21 Thurs Benefit of Two Widows. *Lady Audley's Secret*. Rest as on Monday (all except *Dying Flower*).

23 Sat Change of Bill. *Slave of Crime* (1st night). Mesdames Losebini & Constance. *Tally-Man*.

25 Mon *Slave of Crime* (or, *Sowing the Whirlwind & Reaping the Storm*). Mesdames Losebini & Constance. Mr H.Baker (Irish Vocalist). *Tallyman*. Immense House.

27 Wed J.Parry's Benefit. *Slave of Crime*. *Hidden Guilt* (ie. *Mr & Mrs*

*E.Harding** was an actor at the Britannia.

Manning).* Mesdames Losebini & Constance . . . H.Baker . . . Indifferent House. Weather close & fine. Had *£20* worth of Tickets in. Total *£49* & a few shillings.

AUG 1 Mon   Slave of Crime . . . Mesdames Losebini & Constance. Mr H. De Brenner (Tenor Singer). Mr H.Baker . . . *Tally-Man*. Very good House.

3 Wed   Own Benefit, told so by Mrs S.Lane on May 7th. *Slave of Crime*. Vocalists, as above. *Green Hills of the Far West*. Weather suffocating hot as it has been this fortnight or more. Total of House *£36.8.0*. Cash *£32.12.0*. Tickets *£2.15.0*. Stage Box *£1.1.0*. Printing *£5.4.0*. Posting, joining &c 9/0 Extra Billing 10/0. One Third Share *£10.5.0*.

8 Mon   Slave of Crime. Mr H.De Brenner . . . Mr H.Baker . . . Mr J.H.Stead (The 'Cure').* *Mary of the Light-House*. Middling House.

10 Wed   Miss S.Miles's Benefit. *Rebecca, the Jewish 'Wanderer'*, 1st time (Effingham). J.H.Stead (the Cure). H.Baker . . . Mr H. De Brenner . . . *Aurora Floyd*. Weather cool & capital. House guessed at *£70*. Miss M. allowed to take the 'Running Piece' out of the bill entirely, while last week it could not be permitted to put the 'Running Piece' second, because it was only its 2nd week. She had an entirely clear bill and the 3rd night of J.H.Stead (the 'Cure') – and yesterday it rained all day after many weeks' drought. Everything in her favour.

13 Sat   Immense House.

15 Mon   Old Swiss Church. H.De Brenner. Harry Baker. J.H.Stead. G.W.Jester ('The Talking Hand').* *Slave of Crime*. (Capital House).

17 Wed   Received present from Mr J.H.Stead, the 'Cure', of Tackle for Jack fishing with Live Bait of peculiar fashion – his own invention and making. (This yesterday) . . . Received today a present of 2 large Roach from Mr J.H.Stead, each weighing rather above than under a pound (1lb), caught by him in the Colne this morning.

20 Sat   Immense House tonight at the Britannia.

22 Mon   Drunkard's Children. H. De Brenner, his last week. J.H.Stead. Harry Baker. G.W.Jester. *Swiss Church*. Immense House. Cool Weather after the Rain.

29 Mon   Drunkard's Children. Mr H.Clifton (Comic Singer)* 1st week. Mr H.Baker. J.H.Stead. G.W.Jester. *Swiss Church*.

Mr and Mrs Manning were notorious for their murder of Patrick O'Connor in Bermondsey, 1849. Mrs Manning had been O'Connor's mistress.

J.H.Stead was famous for his song 'The Perfect Cure' (written by Fred Perry). He wore a striped, tight-fitting costume and a high fool's cap on stage, and after each chorus broke into an extraordinary jumping dance.

G.W.Jester was a ventriloquist who made up his hand as a doll, which looked like the face of an old woman.

Harry Clifton was famous for songs of comraderie such as 'Work, Boys, Work, and be Contented' and 'Paddle Your Own Canoe'.

31 Wed Benefit of J.Metcalfe (young man injured by Machinery at Batey's*
Ginger Beer Manufactory). *The Sea*. Vocal stars as rest of week. *Drunkard's
Children*. Immense House (said to be above £*100*). Proved to be £*116.10.0*.
Rain during the day, at intervals.

SEPT 2 Fri Alfred Davis called at the Theatre and at 91 Nichol's Square. Sat
in Prompt Place a long time. Agreed to go fishing on Sunday to Woodford.

4 Sun Mr Randall – comic singer at the Oxford Music Hall (& sometimes at
the Britannia Theatre) – caught this day in Windsor *127lb 14oz* of Barbel! (83
fish in all) & all caught with worms. NB. Mr W.Randall himself says it was
in July.

5 Mon   Mutiny at Nore. J.H.Stead. Mme. Pleon. Mr H.Clifton. G.W.Jester.
Drunkard's Children.

8 Thurs Mr Donne, Examiner of Plays, Mr Spencer Ponsonby and
Mr . . . Architect came to Britannia to inspect. Attended them with Mr
Crauford, Robert Rowe* and J.Martin.* Their principal suggestions were that
the walls of the Gallery stairs should be lime-washed and the skirting painted,
and the Pit and Gallery floors washed and sprinkled with chloride and lime;
that the screws of the water-cistern be looked to as they were rusting[4].

10 Sat Miss L.Sawford's* last night at the Britannia Theatre. (Left for an
engagement at Dublin – of her own accord) . . . Immense House tonight at
the Britannia.

11 Sun Home all day, making out bill for Piece for Mrs Lane's return.

12 Mon Harlot's Progress. Madame Pleon. H.Clifton. J.H.Stead.
G.W.Jester. *Mutiny at Nore*. Went with Mr Crauford to Mr Donne's & to the
Chamberlain's Office to speak to Mr Donne about a letter he had written to
Mr Lane respecting the lime-washing &c. required in the Theatre – did not find
him. To go again tomorrow.

13 Tues Went again to Mr Donne's private residence (40 Weymouth Street,
Portland Place, W.) & saw him. Found him satisfied with the explanations
given – only requesting that the operations he had suggested for purifying,
should be carried out. Promised they *should* be so (and indeed they are already
begun).

17 Sat Great House tonight, at Britannia.

19 Mon Performances same as last week (except Louis Lindsay 'Ethiopian
Grotesque' instead of J.H.Stead).

21 Wed Benefit of Messrs J.Wade & F.Perry. *Bertha Gray* (H.Young's Piece,
1st & only time). H.Clifton. Mme Pleon. Louis Lindsay. G.W.Jester. Master

---

*Batey's had been founded by W.Batey, a Britannia caterer.

*Robert Rowe had been the theatre's Master Carpenter and Machinist since 1841. John Martin was the
theatre's gasman.

*Lalla Sawford had been in the Britannia company since 1862. She may have been a relative of Sam
Sawford, the melodramatic actor, who had previously been a member of the company in the late 1840s.

Shapcott on the Drum & two Pupils. Brass Bands. *Old Oak Chest.* Tremendous House . . . Mr & Mrs Lane came home.

26 Mon   Three Lives. Mme Pleon. Louis Lindsay. G.Jester. *Bay of Biscay.*

28 Wed   Benefit of Messrs Summers & Light. *Sacred Trust.* Extras as above. *Black Doctor.*

29 Thurs   Went to Lord Chamberlain's Office about License with Mr S.Lane, Mr Beckett, & Son, Charles Beckett. Left the Britannia about 12 a.m. Walked from Chamberlain's Office across St. James's Park & Westminster Bridge. Dined at Simpson's . . . Home about ½ past 5 p.m.

OCT 2 Sun   Went, with Fred, & Mr Thos Rogers (Artist)* & Robt Rowe (stage carpenter) to see the scene of the explosions of Powder Mills . . . at Erith[5].

3 Mon   Tom of Tadcaster. Extras as last week. *Three Lives.*

5 Wed   Mrs Crauford's Benefit. *Mother's Dying Child* (1st night). Extras as last week. *Return of the Wanderer.* House not very great at first. – Filled slowly. Cause perhaps Croydon Fair this week, & the attraction of the scene of the Explosion at *Erith.* Turned out £90.8.0.

6 Thurs   J.Reynolds has been 13 years (this day) in the Britannia Theatre.

7 Fri   Received 3 Comic Scenes from Mrs S.Lane (all it is proposed to do in the Xmas Pantomime.)

10 Mon   Mother's Dying Child (2nd night). Louis Lindsay. *Tom of Tadcaster.*

11 Tues   T.Swaine, Stage (or Bar) Door-Keeper at the Britannia died. He was at the Theatre, keeping the door, on Saturday & Sunday.

12 Wed   Bridgins' Benefit. *Mother's Dying Child* (4th night). Extras as on Monday. Balcony Scene from *Romeo & Juliet. Maid & Magpie.* Indifferent House.

13 Thurs   Received Opening of Pantomime from Mrs S.Lane.

14 Fri   Gave out Scene, Property & Wardrobe Plots of all the Comic Scenes. (1st Hooray).

15 Sat   Tonight at the Britannia put up a Subscription List for John Mordaunt* to aid in the defence of his son, committed to Ilford Gaol to take his trial for Manslaughter, – having ('by accident' it is hoped) fired a fowling piece at another boy, while out sparrow-shooting, and so injured the boy that he died; – brought in by the Coroner's Inquest, '*Misadventure*'. This list closed on Saturday 22nd & the subscription reached £2.11.6.

16 Sun   Read & marked 'Opening' of Pantomime.

*Thomas Rogers had recently joined the theatre as scenic artist.

*John Mordaunt, formerly actor and prompter at the Britannia Theatre, was currently stage manager at the Standard Theatre.

17 Mon   Mother's Dying Child. Mme Pleon. *Miller & His Men.*

18 Tues   Gave out Scene Plot & Mask & Personal Property Plots of Panto-mime – 2nd little Hooray!

19 Wed   Announced as Madlle C.Stephan's Benefit. (In reality bought of her by Jacobs, Carter, Thorne etc.). Performances as on Monday, except (instead of *Miller and His Men*) a *sketch* (3 scenes) from *Dumb Boy of Mill & The Will & the Way.* House guessed about £90.

24 Mon   Mother's Dying Child. Albert Steele (1st night). Annie Radcliffe (from Mrs Howard Paul's Entertainment, 1st night). Madame Conson (Hun-garian Prima Donna, 1st night). *Miller & His Men,* 2nd week.

26 Wed   Benefit of some Society. No change of Pieces. Capital House.

30 Sun   All day making 1st Rough Sketch of Pant. Plot for Bill.

31 Mon   Mother's Dying Child. Madame Donti.* Mr Albert Steele. *Rose Roy.* A very good, but not an immense house. Gave back the M.S.S. of Pantomime to Mrs S.Lane.

NOV 2 Wed   Benefit of the Philanthropical Society. Performances as on Monday, only changing last piece to *Poll & Partner Joe.* House not great.

3 Thurs   Asked by Mr W.Phillips* if we had *more Fireworks than we 'wanted',* to give him some for a Display he is getting up for his children on Saturday.

5 Sat   Immense House at Britannia. (Receipts not known, but see Monday).

7 Mon   Mother's Dying Child. Mr Albert Steele. Madame Donti. *Guy Fawkes* (for tonight only). Rest of week, *Captn John Luck* . . . The greatest number of people at the Britannia this evening – ever known there – *4500* in all. *£128.18.0* & some odd pence taken.

9 Wed   Played *Guy Fawkes* again this evening.

13 Sun   Home all day about Pant. Bill.

14 Mon   Mother's Dying Child. Mrs Howard Paul* (1st night) . . . Madlle Donti. Albert Steele, *Captn John Luck.*

17 Thurs   Mrs Howard Paul not at the Theatre tonight. A letter arrived during the Performances from Mr H.P. addressed to Mrs S.Lane, saying Mrs H.P. had an inflamed '*Uvula*' and could not sing, it would be dangerous. Apologies made by Mr Drummond, who read Mr H.P.'s letter on the stage to the Audience & stated that all who had *paid* for admission & were not satisfied, might have tickets for tomorrow evening. About 2 Dozen Tickets were applied for (only 4 of which were asked for by Gallery people) . . . To the Strand to six newspaper offices to correct error in Advertisements.

*Madame Donti was an operatic vocalist.

*W.Phillips was a neighbour of Wilton's in Nichol's Square.

*Mrs Howard Paul presented an entertainment throughout the 1860s (often with her husband) similar in style to that of the German Reeds'. She often appeared in travestie, as Garibaldi (who had recently visited London) or Sims Reeve, for example, singing in the burlesque mode then popular.

19 Sat Harriet White (Grand-daughter of old Mr Dawson,* my first Manager) called at the Britannia this afternoon to solicit a 'little' Subscription. Did not recognise her – not having seen her since she was a child – at least 30 years ago. Raised 10/– among the Company (6d each) & gave her. She said her uncle, *'James Dawson'* was – dead! & that she had had a terrible 'scene' with her Aunt (Mrs Obaldistone)* last night. (Her aunt now between 70 and 80 years of age!!!!) George Obaldistone (son of Mrs O.) married and in Business as a Navy Agent.

21 Mon   Upside Down (1st night). Mrs Howard Paul. Mlle Donti. Albert Steele. *Mother's Dying Child.*

22 Tues A letter from Mr Rophino Lacy* saying Mr Lane would incur the penalty of 40s. nightly if he allowed Mrs Howard Paul to sing *'Selections'* from *Fra Diavolo.* Mrs H.P. says the Music is *Auber's* & she uses her own words, which she has a right to do, & Mr R.L. cannot prevent her. However Mr Lane would rather not run the risk, so Mrs H.P. has consented to refrain.

28 Mon Mrs Howard Paul for only 4 nights (the 4th being allowed by Mr S.Lane on a/c of her absence from illness on Thursday week last). 1st night of the *soi-disant* 'Great Vance'.*

DEC 1 Thurs Mrs Howard Paul's last night at the Britannia – Has not drawn. Her imitation of Garibaldi not making 'a *hit*', though her *'make up'* very clever. . . . Madlle Celeste Stephan stated tonight that her father was dead (died 20th of November).

5 Mon   Upside Down (for two nights). *Dick Whittington* (1st time) for remainder of week. The 'great Vance'. 'The Little Steele'. Donti. The D'Aubans.* *Mother's Dying Child.* Alfred Davis here, to enquire about Standard. G.Bigwood not at Theatre tonight, supposed to be *ivré.*

7 Wed Mr Drummond's Benefit. *Dick Whittington* (1st night). Vance, Steele, Donti. The D'Aubans (burlesque Dancers & duettists). *Richelieu.* Immense House. Alfred Davis at Britannia tonight . . . on the stage.

8 Thurs Began rough copy of Plot of Pantomime for Newspapers.

9 Fri Worked at Plot of Pant. for Newspapers (2nd day). Received 4 *'Poetical Addresses'*, good for as many 'Britannia Festivals' from Alfred Davis, his own writing, – A great cheer!

10 Sat Finished Rough Outline of Plot of Pant. for Newspapers (3rd day). very rough indeed . . . Mrs S.Lane's Benefit Bill out. *Another cheer.*

11 Sun Polishing Plot of Pant. for Newspapers.

---

*James Dawson Senr** was manager of a West Country circuit based on Devon and Cornwall earlier in the century. His daughter, **Mrs Obaldistone**, was the wife of the actor/manager D.W.Obaldistone.

*Rophino Lacy** was responsible for the English translation of Auber's libretto.

*The Great Vance** (Alfred Peck Stevens) had made his debut only this year as a solo singer in the London music halls. He began as a coster-type comedian, later developing a swell Lion Comique type of act.

*The D'Aubans** were duettists. (See note on Wards).

12 Mon (3 first nights of week, Mrs S.Lane with Mr L being gone to Brighton). *Dick Whittington*. The great 'Vance'. The little 'Steele'. The D'Aubans (duettists). Madlle Donti. *Upside Down* and *Aurora Floyd* . . . Three last nights of week *The Mother's Dying Child* (Mrs S.Lane having returned) instead of the last two pieces.

13 Tues Mrs Crauford gone to Hastings.

17 Sat Mr Drummond opened his Beer shop, 'The Carpenter's Arms', in Central Street, City Road, in partnership with a . . . well, the less said the better. Took Pant. bill to Printer. (A loud Hurra!)

18 Sun All day long from 10 A.M. till 12 P.M. writing manifold copies of Anticipatory Puffs for the Newspapers – finished 20 long ones.

19 Mon Mrs S.Lane's Benefit & Last Night of the Season. *Molly Sullivan*. Vance. Steele. Donti. *"Festival"*. *Lurline*. Miss Esther Jacobs* &, 1st time, *The Work-Girls of London*. £105 received . . . Sent 18 long Puffs (anticipatory) to Newspapers.

20 Tues Britannia closed last night. Another Puff (anticipatory) sent for by *The Age*.

21 Wed Revise of the Pantomime Bill corrected & sent to the printers.

22 Thurs Night Rehearsal of Scenery, – over by 11P.M. or thereabouts. Called at 6; began about ½ past 7).

24 Sat *Anecdote of the Britannia*
In the Old House, when it was called 'A Saloon', it used to be the practice, on first opening the doors of an evening, to admit females first, (women before men), & on one occasion, for the *Benefit of Mr T.Fredericks** there was only one *hat* in the Pit!

25 Sun Wrote with Fred's* assistance 20 short Puffs (post production) for newspapers, with letters to Editors &c.

26 Mon Boxing Day. *Little Busy Bee, or The Old Lady of Threadneedle Street. Work Girls of London*. Morning Performance at 12. Began at ¼ past 12. – Nearly £100 in House. At night, guessed at about £150 by C.Pitt . . . Mr Borrow says: £98 in the morning; £173 at night.

27 Tues Great House again.

28 Wed Great House again, but quiet. The words of the Pantomime listened to by the Audience for the first time.

---

*Esther Jacobs** was engaged for the pantomime. Praised for her attractive figure and strong voice by the *Era*, 1/1/1865, she was considered an admirable representative of modern burlesque 'as expressed in a kind of provokingly good-tempered impertinence and perfect nonchalance'.

*T.Fredericks** was a former Britannia actor.

*Fred Rountree**, Wilton's son-in-law.

1865

JAN 2 Mon   Pantomime. *Little Busy Bee* (Miss Esther Jacobs playing in the Opening). *Work Girls of London*. A great *House*, but not crammed. (No admission under 6d.)

6 Fri   Ballet-girl burnt tonight at the Britannia Theatre (Mrs Geary). Ascending a pillar for the Transformation Scene, alone, in the absence of the man appointed to assist her up, her under-dress caught fire from the Gas wing-lights. Not a minute elapsed, perhaps not above half a minute, before the flames were extinguished, yet she was badly burnt. See *Evening Standard* of tomorrow.

9 Mon   Honble Mr Ponsonby & Mr Donne (Examiner of Plays) from the Lord Chamberlain's Office came to the Britannia Theatre this afternoon at 2 o'clock to enquire respecting accident to Ballet-Girl last Friday night[1]

10 Tues   Mrs Geary (Ballet Girl . . .) still in a precarious state.

11 Wed   Mrs Geary . . . a little better.

13 Fri   Letter from Lord Chamberlain's Office (signed Spencer Ponsonby) desiring Wire Guards to be affixed in Theatre to all lights within reach of Performers. Answered promising it should be done[2].

14 Sat   Immense Houses at the Britannia all this week.

16 Mon   Mrs Fisher's (Miss S.Miles's) daughter 'afflicted with a diarrhoea of words'.

19 Thurs   Mrs Geary, the poor Ballet Girl unfortunately burnt at the Britannia, much better today.

20 Fri   Mrs Geary (burnt Ballet Girl) not so well today.

Mem. January 1866   This poor ballet-girl sufficiently recovered to go on again in the ballet tho' obliged to wear silk coverings (flesh coloured) for her arms, to hide the burns.

21 Sat   Dense fog all day & night . . . The Theatre at night – stage & all – full of fog, producing a curious effect in the Ballet. The Fairies all dancing in a fog!

23 Mon   Immense House. Bigwood ill. Bell obliged to play his part – Self playing Bell's. Mrs Montagu (née Julia Seaman) here to tea and supper, to ask advice about her action against E.T.Smith, Lessee of Astley's, for discharging her and her husband at a fortnight's notice, when they were engaged for the Winter season.*

24 Tues   Mrs Geary (Ballet Girl) much better – can move her arms about and all her fingers, but has had only an hour's sleep these last two nights – has also a troublesome cough. Bigwood ill (Quinsy) not at Theatre.

25 Wed   Bigwood still ill – not at Theatre. Mrs Geary . . . very poorly again – much pain.

---

*The Montagues had joined the cast of *Mazeppa* (in which Menken was playing) during 1864, but were not cast in any further roles subsequent to Menken's engagement.

26 Thurs   Mrs Geary not so well.

27 Fri   Snow all day – Remaining on ground notwithstanding the slush beneath. Hard Frost at night. The worst 'House' a pantomime was ever played to, at the Britannia. Mrs Geary same as yesterday; has had no sleep these two nights.

28 Sat   Mrs Geary no better; can get no sleep. A rushing noise, increasing till nearly as loud as thunder, heard behind the scenes tonight at the Britannia, startling everybody and causing much alarm. It turned out to be a fall of snow from the roof over the stage which had become warm from the gas-lights – on to the glass roof over the Painting Room which it smashed and fell through. A similar fall took place a few minutes after into the Pit refreshment room.

30 Mon   Mrs Geary . . . better today. Had sleep Saturday night – None last night.

FEB 3 Fri   Mrs Geary better again. Was out of bed yesterday & sat a short time by the hospital fire. Amelia, Harriet, Jessie, Milly* & Fred to the Britannia tonight – delighted with the Pantomime. Performers begin doubting to express confidence in her recovery (Mrs Geary's). Rehearsed *20 Straws* again. A pitiable tale told tonight by J.Reynolds (Britannia) of his wife's having taken to drinking & broken up his home, selling & pledging all their furniture and clothes during the last 2 years. Today they were parted – & he had but 2 shirts left '*to his back*!'

4 Sat   Rehearsed *20 Straws* again. Mr S.Lane having been a long time unwell, Mrs S.Lane told Amelia last night, that his spirits had been so depressed at times, that she had seen him, without any cause, cry like a child by the hour! – This, when he has attained what it has been the whole and sole study of his life to gain – wealth! to which he has devoted all his mind, all his thoughts, all his energies! & now he sits down & cries like a child! What did Alexander the Great do, when he had conquered the world?

6 Mon   No further improvement yet reported in the health of Mrs Geary . . . Rehearsed *20 Straws* again.

7 Tues   Mrs Geary much the same . . . Today given for study of *20 Straws*.

8 Wed   Mrs Geary much better – once more able to be lifted from her bed and placed in an arm-chair by the fireside at St. Bartholemew's Hospital . . . - Hard frost tonight. Mrs W.Crauford ill, – unable to play tonight. (Bronchitis) – Her part played by Miss Neumann. Rehearsed *20 Straws* – perfect (1st time).

9 Thurs   Mrs Crauford worse tonight, Dr Forshall attending her . . . Hard frost again tonight. Rehearsed *20 straws* – perfect (2nd time)

10 Fri   Frost & snow on ground still. 5 weeks this day, since the accident to Mrs Geary. Rehearsed *20 Straws* – perfect. Mrs S.Lane did not play tonight. Miss S.Miles played her part. Mrs Crauford prematurely confined (at 4 days

*__Milly Wilton__ was the daughter of Wilton's son George, who was resident in Australia. Milly lived with her grandparents.

less than 5 months). On dit brought on by Prescriptions written by Dr Jefferson in opposition to the judgement of Dr Forshall who had been previously attending her and striving to prevent that result. Dr Edwards afterwards sent for. At night $\frac{1}{4}p.11$ Case almost hopeless.

11 Sat   Frost & Snow on ground still. Mrs W.Crauford died 10 minutes past 3 a.m. this morning. Last Tuesday night she was playing in the Pantomime, singing and dancing; she was standing at the wing, by the side of Mr Drummond, laughing and talking about the Comic Scenes; last night she died – while Mr W.Crauford, her husband, worn out with grief and anxiety, was asleep. On Thursday week she was at a Ball (after the Performance of the Theatre).

13 Mon   Mrs Geary much the same – i.e. getting very slowly better – carried out of bed to the fireside, for an hour, every day – able to feed herself with one hand, – but not without pain. Frost & snow on ground.

14 Tues   Frost & snow on ground, still bitter cold at midnight. Learnt that two young ladies who were companions with Mrs W.Crauford at the ball last Thursday week, and both younger than her, are now both, like her, lying dead!

Mem.   Mr W.Crauford told F.Rountree that he had to pay Mr S.Lane £14 per week by way of Rent for the Bar of the Britannia.

17 Fri   Mrs W.Crauford buried this day at the Great Northern Cemetery, Colney Hatch. (about 8½ miles from Hoxton). Went in Mourning Coach with J.Reynolds, T.Drummond, G.Bigwood, T.Rogers (Artist) & H.Muir (Artist).* Altogether 6 Mourning Coaches & 16 Cabs & Broughams followed the Hearse. A great crowd (many thousands) of people collected in Hoxton to see the Procession start. Hard frost (day of the Funeral) & Snow *4 inches thick* (or more) on the ground. Cold intense in the Church of the Cemetery & in the burial grounds. The reading of the '*Service*' very weak & consequently very unimpressive. Mrs W.Crauford's Uncle John* died at 10 m. past 6 this morning.

18 Sat Paid share of Mourning Coach for yesterday	5 0
Paid share of donation given to Coachman =	6
Paid share of Refreshment at Inn, returning =	5
Paid share donation to Luff (Super) attending coach =	2
	= 6 1

Mrs S.Lane left town this morning.

20 Mon   20 Straws (1st night). Pantomime (1st week at half price).

22 Wed   Miss E.Jacobs' Benefit. *Midas* added to the bill (no other change). House middling.

The Pantomime

This year's pantomime has drawn more money than ever was taken at the Britannia during the run of any previous pantomime, but most disastrous

*Hugh Muir** had been an artist at the Britannia since 1860. **John Borrow**, born 1794, was the elder brother of Sarah Lane's father, William. He had been a bank clerk, according to Crauford.

events have occurred during its career. In the Theatre, on the 6th of January *Mrs Geary* of the Ballet was badly burnt & taken to Bartholomew's Hospital where she was obliged to remain for more than (sic) months.

Mr Bigwood, playing the Principal Low Comedy Part in the Opening (January 23rd) was obliged to absent himself for (sic) days, which greatly mutilated the Cast of Characters.

Mrs W.Crauford died February 11th and a Ballet Girl was obliged to play her part.

Mrs S.Lane, in grief, withdrew from the Theatre & her character in the Opening was assumed by Miss S.Miles, who was compelled to cut out all the singing.

Uncle John (Mrs S.Lane's uncle by the father's side) died.

The Edinburgh and *Surrey Theatres* were burnt down.

The *wife of Mr Buck*, the clown, was burnt to death.

The *El Dorado Concert Hall* was burnt down.

The Side Gallery of the Circus (Liverpool) gave way & loss of life ensued.

The Dundee Concert Room and Catholic School, Westminster, were the scenes of lamentable accidents[3].

25 Sat   Immense House tonight – a Boxing Night – Money refused at the doors at 7 o'clock. At least, people were told 'No Seats', when they advanced to the Money-Takers. A remarkably Fine & Mild Day.

MARCH 2 Thurs   Louis' Benefit. *20 Straws*. 'Drunken Combat' from *Dumb Girl of Genoa*. Pantomime. Characters reversed in 3rd Comic Scene – Clown, R.Bell; Harlequin, J.Louis; Sprite, W.Newham; Pantaloon, F.White.*

4 Sat   Sextillion's (sprite's) Last Night at the Britannia.

10 Fri   Miss Melrose, of the Ballet, had an Apoplectic Fit and Paralytic Seizure; (upset Paraffin Lamp in her Bedroom and falling narrowly escaped being burnt to death); carried to the hospital.

13 Mon   *Wedding Eve* (1st Night). *Midas. Twenty Straws*. Mr Drummond ill – away from Theatre – likely, it is said to be so, all the week. Mr R.Bell playing Mr D's parts in two pieces. Mrs Geary (Ballet Girl) expected by her husband to be out of the hospital in a few days[4].

14 Tues   Mr Drummond still away from Theatre.

15 Wed   Clara Casse with a noisy Companion at Britannia. Mr S.Lane up from country with Mrs S.Lane – the latter not looking well – said by herself to be from affection (sic) of the heart and that she was come up to consult a doctor about her complaint.

20 Mon   *Wedding Eve. Cinderella* (Esther Jacobs). *Twenty Straws*. (Signor Mellick & Sagacious Dog announced but did not come) – came Wednesday. Gave Mrs A.Dyas notice that her Engagement would not be renewed at its Expiration – about a month hence.

22 Wed   Benefit of R.Bell & W.Newham. *Hand of Fate*. Signor Mellick &

*F.White was engaged as Harlequin.

Dog. *Cinderella* (Burlesque). *Twenty Straws*. Supposed to be above £60 in the House.

24 Fri   Amelia & Milly to the Britannia to see *20 Straws* and Performing Dog. Monsr Mellick (Frenchman, Proprietor of the 'Sagacious Dog' showed me his Agreement with the '*Management*', by which he was to receive £6 per week for the services of himself and dog).

25 Sat   Last night of Miss Esther Jacobs' engagement – thank Heaven! Subscribed to a *Raffle* at the Theatre for 2 swords & a Belt said by Mr Bigwood to have been got up for the Benefit of Mrs Vezner, sister of Miss S.Miles.

27 Mon   False Mother & Parent Guardian (1st night). Signor Mellick & his Sagacious Dog. Professor Hilton (Ventriloquist) with his 3 heads. Harriet Coveney. *Twenty Straws*. House but middling.

30 Thurs   Benefit of Jacobs, Carter & Thorne. *False Mother*. Signor Mellick & Dog. Professor Hilton. Harriet Coveney. *Maum Guinea* . . . Mrs Geary, Poor Ballet Girl burnt Jany 6th, home from Hospital – not yet able to straighten her arms, which still pain her.

APRIL 1 Sat   Mr & Mrs S.Lane returned again to London (to see, it is said, a new '*Ghost*' Effect by Professor Pepper).

3 Mon   False Mother. Professor Hilton & 3 Heads (Ventriloquist). Harriet Coveney. Signor Mellick & his Dog. *Maum Guinea*.

4 Tues   Maum Guinea changed to *Tower of Nesle* for Mr & Mrs W.H.Morton* to play Gautier D'Aulnay & Margaret of Burgundy upon trial for an engagement. Did not succeed – not refined enough (save the mark!) 'Of the stage – stagey'. 'Penny plain – two-pence coloured'. (This gent & lady were however ultimately engaged & played through the summer).

5 Wed   G.B.Bigwood's Benefit. *Seven Ages of Man*. Entertainment as above. *False Mother*. Excellent House – £61.17.0.

8 Sat   Subscription for Mrs Geary, of the Ballet, burnt Jany 6th, Mr & Mrs S.Lane giving the poor girl's salary for 14 weeks i.e, from Dec 30th, the Saturday preceding the accident, to this day: at 9/0 per week (the first week having been paid the Saturday after the accident) *6.6.0*. Donations by the Company = (sic)

10 Mon   PASSION WEEK. *Histrionic Tableaux. Julius Caesar. Macbeth. Pizarro. Romeo & Juliet. Henry 4th. William Tell*. Concert: Diamond and Bryant (niggers); Arthur Lloyd;* Madme Losebini & Miss Constance; Sailor Williams.* *Hamlet. As You Like It. Richd Third*. Concert: Harry Baker;

*W.H.Morton was the brother of Charles Morton, founder of the Canterbury.

*Arthur Lloyd was a singer of 'swell' songs, specially noted for 'Immensikoff (The Shoreditch Toff)'. Sailor Williams was billed as the only 'real Jack Tar' on the stage. He specialised in nautical melodies. Mrs W.Randall sometimes appeared with her husband until the act prohibiting the performance of dramatic sketches in music halls put an end to their appearances together.

Professor Hilton (Ventriloquist); Signor Mellick & his Dog; Miss H.Coveney; Mr & Mrs W.Randall.* *Shakesperian Combination Tableau.*

11 Tues   A bad house last night – a wretched one tonight.

14 Fri   Night Rehearsal of Scenery for Easter-Piece called at *6 P.M.* did not begin till near *9.00.*

15 Sat   Mrs A.Dyas's last night at Britannia. Gave Professor Hilton a fortnight's notice of the termination of his Engagement, as desired by Mr Borrow. Scene Rehearsal tonight, after the Performances, of Last Scene of forthcoming Easter-piece, *The Volcano.* Began 11.32 P.M. Over 1 – 5 Midnight.

16 Sun   Mr & Mrs Casse here after tea. Beautiful weather. Amelia up Last Night to Clara Casse to offer her an engagement for 3 months at the Britannia, £5 per week & ½ Clear Ben. to commence tomorrow week. Clara accepted.

17 Mon   EASTER MONDAY. *Volcano of Italy.* Professor Hilton, Ventriloquist, with his 3 Heads. *Maum Guinea.* Good House but not immense. *£11.0.0* less than last year. Fine Midsummer Day.

22 Sat   The Subscription making in the Theatre for Mrs Geary, the poor Ballet Girl burnt last Jany 6th, now amounts to £2.4.0.

24 Mon   Volcano. Hilton the Ventriloquist. *Debo-Lear* burlesque. Clara Casse (1st night). *Eagle & Child.* – a shy monday night's house. Received from Mr Borrow an extract from *Reynolds' Weekly* paper, which had been sent by post from Mrs Robinson (Mr Borrow's daughter).*

25 Tues   Shy house at Theatre. Amelia gave Mr Casse the extract from *Reynolds' Newspaper* reflecting on Clara an infamous slander[5].

26 Wed   F.Frimbley* here; formerly Low Comedian in sharing schemes, now a Pensioner at the Dramatic College. Had not seen him for 25 years! Came to ask interest to get votes for his wife's admission to the college next month. Recognised him with some difficulty. Promised to ask Mr Lane . . . Mr Casse & Mr Graham here at night about libellous aspersion on her in Reynolds' paper, 3 weeks ago.

27 Thurs   Mrs S.Lane promised Mr Lane's *votes* for Mrs Frimbley.

30 Sun   Apology in *Reynolds's Weekly Newspaper* (Answers to Correspondents) to Clara St. Casse for slander published in that paper April 2nd[6].

MAY 1 Mon   Volcano. Templeton Minstrels (niggers).* *Debolear* (Burlesque). *American Slavery.* – House not so good as on Saturday.

2 Tues   Wretched House. Worst Business ever known at the Britannia.

*Mrs Polly Robinson** was married to William Robinson. She had previously appeared on the Britannia stage.

*F.Frimbley** had acted with Wilton in Honiton in the late 1830s.

*The Templeton Minstrels** were billed as the 'Original African Opera Troupe'.

6 Sat   Wretched Business at the Britannia for weeks – the worst I have ever known there.

8 Mon   *Volcano*. Templeton Minstrels. *Beauty & the Beast*, (1st night here), Clara Casse. *American Slavery*.

10 Wed   A Ticket night for two of the Ballet Girls.

15 Mon   Performances same as last week (changing *American Slavery* to *Abel Flint*).

Mem.   Horrid Business at the Britannia for weeks & weeks past: worse than has ever been seen there (at least these 18 years, for certain).

20 Sat   Subscription in Theatre for Mr & Mrs Coates – (the latter formerly an actress with us at Yeovil and, once, both of them engaged with Mr Lane). The subscription only amounted to *17s 6d* as nobody (or only one or two) knew them.

22 Mon   Same Performances as last week except changing *Abel Flint* to *Barnard du Val*.

29 Mon   *Bottle. Beauty & the Beast*. (Clara Casse). *Charlotte Corday*.

Mem.   Mrs S.Lane away all this week. Business at the Theatre still wretched – worse than ever before known at the Britannia.

JUNE 3 Sat   Mr & Mrs S.Lane returned home after a week's absence.

5 Mon   WHIT-MONDAY. *Victim of Delusion* (1st time). *Magic Wishing Cap* (new burlesque, 1st time) with Clara Casse & Mrs S.Lane. *Barnard du Val*. Great House. Hot & close.

6 Tues   Capital House (Hot weather).

8 Thurs   Mr S.Lane very unwell – not at the theatre for several days.

13 Tues   1st Letter from Alfred Davis about his right to play *Faith, Hope and Charity*, wishing to have authority in Mr Lane's own hand-writing. Mr S.Lane complaining in Prompt Entrance of young Gregory's* gagging & over-doing on the stage.

14 Wed   Mr T.Drummond's Benefit. *Victim of Delusion. Magic Wishing Cap. Lucrezia Borgia*. Receipts *£45.14.0*.

16 Fri   2nd Letter from Alfred Davis . . . enclosing my letter to him of last Augt 22nd which gave him a copy of the scrap of paper conveying to him the right to play *Faith, Hope & Charity*.

19 Mon   *Lucrezia Borgia. Magic Wishing Cap. Victim of Delusion*. . . . Wrote 2nd Letter to Alfred Davis, naming towns for which Mr Lane had sold '*right*' to play *F.H & Charity* . . . Those towns being Liverpool, Hanley, Sheffield, Hull & Plymouth, besides all Ireland, & London – also returned him my letter of Augt 22nd.

*Gregory, a Super, was a cousin of Sarah Lane's.

21 Wed B.Ellis & Miss E.Scott's Benefit. *Female Detective. Magic Wishing Cap. Lucrezia Borgia*, Failure – only £37 odd in. Woodcuts & Pictures plenty. A great House expected. Tremendous hot day.

24 Sat Addressed by Robert Borrow* on my way home from the Treasury. 'He had a favour to ask of me'. – 'Would I lend him a shilling till next Saturday?' – He had a *pal in distress* and he 'didn't like to see a *pal* in distress'. He 'would be sure to repay me next Saturday', &c. Lent him the shilling and bade good bye to it! Letter from Mrs MacKney (the actress) to Martin the Gas-man asking him to try & get her a small subscription.

26 Mon Female Detective. Magic Wishing Cap (Clara Casse). *Lucrezia Borgia.*

28 Wed Mr J. Reynolds's Benefit. *Man of Red Mansion. Magic Wishing Cap. Female Detective.* Weather a little cooler. House guessed at about £60. Proved £61.

JULY 3 Mon   Man of Red Mansion. Magic Wishing Cap. Clara Casse. *Female Detective.*

4 Tues Mrs Lingham* lent us James Dawson's Auto-biography (Truro, J.R.Netherton, Lemon Street, 1865).

5 Wed J.Parry's Benefit *£56 in house. Herne the Hunter. Magic Wishing Cap.* (Clara Casse) *Female Detective.* A very sultry day. Received a letter from Mr Moffat* consenting to lend his black mare for my *Benefit* next Wednesday week for Drummond to ride in *Dick Turpin.*

8 Sat Mr & Mrs S.Lane left town for *Dublin*!

9 Sun Home all day making own Benefit bill.

10 Mon   Hebrew Diamond (1st night). Clara St. Casse. *English Hawks & Irish Pigeons.* (Bad farce) & *Herne the Hunter.* Immense House.

12 Wed Clara Casse's Benefit. *Hebrew Diamond. Organ Boy. English Hawks & Irish Pigeons.* Wet Saturday & Sunday previous – Good House – guessed between £50 and £60. Proved to be only £45.15.0 – Tickets little more than £3. Weather very favourable. Letter from Mrs S.Lane to her father & mother saying she is safe in Dublin.

17 Mon   Hebrew Diamond. Volunteer. Herne the Hunter. Clara Casse. Mrs W.Crauford's Portrait. Life size – oil Painting. Mr & Mrs Borrow said the Artist only charged them £8 for this.

19 Wed Own Benefit. Beat *String of Pearls* by *£1.15.4.* Ride to York*, Mr

---

*Robert Borrow** was Sarah Lane's brother. A.L.Crauford (p.312) described him as 'the black sheep of the family: an idler and constant frequenter of public houses. He was always cadging from his mother and father'.

*Mrs Lingham** was an actress engaged at the City of London Theatre.

*Mr Moffat** was an equestrian.

*The diary entry [27/9/1865] for *String of Pearls* seems to contradict this.

Moffat's horse 'Koh-i-Noor'. *Hebrew Diamond*. Weather favourable ever since Sunday. Receipts – Total *£82.14.4* Cash *£79.6.10*. Paid Mr Moffat for Horse *£2.10.0*. Borrowed 9 Woodcuts from Mr Harrison (Publisher of 'Black Bess', Merton House, Salisbury Square, Fleet Street, E.C.). Mr H also gave us 250 large cuts (printed in 4 colours) for the Posters & youth at his branch shop in Kingsland Road gave us 14 steel engravings of Dick Turpin standing holding his horse by the bridle. Had these coloured and – with a little type around them – hung up in the Tradesmens' shops. Had also 300 of the bills containing the nine woodcuts coloured by 'Chamberlain' (whilom super at the Britannia). Paid him 6/0 for doing etc. Treating: supers 1s.10d – Carpenters 2s.2d. – Robert Rowe 3d. – Martin 3d. – Cecil Pitt 6d. – Self 2d. – Mr Moffat 8d. – T.Drummond – Property Boy 2d. – Gas Boy 2d. &c – about 10/0. Printer's Bill *£6.14.6*. Painting Lithos (Chamberlain) 6/0 – Paid for Donkey 1s/6d. Two Horses for Simon & Sammy 4s.0d. Mr Moffat's horse 'Koh-i-Noor' for Black Bess *£2.10.0*. My share from Mr Lane *£20.7.1*. Over 1,000 persons in the Gallery. About 30 boys waiting outside the gallery door at a quarter before 4 o'clock in the afternoon – a sight which has not been seen since Xmas last.

21 Fri　Wrote Letter, by desire of Mr Borrow, offering £40 & no Benefit Terms to Mr R.Moffat for his black horse 'Koh-i-Noor' to perform *The Ride to York* at the Britannia, for 3 weeks, commencing September 4th next. Mr Drummond to ride the horse, and Mr Moffat to provide two other horses, one for Tom King, to be doubled for Simon, & another for Sammy, all to be included for the £40. Received a reply from Mr Moffat at night, saying he agreed, only stipulating that the Dance by the horse should be cut out. Wrote replying saying 'no – we must *stipulate* for the dance to be done', as Mr B considered its omission would be injurious to the attraction.

22 Sat　Mr Borrow received this day an answer from Mr Moffat agreeing to instruct Mr Drummond at two rehearsals & to bring 'Koh-i-Noor', one other horse & a pony, for the sum offered.

24 Mon　*Third Class & First Class. Volunteers. Hebrew Diamond.*

26 Wed　Weather very hot & fine – forbidding for the house, Miss Miles's Benefit, *Hunchback. Volunteers. Blanche Heriot*. House guessed at between £60 & £70. Proved to be only *£57*. (*£10* of which were tickets).

31 Mon　*Third Class & First Class. Where Shall I Dine? Hebrew Diamond.* (Clara Casse). Last week of her Engagement.

AUG 1 Tues　Chantrell's 2 children* (acrobats/tumblers) gave a Trial Performance for an Engagement. The children threw somersaults etc. on a Platform some 10 or 12 feet high – well done, but believe the danger is the only attraction.

2 Wed　3 Gymnasts played a Tryal Performance (for an Engagement) on the

---

***The Chantrell Children**, Carl and Fritz, claimed to be 'the youngest trapeze performers in the world'.

Horizontal Bar. Not engaged. Wanted £12 p. week (Mr Borrow said) – & nothing extraordinary in their performance.

4 Fri To the British Museum. Got Reading Ticket changed (or renewed) . . . Met Mr Thompson Townsend, the Dramatic Author for Minor Theatres, and put my name down as a subscriber to a new work he is getting up (Anecdotes of celebrated Actors from the earliest times!) Terms of subscription *2s/6d.* (did not pay the money – left that to be done when book delivered).

5 Sat Observed today for the first time Mr Crauford's hair turning grey!

7 Mon Confederate's Daughter. (1st week) *Where Shall I Dine? Third Class & First Class.*

9 Wed Mrs Barrowcliffe* intoxicated in the Prompt Entrance of the Britannia wanting information as to how she could find Mr Cullenford to pay him her arrears due to the 'Royal General Theatrical Fund'.

12 Sat Action for Libel. Clara Casse v. Reynolds tried today, at Croydon. Damages laid at *£1000.* Verdict for the Plaintiff *£60.* Mr G.Ellis (last Saturday, Augt. 5th) gave in Notice for himself and Miss E.Scott to leave in a fortnight.

14 Mon Confederate's Daughter. Blight & Bloom (1st night of Revival) and *Where Shall I Dine?*

19 Sat Last Night of Miss Scott & Mr B.Ellis at the Britannia.

21 Mon Confederate's Daughter. The Hicken* Family or Troupe (3 children on Pedestals). Mr & Mrs Bland (Comic Duettists). Chantrell's two children. *Blight & Bloom.*

23 Wed Rain all day till midnight & poor Mrs Lingham's Benefit at the City Theatre!

24 Thurs Gave notice to Miss Butler* (the Lady of the Combat!) that her Engagement which was only a 'Week for Trial', could not be extended beyond next Saturday.

26 Sat Miss A.Butler's last night at the Britannia.

28 Mon Last Shilling. The 'Hicken Troupe' on Pedestals (3 children). Albert Steele (comic Singer). Chantrell's two children, 'Carl and Dipple'. *Confederate's Daughter.* Immense House.

30 Wed Mrs E.Yarnold's Benefit. *Heart of London* (a Piece written by Moncrieff & brought out many years ago, in F.Yates's time, at the Adelphi). The name of this Piece altered by Mrs Yarnold to the title of *Blueskin*, (Drummond playing in it the part of 'Covey' called in the bills, 'Blueskin').

*Mrs Barrowcliffe's intoxication may have been behind her request in 1867 for the return of part of her subscription to the Fund, as she was without food and drink. (Trewin, p.40).

The Hicken family had been noted equestrian performers earlier in the century. The playbill gives Hicking.

*Miss A.Butler has not been identified. She may have been connected with one of the two actors named Butler employed at the City of London Theatre in the early 1860s.

Extras as on Monday. *La Traviata* (by permission of Lord Chamberlain) for this night only[7]. Dagger Scene in *Macbeth*: Macbeth, J.Reynolds; Lady Macbeth, Miss S.Miles. Cash *£58*.

SEPT 3 Sun Home all day, working at Piece for Mrs S.Lane's re-appearance.

4 Mon Ride to York (T.Drummond as Turpin) Mr Moffat's Arab horse 'Koh-i-Noor' as 'Black Bess'. *Love's Dream. Confederate's Daughter*. Hicken Troupe. Chantrell's. House not so great as on July 19th but still excellent.

8 Fri C.J.Hazlewood, Dramatic author, in trouble about an accident occurring to his wife, a drunken woman, from whom he has been a long time separated. It appears that she had come to his house in the City Road and attempted to get from the next garden into the one belonging to his house and that as she crossed the wall he pushed her back. She fell on some spikes and received a serious wound in the thigh. He was brought to Worship Street today & remanded till it be seen whether the woman lives or dies. See *Times* of tomorrow[8].

11 Mon Ride to York. 'The Chantrell Troupe'. *Heart of a True British Sailor* (J.Parry playing the Commodore for the 1st time). *Last Night & Last Morning*.

13 Wed C.Pitt & E.Harding's Benefit. *Black Rollo* Woodcuts borrowed of Publisher. Chantrell's Troupe. *Henry 4th* (Scenes only as done in *Histrionic Tableaux*). *Ride to York. Famished City, or Patriot's Doom* (*Surrender of Calais* cut down to one Act). Day most oppressively hot & unfavourable. House guessed about *£77*. Proved to be – Tickets *£32* Cash *£52* Total *£84* odd.

14 Thurs Super *Chamberlain** (nicknamed 'Immense') died yesterday.

15 Fri Theatre inspected[9].

16 Sat Letter from Mr Donne (Examiner of Plays) recommending that the Theatre undergo a complete 'purgation'.

18 Mon Jeannie & Effie Deans. Chantrell Troupe. *Ride to York* (last week of Moffat's horse 'Koh-i-Noor').

19 Tues Last Scene of new Piece, *Poul a Dhoil*, rehearsed today, tomorrow & next day with Scenery. Sent Alfred Davis 100 2 sheet (Posters) Woodcuts to the T.R. Cambridge for *The Message from the Sea*, selected & printed by Beckett, price 14/0, for A.D's Benefit next Friday. Paid Mr Beckett 14.0.

20 Wed Benefit of Summers & Light. *The Lost Fortune*, Faucquez's piece about which Mr Donne (the Examiner of Plays) expressed himself highly displeased when he came to inspect the Theatre on Friday last, and said he would not license it; though Summers, by taking up the licensing fee of 2 guineas, got permission to play it tonight unlicensed. (NB. The piece is announced all this week at the Grecian!!!) *Ambrose Gwinett. Ride to York*. Chantell's Troupe & One-Legged Dancer. Capital House.

---

*E.Chamberlain had been a Super at the Britannia since at least 1862.

24 Sun   Home all day, about M.S.S. of *String of Pearls* & Bill of *Poul a Dhoil* . . . Mrs Lingham called to bid us 'goodbye', going to North Shields on an Engagement at the Theatre there. Mr Lingham going to Stockton on Tees on another Engagement. About an hour after, Mrs L. returned with her children & Boxes in a cab, having found on arriving at the wharf that there was no boat till Wednesday next.

25 Mon   Jeannie & Effie Deans. Chantrell's . . . Don Pattos, one legged Dancer.* Bevan & his automata.* *Rescue of the Orphans* . . . Last Scene 2nd Act (*Poul a Dhoil*) rehearsed today & tomorrow with scenery.

26 Tues   Accident – broke down 'John', highest Dahlia in garden, fell on him & *Mr & Mrs Lane returned from country* – Is it ominous?

27 Wed   Benefit of Messrs Wade & Perry. *Lady in Black.* Chantrell Troupe. Don Pattos, one legged Dancer. Bevan & his Automata. Concert (Brass Bands) 100 Performers. *String of Pearls.* Receipts *£84* odd.

28 Thurs   The whole Piece (*Poul a Dhoil*) called today – with Mrs S.Lane.

29 Fri   Went to the Lord Chamberlain's Office for the License (of the Britannia Theatre for next year). Not told I was to go till late last night. Went with the 2 Becketts, father & son. Paid *£4.14.0* for the license, & was entrusted to bring home that & the bond for Mr S.Lane's signature. Mr S.Lane bound on £300 to obey the behests of the Lord Chamberlain – The two sureties in £50 each. Dined at *Simpson's* as usual – Ox-Tail Soup – Fried Sole – Goose – Celery & Cheese – Sherry & Port. Drank only 4 glasses, with one glass mild Ale, & came home *tight*!!

OCT 2 Mon   Beggar's Petition. Mr Bevan & Automata. Don Pattos 'One legged Dancer!' *Jeannie & Effie Deans.*

3 Tues   Wrote to Alfred Davis to know if he had received woodcuts sent him 19th of Sept.

4 Wed   W.Crauford's Benefit. 1st night of Mrs S.Lane's performing since the Spring. *Poul a Dhoil* (1st night). Don Pattos, One Legged Dancer. Bevan & his Automata. *Rip Van Winkle* with a tremendous 2 Sheet Poster Woodcut. Day fine. House great, but not so immense as on former similar occasions. Guessed between *£80* & *£90*. Performances not over till 3 m *past 12.*

9 Mon   Poul a Dhoil. Mrs S.Lane. Don Pattos, One-legged Dancer. Signor Bevani (Automata). *Fanny, the Fox-Hunter* (? *Fox-Huntress!*) Miss Cornelia Clinton* (1st night). *Jenny Foster, or The Winter Robin.*

12 Thurs   Don Pattos, the one-legged Dancer, engaged for 6 nights more (i.e. for next week) his salary for the week to be *£3.0.0* – it having hitherto been £6 per week (as told me by both himself & Mrs S.Lane). Wrote to Alfred Davis sending him authority for himself & father to play *Faith, Hope & Charity.*

---

*Don Pattos** was performing his 'Bolero Schake Dance'. **Bevani** was a French clown. The automata were small wooden-headed clowns, presumably puppets, which he made tumble in a ludicrous fashion.

*Cornelia Clinton** had just been engaged as an actress at the theatre.

Received letter from him acknowledging his receipt of Woodcuts for his late Benefit at Cambridge 19th Sept.

18 Wed   Benefit of Madlle C.Stephan. (The use of her name purchased by Jacobs, Carter &C – for £5 it is said). *Poul a Dhoil*. Signor Bevani & Automata. Don Pattos (one legged Dancer). Master & Miss King in the *Gipsy Countess,** &c. Songs by Mr Leslie* and Miss McCarthy*. Recitation, *Henry 5th*, Mr Drummond. *Grace Darling* . . . Got 1st Comic Scene this day. Receipts £85 odd.

21 Sat   Received 2nd Comic Scene from Mrs Lane.

23 Mon   *Poul a Dhoil*. 'The D'Aubans' (Duettists). Signor Bevani & Automata. *Dell of Palms. Poll of Horsely Down*.

30 Mon   *Poul a Dhoil*. Signor Bevani & Automata. *Trafalgar, or The Last Days of Nelson*. The D'Aubans, Duettists & Dancers . . . Gave out Property Plot of Pantomime (Opening).

NOV 1 Wed   Gave out Wardrobe & Scene Plots of Pantomime.

4 Sat   Played *Guy Faux* tonight (*£121* tonight) & Monday next, with 'Fireworks'. Immense Houses both.

5 Sun   Home all day about Pant. bill, taking rough sketch, (finished it by tomorrow at tea-time).

6 Mon   *Infanticide* (1st time for many years – bills say 15 – but that is only a guess). The D'Aubans (Duettists & Dancers). Signor Bevani & Automata (his last week). *Poul a Dhoil* – with, announced as for the last night, *Guy Faux* & Fireworks. *Mem*. An Immense House tonight, *£117*, determined the Management to give the same Entertainment next Thursday & Saturday Evenings.

7 Tues   Heard yesterday that Tom Sayers, the celebrated Fighting Man & Ex-Champion of England, died on Sunday last at 20 m.p. 3 P.M. of Consumption! Also that poor little *Carl* (see Augt 28th) was dead, having by some accident (not described) broken his back, or hurt his spine so much that he had died of the injury somewhere in Birmingham. (This afterwards proved untrue.)

9 Thurs   Fireworks again tonight at the Britannia – not a great house.

13 Mon   *Infanticide*. The D'Aubans. *Poul a Dhoil. The Warrior's Return* (revised).

19 Sun   Home all day, about Pant. bill.

20 Mon   *Kerim the Pearl Diver*. The D'Aubans. Olmar the King of

---

***Harry and Katty King**, who were the offspring of tragedian, T.C.King, were duettists. They also performed Irish songs and jigs. **Reubin Leslie**, who came from an acting family named Hill, had joined the Britannia in July 1865 to play leading roles. **Miss E.McCarthy** had just joined the Britannia Theatre as an actress.

Gymnasts* (1st night). *Poul a Dhoil*. This change of performances (all except Olmar) made on Saturday last.

22 Wed   Benefit of the 'Clickers'.* *Warwick, the King Maker*. Intermediary Entertainments as above – Trombone Solo by Master Rogers. Song by a Mr Garrett. *Poul a Dhoil*. Very good house.

27 Mon   Rosalie Mortimer (formerly, in 1857, called *Fate & its Victims*). Olmar. D'Aubans. *Kerim, the Pearl Diver* . . . Rehearsed Opening of Pantomime.

28 Tues   Gave Mrs S.Lane her Benefit bill. Musical Rehearsal of Opening.

29 Wed   Rehearsed music of Opening.

30 Thurs   Rehearsed Words & Music of Opening.

DEC 1 Fri   Mr Prynne, claiming to have been formerly an intimate & protegée of the family of Mr Sandford, Manager of the Plymouth Theatre somewhere about 1832-3 – found his way into the Prompt Entrance of the Britannia Theatre (to my horror) & begged of me first something to help him to exist till next Monday when a lady would procure him two pupils to teach *French* – then a shilling or sixpence for a lodging. I told him (which was the truth) that I had but 3d in my pocket – that he must be aware that he had no claim on me, that I had never seen him in my life till he called on me a few weeks ago, when I gave him 2/0 solely because he appeared in great distress, and made use of an exactly similar tale. When I had said this, he asked again for a shilling or a sixpence. I repeated that I had but 3d in my pocket. Then he said, would I *benevolently* give him that? and perhaps some other kind friend would pay for his bed – His Landlady, he said, charged him 4d for his bed nightly – I gave him the 3d, and then he asked, – had I got – and could I give him – such a thing as an old shirt! – With difficulty I broke away from him. Poor wretch! never was there such a perfect impersonation of Jeremy Diddler,* so gentlemanly in his manner, so well educated – so clean & – oh so thin! a mere shadow – I *believe* he is starving!

3 Sun   'My birthday! I confess' (as James Dawson says) 'I never thought I could have lived so long!' . . . Home all day concocting a description of Pantomime for the newspapers.

4 Mon   Warwick, the King-Maker. Olmar, King of Gymnasts. D'Aubans. *Rosalie Mortimer or, Fate & Its Victims*. (Decent House – middling).

6 Wed   Benefit of Drummond & Bell. *Skeleton Horseman*. Olmar, D'Aubans, *Rosalie Mortimer*. House said to be *£107* or *£108*. Cash *£70* odd. Exact receipts as stated by Mr Borrow Money *£69-9-3*. Tickets *£37-16-0*. *£107-5-3*.

10 Sun   Home all day, polishing Pant. bill.

---

*Olmar** had created a sensation in 1862 at the Alhambra by walking upside down some 90ft above the floor by hooking his feet into a series of large rings.

*The Clickers** were the Leather Cutters & Assistants Philanthropic Society.

*Jeremy Diddler** is a character in *Raising the Wind* (James Kenney).

11 Mon   Mrs S.Lane's Benefit & Last Night of the Season. *Flirt. Festival.*
D'Aubans (Duettists). Monsr & Madme Stertzenbach.* Olmar. *Jessie, the
Mormon's Daughter* (1st night). Immense House (Heard upwards of £120). £50
taken in *shillings* before the doors were opened . . . & Mrs S.Lane's Benefit is
over! thank Heaven – a little Hooray here!

12 Tues   Rehearsal of all the children at 10 – Comic Scenes after. With Jessie
to Prince of Wales's Theatre (late Queen's) to see *Society* (new comedy by
Robertson) & *Lucia di Lammermoor* (burlesque by Byron). Called at Fred
Dewar's* lodgings, & saw his mother & Rose*. Johnny Dewar* going to play
Harlequin! at Whitehaven. Had to walk home at midnight – every step of the
way. Gave Pantomime Bill to Mrs S.Lane.

13 Wed   Rehearsal same as yesterday. Mrs S.Lane said she thought the
Pantomime bill would do *very nicely*, – a loud Hooray here!

MEM.   Theatre closed all this week (Monday excepted).

14 Thurs   Pantomime rehearsed all through, with Principals (3 were absent),
supers, Ladies, Children. Mrs S.Lane said the Puff for newspapers would do
very well – Another hooray here.

15 Fri   Rehearsal same as yesterday, 5 absent . . . To the Adelphi Theatre
with Amelia to see Mr Jefferson* in *Rip Van Winkle* – a beautiful piece of
acting. Splendid House.

16 Sat   Rehearsed Pant. all through (4 absent). Received Half Salary
(Theatre being shut). Began writing Plot of Pantomime (in manifold) for
newspapers – at it from 6 o'clock tonight till ½ past one in the morning.

17 Sun   At work all day unceasingly from 11 o'clock A.M. till Midnight, –
& then another hour till One (Midnight) finishing Manifold Copies of Plot of
Pantomime for newspapers, and enclosing them in envelopes. Wrote 20 long
ones – no short ones.

18 Mon   Rehearsed *Comic Scenes* at *10 A.M.*, & Opening at ½ past 11. (These
hours were the same as all last week). R.Bell, Miss Florence Johnson* absent . . . Gave up Newspaper Puffs to Mr Borrow. Another loud Hooray!

19 Tues   Kept at home tonight correcting Proof of Pant. Bill.

20 Wed   Rehearsal again as yesterday, Comic Scenes at 10, Opening at ½ past

---

*The Stertzenbachs were gymnasts engaged to play Sprites in the pantomime. 'Madam is said to be the
only lady gymnast in the world, and she is, perhaps, the first and the only one that has ever appeared in
such scanty clothing . . . M.Stertzenbach shows a marvellous display of power and muscle, and in this
respect he, probably, has no rival in the world'. (*Era*, 28/1/1866).

*Fred Dewar, a close friend of the Wilton family, was currently engaged as stage manager and actor by
Marie Wilton at the Prince of Wales's Theatre. Rose Wilton was Fred Dewar's sister. She had recently
returned from Malta. She may have been the widow of Wilton's brother, James, but there is no definite
evidence of a relationship with Wilton's family. A Rose Wilton is listed as appearing at Wilton's Music
Hall in 1879, but again it is impossible to corroborate any relationship between the two. Johnny Dewar
was Fred Dewar's brother.

*Joseph Jefferson, the American actor, first played the title role in Boucicault's play in 1860. He first
played the role in England, to unanimous acclaim, on 4/9/1865.

*Florence Johnson a 'spirited young burlesque actress' had been engaged to perform in the pantomime.

11. Only today succeeded in getting the third & last Comic Scene perfect. Mr R.Bell absent from Opening, Mrs S.Lane offended. Employed 6 Hours incessantly tonight in writing Advertisements for next week, 3 sets for the dailies.

21 Thurs   Rehearsal again as usual . . . Miss F.Johnson, Miss Macarthy & Miss Clinton absent . . . With Amelia to the Haymarket Theatre: saw *Overland Route. Used Up.* Charles Mathews in each. Buckstone, Chippendale & Mrs C.Mathews in 1st Piece.

22 Fri   1st Scene (night) Rehearsal. Began tonight at 6 (at least called for 6 o'clock). *Over 12 minutes before 11.*

23 Sat   2nd Night Rehearsal of Scenery begun at past 6 (at least called at that hour) – *Over 11.50* . . . Received Half Salary, the Theatre being shut.

24 Sun   Christmas Eve. Writing Critiques for newspapers. Wrote 15 short ones, all at once (manifold copies) by putting two '*oils*', instead of 1 Tissue, between two blacks.

25 Mon   Writing two extra copies of '*critiques*' (!) for newspapers, making 17 in all – not abed till 2 o'clock.

26 Tues   Boxing Day. Pantomime produced – Morning Performance at 12. *Old Daddy Longlegs.* Olmar. Mme & Monstr Stertzenbach (from the Alhambra) as Sprites. Bevani & Automata & *Jessie, the Mormon's Daughter*, Immense Houses, both Morning & Night Performance.

30 Sat   House by no means great . . . Weather not unfavourable.

1866

JAN 1 Mon   House not great.

Wed 3   To the Princess's Theatre to represent Mr S.Lane at a Meeting of the Managers of the Metropolitan Theatres to consider a printed circular issued & sent (one to each manager) by the Committee of the Scene Shifters & Employees of the London Theatres, demanding a rise of 6d a night in their salaries: i.e. from *1s.6d.* a night to *2s.0d* per night. There were present:
Mr Vining Manager of the *Princess's Theatre*
Mr Horace Wigan Manager of the *Olympic*
Mr Chatterton Manager of the *Drury Lane*
Mr Swanborough Manager of the *Strand*
Mr Kinloch (for Mr Webster) *Adelphi*
Mr J.Douglas Manager of the *Standard*
Mr Fenton Manager of the *Victoria*
Mr Conquest Manager of the *Grecian*
Mr Morris Abrahams Manager of the *Effingham*
Mr Powell Manager of the *Pavilion*
Mr F.Wilton (for Mrs S.Lane) *Britannia*
Miss Marie Wilton Manager of the *Prince of Wales's*
& *Mr_____* (for Miss Herbert) *St. James's*

It was unanimously agreed to resist the demand.

Mr Vining said he had already, some time since, agreed to give (*& is giving*) an advance of 3d. (i.e. *1s.9d.*) a night to his men, because he had found that the same class of men were receiving 2s. a night at Covent Garden Theatre.

Mr J.Douglas said he had always been in the habit of giving (*& is giving*) 2s. a night to his principal flat-man, his principal fly-man & his principal cellar-man. He added that he would answer for *Mr Powell* of the *Pavilion*.

Mr Morris Abrahams hesitatingly said that *his* men had compelled him to give the advance, on *Boxing-night* (or morning) last, by striking when the overture was on, & sending him word that unless he consented they should leave the theatre then & there.

Mr M.A. said: *Under the circumstances* he had agreed, *pro tem*. But now he would do the same as other managers.

Mr Horace Wigan was very determined. He said – if necessary, he would appeal to his audience – explain the occurrence, pull off his coat before them & say, by the aid of his performers & supers, he was going to work the scenery himself, & would trust to their generosity to excuse any little deficiencies they might observe. He was fully determined, he said, to do this.

Mr Conquest answered readily that he would refuse to make the advance.

Miss Marie Wilton freely assented.

Miss Herbert (Mr Vining said) had only consented to give the men the advance till she could learn what other managers would do – &, of course, would now resist the claim.

Mr Chatterton was also resolved to resist.

About a week after this Meeting, Mr S.Lane received a Letter from Mr Vining, Manager of the Princess's, to say that after discharging 29 of his *employees*, the remainder of the men had consented to work on the old scale of wages & the work-people of the St. James's, Olympic, Drury Lane &c.&c. had also agreed to the terms.

J.B.Howe behind the scenes of the Britannia Theatre. Introduced to me two American Gentlemen. One, he said, was Mr Jarrett, Manager of the Boston Theatre, the other an American agent (name forgotten).

4 Thurs   Robt. Rowe (Master Carpenter) fell down a 'Cut', through the stage.

5 Fri   Mr Prynne (the 'Jeremy Diddler') pestering me again at the Theate, got behind the scenes by the connivance of Mr Borrow & suddenly showed himself in the Prompt Entrance – to my horror! Gave him nothing – but got in a passion. He appeared thinner than ever – a perfect shadow!

8 Mon   This night the celebrated *Amateur Casual** slept in the Casual Ward (or Shed) of Lambeth Workhouse. His experiences of which were afterwards published in *The Pall Mall Gazette*.

---

*James Greenwood** was the 'Amateur Casual'. His books include *The Seven Curses of London* (1868).

11 Thurs The steamship *London* sank this day (foundered at sea) with about 270 souls on board, Gustavus.V.Brooke, the actor, among them.

17 Wed Sarah Thorne* behind Scenes.

18 Thurs Miss Lacey's husband* behind the scenes.

22 Mon 1st week of Johnny Day,* aged 9½ years, the Champion Walker. No alteration yet since Xmas.

27 Sat 3 of the Crew & 2 of the Passengers saved from the wreck of the *London* at the Britannia Theatre tonight. The three of the crew led on the stage & introduced to the audience by Mr T.Drummond, who made a long, rambling, inconsequent and very foolish speech about them, saying these brave men had – with the truly great & noble courage characteristic of Englishmen, bravely _____ saved_____ *themselves*!

29 Mon Pant. *Old Daddy Longlegs*. First change of Performances since Xmas. 1st night of *Bitter Cold or, The Secret of the Holly-Bough*. Olmar, King of Gymnasts. 6 of the Rescued Crew of the steamship, *London*, appeared on the stage – (engaged to appear every night this week). Their names: D.T.Smith (Bosun's mate); Wm Daniels (Quarter Master); Benjm Shields A.B; Richd Lewis, A.B.; Jas Gough, A.B. & Alfred White (aged 15).

30 Tues Sent to Mrs B.Ware* . . . in Postage Stamps 1.6 in consequence of a Letter received from her yesterday, saying she was in Whitechapel Union, Mile End, New Town. Amelia to *Whitechapel Union* to enquire about the truth of Mrs B.Ware's letter. Saw the Porter & the Doctor who knew nothing about her, but would enquire tomorrow. Subscription collected for her in the Theatre, all paid, amounted to *1.12.0.*

31 Wed T.G.Drummond said tonight that Mr S.Lane was giving the six shipwrecked sailors from the *London* . . . £10 for appearing 6 nights on the Britannia stage.

FEB 2 Fri John King, Coxswain of the late steamship, *London*, on the stage tonight, introduced to the Audience.

3 Sat Amelia again to Whitechapel Union to enquire about Mrs B.Ware – was told by the Doctor that she might partially, but never perfectly, recover. That we might depend on it everything conducive to her recovery, everything she ought to have, would be supplied to her while in the Infirmary of the Union – that – perhaps – the tea she got might not be so good as she had been accustomed to – and that if we sent her a trifle weekly to enable her to get a

---

*Sarah Thorne, manageress of the Theatre Royal, Margate, sometimes made starring appearances in the East End; she had commenced her career at the Pavilion Theatre in Whitechapel and had played at the Britannia in the 1850s.

*Miss Lacey is presumably Miss Marian Lacey, a popular East End actress. Her husband was a Mr Cuthbert.

*Johnny Day's act involved walking 1 mile in 9 minutes around a circle especially arranged for that purpose on the stage.

*Mrs B.Ware was a former Britannia actress.

little better tea & a little sugar – we could do no better. He asked if Amelia thought, should she recover, she might obtain an engagement on the stage. Amelia replied, 'Not in London'. He then alluded to the possibility of the 'Guardians' not allowing her to remain in the Union, should she recover sufficiently to leave the Infirmary, but added 'Time enough to consider such a gloomy subject when necessary'.

5 Mon   1st Appearance of John King, coxswain of the boat saved from the *London* & of 3 other seamen (one being carpenter's mate). Mr Drummond says that he engaged John King (who is to have £10 for the week), and the carpenter's mate (£4 per week); another of the seamen, A.B. – £2 per week and the third, an ordinary seaman, £1.10.0 for the week. (He says) that Mr Lane has promised to give him (Drummond) £5 for his trouble – and that, tonight, when John King was saying he did not know that he had as much as he ought to have for going on the stage since, all day long, gentlemen were giving him sovereigns, Mr Lane put his hand in his waistcoat pocket & saying, 'Well, & I can give you sovereigns too' – gave him one!

Mem.   The wages of common seamen (T.Drummond says) are now £2.15.0 per month. In engaging this party he had Morton of the Canterbury and Weston of Weston's Music Hall, with others, eagerly competing against him & in treating them (with bottles of wine &c) he incurred expenses (cabs included) amounting to £4.10.0, which Mr S.Lane cheerfully allowed, saying he expected his expenses would have been much more.

6 Tues   Mr T.Drummond told me tonight that John King is to have £30 for appearing next week. Johnny Day, the boy 'Champion Walker' 9½ years of age, & his father both recognised the Photographic Portraits of Edward & his son, Charley.*

7 Wed   Speaking of the demerits of the present *Britannia Pantomime*, Mr C.Beckett (Printer) informed me today, that an acquaintance of his took his children to see it a few evenings since – and that the children cried 'to go home' before the Pantomime was over – which he (C.Beckett) considered decisive as to its merits.

8 Thurs   Shook hands tonight behind the Scenes with Miss Melrose, the poor Ballet Girl, who had a paralytic seizure last year. She is now a pitiable object – one of her sides being still paralysed, her speech thick & her intellect confused. God forgive me! If I could have avoided her, I would – And I got away quickly under pretence of having stage Business to attend to. She was extremely well dressed & looked very healthy. She seemed even in high spirits – probably at finding herself once more behind the scenes, but there was a painful expression of half idiocy in her face! God help her!

14 Wed   (*Ash Wednesday*) A Concert tonight at the Theatre – same as last year. Not a very good house – but an excellent entertainment. Not a muff among the singers.

---

*Edward and Charley were Wilton's son and grandson, resident in Australia. It later emerged that Day and his father did not know them; they were merely trying to ingratiate themselves with Wilton.

16 Fri   Gave a fortnight's notice to Olmar, King of Gymnasts, & Bevan (called in the bills, Signor Bevani, with his Automata) of the termination of their present engagement – it having been made for 10 weeks, which ten weeks will have expired on March 3rd.

17 Sat   Immense House tonight at Britannia. First night of *Casual Ward.**

19 Mon   Immense House. *Casual Ward*. Mrs Howard Paul (1st night). Johnny Day. Mr John King & Crew of wrecked *London*. *Old Daddy Longlegs*. Signor Bevani & Mons. & Mme Stertzenbach, – And, after the Pant., Olmar.

20 Tues   1st Piece at Britannia changed tonight & next 3 nights to *Bitter Cold*.

21 Wed   Charles Pitt (Tragedian) died – Manager of Theatre, Sheffield – brother of Cecil Pitt (prompter of the Britannia). Had to write 34 Advertisements today, and to *alter them all at night*, to put in John King & omit the crew. And had to alter 24 Dailies again next morning & entirely re-write 12 weeklies to insert *J.G.Forde* for 3 nights.

22 Thurs   Mrs S.Lane ill of Quinsy, unable to play tonight. Went to Clara Casse (Euston Road) to get her as a substitute. Found her laid up with a cold. Went in search of Miss S.Miles – could not learn her address. Finally Miss F.Jones* *went on* for the part, wearing Mrs S.Lane's dress.

24 Sat   Mrs S.Lane better but not playing tonight. An Immense House again at the Britannia – drawn by the change of *Bitter Cold* again to *The Casual Ward*.

MARCH 1 Thurs   Louis' Benefit. No Change of Pieces – Double Violins played by Louis & F.White.

2 Fri   An adverse *Notice* of the *Britannia* (bitterly condemning the exhibition of the *Rescued Crew* of the *London* on the stage) in the number of *All the Year Round* of tomorrow, March 3rd[1].

3 Sat   Last Night of Johnny Day (the Boy Pedestrian from Australia). Last Night of the Pantomime. Last Night of Olmar, King of Gymnasts. Last Night of Bevan (Signor Bevani) & his Automata. Last Night of John King, Coxswain of the *London*. Wrote Week's 'Notice' & gave to Miss Florence Johnson . . . James Anderson (Tragedian) behind Scenes tonight.

Mem.   Cecil Pitt said today that Mr Borrow told him the taking of the Pantomime out of the bill would make the expences next week £110 less than this week. And that Mr S.Lane is to give Colonel Stodare,* the conjuror, who is engaged to appear at the Britannia on Monday, March 12th, two hundred pounds (£200) for a fortnight.

*The Casual Ward (Colin Hazlewood), based on Grenwood's 'A Night in a Workhouse', recently published in *The Pall Mall Gazette*, simultaneously played at the Marylebone Theatre, where it had been originally commissioned by J.A.Cave.

*Fanny Jones had joined the Britannia as an actress in May 1865 from the Theatre Royal, Cheltenham.

*Colonel Stodare, actually Mr Alfred Inglis, had presented his sensational effects in 1865 at the Egyptian Hall.

4 Sun Miss E.Macarthy said one night this week that her salary at the Britannia was 32/6 per week.

5 Mon   Casual Ward. J.G.Forde. Miss Kerridge.* *Cinderella* (Burlesque), Cinderella, Miss Florence Johnson. Mons & Mme Stertzenbach. *The Creole, or Love & Duty.*

6 Wed Miss Florence Johnson's Benefit. *Better Late than Never* (1st time). J.G.Forde. Miss Emma Kerridge. *Cinderella* (Burlesque). Mons & Mme Stertzenbach. *Casual Ward.* Fine day, but house very slack at first – 'pulled up' at last. Guessed it at about £55. Miss F.Johnson said it was near £67.

9 Fri Tom Attwood died this day of Typhus Fever in the Hospital, after about a week's illness, – leaving 5 children.

10 Sat Jas.Anderson* at Theatre today, brought his book of *The Scottish Chief* (Parts & Music); also books of *Hamlet, Macbeth* – . . . Subscription making in Theatre to bury Tom Attwood &c . . . reached £3.1.0. leaving many of the employees yet to subscribe. (These, by this day week, made the sum £4.10.0) with the aid of Friends, Strangers &c.

12 Mon   The Castaway, 1st night. J.G.Forde. Miss Emma Kerridge (Comic Singers). Colonel Stodare (Conjuror) 1st night, preceded by *Casual Ward* (Stodare not arriving till ½ past 10 every night after his performance at the Egyptian Hall).

16 Fri Colonel Stodare, the Conjuror, told me that his expences at the Egyptian Hall were fully £100 a week, for Rent, Advertising, Assistants &c. But his two Morning Performances paid it always within £4, he said i.e. he took £48 each Wednesday & Saturday morning. He could take £150 a Performance, if he had room: hundreds went away at each – unable to find a seat – & as his morning performances so nearly cleared his weekly expences, his evening receipts were *all* profit. In fact, he said, he could not close the 'two shows' (meaning, I suppose, the Egyptian Hall & the Britannia) without a loss of £400 a week!

18 Sun Home all day – plots of Burlesque for Easter.

19 Mon Performances same as last week, adding a boy singer named 'Edwin Sanders'.* Row with Jas.Anderson about his being expected to open in his new(?) tragedy of *The Scottish Chief*, next Monday (Passion Week) instead of in *Macbeth*, as he supposed, keeping the new(?) tragedy for Easter Monday. Of course he gave way.

25 Sun Forgot all about Puffs for the newspapers for Easter till past 12 o'clock Thursday night in this week, then too late.

*Emma Kerridge** was a popular serio-comic vocalist.

*James Anderson** (1811–1895), the tragedian, was a frequent visitor to the Britannia Theatre. He had acted with Macready, played leading Shakespearian roles at Drury Lane and Covent Garden Theatres and was also a popular performer at the minor theatres and in the provinces. He was also very effective in melodramatic roles such as Claude Melnotte. See, James Anderson, *An Actor's Life*, 1902.

*Edwin Sanders** was billed as from Covent Garden and styled as the future Sims Reeve. He 'has a nice voice and sings with much propriety'. (*Illustrated Sporting and Theatrical News*, 21/7/1866).

26 Mon   Passion Week. *Harvest Storm. Scottish Chief* (the old Tragedy of *Wallace* with One Scene from the Melodrame), James Anderson (1st night). Miss E.Kerridge, Master Edwin Sanders (Vocalists). *Where Shall I Dine?*

APRIL 2 Mon   Dark King of the Black Mountains, or The Newly Married Man (Clara St. Casse & Mrs S.Lane). Master Edwin Sanders. *Scottish Chief* with Jas Anderson.

5 Thurs   Received Income Tax Paper at Theatre demanding 13/4 from March 1865 to March 1866 to be paid to *P.Bartholemew*, Collector, 259 Hackney Road, N.E. (Two doors from York Street).

Mem.   Never paid any to any person of that name or at that place before.

6 Fri   Jas.Anderson talking of taking Drury Lane Theatre. Went to Mr Hammond, Hoxton Old Town, (to whom our income tax has always hitherto been paid) respecting the above demand. He said he had resigned, consequently, in future, payments must be paid to Mr P.Bartholemew. 'But', he added '*any time before the 20th June will do*', and also said that he had told Mr Bartholemew that there were 'two or three of the Britannia company who would bring their money when convenient', & he need not trouble about them.

9 Mon   Shy house tonight, after a day of cold rain.

10 Tues   Mrs Borrow very unwell.

12 Thurs   Tonight at Theatre Mrs S.Lane ordered a Call of new Piece tomorrow! Afterwards settled with Mr Jas.Anderson to call for rehearsal the new Piece (*Cloud and Sunshine*) on Monday next. Afterwards Mrs S.Lane insisted on its being called without Mr A. for the Performers to read their parts. The *Call* having been put up & Mrs S.Lane gone home, Mr.A., in a passion, refused to allow it to be called, – said he would not have the piece done at all, if the Call were insisted on. He wished to be present at the first rehearsal '*to prevent the actors getting wrong impressions of their parts*'. He wished to have it called on Saturday, when he would '*read the piece to the Company*'. Mr Borrow assented & the call was taken down.

13 Fri   Mr Lane unwell – not at Theatre tonight – was last night spitting blood.

16 Mon   Performances same as last week with 'James Anderson'. – Wretched House.

18 Wed   Business very bad at Theatre all this week. Mr Lane very dissatisfied at being *compelled* to play the Burlesque first – which he says he will never do again.

21 Sat   Mrs Borrow ill – not behind scenes.

23 Mon   Sailor's Return. Cloud & Sunshine (1st time here), Jas. Anderson. *Dark King of Black Mountains* Burlesque (Clara Casse). Bad House.

24 Tues   Bad House. Mrs Borrow ill – confined to her bed.

25 Wed   Benefit of Society, but No Change of Pieces, thank Heaven! James

Anderson and Clara Casse both with bad colds, James Anderson scarcely able to speak. Clara unable to sing. Gallery calling out to Anderson to '*speak up*', Clara cutting out all her songs. Mrs Borrow still unwell – but a little better.

28 Sat Mrs Borrow worse again. Heavy Rain all afternoon & evening. Capital House in spite of rain – though bad business every other night during the week.

30 Mon Bitter cold. Horrible to face, coming home at midnight.

MAY 2 Wed Benefit of Jacobs, Carter & Thorne, Bill Inspector & Door-Keepers or Check Takers. *Swiss Cottage* (*Why don't She Marry?*) Clara Casse. *Cloud and Sunshine* (James Anderson). *Marriage á La Mode*. Cold weather & clear after much rain. House about £67.17.0 (not considered good). Frightfully cold at night.

4 Fri Wretched, bad house again at Theatre. Bitter cold at midnight.

5 Sat Better 'house' tonight at Britannia. Last night of 'Woppets' brother of Mr Jas.Greenwood (the 'Amateur Casual' – author of *A Night in the Workhouse*). Had to pay him his salary tonight (about 10/0) and give him a week's notice. But he sent a note on Monday (May 7th) to say he felt unwell and feared he should not be able to play at night – but would if he felt competent. We saw him no more! –

7 Mon *Last Appeal.* 'Echassé Family' on stilts. *Cloud and Sunshine. Dark King of Black Mountain*. Business at Theatre still wretched as it is everywhere.

9 Wed Mr Jas Anderson's Benefit, (nominal Ben.) *Last Appeal.* Echassé Family. *Civilisation* (1st time here, under the title of *The Huron Chief or The Savage and Civilisation*). *Dark King of the Black Mountains* (Burlesque) Clara Casse.

14 Mon *Corporal's Daughter* (Clara Casse). Echassé Family. *Civilisation* (Jas Anderson – his last week). Shy House – Weather cold.

Mem. Weather unnaturally cold these last 3 weeks – obliged to wear a great coat to rehearsal. No sun – or, if there is, no warmth in it. At night a great coat feels like a shirt of calico, thin & cold.

17 Thurs Mrs S.Lane told me to announce on the bills the week after Whitsuntide that during the summer months the performance would not commence until a quarter before 7 o'clock.

19 Sat Last Night of James Anderson who has 'drawn' very little, if at all, during his engagement. Have had very little trouble, comparatively, in 'getting up' his pieces, the management 'eschewing' the 'legitimate', & avoiding *Hamlet, Macbeth, Lear, Richard* &c, believing they would keep money out of the house.

21 Mon Whit-Monday. *Rich & Poor* (1st night). *Corporal's Daughter* Clara Casse. Master E.Sanders (singer). Hungarian Dancers* between. (About £100

*The Hungarian Dancers Kiralfy (two brothers and two sisters), who had appeared at the Oxford and Alhambra, created an impression with their brilliant costumes and energetic movement.

in house). Tonight a new Waiter being sent from the bar with a glass of Rum & Water to Mr W.Crauford behind the scenes – carried it on the stage to him, before the audience! His wild and eccentric conduct afterwards in the bar led to the conclusion that the poor fellow was going out of his mind.

22 Tues   House, within £3, as good as last night.

23 Wed   Capital House again – supposed to be the *Corporal's Daughter* drawing.

24 Thurs   Bitter cold night – with a killing East Wind. House not so good tonight.

25 Fri   Mr S.Lane complaining of violent head-aches.

26 Sat   Mr S.Lane unwell – spitting blood again – leeches.

28 Mon   *Rich & Poor*. Hungarian Dancers (stuff! – German Jews). Master E.Sanders (Singer). *Corporal's Daughter*.

JUNE 1 Fri   No heat in the sun all day. The infernal N.E. wind still. Wished for a great coat coming home from Theatre at night.

2 Sat   A fine, Summer's day at last. Good house at night.

4 Mon   *Rich & Poor*. Hungarian Dancers. *Belphegor* (burlesque) 1st night, Clara Casse. *Black Domino*. Excellent House . . . Very heavy Rain tonight again during performance at Theatre. Burlesque went off lamentably flat, contrary to expectation. Weather still chilly & gloomy.

11 Mon   *Lady Audley's Secret*. Hungarian Dancers. Burlesque *Belphegor*, Miss Clara St Casse. *Rich & Poor*.

13 Wed   Mr Bigwood's Benefit. *Peerless Pool*. Hungarian Dancers. Burlesque, *Belphegor*, Clara Casse. *Dominique the Deserter*. Day cold, chilly & cheerless. Rain at intervals – sky murky – streets mucky. Tickets *£11 odd*. Cash, between *£46 & £47*. Weather so chilly – glad to sit by the back-kitchen fire to write Advertisements and for meals.

18 Mon   *Devil's Punch Bowl* (1st week). Joe Lund (Nigger Grotesque).* Mme Ramsden (Skipping Rope Dancer), her 1st night. The Comic 'Shadow' (his 1st night).* Burlesque, *Belphegor* (Clara Casse). *Lady Audley's Secret*.

20 Wed   Mr T.Drummond's Benefit. *Lady of Lyons*. Extras as on Monday. Burlesque *Belphegor*. *Wenlock of Wenlock* called *The Prophecy, or The Black Mantle*.

25 Mon   *Devil's Punch Bowl*. Same Intervening Entertainments as last week. Burlesque *Belphegor*. *Betty Bolaine*.

27 Wed   Clara Casse's Benefit. No change in the Performance owing to a dispute between Clara & the Management – Clara wishing to play 'Lady

---

*Joe Lund** performed a grotesque American minstrel act. **Frank Williams** was billed as 'The Evening Shadow' (from the Alhambra) who will 'vocalise his own personal experiences'.

Teazle' in the *School for Scandal*, which the management declined doing because it would involve the painting of a 'Picture Gallery' Scene. Clara therefore refused to take any other piece – or to have any bills printed, or even any tickets. The result was a wretched bad House. At ½ past 8, or thereabouts, when Clara first went on the Stage for the Evening, in the Burlesque, Mr Rogers, the Bass Violin of the orchestra, counted the audience in the Boxes and stalls. There were 20 in the Boxes & 37 in the Stalls. The Stall-Door keeper said to the best of his belief there were never more than 600 people altogether in the house. Between *£13.0.0* and *£14.0.0*.

30 Sat   Clara Casse's last night. Mr S.Lane vowing she shall never again be engaged in the Britannia Theatre, & alledging that the badness of the house on her Benefit night showed she was no attraction.

JULY 2 Mon   1st week of Mr & Mrs S.Lane's absence. *Downfall of Pride*. Intervening Entertainments same as last week. *Devil's Punchbowl*. Better house than last Monday; Perhaps because weather cold & wet (at least in showers).

4 Wed   Mr J.Reynolds' Benefit. *Cartouche* 1st night (Mr Travers's* piece). Joe Lund (Nigger). Madame Ramsden (Skipping Rope). Mr F.Williams (the Evening Shadow). Master E.Sanders. *Downfall of Pride* – Weather cold and showery (wonderfully favourable) – Total between *£79 & £80*.

5 Thurs   Wrote to Charles Dickens for Mr Lane, asking permission to play a Dramatised Version (offered by Hazlewood) of Mr Dickens's Tale, *Our Mutual Friend*. Signed the letter S.Lane (Mr Lane being in Scotland) & addressed it to Gadshill, near Rochester, Kent.

7 Sat   Answer recd. from Charles Dickens about *Golden Dustman** saying he can't give permission to use his name – but gives a 'private assurance' that he will not obstruct our acting the piece or interfere in any way. The letter began 'Dear Mr Lane'.

8 Sun   Home all day, at work at *Our Mutual Friend*.

9 Mon   *Cartouche*. Mme. Ramsden (Skipping Rope). Joe Lund (nigger). F.Williams (the Evening Shadow). Master E.Sanders. *Downfall of Pride*. Fair House – Fine hot day. Letter from Mr Moffat. His son, Alfred, killed by Elephant at Morat in Switzerland. Particulars to send to *Era*. Copied them ship-shape & Posted to him at Leeds.

11 Wed   Miss E.Macarthy's Benefit. *Sixteen String Jack*. (Extras as on Monday). *Effie & Jeannie Deans*. Very hot day. House a failure – not *£25* in house! Poor girl! married – 4 children – her husband been 3 months out of an engagement!

---

*William Travers** was a versatile leading man and resident dramatist at the City of London Theatre. He played Irish, comic and heroic roles. He had played the lead in *Cartouche*, the French Jack Sheppard, and in another of his plays, *Kathleen Mavourneen*, as the hero Terence O'Brien.

*The Golden Dustman** was, in fact, the title given to the Sadler's Wells' adaptation of *Our Mutual Friend*. Wilton is here referring to the Britannia version, *The Dustman's Treasure*.

14 Sat   Miss E.Macarthy taken ill. Miss F.Jones obliged to go on for her part in *Downfall of Pride*. Mr Borrow says, Master E.Sanders engaged for 6 months, at *£3 per week*! Fred & Harriet to Sadler's Wells Theatre to see *Golden Dustman*. Delighted with Belmore* as Wegg – excited about Rogue Riderhood & Bradley Headstone – enraptured with Boffin – and in ecstacies about the whole piece.

16 Mon   *Dustman's Treasure*. Herr Susman (Imitator of Birds). Joe Lund. Mark Floyd.* Master E.Sanders. *Cartouche*.

17 Tues   Mr & Mrs S.Lane at Edinburgh – going to Wales – Mr Lane no better! – and there are his two yachts – rotting at anchor! & (Mrs Borrow says) he is paying £2 a week to his Captain to 'take care of her'. (I presume meaning the larger one). Jessy to Sadler's Wells to see *Golden Dustman*. Disappointed, Dissatisfied, – Disgusted.

18 Wed   Mr R.Leslie's Benefit. All 3 Pieces changed. *Trail of Sin*. Mark Floyd. Herr Susman. Joe Lund. E.Sanders. *Confederate's Daughter*. *Matteo Falcone*. House very shy at first – afterwards pulled up to (at a guess) about *£50*. Fine, bright day. Sally Vivash here – no longer 'Sally Vivash', but married – and now Mrs Buchanan.*

21 Sat   Capital House tonight.

23 Mon   *Dustman's Treasure*. Joe Lund. Herr Susman. Master E.Sanders. *Dark House*.

25 Wed   Mr J.Parry's Benefit. *Kathleen Mavourneen* (Mr Travers's Piece). Herr Susman. Joe Lund. Master E.Sanders. *Dustman's Treasure*. Cloudy sky. Weather favourable. House nearly *£57*.

27 Fri   Mr S.Lane no better.

29 Sun   Mr Crauford & Miss Ellen Watson* married this day.

30 Mon   *Jolly Dogs of London* (1st week). Chris Brown (Ethiopian)* 1st Appearance in London. Herr Susman. Miss Lydia Latimer* (George Harding's 'soi-disant' wife). Master E.Sanders. *Dustman's Treasure*.

AUG 1 Wed   Own Benefit. *Jolly Dogs*. Herr Susman. Miss Lydia Latimer. Mr C.Brown. *Ballet Girl's Revenge*. *Blackbeard*. Weather all that could be wished. Wet Sunday. Gloomy Tuesday. Murkey Wednesday up to noon. Total. *£57.7.1.* Cash *£49.16.1.* Tickets *£1.11.0.* Half Price *£12.0.9.*

*George Belmore** was a low comedian; he had previously been a great favourite at the Marylebone Theatre.

*Mark Floyd** was a burlesque singer and dancer, noted as a female impersonator. The *Illustrated Sporting News*, 21/7/1866, praised his imitation of the 'pets of the ballet', but thought his delineation of 'Dandy Sall', a Haymarket prostitute, highly discreditable.

*Sally Vivash** was probably the daughter of an actor named Vivash, whom Wilton had known in Plymouth in the 1830s.

*Ellen Watson** was a cousin of Sarah Lane.

*Chris Brown** was billed as an 'Ethiopian Grotesque and Eccentric Dancer'. **Lydia Latimer** was a serio-comic vocalist.

6 Mon   Performances same as last week, but no *Susman*.

7 Tues   Letter from Mrs Lingham asking loan of £1. Address 35 Great Osmonde Street, Yarrow on Tyne, Durham, near Newcastle. Declined!

8 Wed   Miss S.Miles's Benefit. *The Wife*. Mr C.Brown. Miss Lydia Latimer. Master E.Sanders. *Minnie Grey*. Weather for several days and today highly favourable. House about £87.

11 Sat   Performances changed tonight. *Jack Mingo, the London Street Boy* (1st night). Miss Lydia Latimer. Mr C.Brown (Nigger). Master E.Sanders. *Jolly Dogs*. Capital House.

13 Mon   Miss Lydia Latimer. Mr C.Brown (Nigger). Master E.Sanders. Mr F.Evans (his first night tonight, Monday). Miss Amy Rosalind (his wife, her first night also).*

19 Sun   Home all day. Principally about Bill for Mrs S.Lane's return.

20 Mon   *Jack Mingo, the London Street Boy*. Mr & Mrs F.Evans (Duettists & Dancers; FE formerly 'Harlequin'). C.Brown (nigger). Lydia Latimer (Serio-Comic Vocalist). G.W.Jester (Ventriloquist). Master Edwin Sanders. *Diogenes*.

25 Sat   Last Night of Messrs G.W.Jester & C.Brown. *Mutiny at Nore*. Jester, Brown, Miss Lydia Latimer (Mr Geo. Harding's 'soi-distant' wife). F.Evans & Wife (Miss Amy Rosalind). E.Sanders. *Jack Mingo, the London Street Boy*.

29 Wed   No Benefit. But change of Performances! *The Wife* & *Mutiny at the Nore*.

31 Fri   Wrote reply to a Letter from Mr W.Donne (Examiner of Stage Plays) – saying for Mr S.Lane that Monday Septr 10th *would* be convenient for him and Mr Spencer Ponsonby to inspect the Theatre.

SEPT 3 Mon   *Drunkard's Children*. Miss Lydia Latimer. Mr H.Macarthy. Master E.Sanders. The 'Martinettes'* from the Hippodrome (1st week). *Mutiny at the Nore*.

5 Wed   Mrs E.Yarnold's Benefit. *Orange Girl*. H.Macarthy (American actor & singer). Miss Lydia Latimer. The Martinettes. Master E.Sanders. *Guilty Mother*. Dully, gloomy, heavy, rainy, windy morning, clearing up to fine afternoon. House guessed at above *£80*. Mrs E.Y. played Orange Girl – shamefully imperfect, did not know a word – cut up everybody. Jacobs put in tickets . . . House finally proved to be above *£97* – Cash *£60* odd.

7 Fri   Wrote to the new Lord Chamberlain, Earl of Bradford, in Mr S.Lane's name for a renewal of the License for the Britannia Theatre for the next year.

*Fred Evans and Amy Rosalind were burlesque duettists and dancers, who had formerly played Harlequin and Columbine at Drury Lane. They had appeared at Wilton's Music Hall the previous year.

*The Martinettes, from the Hippodrome, Paris, cannot be associated with the great pantomimist, Paul Martinetti, who did not make his debut in London until 1876. The Martinette family had appeared at Wilton's Music Hall in April this year.

Did not know whether the Earl was an 'Honourable' or a 'Right Honourable', but dubbed him Right Honourable on the address of the envelope as well as in the inside of the letter – which, it seems, is correct.

8 Sat   Immense House at Britannia after a miserably wet day . . . Recd 2 Comic Scenes from Mrs Lane with a desire expressed that the plots might be got out quickly, especially for Mr Muir (Scene Painter) to model, for Robt Rowe (Master-Carpenter) to have them by 25th Septr, that he might have 3 months to get up the Pantomime.

9 Sun   Home all day about Scene & Prpy Plots of 2 comic scenes recd yesterday.

10 Mon   Gunpowder Tom. Martinette family. Master E.Sanders. G.W.Ross.* *Drunkard's Children*. Tuesday & Friday, *The Wife & Drunkard's Children*, Gave out Scene Plot of 1st Comic Scene. Inspection of Theatre (Britannia). Attended the Honble Mr Spencer Ponsonby & Mr Donne (Examiner of Plays) today in their inspection of the Theatre[2].

11 Tues   Gave out Property Plot of 1st Comic Scene & Scene Plot of second.

12 Wed   Benefit of F.Perry, Drummer & J.Wade (his friend). *Sempstress & Duchess or, Pride, Poverty & Splendour*. G.W.Ross. The Martinettes. Master E.Sanders. *Ocean of Life*. House guessed – between £60 & £70 . . . Gave out Property Plot of 2nd and 3rd Comic Scenes & Scene Plot of 3rd ditto. Thurs: All the Scene & Property Plots of Comic Scenes (Three) have now been given out.

16 Sun   Home all day, working at Comic Scenes & the bill of new Piece for Mrs Lane's return.

17 Mon   Gunpowder Tom. G.W.Ross. The Victorellis (Gymnasts). *The Castaway*. Changing on Tuesday & Friday to *The Lady of Lyons & Castaway*.

19 Wed   C.Pitt's Benefit. *Wild Boys of London* (1st night). 12 woodcuts. G.W.Ross & the Victorellis. *Varley the Vulture*. Fine morning. Wet afternoon. Said to be £85 by Mr Borrow, proved to be £97.

24 Mon   False Mother. Victorellis (Trapeze). The 'Great Vaulting Troupe' from the Alhambra & Cremorne, Double somersault by H.Wardini, Clown the 'Little Delavanti'.* *Gunpowder Tom* changed on Tuesday to *The Lady of Lyons & False Mother*.

25 Tues   Mr & Mrs S.Lane returned from Llandudno, North Wales. Harriet* in Hysterics at the Theatre, frightened by the muskets firing when the Vaulter (Wardini) threw his somersault. Mrs Borrow very kind to her – very assiduous in trying to recover her.

*W.G.Ross had made a sensation with his dramatic rendering of the 'Ballad of Sam Hall' at the Song and Supper Rooms in the 1840s. It told of a chimney sweep who was hanged, unrepentant, for murder. Ross was never able to repeat this success, and died in 1873.

*The Delavanti acrobatic troupe, known as the Kings of the Carpet, had been founded by John Bowden in the mid-century.

*Harriet is Wilton's daughter, Harriet Rountree.

28 Fri   To St. James's Palace with Mr S.Lane, Mr Beckett & Mr Boyce* (his 1st time as a surety) to get the license for the Britannia Theatre from the Lord Chamberlain for the ensuing year. Mr Beckett & self dined at the Pall Mall Hotel . . . Mr Lane & Mr Boyce stayed to luncheon only.

OCT 1 Mon   Mary Edmonstone. Victorelli Brothers. Great Vaulting Troupe. 'The Stonettes'.* Clown, the Little Delavanti. Double somersault, H.Wardini. *False Mother*. First Piece changed Tuesday & Friday to *The Stranger*.

3 Wed   W.R.Crauford's Benefit. *Old Cherry Tree* (1st time). (Extras as above). Mrs S.Lane's 1st appearance since her return from the provinces. *Black Eyed Susan*. Great House – Weather very close – Performances not over till 20 minutes 12. Receipts *£110 odd. £87 cash*.

4 Thurs   Received Opening of Pantomime.

5 Fri   Gave out Scene Plot of Opening to Mr Muir in Painting Room. Told by Mr Borrow that Mr Muir must be set to work tomorrow morning; that Mr S.Lane had heard of his being *ivré* on the premises &c. Told Mr Muir so in as gentle a way as possible – He fires up indignantly & has words with Mr Borrow; says he will leave the Theatre.

6 Sat   Mr Muir gave in his Discharge to Mr Borrow in the Theatre. Mr & Mrs S.Lane returned home at 8 o'clock tonight (not expected till tomorrow night). Mr Lane ill – did not come behind the scenes . . . Found 1/0 in box at Theatre! Subscription in the Theatre for Mr Light, another for Mr . . . * the later Prompter of the City Theatre. Another solicited by Mrs Paul*, late Miss E.Green.

7 Sun   Home all day working at Property Plot of Opening of Pantomime.

8 Mon   Old Cherry Tree (Mrs S.Lane's 1st week). Brothers Victorelli (Trapeze). Great Vaulting Troupe, Clown Delavanti, Double Somersault H.Wardini. *Mary Edmonstone*.

10 Wed   Benefit, Messrs Summers & Light. *Old Cherry Tree*. Extras, as rest of week. *Ivan the Terrible* (1st night). About *£107*, over two or three minutes past 12.

14 Sun   Home all day working at Plots of Opening.

15 Mon   Old Cherry Tree. (Extras as last week). *Mary Stuart, Queen of Scots*.

17 Wed   W.Newham's Benefit. *Old Cherry Tree*. (Extras same as rest of week & a Pantomime sketch called *Mother Goose* – Clown, Mr R.Bell; Harlequin, Mr R.Leslie; Pantaloon, Mr W.Newham; Columbine, Madlle C.Stephan). *Nat Graves* Nat, Mr Drummond (1st time). House appeared middling.

22 Mon   Old Cherry Tree. Victorellis (Gymnasts). Paul Deulin (Nigger).

*Robert Boyce** was an estate agent and auctioneer of 94 Hoxton St.

*Stonette** was a noted Shakespearian-type clown with Circus Renz. It is not clear whether there was any assocation with this troupe.

*J.C.Symondson** may have been the prompter referred to here. (See City of London Playbills). **Mrs Paul** was a former ballet girl from 1856–1862.

N.Ogden ('Kind, old Daddy').* Master George Perks & his Pony, 'Black Diamond'. *Bride of Aldgate.*

29 Mon   Old Cherry Tree. Paul Deulin (Nigger). N.Ogden ('Kind, old Daddy'). Master George Perks & his Pony, 'Black Diamond'. Emma Mowbray (singer) her 1st night. *Edward, the Black Prince.*

31 Wed   No Benefit, but last piece changed to *Black Doctor* – decent house. Mr J.Mitchell of 5 Marlborough Street, Dalston called & left a specimen of an 'Advertising Curtain' which he wished Mr Lane to exhibit at the Britannia Theatre. Showed me an agreement with Mr B.O.Conquest* for a similar accommodation at the Grecian, signed by Mr Conquest & himself – & by which he had agreed to pay Mr Conquest £80 a year – paid quarterly in advance. Mr S.Lane declined. Mr J.M. offered to give me £5 if Mr Lane agreed.

NOV 3 Sat   Last Piece changed to *Guy Fawkes* and *Fireworks.* Immense House, a Boxing Night. *£126* in house before Curtain rose & great at Half-Price.

5 Mon   The What Is It?. Ogden. Deulin. Master George Perks & his Pony, 'Black Diamond'. Miss K.Garstone.* *Old Cherry Tree.* Drama of *Guy Fawkes & Fireworks* for Monday, Wednesday & Saturday, to be changed on Tuesday, Thursday & Friday to *Edward, the Black Prince* & no Fireworks. (Great House).

7 Wed   Fireworks – Excellent House – though not so good as Monday's.

11 Sun   Home all day, cutting down Dahlias and working at story of Panto-mime Opening for the Newspapers.

12 Mon   The What is it? Mr 'Dancing Mad' Brian.* Miss K.Garstone. Deulin. Mastr Geo Perks & Pony. *Old Cherry Tree. Mary Livingstone.*

17 Sat   Last Night of Mr & Mrs W.Morton at the Britannia.

18 Sun   Home all day, preparing plots, bill etc. of new Piece, *Laurette's Bridal.*

19 Mon   Some Bells that Rang. Miss K.Garstone. *What Is It?* 'Dancing mad' Brian. Master Perks & Pony. *Old Cherry Tree.*

21 Wed   Benefit of the 'Clicker's Club'. *Some Bells that Rang. What Is It?* Extras as on Monday, & Master Perry (Drummer) & a Mr . . . who sang two songs. *Thirteenth Chime.* No great things of a 'house'.

24 Sat   A vile night, after a sternly cold day. Horrid cold rain to come home through at midnight. Bad house at Theatre.

---

*Nat Ogden was a character and 'costerial' singer whose song was based on a character in Greenwood's 'A Night in a Workhouse'.

*Benjamin Oliver Conquest had been manager of the Grecian Theatre since 1851.

*Kate Garstone was a serio-comic vocalist.

*'Dancing Mad' Brian. Despite his nickname, Mr J.F.Brian was a singer who made numerous appearances at the Britannia with his wife.

26 Mon   Laurette's Bridal (produced on Saturday last). Miss K.Garstone. Mr 'Dancing Master' Brian. Master George Perks & Pony. *What Is It? Some Bells that Rang.*

27 Tuesday   1st Rehearsal of Opening of Pantomime.

DEC 2 Sun   Home all day about new Piece for Mrs S.Lane's Benefit & her Bill.

3 Mon   Laurette's Bridal. Miss Kate Garstone. Mr 'Dancing Mad' Brian. Mr Laburnum.* Mr Dugwar*, 'Indian Juggler'. *Mother Brownrigg.* Shy House for a Monday.

5 Wed   Benefit of Messrs Drummond & Bell. *Roving Jack, the Pirate Hunter.* Extras as on Monday. *Laurette's Bridal. Paved with Gold.* Plenty of woodcuts, borrowed from Mr Brett.* Great House in spite of horridly wet day *£101-7-0*. Heavy Rain at intervals more or less all day – the worst of miserable weather for a Benefit & it rained all night after. Upwards of *£40* worth of *Tickets*, Upwards of *£60* cash!

8 Sat   Mrs S.Lane's Benefit Bill out.

9 Sun   Home all day, writing Super Plot in *Wildfire Ned* for Mrs S.Lane's Benefit, marking own Part! and preparing comic scene to rehearse tomorrow.

10 Mon   Belinda Seagrave. Mr 'Dancing Mad' Brian. Mr Laburnum (Comic Singer). Dugwar (soi-disant) Indian Juggler. *Laurette's Bridal.*
Error   (NB. *Laurette's Bridal* should have been entered here as the 1st piece & *Belinda Seagrave* as the last) to be changed to *Black-eyed Susan* on Wednesday.

12 Wed   Gave *Pantomime Bill* to Mrs S.Lane – having little opinion of it myself.

13 Thurs   Mrs S.Lane expressed herself pleased with the *Pantomime Bill* and said she had sent it to the Printers.

15 Sat   Rehearsals very heavy all this week.

16 Sun   Home all day writing 20 Long Plots of the Pantomime for the newspapers.

17 Mon   Beauty & the Beast. Dancing Mad Brian. Laburnum (soi-distant 'The Leviathan Comique'). Dugwar, the Indian Juggler. *Laurette's Bridal. Bitter Cold.* Bad house – notwithstanding the change of two pieces.

18 Tues   Mr S.Lane ill at Brighton – Mrs S.L. going down there every night after Performance at night. Not up today to rehearse.

---

*Walter Laburnum was a 'Lion Comique' in the style of George Leybourne. He parodied Leybourne's coach and four by driving a donkey cart through the streets of London. Dugwar, probably Dungwar, a juggler who made use of everyday objects rather than the traditional clubs, included Top-spinning and a Japanese Butterfly Trick in his act.

*Edwin J.Brett was a publisher of popular boys' journals. Next year he was to take over publication of *The Boys of England*, which furnished the raw material for a number of Britannia melodramas.

19 Wed Mrs S.Lane's Benefit and Last Night of the Season. *Kathleen. (Why Don't She Marry* – Miss Esther Jacobs). *Festival. Wildfire Ned.* Extra Dances. Capital House, after a fine, clear, warm & sunny day. Halberds fell in Act 3 Sc. 3 of *Kathleen,* & spoiled scene. Great row about it & 'Insult' in Prompt-Entrance before Mr Superintendent Mott,* Miss Lyon & Supers.

20 Thurs Corrected Proof & Revise of Pant. Bill. Pant. rehearsed all through, Comic Scenes & Opening.

21 Fri Pant. Bill printed last night. Pant. rehearsed all through again.

22 Sat Scenic Rehearsal, began at 6 o'clock (nominally); over at, or about, 10 or ¼ past.

23 Sun Hard at work all day, from ½ past 11 A.M. till ½ past 11 P.M., writing 20 Long Puffs (in manifold) for the Newspapers. Jessie writing the letters to accompany them. (Entered here by mistake – should have been entered last Sunday, Decr 16th.)

26 Wed Boxing Day. Morning Performance of the Pantomime at 12. *The Princess of The Pearl Island, or, The Three Kingdoms of Pearl, Gold & Silver.* (Miss Esther Jacobs). Guessed by Geo. Taylor at above *£100.* At night supposed to be above *£150.*

27 Thurs Immense House again – greater it is said than last night!

1867

JAN 2 Wed Heavy fall of snow during last night & today. Mr Borrow anxious to close the Theatre & not to play. Mrs S.Lane expressed herself determined to play if there should be no more than 20 people in the house. The result was, *we played* – and there was a very decent house!

6 Sun Yesterday, Saturday, Mrs E.Yarnold too ill to act. Came to the Theatre but unable to go on the stage, Miss M.Booth* playing her part in the *Skeleton Crew.*

7 Mon Pant. *Princess of Pearl Island.* . . Miss Esther Jacobs; Harlequin, Fredericks; Clown, Louis; Pantaloon, W.Newham; Columbine, C.Stephan; Sprites, the Dusoni Family (5 in number). *Skeleton Crew.* Capital House in consequence of the magical thaw which took place last night. All the snow gone off the ground in one night! The weather today, wondrously mild & even balmy! a heavy rain during the night having washed both the streets & the air! Mrs E.Yarnold not able to act again and not to play any more during the run of the piece.

10 Thurs W.Newham, bad cold, did not play in Opening. A Super sent on for his part, with the speaking all cut out, or where possible, spoken by Mrs Newham, Mr Bigwood &c.

***Superintendent Mott** was in charge of London's N Division of Police.

***Mary Booth** was an actress who had joined the Britannia company on 2 July 1866. She had been engaged at the Standard in the early 1860s.

12 Sat Hard frost again during last night. Snow (a little) – this morning, resting on ground all day. Hard frost again at midnight . . . Great House again tonight at Theatre in spite of weather.

14 Mon Harriet went to Moorgate Street to buy a diary for me as usual (like this book) for 4d. On getting it home, found it had neither January, February or March in it. She went back and changed it.

17 Thurs Dreadfully cold in Theatre at night. Everybody of the opinion this is the coldest day & night we have had.

22 Tues Extraordinary weather tonight at Midnight. Rain freezing as it fell. The streets, roads and pavements one sheet of ice. No running – scarcely any walking – no getting home from the Theatre without sliding. Street one black slippery sheet of ice. Fell 3 times in sliding home.

26 Sat Mrs S.Lane ill (Quinsy), unable to play tonight. Miss E.Macarthy played her part.

30 Wed Very bad 'House' tonight (said by J.Parry to be the 'worst he had ever seen'). *Mrs S.Lane* still unable to play – *Mrs E.Yarnold* away (says she will not be able to come for a fortnight). *Miss M.Booth* unable to sing in Pantomime (from bad cold), let out of afterpiece. *Miss E.Macarthy* playing Mrs Lane's part in the Pantomime, but very ill tonight, yet obliged to receive Mrs Yarnold's part to study for next Monday; & *Miss S.Miles & Mrs Newham* also both very ill tonight.

31 Thurs Mrs S.Lane better, but her name taken out of the bill – not going to play either this week or next. Miss S.Miles asked that her part might be given to Mr R.Leslie that he might be able to go on for it tomorrow night if she is worse.

FEB 1 Fri Miss S.Miles better. Miss E.Macarthy no better. Mrs S.Lane worse – a third ulcer forming in her throat.

2 Sat Mrs S.Lane no better. . . . Have had no Bills of the Performances at the Theatre since Boxing-Day – unable to get them from Jacobs (Bill Inspector) though asked for repeatedly.

3 Sun Mrs S.Lane better – third tumour burst this morning.

4 Mon 1st Change of Performances since Xmas. Pantomime. *Widow's Fireside*. Mrs S.Lane's name taken out of the bill . . . Polly Robinson* (née Borrow), came home from Russia, brought a beautiful pair of Russian boots for her mother, lined with sheepskin & ornamented with Astracan fur, double soled, with velvet uppers, lace up front & Velvet Rosette with steel buckle.

6 Wed Lord Alfred Paget* & party in Mr S.Lane's private box this evening to see the Pantomime – did not arrive till 6th scene was over. His Lordship

*Polly Robinson's husband, **William**, had been engaged as foreman by the railway contractor, John Aird, to supervise the laying of the railway line in Moscow.

*Lord Alfred Paget was Commodore of the Royal Thames Yacht Club, to which Samuel Lane also belonged.

grown much stouter than when there last . . . Miss S.Miles worse – unable to play tonight – (Doctor's certificate). Miss M.Booth played her part.

7 Thurs   Miss S.Miles not at rehearsal this morning; Mrs E.Yarnold read the part of 'Jessie Vere' (instead of the part of 'Emily', which she is cast) lest Miss Miles should be unable to play next week. Miss S.Miles tonight sent for the part saying she would be at the Theatre on Saturday next to rehearse it – & – would play it next week. Forwarded the part to her, with the assent of Mr Borrow, having had it in my possession since the morning to write *in* a leaf which had been torn out. Mrs E.Yarnold later in the evening sent for the part as she had promised in the morning she would. Gave the part of Emily to Miss Beaver* to carry to Mrs Yarnold . . . Lord Alfred Paget in Stage Box tonight.

8 Fri   Mrs S.Lane better. Miss S.Miles better. Miss S.Miles played tonight.

9 Sat   Capital House. Mrs S.Lane better – in the Stage Box to see the Pantomime.

11 Mon   Pantomime. (Mrs S.Lane not playing – gone down for a few days to Hastings to affirm her health). *Return of Wanderer*.

12 Tues   Mr W.Crauford gave me a splendid meerschaum Pipe subscribed for by several members of the company to be presented to me – more power to their elbows!

16 Sat   Capital House . . . A Doctor Mortimer Glanville behind the scenes wanting statistics of the Theatre for a member of Parliament, to speak in the '*House*', on a new 'Theatre Bill', soon to be 'brought in', & for a series of readable articles in *Once a Week*.* Will come again some Friday & may bring the Earl of Limerick.

20 Wed   Miss Neumann* (Mrs Manning of the Ballet) taken ill, unable to play Miss Macarthy's part (Princess Gold) in the Pantomime. Obliged to give it to Miss Elton* (Ballet Girl also) who has never yet attempted to speak (Miss Pearson* looking too old, as Mr & Mrs Borrow say). Mrs Manning confined of a daughter tonight.

21 Thurs   Quarrel between Miss F.Jones & Miss Esther Jacobs at Theatre tonight. Miss E.J. telling Miss F.J. on the stage that her dress was *dirty*. And Miss F.J. saying there were dirtier things went on *that* stage than her dress, & if Miss E.J. dared make such observations again she (Miss F.J.) would wring her neck for her & pitch her into the Pit.

25 Mon   Last Link of Love (1st night). Pant. *Princess of the Pearl Island*. Mrs S.Lane's 1st night of playing since her illness – since Friday Jany 25th. Very shy House tonight.

26 Tues   Very shy 'House' again tonight. Miss Pearson ill – unable to come

---

*Miss Beaver was a ballet girl.

*Once a Week did not print any articles on the Britannia Theatre in the ensuing months.

*Miss Neumann was married to a super, who seems also to have been employed as a dayman and scene shifter at the theatre. Miss Elton had been a ballet girl since 1859. Miss Pearson had been a ballet girl since 1858.

to Rehearsal. Said, at night, to have burst a blood vessel & vomited a quart of blood. Miss E.Macarthy ill – got Erysipelas in her face – one eye much affected & the disorder said by the doctor to be about to attack the other. Gave notice to Mr Morgan, Proprietor of the Lime Light, & Mr Dusoni, of the 'Sprites', that their engagement terminated next Tuesday. Miss Pearson (of the Ballet) did not come to the Theatre tonight – her illness (see above) said to be premonitory of consumption.

27 Wed   Benefit of J.Louis (Clown). No change in the stock bill of the week, except altering the Cast of 3rd comic scene, and adding 'Three Sensation Scenes' from *The Dumb Man of Manchester*, Louis playing 'the Dumb Man'. In the 3rd comic scene Louis playing Columbine; Leslie, Harlequin; R.Bell, Clown; Newham, Panta-Clown; Fredericks, Harlequina. House only middling.

MAR 4 Mon   Last Link of Love. 11th & Last Week of the Pantomime (*Princess of the Pearl Island*) as a whole. No Comic Scenes after Tuesday . . . C.Pitt writing out tonight an Announce-Bill of a Farewell Benefit for Mrs E.Yarnold, said that she had told him that she had given in her discharge to the Management – not having strength enough to act – at present.

6 Wed (*Ash Wednesday*) Grand Concert . . . Messrs Milburn,* Robt Green,* Connelly & Wilmet,* Buckstone,* Wardes & D'Aubans. Alfred Young, Harry Liston,* Fredk Evans & Rosalind (his wife). Mr & Mrs McHaffie,* Mrs Brian (wife of 'Dancing Mad'), Miss Emma Kerridge, Louie Sherrington,* Dugwar (the Indian Juggler), 'The Marvels of Peru' (acrobats), Mr & Mrs Langham & J.Millicent.* Good House.

7 Thurs   Miss Esther Jacobs' Benefit. *Asmodeus.* Opening (only) of Pantomime. *Last Link of Love* (1st night at Half Price) – Change Piece again tomorrow – Horrid weather – Heavy fall of snow, swift & furious – and *the* abominable N.E. Wind after. Shy House (*£29* only) as there might have been under any circumstances, but this sufficiently accounted for by the weather.

8 Fri   Last Link of Love. Opening (only) of Pantomime, no comic scenes. *Mary Blane* (same performances tomorrow). Mr T.Drummond ill, unable to play tonight (bad leg). Mr R.Bell played his part in *The Last Link of Love.*

9 Sat   Mr H.Muir (Scene Painter) who burst a blood vessel yesterday, unable to come to the Theatre tonight, & said to be dangerously ill. Gave Miss F.Jones a week's notice. *Mem.* Missed her at end of performance, she having gone 'home' a few minutes before, and her crying on receiving the notice at her lodgings, holding the street door in her hand.

---

*J.H.Milburn was a vocalist, whose most famous songs included 'All Among the Hay' and 'On the Beach at Brighton'. **Robert Green** was a baritone. **Connelly and Wilmet** were a comedy duo. **George Buckstone** was a comic vocalist. **Harry Liston**, a comic vocalist from Manchester, first appeared in London in 1865. His songs, some of which were of the 'swell' variety, included 'The Convict', 'When Johnny Comes Marching Home' and 'Nobody's Child'. He was also a competent dancer. **Peter and Amelia McHaffie** were Irish singers who also danced. Their impersonations ranged from swells to convicts. Amelia, who was praised for her fine voice, died the following year. **Loui(s)e Sherrington** was a popular serio-comic vocalist. **Mr and Mrs Langan and J.Millicent**, who were known as the Louisville Minstrels, had first appeared in London the previous year.

11 Mon   Corsican Brothers. Opening of Pantomime. *Last Link of Love.*

12 Tues   *Prynne*
Michael Allen Prynne, a native of Devonport, brought up before the Magistrate on Saturday last at the Mansion House for begging – asked by his
Worship, Mr Alderman Wilson, if he would like to be sent to Plymouth –
answered in the affirmative & was taken to the Workhouse of the City of
London Union, preparatory to being clothed & sent there. (See *Times* of
yesterday). 'He had a worn shawl wrapped about his head & shoulders & was
otherwise in rags, "through which" as he said, "every wind of Heaven . . '

13 Wed Benefit of Gold Beaters' Society. *Corsican Brothers.* Opening of
Pant. *Rose Roy* . . . Same horrid Wind & piercing cold. Hard, black
frost . . . at midnight, horrid cold! Glad to take a glass of Rum at the bar
before leaving – which I have done several times of late! . . . A stranger, a Mr
Frith, of the firm of Frith & Smith (Silk Pressers, Calenderers &c) of Brook
Road, Dalston, came to the Theatre tonight, and was mistaken for Charles
Dickens's brother by Mr S.Lane, who took him into his Private Box – brought
him on to the stage and paid him great attention, but at length suspecting some
mistake, came & asked me if I knew 'the gentleman he had been talking with'
– if I should take him for Charles Dickens's brother &c. & told me to find out
who he was &c. – which I did from John Martin, our Gas-man, who knew Mr
Frith.

14 Thurs Mrs E.Yarnold's Benefit. *Lady of Lyons.* Opening of Pantomime.
Last Link of Love. – This being announced as a *Farewell Benefit* (on a/c of
health) for Mrs Yarnold, all the company desired by Mrs Lane to appear on
stage in Evening Dresses (save the mark!) while Mrs E.Y. should speak her
Address. (See account of another Farewell Benefit of Mrs E.Yarnold's on
April 14th 1858). Tonight, after the conclusion of her Address, a wreath of
Laurel was held over her head by Mr J.Reynolds. A capital House tonight –
notwithstanding the weather.

15 Fri Miss E.Jacobs ill – unable to play tonight. Her part played by Miss
E.Macarthy cutting out the songs.

16 Sat Last Night of the Pantomime. Miss Esther Jacobs away ill – did not
play tonight . . . Immense 'House' tonight. Last Night of Miss Polly Jones
(Miss F.Jones in the bills). – Mr S.Lane said on Thursday night last that,
notwithstanding Mrs E.Yarnold's illness, her Farewell Address &c., &c., he
would bet £1000 to a penny she would be back again to the Theatre in six
weeks!

18 Mon   The Flirt. The Waterman (Miss Esther Jacobs). *Last Link of Love.*
Killing Weather – snow, sleet, rain, slush & piercingly cold wind through all.
At Rehearsal this morning, Mrs S.Lane unable to attend, being ill & having
sent for a doctor, but says she will play tonight – Mr Lane very ill of Ague.
Miss E.Jacobs sent message to say she cannot play tonight being ill. Mrs
S.Lane afterwards arrived from Tottenham, but did not come on the stage.

Miss Ruth Edwin* rehearsed Miss Jacobs's part (Tom Tug in *The Waterman*) & played it at night.

19 Tues   Miss L.Rayner's* 1st Appearance at the Britannia (last night) as Wilhelmina in *The Waterman*. Miss E.Jacobs played tonight, tho' very unwell – probably alarmed by finding we were getting on so well without her.

20 Wed   Benefit of Hand in Hand Society. No change of Performances – no bills out. An excellent House tonight.

21 Thurs   Benefit of Foresters. Last Piece changed to *Robin Hood*. Bad House, after a bright, clear but cold day.

25 Mon   *Faust* Miss Esther Jacobs, & Ruth Edwin. Mrs Lane. *Ticket of Leave*.

27 Wed   Society's Benefit . . . Very fair 'House' tonight – though no change of pieces.

APRIL 1 Mon   *Faust* (Burlesque) Mrs S.Lane, Miss E.Jacobs. Miss Ruth Edwin. *Dustman's Treasure*.

3 Wed   Mr Bigwood's Benefit. *The Vagabonds* (a Victoria Piece, lent by the Author). *Faust* Burlesque. *Jack & Jack's Brother*. House indifferent at first, but pulled up afterwards.

4 Thurs   Miss Esther Jacobs gave notice that she was too ill to play tomorrow night. – Told Mr Elton that he must play her part & rehearsed him in it during the performance of *Golden Dustman*. Found him *perfect* – he having been told a week ago to understudy it. Took Miss Jacobs name out of the proof of the bill for next week.

5 Fri   Very bad 'House' tonight. Mr E.Elton played Mephistophiles tonight, 1st time, instead of Miss Esther Jacobs.

6 Sat   A row between Mr Bigwood and the management about a Poster which appeared this morning announcing *Mr Elton* for *Mephistophiles*, & not mentioning Mr B's name. Mr B wished to resign his engagement – wrote letter to the management to that effect. Management gave way – & had 200 more posters printed with his name in them. – NB. The poster concocted by Mr Borrow or Mr S.Lane, & no proof sent to me – so I was out of the mess.

8 Mon   *Dream of Aileen* (written by J.B.Howe). J.B.Howe's 1st night.* *Faust* (burlesque), Mr E.Elton playing Mephistophiles, in lieu of Miss Jacobs, who left last Thursday night. *Sailor's Return* . . . Miss Macarthy very ill at theatre, wasting daily – not attending rehearsals – yet playing at night.

10 Wed   Benefit of Foresters Lodge 3542. No change of Performances. Shy House, alas.

---

*Ruth Edwin** had enjoyed occasional engagements at the Britannia Theatre since 1860.

*Lizzie Rayner** joined the theatre as a leading actress. She was married to a Mr Morgan (possibly the Limelight Proprietor).

*Howe** had just spent two years at the Effingham Theatre.

11 Thurs   Pieces changed to *Old Mint of Southwark*, *Faust* (burlesque) and *Eagle and Child*, for Miss Clara Griffiths's* Benefit. £47 odd in House.

14 Sun   The Mother of the *Little Xtal Palace Mite* died this day.

15 Mon   *Rob Roy* (2 last Acts) – 20th Grenadiers (1st Battalion) from the Tower. Piece cut – only played *1h.37.m.* Burlesque, *Faust* (no star) & Grand Concert: Mr Robt. Green; Mme Pedley;* Mr & Mrs McHaffie; Little Lotto;* Madme Beatrice Bermond;* Mr W.Adams;* The Four Marvels of Mexico.*

18 Thurs   Subscription making in the Theatre for the 'Little Xtal Palace Mite' & her brother. Gave 2/0. Mrs S.Lane gave £1.0.0. Misses M.Booth & S.Miles 2/6 each.

22 Mon   Easter Monday. *Life Signal*, 1st night. *Cherry & Fair Star* (Burlesque, 1st night). *Dream of Aileen.*

28 Sun   Busy about *The Spinning Wheel* to follow Burlesque? (sic)

MAY 1 Wed   A most wretched 'House' – the worst at the beginning, – I ever saw at the Britannia. Before the curtain rose, it resembled only such bad houses as I have seen in the country, in Teignmouth, to wit.

Mem   . Very bad business at the Theatre all this week – worse I have never seen at the Britannia – nor so bad I think.

3 Fri   Mrs Casse & Bobby (her grandson) here. Bobby (4 years old) recited '*Ladies & Gentlemen, they have sent me out*' and sang *Annie Laurie* in the front parlour.

4 Sat   John Martin said in the Prompt Entrance tonight that Mr Crauford had to pay £12 per week for the Britannia bar, & that Bridgins had to pay the same for the Saloons.

6 Mon   *Old Maid in (the) Winding Sheet*, revived. *Cherry & Fair Star*, burlesque (Miss Ruth Edwin, Mrs S.Lane & Miss M.Booth only in it.) *The Life Signal*. Fine, hot day. The Great Reform Meeting in Hyde Park. Dreadful, bad house tonight at the Britannia, only 2 persons in the Boxes before the curtains drew up!

7 Tues   Prynne, the immortal cadger! called at the Britannia bar during rehearsal.

8 Wed   Benefit of the 'Old Ford' Volunteer Fire Brigade. Performances unchanged, except last piece to *Work Girls of London*, & the bringing of real Fire Engine on the stage, with real horses & real Firemen to extinguish a supposed fire at the end of the 1st act. Bad House. The arranger of the Benefit said they had lost a clear £20, but Mr Lane had given them back £4, 'so they could not complain'.

**Clara Griffiths*, 'the Little Crystal Palace Mite', was a child performer.

Madame Pedley* was a sentimental vocalist. **Little Lotto, an offspring of Madame Pedley, was a serio-comic vocalist. **Beatrice Bermond** was later to be billed as 'the reigning queen of drawing room serio-comics'. **W.J.Adams** was a comic singer. **The Marvels of Mexico** were acrobats.

9 Thurs Horrid bad 'business' at the Britannia all this week – a worse week's business, till Saturday 11th, never seen there – unless it was last week! –

10 Fri Mr Walden, behind the scenes, told me my appeal against the Income Tax was allowed – & added that if the Collector troubled me any further about it, I was to refer him to Spital Square.

11 Sat House, at Theatre, a little better tonight.

13 Mon Performances same as last week, except changing *Life Signal* for *Blue Beard*.

18 Sat Capital House. Pieces changed to *The Shamrock of Ireland* (J.B.Howe's writing) 1st time. *Mayor of Garret*, called on the bills *The Volunteers* & *Old Maid in Winding Sheet*.

20 Mon Performances as changed on Saturday last. Up to Weymouth Street, Portland Place & down from there to Lord Chamberlain's Office, St. James's Palace & thence back to Weymouth Street to see Mr W.Bodham Donne about the piece of *The Old Maid in the Winding Sheet*, which *Mr W.B.D.* did not remember having been licensed. Saw the Queen pass the door of the Chamberlain's office in an open barouche, 2 or 3 other ladies in the carriage with her. The Queen was still in mourning – Came on to rain – Got wet through coming home. Mr W.B.Donne said he did not attach one atom of blame to the management of the Britannia Theatre, nor did he mean to put them to one penny expense – but he feared they had been imposed upon by the author (Hazlewood) bringing them a M.S.S. and saying it had been licensed for, & played at a country Theatre. He asked for Hazlewood's address & to be allowed to retain the bill of May 18th (the first night the piece was acted). Said he would make further enquiries & write again in a day or two, & return the bill – Gave me a glass of wine, – which (being wet through) I accepted. He also spoke of the trouble he had had with *Faucquez & Travers*,* called the former, in jest, & with a smile, 'a slippery rascal'.

27 Mon *Auld Robin Gray*, 1st night of this revival. *The Shamrock. The Volunteers.* House middling.

29 Wed Shy House.

30 Thurs Benefit of a Forester. *The Shamrock. Dark Cloud with Silver Lining. Volunteers.* Shy House.

JUNE 3 Mon *The Gipsy & the Showman. Shamrock. The Clock on the Stairs.*

5 Wed T.Drummond's Benefit. (Rainy Day). *Othello*, 5 acts. *Shamrock.* £73.10.0 in house. Othello, Drummond; Iago, Reynolds; Cassio, J.B.Howe; Desdemona, S.Miles; Emilia, Miss J.Coveney;* Brabantio, J.Parry.

6 Thurs J.B.Howe said in the Prompt Entrance tonight that Mr R.Leslie's

---

*Faucquez and William Travers** were East End dramatists.

*Jane Coveney** joined the Britannia as an actress in April 1867. After extensive provincial experience, interrupted by a short spell at the Victoria Theatre, she had previously appeared at the New Olympic Theatre, the Surrey, Drury Lane and, with her sister, Harriet, at the Grecian.

name ought not to be placed before *his* in the Advertisements for he felt quite certain Mr R.Leslie's engagement did not entitle him to pre-eminence over him (Howe). His own engagement, he said, was for £4 a week, and a share of the 'Leading Business' with Reynolds & Drummond.

7 Fri   Up to British Museum to change reading ticket. Examined a Collection of Garrick's Poetry (3 vols) to find quotation 'A fellow feeling makes us wondrous kind', & his *Lethe* – 'a satire' – did not succeed. Saw a copy of the play-bill announcing *Garrick's 1st appearance* on the stage, *Oct 19th 1741*.

10 Mon   Whit-Monday. *The Marriage Certificate, or A Mother's Honour* (1st night). Hildebrandt & Ormonde (niggers).* *Auld Robin Gray*. Splendid weather – too fine for Theatres. Good 'House' notwithstanding. Went with Amelia to see Rose Wilton just arrived from Richmond to live with her brother, Fred Dewar, at no.12, Canonbury Rd, Islington. Struck with increased look of age about her – & observed that her brother, Fred's, hair was turning from black to grey! Sorry to see it.

12 Wed   Good House – spite of the hot weather. Subscription paper 'put up' last night in the Theatre to bury *George Cooke*, a good actor who was a few months ago playing the principal juvenile parts at the Britannia – but drank himself to death!

17 Mon   *Ding Dong Will. Marriage Certificate. George Barnwell*, (cut into 2 acts). Hildebrandt & Ormonde. Very cold weather, wind N. & N.E. Shivering at Noon coming home from Theatre & hovering over the fire at home. . . Received during rehearsal a Certificate from a Doctor, stating that Miss Booth was too ill of haemorrhagia to follow her usual occupation. She played tonight – notwithstanding.

19 Wed   J.Reynolds' Benefit. *Macbeth*. Hildebrandt & Ormonde. *Moonlight Jack* (Mr Travers's piece). Wood-cuts. House above *£101.0.0*. NB. Last Sunday gloomy, threatening weather with occasional showers. Today overcast – all in favour of the house.

22 Sat   Mrs S.Lane's Last Night for the Season.

24 Mon   *The Ballinasloe Boy* (1st week). Hildebrandt & Ormonde. Mr & Mrs McHaffie. Mr Geo.Buckstone. *Ellen & Susan*.

26 Wed   R.Leslie's Benefit. *The Collier's Strike* (1st night), Hazlewood's concoction & not licensed. Extras as above. *Nick of the Woods* (1st time). Fine Day. House above *£50*.

28 Fri   Bought book of *Lucky Horse Shoe* & went to Bath's to ascertain about woodcuts – found they had plenty.

JULY 1 Mon   *Moonlight Jack*. Mr G.Buckstone (Comic Vocalist). Mr & Mrs McHaffie (Hibernian Entertainment). Messrs Hildebrandt & Ormonde

*Hildebrandt and Ormonde** were much admired for their comic dialogue and singing. Hildebrandt lost his reason and died about 1870 and Ormonde became deaf from a fever and subject to fits of epilepsy.

(Niggers) – The Champion Skaters.* Last 3 Acts of *Macbeth*, with all the singing.

3 Wed   Mr J.Parry's Benefit. *Richard 3rd*, with 3 Richards, 1st & 3rd Acts by Mr T.Drummond; 2nd Act by Mr J.Parry, in imitation of *Edmund Kean* (!!!) 4th & 5th Acts by Mr J.B.Howe. Extras same as rest of week. Two Acts of *Raby Rattler* – Weather favourable, gloomy & overcast – today & yesterday. House (guessed) above £70 . . . Amelia up to Dean Street to see the House just taken by Fred Dewar. Got Proof of Benefit Bill from Beckett's and late at night one sort of Picture Bills (with 7 woodcuts) from Bath's, with promise of the rest – and loan of wood-cut tomorrow.

5 Fri   Amelia, Jessy & Milly to see *Macbeth* (last 3 Acts) & the Champion Skaters.

6 Sat   Robert Bell's mother died at ½ past 9 on this Saturday morning. Sultry weather, a bad omen for my Benefit, next Wednesday. – Remember it.

7 Sun   Blazing hot day. Bad prospect for Benefit on Wednesday next. – A bad omen – Remember it!

8 Mon   *Jack O'Lantern* (1st night). McHaffies, Mr Buckstone. Champion Skaters. *Moonlight Jack*. Blazing, hot day; House guessed at from £70 to £80.

9 Tues   A blazing hot day – Bad prospect for Ben tomorrow.

10 Wed   Own Benefit. Blazing hot day – 29.5.10. *Jack O'Lantern*. Extras as rest of week. 'Jockey Hornpipe' (Leslie). *Lucky Horse Shoe*. Cash £25.15.4. Tickets *1.10.0*. Maria Underhill* here & *paid* to go to the Theatre tonight! Mr Blackett went without Mrs B (the latter being ill). My share £6.8.7. & I believe, all owing to the sultry weather.

11 Thurs   Same weather – bad 'House' at Theatre. Letter from Mrs B.Ware, asking aid to get her son – the son of *Mr B.Ware*, a situation. Spoke to Mr Crauford about it. Mr *C* said, 'Let him come & look at me,' & if he has a good character (!) &c. . .

12 Fri   Same weather – bad 'House' at Theatre.

13 Sat   Rainy Day. Theatre crammed at night.

15 Mon   *Jack O'Lantern*. McHaffies. Skaters. Duett – E.Elton, Miss Macarthy. *Moonlight Jack*. Rainy Day – Immense 'House' at night.

16 Tues   More Rain. Benefit of a Mr Jevons.* Last piece changed to *The Tower of Nesle*. Decent House, upwards of £40 cash.

17 Wed   Stormy (Windy) Day. Miss S.Miles's Benefit. *Hamlet* (Hamlet, 1st time, Miss S.Miles). Extras as rest of week. *Whitehall, or Claude-Du Val*.

The Champion Skaters were M.Elliot and Mme. Fredericka, whose entertainment included a comic episode *Dunreary on Ice*. All such skating acts in theatres at this date were performed on roller skates.

Maria Underhill was a married sister of Fred Rountree.

Mr Jevons was a Loyal United Friend.

Magnificent Weather ever since Friday last. Rainy, Saturday, Sunday & Monday, Tuesday & today. House said to be *£92* and only *£7.10.0* tickets.

20 Sat   Great House at Britannia tonight – *Rain.*

21 Sun   *All The Year Round* of this week gives the quotation 'A fellow feeling makes us wondrous kind' in the Prologue spoken by Garrick (& written by him) previous to the comedy of the *Wonder* on the night he quitted the stage, June 10th 1776.

22 Mon   *Jack O'Lantern.* McHaffies. The Skaters, Niggers, Messrs Williamson & Craven. *Corsican Brothers.*

24 Wed   J.B.Howe's Benefit. *Scarlet Dick.* The McHaffies. The Champion Skaters. *Rip Van Winkle* (Rip by Mr Howe). 3rd & 5th Acts of *Othello.* Favourable weather. House *£85.* His Printing & Posting together cost him above £16! (Printing £11 odd; Posting £5 Odd). Total receipts *£85* odd.

27 Sat   Immense *House* tonight.

28 Sun   Home all day at *M.S.S.*

29 Mon   *Scarlet Dick.* Williamson & Craven (niggers).* The McHaffies & The Champion Skaters. *Jack O'Lantern.*

31 Wed   Benefit of Miss Jane Coveney. *Lady of Lyons* (Pauline, Miss J.C.). Extras as rest of week. *Surgeon of Paris.* Weather favourable today & yesterday, cool & gloomy (or, at least, dull). House between *£60* & *£62.* Mr J.B.Howe after rehearsal today made a communication to me to the effect that Mr T.Drummond & Miss S.Miles were going off together to America; either next Saturday week or the week after; that Drummond had told him so after borrowing five shillings of him; that Drummond & Miss S.Miles were now living together; that he believed they meant to leave abruptly & without giving any warning to the management[1].

AUG 2 Fri   This night, going home after the performances, Mr J.B.Howe and Mr R.Leslie quarrelled & fought on Whitmore Bridge.

3 Sat   R.Leslie's face marked with bruises, a black eye & large scratches . . . - Miss S.Miles saying J.B.Howe had kicked Leslie in the face & scratched him. Howe himself, in my dressing-room, told me that Leslie, as they quarrelled, sprung into the road, took off his coat and challenged Howe to fight; that he (Howe), without taking off either of his two coats, went into the road and gave Leslie a d – d good thrashing, asked him if he had had '*enough of it*', – and declared his determination to serve every other man in the Theatre, who insulted him, the same. And added that if he (Mr Leslie) dared insult him again, he would not only give him another such a thrashing, but that when Mr Samuel Lane came home, he would tell him something that would be the last thing Mr Leslie would like to hear, finishing with the words, 'I know more than you think!' – Today Howe has not a mark on his face.

---

*Williamson and Craven were negro minstrels, billed as 'celebrated American Comedians and Instrumentalists'. They also appeared in a couple of crowd scenes in the Derby Day drama, *Jack O'Lantern.*

5 Mon   Scarlet Dick. The Skaters. Mr J.Plumpton, 1st night. C.Woodman. Little Levitte & Nina the Electric, (Comic singers, mediocre),* their 1st night. *Jack O'Lantern.* Some rain fell at night – middling House. Above *£9* in the Gallery (£13 considered a capital Gallery, George Taylor says).

7 Wed   No Benefit, but Pieces changed to 1st, 3rd & 5th Acts of *Hamlet*, (Extras as rest of week) & *Surgeon of Paris.* Rainy Day – Good House.

10 Sat   Paid J.Parry on a/c of 'Sick Fund' = *3.0* . . .[2] Mr T.Drummond seen coming into Nichols's Square with another man, in a *Hansom* cab, with a huge, new *Box* on the top of it. They went to Mrs Mellon's* where Miss S.Miles was. Huge suspicions extant that Miss S.Miles has left the Theatre clandestinely & without warning . . . She was seen this afternoon kissing her two children in Nichols's Square & bidding them, 'good bye', & her daughter, Sophie, told our Milly tonight that her mother was gone away for a month – that she had brought them such beautiful notepaper, all covered with flowers, to write to her. The new box is supposed to be for the purpose of packing either Mr Drummond's or Miss S.Miles's dresses & properties previous to their flight together for America. After a time Mr Drummond left the Square in the cab, which waited in the Hackney Road till Miss S.Miles came & entered it, & then drove away with her & Mr T.D.

12 Mon   Poll & Partner Joe (1st & 3rd Acts). Bros. Hanlon* (1st week). J.Plumpton. Champion Skaters. C.Woodman. Little Levitte & Jessie Nina. *Jack O'Lantern.* No Miss S.Miles at Rehearsal this morning. But, having sent the part of Mary Maybud to Miss J.Coveney yesterday, that lady rehearsed the part. Mr T.Drummond was seen & spoken to by Mrs Wilton yesterday, and seen again today, 12 o'clock, Midnight. Mr T.Drummond has not appeared at the Theatre tonight. Mr J.B.Howe played his part, & Mr J.Parry played Mr J.B.Howe's. During the evening came a letter (to me) from Miss S.Miles, enclosing the book she had received to study the part of Mary Maybud in *Poll & Partner Joe* and the part of Beatrice in *The Gray Ladye* (a piece not yet acted). The audience took the change of actors very quietly and never called for either of the absentees! So much for popular favour to actors! Two great favourites disappear suddenly, from a London Theatre, & no notice is taken. Coming home, after the performance, nearly opposite the Theatre, I was accosted by Mr Drummond's wife ('Poll Batten' as she is rather con-temptuously called) enquiring whether I knew if Mr Drummond had yet gone home from the Theatre? (i.e. after acting, as she thought he *had* done). I answered that he 'had not been at the Theatre tonight, at all', & got away from her as quickly as possible, fearing a scene. Early this evening a gentleman called on Mr Borrow saying he had taken leave of Mr Drummond at 3 o'clock this afternoon, Mr D saying 'He had left the Britannia "*for good*", – & should not go there again – He & Miss Miles had an engagement of 80 dollars a week

---

*Little Levite and Jessie Nina** were Comic Duettists and Dancers, billed as the Sensational Grotesques.

*Mrs Mellon** was the wife of Henry Mellon, an actor resident at 78 Nichol's Square.

*The Hanlon Brothers** developed a series of acrobatic pantomimes which took London and Paris by storm in the 1870s.

at some *"Gardens"* in America'. (Query, *Niblo's Gardens*, New York?) He (Drummond) owed this gentleman some money ("a *little* money") which he would *"pay as soon* as he could"'.

13 Tues   Row in the Square last night by 2 drunken women, the youngest after Teddy Elton!* . . . At the Britannia Mr C.Pitt sent on to say to the Audience that Mr Drummond having left this Theatre without warning or notice, & with his name in the bills, Mr J.B.Howe had undertaken the part of the Jockey at very short notice & hopes &c. . .

15 Thurs   Petition from Mrs T.Drummond to Mr Borrow for a Subscription! At the Theatre an Apology again made tonight by Mr C.Pitt.

19 Mon   Last Man (altered by J.B.Howe). Bros. Hanlon (2nd week). Mr J.Plumpton. Mr C.Woodman. Champion Skaters. Mr & Mrs Coleman & Mr W.Brown, Niggers,* (1st week). *Last Shilling*.

24 Sat   Capital 'House' tonight.

26 Mon   The Sea. Champion Skaters. The Hanlon Brothers (Acrobats, from the Oxford). Mr J.Plumpton. Mr & Mrs. Coleman & Mr W.Brown (Niggers). *The Last Man*.

27 Tues   G.Bigwood very drunk tonight during Performances, quarrelled with Mr Borrow & said to me he should not come tomorrow night.

28 Wed   Change of Performance (though not a Benefit) to 1st, 3rd & 5th acts of *Hamlet*. Extras as above, and *The Miser's Daughter*.

SEPT 2 Mon   Man of Red Mansion. Skaters. Plumpton. Coleman (Mr & Mrs) & Wood (Niggers). Monsr Coutellier and M.Eugenio, Trapezists. *The Sea*.

4 Wed   Benefit of Perry & Wade, Musicians. *Claude Lorraine*. Brass Bands (Nine). Skaters. J.Plumpton. Mr & Mrs Coleman and Mr W.Brown (Niggers). Monsr Coutellier & M.Eugenio (Trapeze-Men). *The Boy Detective*. Examiners of Theatre, Messrs Ponsonby, Donne & the Architect (Mr Pinch or Pincher) inspected Britannia Theatre this morning – went away very well pleased . . . Mrs J.Martin went to see poor Mrs B.Ware . . . Capital House, said to be above £80.

Examination of Theatre

Honble Mr Ponsonby, Mr Donne & Mr Pinch, or Pincher, examined Britannia today . . . & left suggestions[3].
1.   That Fillets of Wood be put in front of seats (as they already are behind) in Boxes and recommended their being screwed not nailed on. Mr Donne said, 'You can begin with a few & if you don't like them, do away with them'.
2.   That Ventilators (three) be put in the Gentlemen's long Dressing-Room.
3.   That the iron shields above the Gas-lights in & about Lady's Dressing Rooms should be taken away & replaced by Discs. Also that the Gas-Pipes

---

*Edward Elton** was resident with his family at 76 Nichol's Square.

*Mr and Mrs Coleman** and **W.Browne** performed a minstrel act of 'ludicrous grotesquerie'.

leading to the lights should each be lengthened a few inches.
4.   That the floors should be washed. Gallery & Pit.
5.   Mr Donne requested that *M.S.S.* might, for the present, be addressed to his son, the Revd Mr Donne.

5 Thurs   Miss L.Rayner (i.e. Mrs B   )* tumbled to pieces. Jessie talking all day of Going on the stage. Mr Borrow came into the Prompt Entrance & asked why I could not let Jessie become an actress! – & persuaded me to let her *try*! Promised I would think of it.

6 Fri   Consented that Jessie should try her fortune on the stage, next Wednesday night in the part of 'Basil', the boy, in *The Bottle*. Went to the Theatre & told Mr Borrow so. He seemed much pleased – NB. The bills are out with Miss Newham's name *in* for the part, consequently Jessie's name will not appear in print. My reasons for choosing this part, for her debut, were, that it was not 'in possession', that it was conspicuous, & that it was easy and might give no trouble.

7 Sat   Gave out Scene & Property Plot of 1st Comic Scene, 'The House Tops & View of London by Moonlight' . . . Amelia went with Jessie to May's to borrow Dresses for Wednesday next.

9 Mon   1st night of *The Graye Ladye*. 1st night of Mr & Mrs Courtenay.* Coutellier and Ellice (misnomed 'Eugenio'), Gymnasts (from the Hippodrome, Paris). J.Plumpton Mr & Mrs Coleman & Mr W.Brown (Niggers). *Widow's Fireside* . . . In much anxiety about Dresses & Properties for Jessie. Went to Clarkson's* & chose 3 wigs for her. Clarkson very kind, would not state any charge for them. Believe, from his manner, he does not intend to charge. Met S.May* at the door, & found him equally kind & willing to oblige us.

10 Tues   All the family full of worry & anxiety about Jessie's dresses for tomorrow night and we have discovered that the part we have chosen for her, thinking it would give no trouble, is the most onerous.

11 Wed   Jessie's 1st Appearance on any stage. Benefit of R.Bell. *Forest of Bondy*, the dog by Mr Crauford's dog, 'Lion'. Extras as rest of week. *The Bottle*. Capital House. *£93.12.0. £70.17* Cash. *£22.15.0* Tickets. Jessie 'went on' for Basil & got through it very fair for a first appearance, and with more courage than could have been expected, – considering the great disadvantage she had to contend with – before a crowded House, – wearing male attire, – and after only two hurried rehearsals – the piece being full of bustle, and mixed up in eight Tableaux, besides having 2 changes of dress.

16 Mon   Dog of Montargis (Crauford's dog, 'Lion', playing the part of

---

*Miss L.Rayner's married name is given elsewhere as Morgan.

*Mr E.Courtenay and Mrs Eveline Courtenay were from the Theatre Royal Bath. The latter was described by the *Sunday Times* (15/9/1867) as 'not devoid of mannerism and has much yet to learn'. W.Clarkson was a well-known theatrical wig-maker. Samuel May, the theatrical costumier, was responsible for dressing many Britannia productions.

'Dragon'.) American Minstrels and their 'congener', Japanese Tommy.* *Gray Layde*.

18 Wed   Benefit of Miss M.Booth (i.e.) that Lady had *sold her name* to Mr Jacobs & Mr Thorne & a 3rd party. *Alone in the Pirate's Lair*. Coutellier & Ellice, Gymnasts. American Minstrels & 'Japanese Tommy' (a Dwarf). Duett by Mr Elton & Miss Booth. *The Castaway*. Immense House. £116 odd. Cash, £70. Tickets £46. Jacobs sold £21 odd. J.Thorne £18 odd. Miss M.Booth £3.16.0 (Third Party).

23 Mon   Alone in the Pirate's Lair. M.M.Coutellier & Ellice (Gymnasts from Paris). American Minstrels, with 'Japanese Tommy'. *Gray Layde*.

24 Tues   Mr & Mrs Lane came home from the country – for the season.

25 Wed   Benefit of C.Pitt & E.Harding. *Lion Limb* (Written by C.Pitt). Extras as rest of week. Duett, Elton & Booth. Comic Song, R.Leslie. Recitation, '*Jealousy*', J.B.Howe. Pas de Deux, Misses Craddock & Chipps (Ballet Girls). *Red Ribbund, or Soldier's Motto*. £90 odd in the house. Above £60 cash.

26 Thurs   To Clerkenwell Police Court, with Subscription of £3.3.0 from Mr Lane to the Fund raising on behalf of the Wife & Family of Mr Brown, Reporter, who has suddenly (or gradually) lost his reason.

28 Sat   Jessie spoke to Mrs S.Lane last night, asking an opportunity for '*practice*'. Mrs S.L. told her to tell 'her father to cast her whatever he thought best for her' – and today, in the Treasury, before Mr Borrow, said, 'So, Jessy's going to act then?' . . . 'Yes – she is very anxious to try' . . . 'Well – she's quite right – everybody ought to try' . . . 'And very sanguine' . . . 'She wouldn't get on if she wasn't' . . . 'That's true – I believe that – I wish I was as sanguine of her success' . . . 'Well – you don't know till you try – you must try her in everything' . . . 'What I fear most is her voice – yes – & her face' . . . 'Pooh! You can't tell'.

30 Mon Lion Limb (C.Pitt's Benefit Piece). American Minstrels. M.M.Coutellier & Ellice. Japanese Tommy. *Alone in the Pirate's Lair*. Went with Mr Lane, Mr Beckett & Mr Boyce to get License renewed at Lord Chamberlain's Office, at St. James's Palace. Left the Britannia at 12 p.m. After getting the license rode in cab to Brompton (or Kensington) to see the Albert Memorial – now building – through the Park to Victoria Gate & back through Park Lane. Dined at the Pall Mall.

OCT 1 Tues   Recommended Mr S.Lane to eat tomatoes.

2 Wed   Mr W.Crauford's Benefit, & 1st App. of Mrs S.L. (for the season). *Break but not Bend* (new piece by Hazlewood). Extras as rest of week. *Miller & his Men*. House not very great, owing to a Benefit at the Eagle.*

3 Thurs   Mr Borrow showed me the Agreements with 'Coutellier & Ellice' & with the 'American Minstrels & Japanese Tommy' – found that the former had

---

*Japanese Tommy was 33 years of age and only 37 inches high.
*The Eagle was the Grecian Theatre.

£6 per week & the latter £8 per week. 'C'est á dire' £3 each for the former, £2 each for the latter.

*7 Mon	Break but not Bend* (1st Week, Mrs S.Lane). Coutellier & Ellice (before the play). American Minstrels (after the play), with 'Japanese Tommy'. *Lion Limb*, 2nd week.

9 Wed	Benefit of Summers & Light, Waiters. Last Piece changed to *Road to Transportation*. An indifferent 'House'. Wet day . . . The '*Britannia*' Gallery said by George Taylor to be full at £15 though £16 said to have been once in it. Of course at Xmas when the price is raised to sixpence the Receipts are higher. There has been nearly £19 in it.

13 Sun	All day sorting & pasting bills in books.

14 Mon	Performances same as last week, except 'Coutellier & Ellice (Gymnasts) gone & Mr & Miss West, nigger singers, in their place. (Mr West celebrated as a 'Stump orator').*

16 Wed	Benefit of 'Loyal, United Friends'. Performances as rest of week, except last piece changed to *Beggar's Petition*, & an Address spoken by a member of the order. Indifferent House.

17 Thurs	Tonight, at Theatre, received *Opening of Pantomime* from Mrs S.Lane to prepare for Xmas – but not able even to look at it (further than the title) till Saturday next, which see.

18 Fri	Tonight Mr Thos Rogers, Scene Painter, came to me from Mrs S.Lane, requesting I would write out the Puppet Scene from the Pantomime so as to be able to give it to Mr Middleton* (the Puppet Show-Man), whom Mrs S.Lane is to see tomorrow & to meet Mr Rogers & Mrs S.Lane at 4 P.M. tomorrow to explain the requisites of the scene – How can I do this – the M.S.S. having only been given to me last night & I unable from press of business yet to look at it!

*19 Sat	Wrote out Puppet Scene* from Opening of Pantomime for Mrs S.Lane to give to Mr Middleton, but when written requested by Mrs S.Lane to give it to Mr Thos. Rogers (scene painter).

20 Sun	Home all day. Began to read Opening of Pantomime. Mrs Barrowcliffe (née Miss Johnson) came & knocked several times at the door. Did not open it. At length she went away. Saw her face & thought her sober.

*21 Mon	Break not Bend*. American Minstrels. Japanese Tommy. Stump-orator West & Miss Emma West. *Belinda Seagrave*. 1st night of *Miss M.Henderson** from Sadler's Wells.

---

*Will West** was a 'Stump Orator', a performer in black make-up who lectured or harangued the audience, usually on topical subjects, using props such as a table, umbrella etc. West's speeches concluded with the refrain, 'Am I right or any udder man?' Stump is slang for platform.

*Middleton's** marionette theatre was the oldest-established puppet troupe in England, with numerous members of the family involved. (See *The Life and Travels of Richard Barnard*, 1981).

*Marie Henderson** had recently been engaged at Sadler's Wells, but was tempted away by a better offer from the Britannia. 'Possessed of a pleasing appearance, some command of passion and clear pronunciation, this lady is likely to become a very great favourite'. (*Sunday Times*, 1/12/1867).

22 Tues   Miss M.Henderson taken ill at the Theatre – unable to go on the stage – Miss J.Coveney played the part of Belinda Seagrave at a moment's audience (sic).

23 Wed   Mr W.Newham's Benefit. *Wild Charlie or The Link-Boy of Old London* (wood-cuts lent by Brett). American Minstrels & Japanese Tommy. Stump orator, West & Miss Emma West. *Break not Bend. Proud Prudence, or, Captain Hawke the Highwayman.* Fine day. House above *£80* odd.

27 Sun   Home all day – busy making out Property Plot of Pant.

28 Mon   *Wild Charley*. Stump-orator West – Miss E.West. *Break not Bend*. Majilton (Le 'Chapeau du Diable').* Miss F.Phillips.* *Harvest Storm*. Not over till *12.5*.

30 Wed   Benefit of 'Clickers'. *Red Lance*. Extras as rest of week. *Break not Bend*. House middling.

31 Thurs   Mrs S.Lane received a letter signed Marian Bernaschina requesting information of the whereabouts of Mrs B.Ware & giving Address: Music Hall, Middleborough, Yorkshire. Answered stating particulars.

NOV 4 Mon   5th Act of *Richd 3rd*. West & Miss E.West, Niggers. Miss F.Phillips. Majilton Le Grand. *Break not Bend. Wild Charley*, changing the last piece, on Tuesday & Saturday, to *Guy Fawkes*, & giving Fireworks on Monday, Tuesday & Saturday.

5 Tues   Mrs S.May died this day at Tottenham, having been for years subject to falling fits, & being today in a room alone she fell with her forehead on the front bar of the fire-grate & died a few minutes after. The fall was heard by son of the family who were in the next room & who ran to her assistance – but too late.

9 Sat   Gave Mr Clingan Jones* notice that Mr Lane could not continue his & Mrs C.J's engagements beyond Xmas next.

10 Sun   Home all day at Pantomime bill.

11 Mon   *Spanish Page. Marriage Certificate* (Jessy's 2nd appearance on any stage) as Ann Chubb, a few lines only, in 1st scene of Act 2. Dress borrowed of Mrs Shelton. Extras. Majilton Le Grand. Mrs F.Phillips (singer). Mr Langan. & Mr & Mrs Millicent. *Wild Charley*.

13 Wed   Benefit of Leather, Carter & _____*(sic) (Doorkeepers). *Ivan the Terrible* (Extras as rest of week). *Wallace* (The Melo-Drama) & *Wild Charley*. Good house. W.Newham taken suddenly & seriously ill (Violent bleeding at the nose). Doctor attending him 4 times today, unable to stop it. Newham's daughter came crying to our house today to say he could not play tonight, –

---

*Majilton was a professor of 'chapeauography', which consisted in the performer twisting a felt hat into a variety of shapes suggestive of historical styles or personalities, while he struck appropriate poses. Miss F.R.Phillips was a serio-comic and descriptive singer.

*Mr and Mrs Clingan Jones had only just joined the Britannia Company.

*W.Leather, J.Carter and T.Fuller were the benificaires.

& afterwards crying to the Theatre to know the very latest moment that her mother might remain at home before coming to play in *Wallace*. Later Mrs Newham came crying herself, to know if any other lady could play her part that she might stay at home all night with her husband. Mrs Clingan Jones consented to play it & Mrs S.Lane not being at the Theatre, I took upon myself to sanction it.

14 Thurs   W.Newham terribly ill – the bleeding not stopped till 4 o'clock this afternoon – his life in great danger.

15 Fri   W.Newham a little, a shade, better . . . Mr S.Lane ill, gone tonight to Brighton.

16 Sat   W.Newham still a little better . . . Mrs S.Lane at night, 20 m p.10, went to Mr Lane (ill) at Brighton.

17 Sun   Home all day working at Pant. bill.

18 Mon   *Mutiny at the Nore*. Majilton. Mark Floyd. Mr & Mrs P.Langan & Mr J.Millicent (Niggers, their 2nd engagement). *The Marriage Certificate*. Marie Roberts* (née Hayne) here all day making a stage apron for Jessie.

20 Wed   Benefit of Mr J.Reynolds, with (under the Rose) Mr W.Crauford. *George Barrington*. Extras as rest of week. *Black Eyed Susan*. Woodcuts of Jack Sheppard introduced as illustrations of *George Barrington*! with 2 new scenes written by C.Pitt. Immense House. *£70* worth of Tickets. Near *£20* cash . . . W.Newham in the Theatre tonight – looking wonderfully well.

25 Mon   *The King's Death Trap* (1st time). Mark Floyd & the Niggers, Langan, Mrs Langan & J.Millicent. *Rip Van Winkle* and *Mary Blane*, Jessie playing 'Ariadne', Bigwood drunk, not in the Theatre till about 5 minutes before the curtain rose & he having to be discovered as Knickerbocker. Of course he didn't know one line of either that part or of Simon Snipes in *Mary Blane*, – and Jessie's only two scenes in the latter piece being with him! Of course neither she nor J.Parry, who played Sam Spar, could get a cue from him & the two scenes were utterly spoiled. Two letters received from Mrs B.Ware, one written by a pauper friend in the sick ward saying Mrs Ware is dying – the other containing Portraits of Mrs B.Ware's son & daughter & niece to be sent, the son's to her son, the other to her sister, Mrs Bernaschina, Black Horse Inn, Commercial Street, Middlesbourgh.

26 Tues   A Note from Master of Whitechapel Union, saying Mrs B.Ware very ill & recommending a message to her relatives . . . Rehearsal of Mr J.B.Howe's Pieces for tomorrow night not over till half past 3 – The lamps were alight in the streets as I came home. After dinner wrote 4 letters & despatched them about Mrs B.Ware's business.

27 Wed   Mr J.B.Howe's Benefit. *Captain Gerald* (a new Piece, written by Mr Howe), Extras as rest of week, and *Such is Life*, another Piece written by Mr Howe, but first played in America & afterwards at the Effingham. Capital

Maria Roberts was a family friend of the Wiltons.

House, – although neither Mrs S.Lane, Mr J.Reynolds or Miss M.Henderson played – all 3 being left out of the bill. Cash £76. Tickets (sic) . . . Mrs B.WARE DIED this morning at 2 a.m. . . . *Answer of Mr J.W.Anson** to my letter asking if the Association of which he is Treasurer would bury Mrs B.Ware, in case she should die in the Whitechapel Union.

28 Thurs   Another letter from Mr J.W.Anson saying that he had had a letter from the Master of the Union informing him that Mrs B.Ware died yesterday morning, that the Necropolis Company would take a coffin & remove the body to their quiet station in the Westminster Road & would I settle the time of the Funeral? He thought if it were to take place on the Sunday, there might be some of our Company desirous of attending – The Train would leave for Woking Cemetery at 11.30 & return at 3.30, fares 2.0d. . . . Another letter from Mrs Bernaschina (sister of Mrs B.Ware) regretting inability to attend or send money – being, with her whole family, thrown out of a situation by the sudden closing of the Theatre.

29 Fri   Wrote Mrs Bernaschina (sister of Mrs B.Ware) word of her sister's death – Address, Theatre, Nomanby near Middleborough, Yorkshire.

DEC 1 Sun   Mrs B.Ware buried this day at Woking Cemetery.

2 Mon   King's Death Trap (2nd week). Mr Robert Fraser (Boy at Mugby* – announced but did not come – ill of Bronchitis). The Langans & J.Millicent (niggers). Mark Floyd and *Captain Gerald* (J.B.Howe's Piece, played 1st time last Wednesday). Very bad business all the week. Very slight call for Harry Frazer* – no Apology made – He having sent as a substitute Mr Arthur Wyndham. Jessie playing in *Captain Gerald*.

Mem.   Monday Decr 2nd. Sent P.O. Order to Mr J.W.Anson (Mrs B.Ware's funeral), Being Price of 2 Railway Tickets. 4/0 & remnant of Subscriptions 1.9.0.

15 Sun   Home all day writing Puffs for newspapers, 20 long ones anticipatory. Wrote ten at a time, using nothing but Tissue Paper – with mostly new Black Tracing sheets. F.Rountree wrote the Editor's notes & addressed the Envelopes. Began at 10 in the morning – did not finish them till 12 at night.

16 Mon   Othello (J.B.Howe playing Othello on Monday & F.Charlton,* Cassio – and F.Charlton playing Othello on Tuesday & Howe Cassio). Mark Floyd. Robt Fraser (Boy at Mugby). The Langans & J. Millicent (niggers), with *The King's Death Trap*.

18 Wed   Last Night of the Season. Mrs S.Lane's Benefit. *Who Did It*? (new)

***J.W.Anson** was the Treasurer of the Dramatic and Equestrian Association. Formerly of Astley's and the Belfast Theatre, he was the first secretary of the Royal Dramatic College.

***Robert Fraser** was a Buffo Vocalist and Comedian from the Alhambra. He proclaimed himself the original boy at Mugby and sang of his occupation in the railway refreshment room, giving his ideas on what could be done to improve the service. The act was inspired by a story in 'Mugby Junction', the 1866 annual of *All the Year Round* by Charles Dickens. **Harry Frazer** is presumably entered in error for Robert Frazer.

***Frank Charlton**, from the Theatre Royal, Leeds, was engaged to play leading business and had made his debut on 28/10/1867.

1st night. Mr Edwd Deane* (1st appearance) & Mlle. C.Stephan. *Devil to Pay*, Lady Loverule (Miss Ruth Edwin). Jockey Dance (Xtal Palace mite). *Britannia Festival* (Jessy in it) (played before *Devil to Pay*). Rose Nathan* in Skipping Rope Dance (1st Appearance). *Drunkard's Children.* Curtain did not fall till ¼ to One! Not a great house. Weather fine.

19 Thurs   To the Royalty Theatre with Jessy to see Fred Dewar in *Captain Crosstree* a burlesque on *Black Eyed Susan* by Burnand,* and 1st night for a new 2 act comedy called *Humbug* (also by Burnand). Extremely well pleased with F.D. & a new actor of old men Mr G.W.Ray, & with Miss Oliver* as Susan & Mr Danvers as Dame Hatley. Cost me 1s/10d for Buses.

23 Mon   Rehearsal of Opening at 11. Comic Scenes at past 1. Marked comic scenes after – did not get home till 4.35 & had to be at the Theatre again to rehearse Middleton's Marionettes afterwards at 5 p.m. After that a night Rehearsal of Scenery, not over till 11.50 p.m. If that isn't hard work – what is?

24 Tues   Rehearsal at *10 A.M.* to let Supers try on their Masks & Properties for the 'Opening' of the Pantomime. At 11 began rehearsing the 'Opening' itself. At about ½ past 1 began 'Comic Scenes', which lasted till ½ past 2. Then rehearsed the Marionettes – got all over about 4. Then home.

Mem.   George Taylor says that notwithstanding the seemingly bad houses we have had at the Britannia in the fall of this year – every house has been an improvement over the corresponding House of last year.

26 Thurs   BOXING-DAY. Morning Performance at 12 o'clock (Pantomime only) – 20 minutes waiting for carpenters before raising curtain. Opening played *2h 21m.* Comic Scenes *1h 29m.* Total *3h 50m.* Not over till 3.50. Dense Fog – Couldn't see the Britannia from top of Huntingdon Street. Capital House. And another at Night, but the Gallery not equal to that of last year.

27 Fri   Mrs E.Yarnold died last night at 10 o'clock of Dropsy at an Oil Shop in Queen St., Holborn. Tonight wrote Mr J.W.Anson Treasurer of the 'Dramatic & Equestrian Association', by desire of Mrs S.Lane, asking if her funeral would be undertaken by the Association as Mrs B.Ware's had been & stating that Mrs S.Lane would give a sovereign towards the expences.

28 Sat   The first *NOTICE of the BRITANNIA THEATRE* which ever appeared in TIMES NEWSPAPER appeared *yesterday* in the columns descriptive of the Pantomimes, nearly 20 lines all adulatory![4] Received whole salary again today! and so did Cecil Pitt (Prompter). What *does* it mean?

30 Mon   Pantomime *Don Quixote, or Sancho Panza & his wife Tereza*, Miss Ruth Edwin as the Duke. *Who Did It?*

---

*Edward Deane was engaged to play Harlequin in the pantomime. **Rose Nathan** was a dancer, engaged to play Columbine in the pantomime.

*Fred Dewar sang a song in Burnand's burlesque, which had been playing for over a year, entitled 'Captain Crosstree is my name', burlesquing the celebrated 'Champagne Charlie' song of George Leybourne. **Patti Oliver**, a popular burlesque actress from the Strand, was lessee of the Royalty Theatre from March 1866 until May 1870.

1868

JAN 2 Thurs   Mrs E.Yarnold buried this day at Woking Cemetery (by the side or rather at the foot of, Mrs B.Ware's grave). Edwin Yarnold's wife, Margaret, & her sister, with two of Mrs E.Yarnold's younger sons, followed the coffin. Robt. Rowe (stage carpenter of the Britannia) & Mrs Martin (wife of the Gasman of the theatre) were also there.

4 Sat   Subscription for Mrs E.Yarnold's family   3.0.6.
Afterwards added   2.0.

10 Fri   Miss Ruth Edwin ill – unable to come to Theatre tonight – Took M.S.S. of Pantomime to Miss E.Macarthy at her lodgings 61 Lever St., Goswell Road & left it there – her husband saying she was gone out on a visit to her mother, but he would follow & give her the information. About two hours after he brought back the book saying he could not find her. Went to Miss Neumann (at her lodgings) & told her *she* must dress in Miss R.Edwin's dress & go on for the part. The dress proved too small for Miss Neumann, so the part was cut out & the few speeches, imperatively necessary, spoken by Miss M.Booth – This led to the discharge of Miss E.Macarthy.

11 Sat   R.Bell absent from Theatre tonight (swollen foot). Wrote & gave Miss E.Macarthy a *Week's Notice*, on account of the above matter. (See yesterday).

14 Tues   Plaintive letter from Miss E.Macarthy to Mrs S.Lane asking extension of Notice to leave. Answer – Negative.

15 Wed   Miss Ruth Edwin sufficiently recovered to play tonight.

16 Thurs   Miss Ruth Edwin still better tonight than last night – played again.

18 Sat   Last night of Miss E.Macarthy at the Britannia. R.Bell not at Theatre all this week, ill, swollen foot.

20 Mon   Miss M.Henderson did not play tonight – her husband (Mr Gahagan, musician)* died yesterday. Miss M.Booth played Miss Henderson's part in *Who Did It?* Miss E.Macarthy gone from the Britannia . . . Miss L.Rayner played *her* part in *Who Did it?*

21 Tues   Received at the Theatre a M.S.S. (by Book Post) of a one act Drama entitled *The Cardinal of Paris* with Hamilton written as the name of the Author at the end. Addressed to Mr Wilton, Britannia Theatre, but no note or letter with it, nor a single line of explanation. Gave it to Mr Borrow. Mr Sefton Parry* wrote Mrs S.Lane to say Miss L.Rayner had left the Holborn Theatre without a word of notice & he would not allow her to play anywhere. In consequence her part at the Britannia was played tonight & will be played for a fortnight by Miss Neumann (a ballet-girl).

*Frederick Geoghegan, professor of music, aged 28, many years connected with Liverpool, died at his residence, 47 King's Square, London, on 19th January, leaving a widow and two children. (*Era*, 2/2/1868).

*Sefton Parry was lessee of the Queen's Theatre, Holborn.

25 Sat   Mr Gahagan (husband of Miss M.Henderson, actress at the Britannia, and violinist in orchestra) buried today.

31 Fri   One of the Trapeze men (the Victorellis) fell from the Trapeze tonight – but rose, ascended the rope again and repeated the feat.

FEB 3 Mon   First night of Miss M.Henderson's acting after the Death of her husband . . . Mr S.Lane told me tonight, on the stage, that he meant to give up the Britannia Theatre 3 years from next Christmas. He had agreed with Mrs S.Lane to do so at '4 years from last Xmas'.

6 Thurs   Jean Louis (the clown) sprained his left foot badly tonight in the second Comic Scene . . . Wrote a letter for Mr Lane in reply to an application for the loan of the Theatre on sunday mornings to give a Breakfast to the unemployed operatives of the district & preach at them afterwards – declined on the score that it would be a serious task to cleanse, wash & dry the Theatre during sunday afternoons (after the breakfasts) for the reception of our usual evening congregation[1].

7 Fri   Jean Louis (the clown) unable to come to the Theatre tonight. Mr R.Bell obliged to go on for the part of Clown – a destructive change for the pantomime, R.Bell having no fun or humour in him and having never before *seen* the Comic Scenes.

8 Sat   Louis again absent tonight from the Pantomime. Clown played by R.Bell.

10 Mon   Louis sufficiently recovered to play Clown tonight.

14 Fri   Maria Roberts (née Hayne) here to tea – made Jessie a sun-shade to wear in new piece next week.

15 Sat   Performances changed to *All but One* (first night) & Pantomime, *Don Quixote*, with the Echassé Family (instead of the Victorellis) as sprites.

19 Wed   Benefit of J.Louis, clown. No alteration of performance save the addition of the 'Forest Scene' from *Valentine & Orson*. (Valentine, Miss M.Henderson; Orson, Louis). *£44 odd*.

21 Fri   Alfred Davis here. Spoke much of his great success in his new Theatre at Glasgow – Rent £600 per year. Receipts averaging during Pantomime time above £400 a week and (if I recollect rightly) £55 a night for 7 months ! – On a three night's engagement with Sothern* had paid the latter for his share *£250* – had received Presentation Meerschaum Pipe, Cigar Holder and huge Time-Piece from the actors and employees of the Theatre. Showed us the cigar holder & case, but did not mention the 14 shillings he owed us for Wood cuts &c sent him so long ago – nor the article of Fishing Tackle ditto!

---

*Edward Askew Sothern was noted for his performance of Lord Dundreary in *Our American Cousin*.

26 Wed   (Ash Wednesday) *Concert*. Fredk Evans & wife. Jolly Nash.* Great Vance. W.Randall & Wife. Aroun Alrachid Hassan* & wife, Irene Hassan. Miss Fenhoulet*. Dancing Mad Brian & Wife. The D'Aubans & Wardes, Kate Garstone, Clifton* & Santley*, Oceana* &c. An Immense 'House' – like a Boxing night.

28 Fri   Mr G.Bigwood ivré at night – very.

29 Sat   Last Night of the Pantomime! the worst we ever played at the Britannia, in my time.

MAR 1 Sun   In a fever all day yesterday & the day before about the copy of our next new piece lent to M.Faucquez to get printed at Charles Beckett's for a Benefit to come off next Thursday week. Received the copy & Proof last night at *915 P.M.*

2 Mon   Farmer of Inglewood Forest. Miss Kate Clifton (the only female Irish*man*). Mr J.F.Brian (serio-comic vocalist) – Mr J.W.Liskard (the Musical Momus).* *All But One*. Better 'house' than last monday.

4 Wed   Benefit of 'Loyal United Friends' (a Gift Fund Society). *Farmer of Inglewood Forest*. Entertainments same as rest of week. *Dark House*. Capital House – Fine weather . . . *S.May's Benefit* at Drury Lane Theatre on a/c of his great losses by the burning of the opera House. Capital House (Mr Borrow guessed it at *£500*).

7 Sat   Immense House at the Britannia.

8 Sun   *Lloyd's Weekly News* of today contains a/c of James Lee, the poor old actor, being taken up for begging in Burlington Arcade. He was an actor in the Birmingham Theatre the season I was there (1828) with the Bruntons.*

9 Mon   Young Apprentice (1st night). Kate Clifton, the only Female Irishman. Mrs J.F.Brian. Mr J.W.Liskard (the musical momus). *Farmer of Inglewood Forest*. Conference between Mrs S.Lane, Mr J.B.Howe & Mr F.Charlton in Pit Passage.

10 Tues   John Thorne (facetiously called 'Fat Jack') Check-Taker at the Britannia Theatre, and Cab-man, died of *Delerium Tremens* $\frac{1}{4}$ past 4 o'clock this morning.

11 Wed   Benefit of Mr Edwards. Last Piece changed to *Rescue of the Orphans*. Rest of Bill same as Monday. Tremendous House. *£46 odd of tickets.* Was told by Cecil Pitt in Prompt Entrance that there were singular stories

---

*Jolly John Nash** was a comic singer whose laugh was a feature of his act. He was a great favourite of the Prince of Wales. **Hassan** may have been a vaulter of that name who was performing with his wife, a French rope-dancer, at this time. **Laura Fenhoulet** not only mimicked other female singers, but gave 'passable imitations of both Vance and Leybourne'. **Kate Clifton** was a male impersonator of Irishmen. **Kate Santley** was a popular vocalist in burlesque. **Oceana** was a tight-rope artiste, twelve years old at the time, who later married into the famous Renz family of circus proprietors.

*J.W.Liskard** was a musical clown and instrumentalist.

*Richard and John Brunton.** Richard was manager; his father John acted. They moved to Bristol the following year.

telling of the Beneficiaire – which Bigwood knew all about, as a 'mauvais sujet'.

12 Thurs Benefit of a Forester, got up by M.Faucquez. *Guilty Father*. Extras same as rest of week. *Young Apprentice. Volunteers*. Decent House – guessed above £50. . . . Received letter from T.Drummond addressed from Galveston, Texas & dated Feby 21st, 1868, asking me to get M.S.S. for him from Hazlewood of *Downfall of Pride, Aurora Floyd, Jack O'Lantern, Jeannie Deans, Old Maid in Winding Sheet & Auld Robin Gray* &c.

14 Sat Immense House (said to be *£117*). Gave Miss Kate Clifton a fortnight's notice of the termination of her Engagement. The greatest Gallery tonight ever known at the Britannia (says Mr J.Martin) *£19* odd. (Mr George Taylor says *nearly* £19).

15 Sun Mr C.H.Hazlewood (dramatic author) here – agreed to accept *£6.10.0* for the M.S.S. for Mr T.Drummond.

16 Mon Young Apprentice (2nd week). Mrs Brian. Miss Kate Clifton. Mr J.W.Liskard, the Musical Momus – and M.Faucquez' piece of *The Guilty Father*.

18 Wed Benefit of 'Jacobs' (under the fictitious name in the bill of 'Frank Mascati'). New melodrama *He Would Be a Sailor*. Extras same as rest of week. *Young Apprentice. Spanish Page*. Not a Great House. Not over till *11.40*.

19 Thurs Received from Mr Mellon* on a/c of Mr T.Drummond 8.10.0. Paid for *Receipt Stamp* for Do. 1d: Book of *Aurora Floyd* 6d.

20 Fri Paid Mr Hazlewood for 5 M.S.S. for Mr T.G.Drummond, viz., *Auld Robin Gray, Jack O'Lantern, Jeannie Deans, Old Maid in Winding Sheet, Downfall of Pride* 6.10.0.

23 Mon He Would Be a Sailor. Mrs J.F.Brian. Mr C.D.Davies, ventriloquist.* Miss Kate Clifton. *The Young Apprentice* (Mrs S.Lane).

26 Thurs Received Wig from Mr J.Reynolds for Mr T.G.Drummond, paying for said wig 15.0 and 5/0 for a quantity of Crepe Hair of different colours and desired by Mr T.G.Drummond in his letter from Galveston, Texas, dated Feby 21st 1868.

27 Fri Went to General Post Office, St Martin's Le Grand, with Parcel for Mr T.G.Drummond, containing *5 M.S.S.* viz: *Auld Robin Gray, Jack O'Lantern, Downfall of Pride, Jeannie Deans, Old Maid in Winding Sheet*, a printed book of *Aurora Floyd*, price 6d; a wig procured by Mr J.Reynolds, price 15/0 and 5/0 worth of crepe hair – Bought stamps at P.O. office 3/0 – and stamp for Registering 4d – Stuck the stamps on the parcel which weighed something less than 8 lbs. Posted the parcel & was told it would not be despatched on its journey till 7.o'clock P.M. Saturday 28th.

*Henry Mellon was Wilton's neighbour.

*C.D.Davis was probably E.D.Davies, perhaps the first artiste to perform ventriloquism with speaking dolls. His puppets, which do not appear to have had mouthing pieces, were named Tommy and Joey.

30 Mon Posted Letter to Mr T.G.Drummond informing him of despatch of Parcel.

31 Tues Mrs E.Courtenay yesterday received anonymous letter accusing her husband of undue intimacy with a Miss Newcombe, leading actress at Southampton, where he is Stage Manager. Today, by advice of several of the Company, she enclosed the letter to her husband – saying she did not believe it and demanding an explanation – expecting a telegraphic message in reply – none came all day.

APRIL 1 Wed Mr Bigwood's Benefit. *Wait till I'm a Man* (new piece by Hazlewood, 1st time). Extras same as rest of week. *Johnathan Bradford.* Total Receipts about *£73.* Tickets *£26* – Cash *£47* . . . A Telegram received from Mr Courtenay by his wife simply denying . . . Mrs Courtenay went off by night train to Southampton.

2 Thurs Mrs Courtenay not returned . . . Jessie went on, tonight, for her part in *He Would Be a Sailor.*

3 Fri Mrs Courtenay returned with her husband; but scarcely satisfied. Being rallied, she says: 'Sir, you may place the fragments of a broken vase together & cement them, but you can never make them *whole* again.' William Batey died.

6 Mon Histrionic Tableaux *Pizarro* (3 Scenes). Ballet by D'Aubans & Wardes. Singers, A.St.Albyn,* Sydney Franks*. Last Scene of *Jane Shore.* Asa Cushman & Joey Tennyson*. Kate Garstone. Jolly Nash. Dagger Scene of *Macbeth.* Balcony scene of *Romeo & Juliet.* Dance, Celeste Stephan & Ladies of Ballet. 4th Act of *Wm Tell* (beginning 'Double the guards' & ending with 'To kill thee, Tyrant', the Combat & Tableau). Miss Laura Fenhoulet (giving imitations). 3rd act of *Othello.* Fine, hot weather. *Very shy house.*

7 Tues PASSION WEEK. Bad Houses at Theatre all this week.

11 Sat Madlle. Celeste Stephan hissed tonight on going upon the stage to dance, stood still, gazed upon the audience for a few seconds, then walked off the stage . . . Miss M.Henderson ill – did not play tonight – Miss E.Courtenay played her parts.

13 Mon EASTER MONDAY. *Wolf of the Pyrenees.* No Singers. Dance only between C.Stephan & Ladies of Ballet. W.H.Pitt's* 1st appearance. *Wait Till I'm A Sailor.* Capital House. Performances not over till 12 m.p.12 midnight. Miss M.Henderson played, but very ill indeed – not expected to get through – Miss E.Courtenay being detained in the Theatre to finish Miss M.Henderson's part in case she (Miss M.H.) should break down.

15 Wed Shy House.

16 Thurs Bad House at Theatre.

*Alfred St. Albyn was a Buffo Vocalist (Tenor). **Sydney Franks** was a comic vocalist. **Asa Cushman and Miss Joey Tennyson** were billed as 'Transatlantic Duettists'.

*W.H.Pitt was Cecil Pitt's brother. A dramatist as well as an actor, he was engaged to play 'Heavies'. He had appeared at the Britannia in the 1850s and at the Victoria in the early 1860s.

17 Fri   Horrid House at the Britannia.

18 Sat   Very good 'House' tonight, at Theatre.

19 Sun   Home all day marking the M.S.S. of *London by Night*.

22 Wed   Mr F.Charlton's 1st Benefit. *Raising the Wind* (!) No Extras. *Wolf of Pyrenees* (2nd week). *Jack Long* (first time for years). House about £37.

25 Sat   Very *good* house tonight at the Theatre, after another shy week.

27 Mon   *Avarice, or The Miser's Daughter*. *Wolf of the Pyrenees*. *Jack Long*. Shy House for a Monday.

29 Wed   Told by Mrs S.Lane that *she* should have no objection to Jessie's acting the part of Rose Maylie in *Oliver Twist* next week, but that Mr Lane objected so much & had said he would not have people learning their business on his stage.

MAY 4 Mon   *Oliver Twist*. (1st time these 13 years, the prohibition against the piece from the Lord Chamberlain's Office being removed)[2]. *Wolf of the Pyrenees*. . . . Mr Fisher (husband of the soi-disant Miss S.Miles) called with another gentleman (whose name was not mentioned) to ask information concerning the money drawn by me from Mr Mellon by the request of Mr Drummond . . . showed them Mr Drummond's Letter. Mr F-'s friend said there was nothing in the letter. Mr F expressed himself satisfied – but said he must give me more trouble – he was sorry for it – but he intended to apply to the law & would have to summon me &c &c.

6 Wed   Benefit of City Cordwainers. *Man of Red Mansion*. *Oliver Twist*.

11 Mon   *Dark Side of the Great Metropolis*. Title altered after Bills were out & Advertisements (except Dailies) to oblige Mr Boucicault, as intended to be called *London by Night*[3]. 1st Night. *Confederate's Daughter*. Missed _____from L.I.E, while _____ were at R.I.E. Found them afterwards in Prompt Box. This while waiting to begin the rehearsal of *London By Night*. The Rehearsal of *The Confederate's Daughter* being over a quarter of an hour before *London By Night* was called, Query 'Will you rehearse the Duett with Miss Ruth Edwin *now* to save time? *Ans*. 'No, sir – I am trying something else!!!'

13 Wed   Benefit of 'Gold Beaters'. *Dark Side of Great Metropolis*. P.Elbin & Son, Acrobats (who began the Performance, playing for an 'engagement'). *Beggar's Petition*. Shy 'House' at beginning but improved afterwards. During the 1st piece a bit of canvass over the chandalier caught fire (smouldering). John Martin went up to extinguish it & a scrap of it fell into the Pit – & created some disturbance among the audience till Mrs S.Lane, who happened to be on the stage & saw what had happened, re-assured them, – & after a few seconds, they became calm & the play was proceeded with.

15 Fri   Bad 'Houses' all the week thus far & indeed ever since Xmas – Commercial depression the cause.

16 Sat   Packet of Pence received from Treasury today – 4d short! . . . Capital

'House'. Mr Bigwood absent. (In explanation, Mr Borrow sent Jacobs round to the stage. Mr Bigwood had been to the doors '*beastly drunk*' and had gone away saying he 'wouldn't "*go on*" at *all?*' In consequence his part was cut out – the dialogue arranged between C.Pitt & E.Elton & the piece got through as best we could – The audience either did not notice Mr Bigwood's absence, or did not care for it – and never called for him . . . Letter addressed to me from T.Drummond, Galveston, Texas, containing only another Letter in an Envelope addressed to Fredk Matthews – the Painter's Assistant at the theatre – not one word to me!!!

18 Mon   (Shy House).

19 Tues   Amelia & Jessy to Marylebone Theatre to see *Miss Mary Saunders* & to judge (by desire of Mrs S.Lane) if that lady would do for the Britannia. Went up by Underground Railway – saw her in *the Old Mint of Southwark* & *Abyssinian War* & came home with an opinion that she would not do – for 'want of fire' & physical power. Their journey cost 4.7. – Mr S.Lane ill today – spitting blood – saw a quantity in his mouth at night when he came on the stage & spoke to me.

20 Wed   Mrs S.L. says that last night after Mr S.L. got home to his lodgings at Tottenham, he voided not less than 3 half pints of blood. Mr S.Lane much better tonight – has sent for Dr Gowland – who says if he had not lost so much blood, he would have had a fit & died suddenly.

21 Thurs   Bad 'Houses' all this week.

24 Sun   Home all day, making out bill of Whitsuntide Piece – *War in Abyssinia*.

25 Mon   *Jack O'Lantern*. Mr & Mrs P.Langan & J.Millicent. *Dark Side of Great Metropolis*. Shy House – Stormy Wind all day and cold (*nose-cold*) at night. Went to the Tower & got permission for Soldiers 'Scots Fusileers' (1st Battalion) to come as Supers next week from Colonel Gibbs – (Sergt Major McBlane).

30 Sat   Mrs S.Lane's last night of acting.

JUN 1 Mon   Whit-Monday. *Abyssinian War* (1st night). Miss Lydia Latimer. Mr & Mrs P.Langan & J.Millicent. *Jack O'Lantern*. Soldiers from the Tower. 1st Battalion Scots Fusileer Guards, Colonel Gibbs, Sergt Major McBlane. 1 Sergt, 1 Bugler, 20 Soldiers. Good House. Piece Enthusiastically received. Nightly cost of Soldiers for *Abyssinian War* 1.16.0.

6 Sat   Gave a week's Notice (by written order of Mr Borrow) to 3 Ballet Ladies, Misses Johnson, Craddock and Louise, (Madlle Celeste's pupil); & Miss E.Courtenay (leading actress). A fortnight's notice to Miss Lydia Latimer (comic, *very* comic, Vocalist) and a letter to Mr W.Newham (contents not known).

8 Mon   Performances same as last w. except *The Chimes* instead of *Jack O'Lantern*.

10 Wed   Mr J.Reynolds's Benefit. *Man in the Iron Mask*. Miss Lydia Latimer. Mr & Mrs P.Langan & J.Millicent. *Aurora Floyd*. Bad House £48 or £49 odd. Fine day.

13 Sat   T.Drummond & Miss S.Miles called in a cab, just arrived from America, via Liverpool, having taken ship from Galveston, Texas; ostensibly to get possession of Miss S.Miles's two children: brought me a tin case with several Tropical Plants in it, viz. a *Banana*, two red *Mexican Lilies*, a *Feathery Honeysuckle* &c . . . From himself today we received the first acknowledgement of his having received the Parcel sent off to him.

15 Mon   *Frank the Ploughman. War in Abyssinia*. Miss Lydia Latimer. Mr & Mrs P.Langan. J.Millicent. *Abel Flint*. T.Drummond & Miss S.Miles in the Theatre tonight, paid to go into the Boxes. Mr Drummond found his way up into the Long Dressing Room, & afterwards brought Miss S.Miles behind the scenes & took her to the Ladies' Dressing Room, downstairs. Mr Borrow hearing of this sent 'Leather', the Check-Taker at the Stall Doors, to order them out – telling him, if they refused to go, he was to drag them out. They left the stage immediately and Mr T.Drummond then asked Mr B. what he would let him have the house for – for a Benefit. Mr *B* replied – 'Not any sum you can pay', or words to that effect. A conversation ensued in which Mr B. very angrily (as Mrs Borrow told me) asked him how he dared bring such a woman behind the scenes or on the stage, adding 'we have respectable people here now, Sir' &c and further said, 'What have you done with the coat you stole?' alluding to a 'Claude Melnotte'* coat &c – which Mr D had borrowed of Mr May before leaving for America & had not returned. Mr D. said he had brought the coat back to the Theatre before he went to America. 'Did you put it in the hands of the man you had borrowed it of', said Mr B. 'No', replied D. 'I left it on the Dressing-Place'. Mrs Borrow told me that the money Mr D. owed Mr B. was 'a considerable sum – a very considerable sum'.

20 Sat   Change of Performance. *Fred Frolic* substituted for *Frank the Ploughman*. . . . Excellent House.

21 Sun   Made out bill of *3 Fingered Jack* for own Benefit. Thinking of *Ride to York* if could get a horse. Dolly James* (here to dinner) said Mr Moffat was at Xtal Palace with his Blue Horse – Fred* to Nelson Lee's to enquire Moffat's address. He did not know but said a letter to the Xtal Palace would reach him. Went with Fred, in the Evening, over to Mr M's former address – Owen's Yard, Juston Street, Tower Street, Waterloo Rd. Got same answer from there. Coming back through the 'New Cut' Fred had his meerschaum pipe stolen out of his mouth by a fellow who darted like lightning down a bye street & got clear off. Rain came on and having no money we were obliged to walk all the way home to Nichol's Square – wet through. Wrote to Mr Moffat, directing to Xtal Palace, before to bed.

---

*Claude Melnotte** was a character in *The Lady of Lyons*.

*Dolly James** was probably a relative of Wilton's cousin, Richard James. **Fred** was Fred Rountree, Wilton's son-in-law.

22 Mon   Fred Frolic. Miss Emma Alford (Vocalist & Clog Horn-Pipe Dancer).* Mr H.Rickards (Comic Singer)*. *The Three Lives.* Very good House.

23 Tues   Received very friendly letters from Mr Moffat (yesterday) & Mr Nelson Lee today. Mr M saying the horse *Koh-i-Noor* is dead.

24 Wed   J.Parry's Benefit. *Hut of Red Mountains.* (Extras as above). *String of Pearls.* Weather favourable. Rain last Saturday & Sunday & Tuesday. Capital House – most probably drawn by *The String of Pearls.*

28 Sun   Mr Moffat here to tea – from Lower Sydenham, where he is now living – while exhibiting his blue horse at the Xtal Palace . . . Fine, hot, bright day! a gloomy prospect for the Benefit on Wednesday.

29 Mon   Knights of the Road. Mr J.Ryley & Miss M.Barnum* (on Monday & Tuesday only). Miss E.Alford (every night after Tuesday) & Mr H.Rickards. *Fred Frolic.* Hot, bright weather – the worse promise for next Wednesday.

30 Tues   Hot, fine weather – bad prospect for Benefit tomorrow.

JULY 1 Wed   Own Benefit. *Knights of the Road.* Miss E.Alford. Mr H.Rickards. *High Life Below Stairs. 3 Fingered Jack.* Total £34.7.10. Tickets £1.10.0. Cash £32.17.0. Morning overcast, but gloom passed off & day became hot & bright. Sixty Thousand People said to have paid 1/0 each at Alexandra Park today for admission to the Races. This supposed to have spoilt the Benefit in conjunction with the weather. Every vehicle at the East End of London engaged to go to Muswell Hill.

2 Thurs   Very bad House at Britannia tonight.

3 Fri   Very bad House tonight at Britannia.

4 Sat   Mr W.Crauford tonight said he must be absent from Theatre next Tuesday to go to Gravesend – having a risk in Mr Robinson's* venture at the Public House there (ie. had lent) – *400 0 0.*

6 Mon   Knights of the Road. Harry Rickards, Oxford Joe. Miss E.Alford (Vocalist & Skipping Rope Dancer). M.Jean Price* on the Trapeze & leaping from the Upper Gallery to stage. *String of Pearls.* Not a great House.

7 Tues   Received Letter from Mr T.Drummond, at Douglas, Isle of Man, saying 'they' (i.e. himself & Miss S.Miles) were going to play for 6 nights at that town & requesting me to send the balance of his a/c *14s10d* to him there, by P.O.Order.

---

*Emma Alford performed an 'American Boot and Skipping Rope Dance'. Harry Rickards, known as 'Oxford Joe' after one of his popular songs, sang military and 'masher' songs. Eventually he went to Australia where he was very successful.

*J.H.Ryan and Marie Barnum, comic duettists, were known as 'The Dancing Quakers'. They were noted for their lively, burlesque acting and clever, eccentric dancing, the briskness of which was phenomenal.

*William Robinson, Sarah Lane's brother-in-law.

*Jean Price developed an unusual feat on the flying trapeze by performing without a partner. Instead of relying on a catcher, he caught the second trapeze with his legs.

8 Wed   Posted Letter to Mr T.Drummond with Postal Order as desired above 14s.6. Miss J.Coveney's Benefit. *Nelly, or The Companions of the Chair*, (1st night). Miss E.Alford. M.Jean Price. *Lady Audley's Secret*. House very bad at beginning – pulled up afterwards, proving that *Nelly* did not draw. Total said to be *£32.19.0*. . . . Told Mr F.Charlton by Mr Borrow's desire that he must play the part cast him in the *Blue Dwarf* or quit the Theatre at a week's notice.

11 Sat   Great House at Theatre tonight – Principally Gallery People.

13 Mon   *Life of a Weaver*. H.Rickards. Mons. Jean Price, on the Trapeze. *Knights of the Road*.

15 Wed   Miss M.Henderson's Benefit. *The Wife*. Extras as rest of week. *Blue Dwarf*. Excellent House in spite of the intensely hot weather.

18 Sat   Good House but not great.

20 Mon   1st night of *Lady Anne's Well*. American Minstrels & Japanese Tommy. Miss Louise Austen (Imitator of Concert-Room & Music Hall celebrities). Jean Price (Aerial Gymnast). *Life of a Weaver*.

22 Wed   No Benefit but altered the Pieces.

24 Fri   The yacht, *Phantom*, for sale. Price *£600* as per printed list, issued by Yacht Club.

25 Sat   Gave notice to M. Jean Price by desire of Mr Borrow (conveyed through Jacobs) that next week must be the last of his engagement – & the words were scarcely uttered, when Jacobs came with another message & counteracted the order.

27 Mon   *Lady Anne's Well*. Japanese Tommy & his Party. Mons. Jean Price (Aerial Gymnast). *The Sea*. Good half price.

29 Wed   No Benefit, but altered Pieces to *The Wife* & *Lady Anne's Well*.

AUG 3 Mon   *The Gorilla Hunt*. Miss A.Anderson, serio-comic vocalist. American minstrels & Japanese Tommy, & Mons Jean Price & *Lady Anne's Well*.

5 Wed   *The Lady of Lyons*. Extras as above, and *The Gorilla Hunt*. (No Benefit).

10 Mon   *The Dead Reckoning*, 1st night. Miss A.Anderson. Japanese Tommy & American Minstrels. *Lady Anne's Well*.

12 Wed   No Benefit, but changed last piece to *Man of Red Mansion*.

15 Sat   Great House.

17 Mon   *The Dead Reckoning*. 1st week. Miss A.Anderson (Singer & Dancer); H.Rickards (Oxford Joe). *Phoebe Hessel*. Good but not great house.

19 Wed   No Benefit, but changed bill. *Fazio*. (Extras as above). *Dead Reckoning* – very good house.

20 Thurs   Supers' Ticket night – A Ballet played by them – lasting 14 minutes only – and going extremely well. Miss Beaver playing the heroine & the Ballet having been written by Joseph Pitt (son of Cecil Pitt, the Prompter).

24 Mon   Spring-Heeled Jack (produced on saturday last). H.Rickards (Oxford Joe). The Boss, Orville Parker. *Dead Reckoning.*

26 Wed   No Benefit, but changed *Dead Reckoning* to *Bride of Aldgate.*

31 Mon   Terror of London. H.Rickards (Oxford Joe). The Boss, Orville Parker, (on Monday & Tuesday only). A.Cox, nigger,* (after Tuesday). Charles Woodman. *Bay of Biscay* (changed to *Hut of Red Mountain* on Wednesday night).

SEPT 2 Wed   Received 1st act of Mrs S.Lane's 'Opening' Drama. No Benefit, but changed *Bay of Biscay* for *Hut of Red Mountain* which we played.

Mem.   A Board, written by Mr Thos. Rogers our Scene Painter warning strangers from entering the Painting Room and couched in these words: 'No Admission. Except no Person' and a Paraphrase of it in the long Dressing Room, saying 'No Admittance – except Nobody!'

3 Thurs   Received 2nd Act of Piece for Mrs S.Lane's opening, called *The Old, Old Story* . . . To Harriet's to tea, with Amelia, Jessie & Milly, met there Fred Dewar & Rose & their brother John. Afterwards they all came to the Theatre, Fred in the Prompt-Box. Took him into the Painting-Room & up into the long Dressing-Room.

5 Sat   1st night of *Wedded & Lost.* Capital House. *Terror of London* last.

7 Mon   Wedded & Lost produced last Saturday. H.Rickards (Oxford Joe). C.Woodman. *Terror of London.*

9 Wed   Benefit of Messrs Summers & Light. *Virginius.* H.Rickards (Oxford Joe). Charles Woodman. Band of Dyers. *Ballet* by supers & Miss Beaver (Ballet Girl). *Nat Graves.* (Nat G. by Mr F.Charlton, 1st time). Capital House.

10 Thurs   T.Drummond & Miss S.Miles Benefit at the 'Grecian' (they having taken the house for the purpose). Immense *House.* Many different rumours as to the amount – J.Martin informed by the Bill Inspector, who counts the checks there, that there was in fact *£103* in the house & no more – of which *£10* Only was in Tickets, all the rest, cash.*

12 Sat   Letter from Mr Donne Examiner of Plays (opened by Mr Borrow, tho' addressed to me) putting off the Inspection of the Theatre from next Monday 14th till Thursday the 17th.

14 Mon   Wedded & Lost (2nd week). H.Rickards (Oxford Joe) till Saturday & C.Woodman. *Corsican Brothers.*

16 Wed   Perry & Wade's Benefit. New Piece, *Wild Will, or The Pirates of the Thames*! (1st night). Oxford Joe. C.Woodman. Several Brass Bands. *Dark*

---

*Abe Cox** was billed as performing sketches.
*Drummond** was billed as Mr Raymond. Pieces included *Hamlet* and *The Reprieve.*

House. Great House – *about £90. NB*. They paid Travers £5 for the new Piece which played 1 hour 15 minutes.

17 Thurs   Annual Inspection of Theatre by officials from Lord Chamberlain's Office took place this day. Hon. Mr Ponsonby, Mr Donne, Mr Pince (or Pinch, or Pincher) & another Architect. All seemed very much pleased – said we had a 'clean bill this year' & that they supposed we did not like being found fault with last year. The Architect pointed out a Damaged Seat in the Upper Gallery, a Gas-pipe hanging down in urinal back of Painting Room, and one or two pieces of profile over some spaces that had been cut for ventilation in Mlle Celeste's Dressing Room and recommended pieces of perforated zinc to be put in their stead & also in the Supers' Room over the window.

19 Sat   1st night of *Admiral Tom*. Mr C.Woodman only. *Wedded & Lost*. Immense House. Got up subscription for Joe Short, Assistant Property Man-Boy. (He is married & has 2 children) – has been 3 weeks ill — gathered £1.10.2 for him. Gave his wife £1 – not having collected all the subscriptions.

20 Sun   Home all day writing (letters) and finishing Bill of new Piece for Mrs S.Lane's return, *The Old, Old Story*.

21 Mon   *Admiral Tom*. C.Woodman. Jas. Doughty & Dogs. *Wedded & Lost*.

23 Wed   Benefit of Messrs C.Pitt & E.Harding. *The Night Guard* (new Drama by C.Pitt). C.Woodman. J.Doughty & Dogs. 5th Act of *Richard 3rd* (Richard 3rd, Mr W.H.Pitt). *Eliza Fenning*. Great House.

27 Sun   Home all day writing Super Plot of Mrs S.Lane's piece.

28 Mon   *Admiral Tom*. J.Doughty's Dogs. *Return of the Wanderer* . . . Mr & Mrs S.Lane came back from country – has not acted since May 30th.

29 Tues   LICENCING DAY. To St.James's Palace with Mr Beckett & Mr Boyce (Mr S.Lane's *Sureties*) to sign the Bond for the Licence of the Britannia Theatre & pay the Fees *£4.4.0* and stamp Duty on the Bond = *10.0*. Mr S.Lane did not go. Lunched at Simpson's . . . before boing to the Palace . . . Then . . . to Simpson's to dinner . . . Gave W.Borrow,* who drove cab, 1s6d.

30 Wed   Benefit of Miss M.Booth & D.Jacobs, Bill Deliverer. *Idle Apprentice* (Jack Sheppard *redivivus*) written by F.Marchant & played at the Victoria Theatre; Doughty's Dogs. 5th Act of *Macbeth*. *Blanche Heriot*. Capital House.

OCT 1 Thurs   After rehearsing *The Old, Old Story* 20 min. by watch in Prompt Entrance, Mr J.Reynolds laughing said, 'They've had a long stretch; I say, you ought to charge' & at night 'á ses années! S'amouracher!'

3 Sat   Gave out Scene & Propty Plots of 3rd Comic Scene & wrote Dress Plots of all three.

5 Mon   *Idle Apprentice* (Alias *Jack Sheppard* by F.Marchant). J.Doughty's Dogs. *Admiral Tom*. △By Elton. Ainsi dit John Martin[4].

---

*William Borrow was Sarah Lane's brother.

6 Tues   Disturbed △L.I.E. twice.

7 Wed   W.Crauford's Benefit. Immense House. *The Old, Old Story* (new Piece, 1st night of Mrs S.Lane this season). Play Scene of *Hamlet* (Hamlet, 1st time, J.Reynolds). *Waiting for the Verdict*. Cash £84 odd. Total *£108.10.0d*. △L.I.E. twice.

12 Mon   *The Old, Old Story*. Mr Rennolf (Versatile Baritone). *Idle Apprentice, or Orphan of the Storm* (F.Marchant's version of *Jack Sheppard*). Mr S.Lane ill – not able to come up from Brighton. Mrs S.Lane up without him to rehearsal & to perform at night – then returning to Brighton.

Mem.   Monday Oct. 12th – at night. △L.I.E. at rehearsal. *Martin disait qu'il trouvait ** baisant au derriere de L.I.E. et G Bd disait 'qu'il, est embarassant pour, encore, se trouver, continuellement, courant dans, les bras, de monde, embrassant, l'un, l'autre*[5].

13 Tues   Mr S.Lane better & in the Theatre.

14 Wed   Benefit of Loyal United Friends. *Old, Old Story*. Mr A.Rennolf. La Petite Taglioni. Address by a 'Loyal United Friend'. *Mutiny at Nore*. Good House (not over till one minute to 12).

19 Mon   *Old, Old Story* (2nd week). Mr Rennolf (Versatile Baritone). *All But One*.

21 Wed   Benefit of Check Takers, J.Carter, Leather &c. *Old, Old Story*. Mr Rennolf. Trial Scene of *Merchant of Venice*. *Maum Guinea*. Total £95.0.0.

23 Fri   Received Opening of Pantomime from Mrs S.Lane.

25 Sun   Home all day, working at Property Plot of Pantomime.

26 Mon   4th Act of *Virginius*. *The Old, Old Story*. Mr A.Rennolf, Baritone Singer. *Blue Beard*. E.D.Davis here. At his request, George* & Fred Rountree went to Nelson Lee to enquire about some *Crystal Glass Drops* which he had for sale, Mr E.D.Davis wanting enough to cover a space of from 30 to 45 square feet. Nelson Lee's drops of no use because of their sizes, while Mr Davis wanted only those about an inch square & N.Lee had only about 2 Gross altogether . . . Gave out Scene Plot & Property Plot of Pantomime.

27 Tues   Mr E.D.Davis here after dinner, wants some xtal drops. George & Fred went to Nelson Lee's about some – wouldn't do.

28 Wed   Benefit of *Hand in Hand Society*. No change of Pieces. Capital House. Amelia and George at night to the Britannia – came behind the scenes . . . Gave May Wardrobe Plot of Pant. yesterday (to read only) without the cast, & received it back tonight.

NOV 2 Mon   Performances varied during this week. Monday, Tuesday & Friday 4th Act of *Virginius*, M.Rennolf, *Old Story*, *Blue-Beard*. Wednesday *Katherine & Petruchio*, Mr Rennolf, *Old, Old Story*. Thursday & Saturday *The Old, Old Story*, Rennolf, *Guy Fawkes*. Fireworks.

---

*George Wilton, one of Wilton's sons, had recently returned from Australia.

3 Tues   Gave Hart* alteration of Property Plot for 1st Scene of 'Opening'.

4 Wed   No Benefit but Change of Pieces. *Katherine & Petruchio* (Miss Harcourt's* 1st appearance). Mr Rennolf. *Old, Old Story*.

5 Thurs   *Old, Old Story*, & *Guy Fawkes*. Grand Display of Fireworks. Mr A.Rennolf sent excuse, had 'utterly lost' his voice – did not come. Was not called for by the audience. Immense House. Fireworks better than ever before.

8 Sun   Home all day at Pantomime Bill.

9 Mon   Performances varied during week. Monday *Old, Old Story*. A.Rennolf, *Guy Fawkes* and Fireworks. Wednesday Benefit of Mr Teddy Mills. Tuesday, Thursday, Friday & Saturday *The Alchemist* (1st time) A.Rennolf. *Old, Old Story*.

11 Wed   Benefit of Mr Teddy Mills, The Swift Runner. *Il Trovatore*. A.Rennolf. Harry Kelly (Champion of the Thames). G.Davison, a walker. Teddy Mills. W.Randall (Comic Singer). Chas Sinclair, Harry Baker, Frank Percival (vocalists). *The Old, Old Story*. House not full, but a great many tickets sold at high prices, 5/0 & even £1 each.

14 Sat   Tonight, enquired of the company & others in the Establishment (by desire of Mr Lane) who among them were willing to vote for Mr Butler (candidate for the Borough of Hackney) at the Election to take place next Tuesday. Received promises from Robt Rowe (Carpenter), Thos Rogers (Scene-Painter) who says he has promises from 60 friends; W.Hart (Propy man) a split vote; G.Bigwood (a Plumper); J.Martin (Gas); W.Newham (a split vote); E.Elton (split vote). In the orchestra Rogers, Groves, Perry. Buck (scene painter) has promised Holmes his vote. The rest not qualified. J.Reynolds, E.Harding, R.Leslie, W.H.Pitt, R.Bell, R.Leslie not qualified to vote for Parliament – Non-resident[6].

15 Sun   Home all day. Announce Bill of Mrs S.Lane's Benefit.

16 Mon   *Alchemist of Modena*. (No Extras). *Old, Old Story* . . . A notice put up tonight at Theatre requesting all those agents who felt desirous of voting for Mr Butler tomorrow to meet Mr S.Lane on stage tomorrow morning at $\frac{1}{4}$ before 10.

17 Tues   Election Day (General). Voted for Mr Butler, – a Plumper. Mr Butler lost the day . . .

18 Wed   Mr John Ingram's (Friend of Bigwood's) Benefit. *Scarlet Mark* (1st night) Mrs S.Lane. *Wait Till I'm a Man* . . . Mr T.Drummond arrested at Grecian Theatre tonight – before Performance. Said to be for £400.

23 Mon   *The Scarlet Mark*. Louie Sherrington. Mr McHaffie, Irish comic singer. *Wait Till I'm a Man*.

---

*W.Hart had been engaged as Property Man at the theatre since 1865.

*Miss Harcourt was from the Theatre Royal, Princess's, according to the playbills; from Edinburgh, according to the *Era*.

25 Wed Mr R.Bell's Benefit. *The Headless Horseman.* Miss Louie Sherrington, Mr P.McHaffie. *The Scarlet Mark* (in which Mrs S.Lane plays). 3rd Act of *Lady of Lyons.* Capital House guessed at above £90 – upward of £60 cash.

30 Mon The Scarlet Mark. Louie Sherrington. Mr P. McHaffie. *Headless Horseman.*

DEC 1 Tues Wretched *House* at the Britannia tonight.

2 Wed No Benefit, but the 1st Piece changed to *Ingomar* (Ingomar, W.H.Pitt).

3 Thurs 1st Rehearsal of Opening of Pantomime.

4 Fri Called alone with Mrs S.Lane to meet Mr F.Marchant at Theatre to alter words of songs in Pantomime – Mr F.Marchant did not come.

5 Sat Bad House at commencement, very bad, but filled during the Evening & became first rate . . . △in Prompt Entrance for 25 minutes, timed by watch after Rehearsal of Opening of Pantomime.

6 Sun All day concocting Description of Pantomime for Newspapers. Succeeded in getting the rough sketch finished – in 72 lines.

7 Mon David Hunt. Louie Sherrington. Mr P.McHaffie. *Scarlet Mark* (Mrs S.Lane) – changed on Wednesday to *Beggar's Petition. Ballinasloe Boy.*

9 Wed No Benefit, but *Scarlet Mark* changed to *Beggar's Petition.*

11 Fri Mrs S.Lane's Benefit Bill printed and out. 1st Rehearsal of Comic Scenes.

13 Sun Wrote 20 long Puffs of Pantomime with manifold for newspapers, – began at 11 a.m. & had finished all but directing them at 20 minutes past 12 midnight – not putting any letters to editors in them but simply writing on the latchet of the envelope 'With Mr S.Lane's respectful compliments.'

14 Mon Lion Limb. Miss Louie Sherrington. Mr P.McHaffie. *Scarlet Mark* (Mrs Lane). Bad House – Rain. Gave Pantomime Bill up to Mrs S.Lane.

15 Tues Heavy Rain at night. Wind S.W. A most wretched bad 'House' at the Theatre tonight, one of the worst ever seen at the Britannia.

21 Mon Mrs S.Lane's Benefit & Last night of the Season. *Old Cherry Tree.* Monsr & Madame Boisset (Gymnasts).* Professor & Mme Thomas (the Professor being an extraordinary marksman & swordsman). The Acrobats, called The Brothers Carlotte (Juan, Pedro & Gomez). The new, Poetical 'Britannia Festival' & a new Drama (by C. & W.H.Pitt) called *The Harbour-Master's Secret.* (Above £100 in the 'House' and more than 4,000 persons.)

22 Tues With Amelia, Fred & Harriet to the Royalty Theatre to see Fred

---

*M. and Mme. Boisset** were for years celebrated for their 'graceful and daring acts of strength, acrobatics and gymnastics'. They spawned a lot of imitators in England.

Dewar play *Richard 3rd** (Burlesque) (for which he sent us an order for a Private Box). 1st Piece *A Loving Cup*. Last Piece, *The Clockmaker's Hat*. Rainy night, Bad House.

24 Thurs Christmas Eve. A Scenic Rehearsal called at *6 p.m.* Did not commence till *7.30*. Over at *fifteen minutes past one*, midnight. Fine night. Transformation Scene splendid.

26 Sat BOXING-DAY. Morning Performance began *12.30* over at *3.45* Great House. Pantomime, only, played. Transformation Scene, as usual, not ready – Could not be worked – obliged to show it all at once. T.Rogers, the Scene Painter, burst into tears in the Prompt Entrance & cried like a child. 'The best scene I ever did', he said, 'spoiled by those humbugs' (meaning the stage carpenters). At night the Pantomime repeated, *Blutzerranbothrumb*, with Monsr & Madame Boisset, Gymnasts; Professor Thomas the wonderful marksman & Mme Thomas á la Wm Tell & Son. *The Harbour Master's Secret*. Great House.

28 Mon Pantomime *Bhlutzherranbothrumb*. Monsr & Mme Boisset (Gymnasts). Professor Thomas (Wonderful Marksman & his wife á la Wm Tell & Son, shooting the apple off boy's head). *Harbour-Master's Secret* (C.Pitt's Piece). *Morning Performance* at 12 (*very bad house*). At night a Great House.

Mem. Door Keepers at Britannia (Cox & G.Taylor) say that 3500 shillings were taken before the doors were opened (i.e.) for Admission at the side of the Box Entrance on Saturday night & that after the doors opened Cox took £25 more – & that besides more was taken by other money-takers. G.Taylor adds that he believes *more* than 3500 shillings were taken *this* (*monday*) night before the doors were opened.

1869

JAN 2 Sat By desire of Mrs S.Lane suddenly at night, gave Mr C.Grimani (Assistant Painter) a week's notice. Her wish being only communicated at the last moment thro' Mr C.Pitt, with a request that the notice might be given before he left the Theatre, was under the necessity of giving a Verbal Notice *á l'instant*. Mr C.Grimani received the notice with tolerable equanimity. Asked him if he would prefer having a written one. He said, 'Well, it did not matter – but perhaps – if I did not mind the trouble it might be as well'. – In consequence, I wrote him one *while he waited*, in the Prompt Entrance!

12 Tues Meeting of the '*Britannia Sick Fund*' Association this day – Only 8 members attended. Mr J.Reynolds proposed that, instead of breaking up the fund, £10 should be left in the Treasurer's (Mr Crauford's) hands, that the rest of the fund be equitably shared & the Association should continue. It was agreed to call another meeting this day fortnight for which a strenuous effort

---

*Richard** was played by Fred Dewar in Burnand's *The Rise and Fall of Richard III or, A New Front to an Old Dickey*.

should be made to get every member to attend, & then the matter should be decided.

16 Sat   Capital House tonight . . . Some members of the Britannia Sick Fund having borrowed loans from it some two or three years ago – and having not only never repaid the loans, but having also ceased for the same period to pay their subscriptions to the Fund, I was told in the Treasury by Mr Borrow & Mrs S.Lane today to inform every member of the *Sick Fund* that all those who are in debt to the Fund for Loans must pay before the 'run of the Pantomime' is over or they will then be discharged. Told Messrs Radford,* Newham & Harding accordingly tonight. Harding & Radford acquiesced – Newham, excited & passionate, said he would pay, but not on account of the menace – no! – but because he would not have his name disgraced &c &c.

19 Tues   Received 2 Newspapers last night from Alfred Davis, containing accounts of the destruction of his Theatre (the 'Prince of Wales', Glasgow) by fire. A Relief fund for the actors forming. £100 subscribed the 1st day (£20 by Theatre Royal).

26 Tues   Grand Meeting of Sick Fund. Only 9 members present . . . viz: W.Crauford, J.Parry, J.Reynolds, C.Pitt, J.Martin, R.Rowe, Thos Rogers, Mrs J.Parry & F.Wilton . . . Received this night from Mr W.Crauford a Cheque for the sum agreed to be divided at the above meeting *15.14.11.*

27 Wed   Jessie up to Fred Dewar's – & to the new Gaiety Theatre with Rose. No Fees – Programmes given – The visitor walks in & takes whatever seat he likes – A Hassock to sit on upon each seat. Principal Pieces *The Two Harlequins* & the Burlesque of *Robert the Devil.*

FEB 1 Mon   1st change of Performances since Xmas. *Love's Dream.* Pantomime, *Bhlutzherranbothrumb.* Professor Thomas, the Wonderful Marksman. *Sailor's Return.*

4 Thurs   Wrote Receipt in Mrs S.Lane's Dressing Room for _____ 5000 for '*Special Services*' giving credit for that sum to Mr Chas M.Sawell* & signed 'for Mr S.Lane, – Fredk Wilton'.

8 Mon   2nd change of Performances since Xmas. *Love's Dream* (played last week). *Bhlutzherranbothrumb* (Pant). *Death of Sikes* (A concoction of a few scenes from 3rd Act of *Oliver Twist* for W.H.Pitt).

9 Tues   Missed M.S.S. of *The Snow Drift*, new piece to be produced next monday[1].

10 Wed   (Ash Wednesday) Concert, as usual, at Britannia Theatre . . . Very good 'House' & all went off well.

11 Thurs   Ascertained beyond a doubt that the M.S.S. of *The Snow-Drift* is lost.

15 Mon   *The Snowdrift, or The + on the Boot* (1st week). Amazed by finding

*John Radford** was a dayman and super with the Britannia company.

*Charles M.Sawell** has not been identified.

the lost M.S.S. in old jacket pocket! *Bhlutzherranbothrumb* (Pantomime) – 8th Week of the Pant. First Week of Reduction in Price – 3d. to all parts of the Gallery.

24 Wed   Benefit of Louis, the clown. *Kerim the Pearl Diver*. Monsr & Mme Boisset. *Pantomime* (omitted 2nd comic scene). *Sketch* from *Maid of Genoa* with *Drunken Combat*, preceded by Professor Thomas (the marksman). Receipts about £45 – spoilt by Heavy Rain.

25 Thurs   Gave notice to Mons. & Mdme Boisset & Professor & Mdme Thomas that their Engagements would cease with the Run of the Pantomime on Saturday March 6th. Professor Thomas said that Mrs S.Lane had *previously* told him . . . Mons & Mme Boisset said they could not play after saturday night next – as their Agent, Mr Roberts, had informed Mrs S.Lane – and that they were engaged & announced to appear at Bristol on monday night next. Mrs S.Lane & Mr S.Lane agreed that they might go – it was of no consequence.

MAR 1 Mon   Snow Drift. Great Gorilla, 'Olma', & man-monkey 'Le Main'* (who appeared 1st time one night last week – then playing for an Engagement). The 3 Sisters Claribel (novices – wives of the Brothers Carlotte – Acrobats) with their husbands. Professor Thomas, the marksman, last week. *Pantomime*.

3 Wed   Mr G.Bigwood's Benefit. *White Squaw. Siamese Twins* (Farce). Extras as rest of week. *Bhlutzherranbothrumb*, Pantomime. Cold, clear & bright day. Immense House. *£83* cash. *£113.0.0*. . . . Money turned away at the Britannia tonight as much, Louis the clown was told (by one of the door-keepers, Mr Leather) as was in the house altogether!

4 Thurs   Mr Borrow engaged the Siamese Twins for two nights next week (Tuesday & Friday).

6 Sat   Last Night of Pantomime. Capital House.

8 Mon   When the Clock Strikes Nine. The American Gorilla Olma & man monkey Le Main. *The Volunteers. The Snow-Drift*. 'Shy House' & no wonder – the real Siamese Twins announced for Tuesday & Friday.

9 Tues   THE SIAMESE TWINS, THE CIRCASSIAN LADY & THE NOVA SCOTIAN GIANTESS* appeared at the Britannia tonight, apparently an enormous house – but the returns only *£113.14.0*, about the same as Mr Bigwood's last Wednesday night. After the Exhibition the Wonders all went

---

*Olma and Le Main 'appear in hairy-looking coverings like baboons, and jump about and mimic the acts of those creatures pretty closely. One of them holds a long pole upright, with the lower end of it resting on his stomach, and the other runs up it, and balances and twirls and hangs on the top of it in a very daring and clever manner'. *Era*, 14/3/1869.

*The Siamese Twins, Chang and Eng, had first visited England nearly 40 years before. Joined by a ligament under the breastbone, they had in the meantime each raised families, having married two American sisters, and settled as planters in North Carolina. Ruined by the American Civil War, they had been forced to tour yet again. **The Circassian Lady**, Zobeiede Luti, allegedly rescued from slave dealers and reared by an Austrian nobleman when a child, was famed for the vigorous mass of brown hair which stood out from her head. **The Novia Scotia Giantess** was Anna Swan.

9. Cecil Pitt. A Redington portrait.

10. Playbill for the Hanlon Brothers, 1867.

11. Playbill for Lu-lu, 1871. Note the woodblock illustrations for the plays, which were not specially made for the theatre but borrowed from the publishers of journals.

12. Tom Sayers, a pugilist-clown, 1863.

MONS. LOUIS AS CLOWN. 44.

London Published by J. REDINGTON, 73 Hoxton Street, Formerly called 208 Hoxton Old Town.

13.   Jean Louis, the resident clown. Both Redington portraits.

14. A typical pantomime playbill, 1867.

15.   A typical transformation scene, probably for *Little Busy Bee*, in which a ballet girl was badly burnt, 1865.

16. The toy theatre shop in Hoxton Street, a few doors from the Britannia Theatre, from which the Redington portraits of many Britannia actors were published between 1850 and 1876. The photograph shows Benjamin Pollock, John Redington's son-in-law and successor, in about 1930. The appearance and stock of the shop remained unchanged from Redington's time.

into Mr Lane's Private Box & sat to see a considerable portion of the last piece – all went off well.

10 Wed   Mr R.Edwards' Benefit (Mr E. late of Xty Minstrels). *Snow-Drift* changed to *Mary of the Light House*. (Gorillas &c. as rest of week). Several Concert Singers (strangers) between the Pieces. Good, but not great, House.

12 Fri   SIAMESE TWINS &c at Britannia tonight, same as Tuesday last, an enormous 'House'.

15 Mon   Performances on Monday & Thursday, *When the Clock Strikes Nine*. The American Gorilla 'Olma' and man monkey 'Le Main'. SIAMESE TWINS, Circassian Lady & Nova Scotian Giantess, preceded by *The Mayor of Garrett* (called *The Volunteers*) & *The Snow Drift*. On every other Evening during the week, only *Mary the Lighthouse Keeper's Daughter* after the 1st Piece & the monkey-men. Immense House again.

16 Tues   Wretched 'House'.

18 Thurs   The SIAMESE TWINS &c. at Britannia tonight. Immense House tonight.

20 Sat   Collected 12/0 for a Mrs Chester, Widow of a Mr Harry Chester, on a letter sent to Mrs S.Lane who gave 2s/6d – sent it by Fred to Mrs Chester (tomorrow morning) at her address, 80 Nichol's Square.

22 Mon   Mr & Mrs Howard Paul's Entertainment, being PASSION WEEK. *Devil to Pay*. Monkey Men (as last week). SIAMESE TWINS (tonight, Wednesday & Saturday). Circassian Lady & Nova Scotian Giantess. *Lady Audley's Secret*. House very good – but not so great as last week.

23 Tues   Bad House, with Mr & Mrs Howard Paul.

24 Wed   SIAMESE TWINS &c. again at Britannia tonight – Capital House, but not so immense as last week.
△Mr S.L. gazed sternly into L.I.E. from middle of stage for some time after # had left it & walked up stage – This occurred during Rehearsal of new Piece for next Monday – in which both ⊗ and ⊗ were engaged.

26 Fri   (Good Friday) Britannia open tonight. Oratorio (Handel's) Messiah. Principal Vocalists Mr Lew Thomas, Mr Vernon Rigby, Madlle Liebhart, Miss Julia Derby – 300 (on dit) choristers. F.Kingsbury, Leader. Very good, but not great House. All over at *10h.20m*. Mrs S.Lane & Mr Borrow declared themselves satisfied.

29 Mon   *Biddy O'Neil* (1st time). *Gorillas* (a Monkey Ballet), written by F.Marchant (1st night). *Kerim the Pearl Diver* (the Monster by W.H.Pitt, 1st time). Immense House. No Siamese Twins tonight.

APRIL 1 Thurs   SIAMESE TWINS at Britannia tonight, with the Circassian Lady & Nova Scotian Giantess. House not great – and, for the first time since their engagement, plenty of room for the audience in the audience part of the Theatre – not one was admitted on to the stage.

2 Fri   SIAMESE TWINS & Circassian Lady at the Britannia tonight. The Nova Scotian Giantess ill – did not appear. Not a great 'House'.

3 Sat   SIAMESE TWINS & Circassian Lady at the Britannia Theatre tonight. End of their Engagement. The smallest of the twins ill, scarcely able to stand – The Nova Scotian Giantess, ill (dangerously so of Pleurisy) not able to appear – did not come.

4 Sun   Home all day – sorting Play-Bills! Wrote letter at the entreaty of W.H.Pitt to Mr T.Crane of the *Sunday Times* asking him to take the sting out of a critique which appeared in *Sunday Times* yesterday (on *Biddy O'Neil*)[2].

5 Mon   *Biddy O'Neil*, *Gorillas* (Ballet) & *The Bottle* – shy House.

6 Tues   Very shy 'house'. Soft Rain all Day. Received letter from Mr T.Crane of *Sunday Times* . . . half apologetic & enclosing stamped envelope for reply – evidently that I might give him a hint or two as to what he may fairly praise.

7 Wed   Mr Casse here later, says the charge for SHOREDITCH TOWN HALL is (with the Footlights) £7 a night.*

8 Thurs   Very bad 'House' again tonight.

9 Fri   1st Rehearsal of *The Very Grand Dutch-S* for the Christy Minstrels next Monday.

10 Sat   'House' bad at opening of Theatre tonight, but filled up afterwards.

12 Mon   Royal, Original *Christy's Minstrels* from St. George's Hall & Drury Lane Theatres (advertised as 100 Performers!) *Part 1* Ethiopian Entertainment. Songs, Dances &c. *Part 2* Opera Bouffe *The Very Grand Dutch S. Biddy O'Neil*. *Lone House on Heath* (*Rendezvous*). Shy House – All over 11.40 . . . Mr Crane, Reporter of *Sunday Times* in the Prompt-Box.

14 Wed   June Weather, hot & sultry. Robt Rowe, Carpenter of Britannia Theatre, had his hand blistered today by placing it on the slates of the roof of the Theatre (a blister over the size of a hazel nut). Thermometer 71° exposed, in shade.

17 Sat   Great House & noisy at Britannia tonight. In Mrs S.Lane's best scene, *Biddy O'Neil*, such a hubbub that '*not a word was heard*', except occasionally some stentorian voice, in the gallery, shouting out 'speak up!' or 'chuck it out!' Mrs S.Lane, Miss M.Henderson & Miss J.Coveney, 3 Favourites of the public, all well dressed & all good-looking, being on the stage alone all through the scene.

19 Mon   Good House – not great.

20 Tues   The Duke of Sutherland & 2 Ladies in the Prompt Box, at the Britannia tonight.

21 Wed   Benefit of Philanthropist Society – but no change of Pieces – only

*Clara St. Casse** was looking for a venue for her entertainment, 'The Songs of Shakespeare', which she eventually performed in the Manor Room, Hackney.

Louis the Clown & his Partner, or Friend, suddenly made their appearance in the course of the 2nd Piece, *Biddy O'Neil*, & asked if they might go on between the acts, or if they *must* wait till the end of the piece, as they had to be at the Alhambra for another Engagement by 20 m. past 11. – and not a soul behind the scenes had ever heard that they were to appear tonight at the Britannia.

26 Mon   Xty Minstrels. *Grand Dutch S. Marriage Certificate.* 5th Act of *Jane Shore.* House bad at beginning – filled up at half price.

27 Tues   Wretched House tonight at Britannia.

28 Wed   Benefit of Widow of late Mr Henshaw. Performances same as rest of week except *Prairie Flower* instead of 5th Act of *Jane Shore* & 'The Great Evardo' on the Flying Rings. Bad House.

MAY 1 Sat   Performances altered. Burlesque of *Grand Dutch S* changed to Burlesque *Il Trovatore* & 5th Act of *Jane Shore* changed to *Prairie Flower.*

3 Mon   Xty Minstrels. *Il Trovatore* (as on Saturday last). *Marriage Certificate. Prairie Flower.* Shy House.

4 Tues   Wretched House at the Britannia again. Mrs Honner* (now Mrs Morton) said by Bessy Rogers* to be *Paralysed*! may live a long time but is not expected to be ever able to get out of bed again.

5 Wed   Wretched House at the Britannia. Believe the Xty Minstrels are keeping money out of the House.

6 Thurs   *Lady of Lyons* played tonight instead of the *Marriage Certificate* . . . 'House' better tonight at Britannia – drawn by the *Lady of Lyons* – being also the 1st order night of the week.

7 Fri   The nigger Performance changed to *Il Trovatore* & *The Very Grand Dutch S* . . . with *The Marriage Certificate.* House nearly – not quite – as good as last night.

8 Sat   Performances same as last night . . . Middling House –. Last night of the Royal, Original Xty's minstrels! . . . △50 m. L.I.E. after rehearsing *The Old, Old Story* while *The Lord and the Lout* was being rehearsed, till old Saville* came to call to dinner – observed by C.Pitt. One hour one morning before, & 2 hours another morning, when female servant came to call & Mr Bigwood called attention . . .

10 Mon   *The Lord and the Lout.* Mr C.Woodman (for 6 nights only). Monsr & Mme. Marten, the celebrated 'Cat' Duettists & Mdlle Marten.* T.Carey, Irish singer (á la Collins & Ogden). *Old, Old Story.* Wretched House at beginning – improved afterwards, but to the last *shy* for Monday. Bought pair of Spanish leather Boots for stage 10.0.

---

*Mary Honner, widow of the tragedian Robert Honner, had previously acted at the Pavilion, the City of London and the Britannia Theatres. Bessy Rogers was presumably wife or daughter of one of the musical Rogers in the orchestra or of scene painter Thomas Rogers.

*Thomas Saville was a servant of the Lanes and Craufords, resident at the theatre.

*The Martens, from the Alhambra Palace, sang 'Trio Tyrolese', expressly composed for them by Offenbach and the Grand Duet from *Othello*.

11 Tues Most wretched House again. A Mr C.A.Booth* (soi-disant the Champion Skater) appeared & performed for an engagement on the new, patent velocipede – a very clever performance.

12 Wed Wretched 'House' again – Evidently we have not gained by parting with the X̊ty Minstrels.

13 Thurs Dreadful bad business at the Britannia all this week.

14 Fri Wretched House again at the Britannia.

15 Sat 'House' better at Britannia (as usual on a Saturday) but not equal to the average saturdays.

17 Mon WHIT-MONDAY. *Hop-Pickers and Gypsies.* Mr T.Carey (Irish Comic Singer). Mons M.me & M.mlle Marten ('Cat' Duettists & Trio Singers). Mr C.A.Booth, velocipedist. *The Lord and the Lout* (W.H.Pitt's piece).

18 Tues Rainy Day. Immense House at Britannia.

19 Wed Benefit of Clickers. Last Piece changed to *Fazio*. Immense House.

22 Sat Immense 'House'. Sultry weather again. Gave a week's notice to Mons Martin (written in French, very *English* French). '*Mr S.Lane doit faire, respecteusement savoir á Mons Madame, et M.ddle Marten qu'il ne peut continuer (pour le present) leur engagement apres Samedi prochain (Mai 29). Des autres engagements formés avant que cela de Mons. Mme, et Mdlle Marten étant la seule raison*'. Theatre Britannia le 22 ieme Mai 1869. Frederick Wilton (Regisseur).

23 Sun Home all day arranging scenes from *School for Scandal* for Benefit. Tried to condense *Louise Durand* into one act – failed (too long).

24 Mon Performances same as last week, except Mr T.Carey – not by any means a *good* monday night's house.

25 Tues Rumour of a Balloon Accident – Heard tonight in the Theatre that a Balloon in Cremorne Gardens had broken its ascending rope & escaped, carrying away 35 Passengers! Later in the evening it was said there was nobody in the Balloon at the time of the escape – & this afterwards proved true.

31 Mon 1st night of J.D.Beale's *Ghost Company. Man of Mystery & The Phantoms.* Mr C.A.Booth (Velocipedist). *Hop-Pickers & Gipsies. Mem.* Preparations took so long (i.e. till Performance commenced) that no rehearsal could be had of the Ghost Piece. At 4 P.M. the GLASS CRACKED to the consternation of everybody. Shy House & Performance at night half a failure.

JUNE 1 Tues Last night the House reached nearly £100 and very good tonight at half-price.

3 Thurs House still indifferent.

---

*C.A.Booth 'changes his coat, carries a lad on his shoulders, and stands with one foot on the back of the machine while he is careering around the stage with great swiftness.' *Era*, 20/6/1869.

5 Sat   First really hot day since April 14th. Immense House at Britannia . . . Mrs S.Lane's last night this Season.

7 Mon   Performances same as last Week – changing only last Piece to *Gipsy Twins*. Mr & Mrs S.Lane left for the Summer.

12 Sat   Bill changed to *Gratitude* (1st night). C.A.Booth (Velocipedist). *Village Lawyer & Man of Mystery* – Ghost Piece . . . *The Village Lawyer* badly played tonight & Mr Borrow saying it was 'imperfect' which it was not.

14 Mon   Fair House. Miss M.Henderson very ill.

15 Tues   Miss M.Henderson worse, scarcely able to stand – yet played her part in W.H.Pitt's piece called *Gratitude*.

16 Wed   First of the Actors' Benefits for the season. F.Charlton's Benefit. *Blue-Eyed Witch*, new drama (1st night). C.A.Booth (velocipedist). *Sons of Freedom* (Piece of Facquez'). *Man of Mystery & the Phantoms* (Ghost-Piece by J.D.Beale's Company) – Good House (guessed between £60 & £70 – Weather having been exceedingly favourable for several days – i.e. wet & cold). Miss M.Henderson very ill, did not play tonight – Miss M.Booth undertaking Miss Henderson's part. Receipts £60.4.0.

17 Thurs   Jessy over to Westminster Theatre to see Mr Jas Harwood* & ask his Terms for allowing his mare to play Turpin's *Black Bess* in *Ride to York* for my Benefit July 14th. His answer was £10!!!!!!

18 Fri   Mr Grosvenor (Stage Manager of the Spectral Company) not arriving at the Theatre tonight in time to play his part, their ghost played it, C.Pitt going on for the Ghost. On Mr Grosvenor arriving too late, Mr J.D.Beale (Proprietor of the Exhibition) discharged him on the instant.

19 Sat   Last Night of J.D.Beale's Spectral Company. Another gentleman played the Ghost – a young man who had formerly belonged to their company.

20 Sun   Home all day cutting *Red Rover* for Leslie's Benefit. Over to Mr Parkes (at cigar shop, Westminster Bridge),* to learn terms of Mr Samwell* for Loan of Horse for *Ride to York*.

21 Mon   *Blue-Eyed Witch*. C.A.Booth (Velocipedist). *Gratitude* (W.H.Pitt's piece).

23 Wed   Mr J.Reynolds's Benefit. *Louis XIth*. C.A.Booth (Velocipedist). *Poor Ray, the Drummer Boy*. Favourable weather preceding the day – but a fine morning. Receipts above £60.

Mem.   Miss M.Henderson ill and away from the Britannia Theatre all this week.

---

*James Harwood, a popular equestrian performer, was currently performing at the Westminster Theatre (Astley's) in *The Mare and Her Master*. Of good height, with a strong voice and a manly bearing, he was very successful in roles such as Dick Turpin.

*The Westminster Bridge Road was a well known venue for theatrical agents. Mr Samwell was an equestrian. He may also have been the Professor Samwell who appeared with performing dogs at Wilton's Music Hall in 1869.

24 Thurs   Bad 'House' at Britannia.

25 Fri   Bad House at Britannia.

26 Sat   Last night of *Gratitude* (W.H.Pitt's piece) . . . Mr Samwell & friend called at the Britannia today, during rehearsal, & promised the use of his black mare for my approaching Benefit (July 14) & offered to send her by his groom, at his own expense, on any day to rehearsal! –

28 Mon   *Sons of Freedom* (Faucquez' Piece, now played in 3 acts – last Wednesday, played two only, cutting out the first, for lack of time). Mr C.A.Booth (velocipedist) his last week. Miss Sophia Ogilvie, Violinist (the 'Signora Paganini'). Messrs Persivani & De Ronde (Acrobats from Alhambra Palace).* *Blue-Eyed Witch.*

30 Wed   R.Leslie's Benefit. *King Lear.* Miss Sophie Ogilvie (The 'Signora Paganini' – violinist). Mr C.A.Booth (velocipedist). *Wanted 1,000 Artificial Flower Makers. Red Rover.* Fine weather (too fine). Amount of House £51 odd.

JULY 5 Mon   *Hagar, the Jewess.* Miss Sophie Ogilvie (violinist). Messrs Persivani & De Ronde, acrobats (the Poetry of Acrobacy). *When the Clock Strikes Nine.* First Appearance of Miss Adelaide Ross* in London & at the Britannia. (She played Hagar in the *Jewess*). Miss M.Henderson played again tonight after being absent from illness ever since June 15th.

7 Wed   Mr J.Parry's Benefit. *Love's Sacrifice.* Miss Sophia Ogilvie (Violinist). Messrs Persivani & De Ronde (Acrobats). *Jolly Dick the Lamplighter.* Weather too fine last Sunday & today. Total Receipts £44.18.0.

8 Thurs   R.Leslie went today to the X-tal Palace to try the Mare, *Alma*, promised for the Benefit next Wednesday. Rode the mare & took the leap 8 times. Paid Mr Leslie's expenses only = 2.6. (viz. 1/6 his fare down, & 1/0 the groom).

11 Sun   Weather very sultry, – bad for the Benefit.

12 Mon   *The Victim Patriot* (1st Time) – played under the title of *Barnard* some 25 years ago under Osbaldistone's management at the Victoria when it shut the Theatre up. Miss S.Ogilvie (Violinist). Miss Jenny Franklin (Serio-Comic Vocalist & Dancer).* *Hagar the Outcast Jewess* (Miss Adelaide Ross's 2nd week).

14 Wed   Own Benefit. Sultry weather. *Ride to York* (Dick Turpin, Mr R.Leslie). 'Black Bess' by Mr Samwell the Equestrian's black mare, 'Alma', kindly lent gratis for the occasion. Extras as rest of week. Scenes from *School*

*Persivani and De Ronde** were equilibrists. De Ronde was able to throw a double somersault from a side balcony on to the stage.

*Adelaide Ross** had played in the provinces, including engagements at Glasgow, Aberdeen and Liverpool. 'Young, tall and graceful, her face pleasing and of a refined character, and her voice clear and agreeable'. *Era*, 11/7/1869.

*Jenny Franklin** was an American.

for Scandal (Sir Peter, 1st time Mr J.Reynolds; Lady T. ditto Miss M.Henderson). *Lady Hatton*, Lady Hatton, Miss A.Ross (1st time). Total receipts £72.8.9. Tickets *£4.3.0.* Expences, Printing £6.13. Posting £2.10.8. Horse expences £1.14.4. 2 horses & a Donkey 5/6 (W.Borrow's horses) besides *Alma* the mare. This House obtained in spite of Sims Reeves at the Standard and James Anderson at the Grecian.*

15 Thurs Hundreds of people last night turned away from the doors! Mr Borrow laughed & said he felt really ashamed last evening when he looked out of his window before the Doors were opened to see the mob waiting for admission (ragged shoe-less boys). If Mr Lane had been at home he (Mr Borrow) did not know *what* he would have said. During the Performance Fred Rountree saw a man in the gallery, after drinking a pint of Beer, throw the empty pot over his head behind him and as it flew through the air, the other people in the gallery did not seem at all surprised but quietly raised their eyes & watched its flight! The Gallery was filled in half an hour after the doors were open & then the doors were closed, & there was such a number of people disappointed & grumbling at not gaining admission that there were 3 Policemen appointed to pace the pavement & keep the people quiet. During the dialogue of *The School for Scandal*, the boys in the gallery were singing *a rousing chorus*! & scarcely a single speech was heard from beginning to end of the piece (*School for Scandal*).

19 Mon Luck, a Story of Pastoral Life (1st week). Miss S.Ogilvie (female Violinist). Mr H.Watson (Nigger)* 1st week. *Lady Hatton . . .* Shy House.

20 Tues Fred brought for me a *Pipe* to give to Mr R.Leslie as a little present for playing Dick Turpin = 11.3. NB. Mr R.Leslie had a narrow escape from being crushed during the performance of Dick Turpin by the mare rearing & falling backwards upon him. He escaped with whole bones to the wonder of all who saw the accident, but was seriously bruised all over & has not yet quite recovered. His right arm, he thinks tonight, is getting worse. He had not thought anything of that before today. His leg, which is now well, had engrossed all his attention.

21 Wed Miss J.Coveney's Benefit. *Luck!* Miss S.Ogilvie (Violinist). Mr H.Watson (Nigger). *Paul Derwent The Renegade* (new Drama by C.Pitt) with Wood-Cuts. Weather too bright though cool with East Wind . . . Shy House.

26 Mon Luck!, a Story of Pastoral Life. Mr H.Watson 'nigger'. Mr G.W.Lewis,* Comic Vocalist. *Poor Ray, the Drummer Boy.*

27 Tues Mr R.Bell refused yesterday to play the part of Otto in *The Demon Bracelets* – cast him by Mr Borrow.

*Sims Reeves was playing in a revival of *Guy Mannering* for a limited season; James Anderson was appearing in *Ingomar* for one night only.

*Hubert Watson was a Stump Orator, made up to look African in appearance. From the Broadway Theatre, New York, he was an eccentric comedian, who also danced and sang. His oration 'Men, Machinery and Rheumatism' was considered very amusing.

*G.W.Lewis was a comic vocalist known as 'Jolly Little Lewis'. His songs included 'Poor Old Stable Jem' and 'The Girl Who Stands No Nonsense'.

28 Wed   Miss M.Henderson's Benefit. *Hamlet* (Hamlet Miss M.H.). Mr H.Watson (Nigger). *Falsely Accused, or The Boys of Bircham School*, new Piece lent by Mr W.Travers. Rainy Day – cleared up in the afternoon (– greatly in favour of the house). Capital House. Total amount £85.3.0. Tickets £11.11.0. Cash £73.9.0.

29 Thurs   Told by Mr Borrow to give Mr R.Bell a week's notice – & to give him a hint that I had orders to do so – & 'see how he took it'. Told Mr R.Bell during the rehearsal – & he treated the matter with derision. Said also he would not play Benvolio – nor would Miss M.Henderson play Juliet – next Wednesday.

30 Fri   Miss M.Henderson tonight at the Theatre appeared the worse for liquor!!! At least Mrs Borrow thought so & directed my attention to the looks of Miss M.H. At length the latter lady fell off a Platform on which she had to struggle, while acting with Miss A.Ross, & abused the Carpenters, saying they had not properly secured the platform – Then I saw it was as Mrs Borrow thought.

31 Sat   Gave Mr R.Bell a week's verbal notice of discharge – after offering him a written one which he refused to take, saying a *word* was '*enough*' for him – *he* didn't want to stay – & he would not promise to stay the week out – that would depend on circumstances, he said. He had been to Bow Street & entered his name on the books of two agents, promising them a sovereign if they obtained him an engagement at Marie Wilton's or the Strand – or 'any of *them*' Theatres.

AUG 2 Mon   *False Mother*. Mr H.Watson (Nigger). Mr G.W.Lewis (comic singer, very –). *Luck*. Poor House.

4 Wed   No Benefit – but change of 2 Pieces. *Romeo & Juliet* (Romeo, 1st time here, Miss A.Ross) (Juliet, 1st time here, Miss M.Henderson). *Mary Stuart*. House but middling. Pieces not so attractive as expected – but, Mr Borrow said, a very large proportion of the audience highly respectable. Had a night Rehearsal of 'Ghost Effects' in the forthcoming, new Spectral Drama (not over till about ½ past 2 in the morning!) – found the 'Effects' so ineffective that Mr Borrow considered it undesirable to think of producing the piece next week.

5 Thurs   Tried again this morning the 'Ghost Effects' rehearsed last night after the performances . . . Mr Rogers (Scene Painter) thought cleaning the glass would remedy all defects – & set the men about it – but Mr Borrow determined to postpone announcing the production till rehearsals could *assure* us the effects were *effective*. So, though the bill is printed, it is not to be issued.

9 Mon   *The Castaway*. Paul Deulin. *Luck*.

11 Wed   No Benefit but 1st Piece changed to *Alexander the Great*, Alexander, Mr J.Reynolds (1st time); Hatira, Miss M.Henderson (1st time); Roxana, Miss A.Ross. *Luck*.

14 Sat   *The Demon Bracelets, or, the Mystic Cypress Tree* (1st night) (Ghost Piece with Spectral Illusions). Paul Deulin. *Downfall of Pride*.

18 Wed No change of Pieces whatever tonight – thank Heaven! – a most welcome relief to the actors!

25 Wed No Benefit – but Pieces changed to *Othello*. Desdemona, Miss M.Henderson; Emilia, Miss A.Ross. Deulin & *The Demon Bracelets*.

28 Sat Pieces changed. *Jack Stedfast*. Deulin. Messrs Herbert, Frank & John Lenton* Gymnasts (the two latter – boys). *Diamond Bracelets*.

30 Mon Jack Stedfast. C.Burton* ('Transformation' Dancers). Herbert, Frank & John Lenton (Gymnasts á la Risley).* *Demon Bracelets* (Ghost Piece). Capital House – Immense Half Price.

SEPT 1 Wed Benefit of Perry & Wade. *Clerk of Clerkenwell* (an abortion of Almar's). C.Burton ('Transformation' Dancers). H., F. & J.Lenton (Gymnasts). Numerous Brass Bands. *Raymond & Agnes*. House not so good by £20 as last year. Receipts £66.

6 Mon Performances same as last week, except Mr C.Burton gone, & replaced by Madme Pleon, Major Mite & General Tom Dot.*

8 Wed Benefit of W.Newham & Jacobs. *Prince Hal* (new Drama by Hazlewood). Extras as rest of week (besides Newham Junr* & his 'Partner' in a comic Duett). Scene from *Macbeth* (Lady M reading the letter). Scene from *King John* (Hubert & Arthur). *Twice Dead*, or, *Trail of the Serpent*, (Charlton's piece). Capital House £87.0.0. Cash £43. Tickets £44.0.0.

11 Sat Performances changed to *Good as Gold* (first night). Madame Pleon, Major Mite & General Tom Dot. The Lentons (Gymnasts). *Demon Bracelets*. (Not what is called a very great house).

15 Wed Benefit of 'Loyal United Friends'. *Good as Gold*. The Pleons. The Lentons (Gymnasts). Grand Banquet Scene & Address. *Loss of the Ocean Monarch*. (Middling House).

18 Sat Last Piece changed to *Jack Stedfast*.

20 Mon Good as Gold. Madame Pleon, Major Mite & General Tom Dot. *Jack Stedfast*.

22 Wed Benefit of C.Pitt & E.Harding. *The Black Tower of Linden* (new piece, written by C.Pitt). Extras as rest of week. Trial Scene of *Merchant of Venice*. *Wild Boys of London*. Total Receipts £81.12.0. Cash £50 *odd pounds*.

27 Mon Poor Parisheen. Mme Pleon, Major Mite, General Tom Dot. *Good as Gold*.

---

*The Lentons, under the patronage of the Duke of Edinburgh, were from Australia.

*Charles Burton appeared in an entertainment entitled 'The Carnival Fete'. Risley and his son (then little more than six years old) performed an act at the Strand Theatre in 1843, in which the son turned a number of somersaults in the air and landed on his father's hands; later, he stood on his father's feet, turned a number of somersaults, and landed on his father's feet again.

*Major Mite and Tom Dot were Madame Pleon's children, who 'gave some amusing caricatures of celebrated music-hall performers'. (*Sunday Times*, 19/9/1869).

*Billy Newham was the son of W.H.Newham. Newham and his partner, Wilford, had been billed at MacDonald's Music Hall in Hoxton High Street in 1868.

29 Wed Benefit of Summers & Light. *Iron Chest*. Extras as rest of week & The Hoxton Dye Works Band. Scene from *Tower of Nesle* & *Hidden Guilt* (Mr & Mrs Manning murder). Capital House.
Went to the *LORD CHAMBERLAIN'S* for the *LICENCE* with Mr Beckett & Mr Boyce as sureties. Paid the fees of *£4.14.6.* and was permitted to bring home the Bond after the sureties had signed it, for Mr Lane to sign it at home (as he was ill); with instructions for me to see him sign it, & sign it myself as a witness, & then to bring it myself on Friday here to the Lord Chamberlain's office. Afterwards went to dine at the *Star & Garter*, Kew. The Dinner with wine costing *£1.4.0.* The whole day's expenses being *£1.16.0³*.

OCT 1 Fri Went to the Chamberlain's Office & got LICENCE for Theatre . . . Charley Wallace, Flyman at the Britannia Theatre, found DEAD in Scene Dock at back of stage, supposed to have fallen from the Flys. Doctor said he had been dead 2 hours. He had been a teatotaller for upwards of 9 (nearly 10) years & had just taken to drink again – was drunk in the bar only about 2 hours & a half before he was found dead with two bruises on the top of his head.

4 Mon   The Poor Parisheen. The Pleons (as last W.) Mr F.Foster.* *Good as Gold*.

6 Wed   Mr W.Crauford's Benefit. *Far Away Where Angels Dwell* (1st time), Mrs S.Lane's 1st appearance for the season. The Lentons (á la Risley), for this night only. The Pleons . . . Fred Foster. *Ding Dong Will. George Barnwell* (George B., Miss M.Henderson, 1st time). Receipts not *£90*. Cash only *£52*.

9 Sat   Pieces changed to *Far Away Where Angels Dwell* and *The Poor Parisheen*. Extras as rest of week . . . Rehearsed *Far Away Where Angels Dwell* ½p.10. *Work Girls of London* 12 o'clock. Finished rehearsal 1st Piece at _____(sic) ∆L.I.E. till _____(sic).

11 Mon   Far Away Where Angels Dwell. The Pleons . . . Mr F.Foster ('The Girl of the Period'). *The Poor Parisheen*. House only middling . . . Received 2 Comic Scenes (the first).

13 Wed   Benefit of 'Loyal United Friends'. Last Piece changed to *The Work Girls of London*. Great House.

18 Mon   Far Away Where Angels Dwell. The Pleons. J.Ryley & La Belle Marie Barnam, their 1st night. F.Foster. *Work Girls of London*. House middling.

20 Wed   Benefit of J.Carter & T.Fuller. 3rd act of *Hamlet*. The Pleons. J.Ryley & La Belle Marie Barnam. F.Foster (the Girl of the Period). *Far Away Where Angels Dwell*. Shy House, only *£21* cash at first price.

22 Fri   Got Opening of PANTOMIME.

24 Sun   Home all Day about Property Plot of Pantomime. Wrote to

---

*Fred Foster, billed as 'from the Oxford', was a comic singer, whose most popular song was 'The Girl of the Period', which he performed in character.

E.D.Davis about Female Dancers of whom he wants four – & none to be had – and to Marchant, author of forthcoming Pantomime, complaining of there being no punning descriptions of characters in his opening.

25 Mon   Far Away Where Angels Dwell. The Pleons. Mr F.Foster. *Rag-picker of Paris.* Shy House – the cause, Fine Days yesterday & today!

27 Wed   Benefit of Shoreditch & Finsbury Provident Society. Last Piece changed to *Rescue of the Orphans.* Shy House.

28 Thurs   Had to write a fresh lot of Advertisements for next week.

29 Fri   Breakfasted with Mr E.D.Davis & his daughter Emily at 2 Norfolk Street Strand . . . Saw Mr E.Stirling* at Drury Lane Theatre by desire of Mr Borrow about the piece of the *Rag-Picker of Paris* which we have been playing all this week, & which Mr S. claims as his own. Mr Stirling said Mr Lucas* translated it for him & he paid him for translating it. Showed him our old M.S.S. & a bill of 1847 to show we were then playing it. He said Mr Lucas had no power to sell us the right of acting it. It was licensed in his name & printed & published in his name. He allowed that we were infringing his right by error, & he should not charge us anything for having acted it this week, but if we played it afterwards, it must be under an agreement with him alone & then his charge would be 10/0 per night for a single night, or £2.2.0 for a week or he would sell us the right to act all his pieces (& he possessed the right of 100) for £90 a year. This conversation took place on the stage of Drury Lane Theatre at about ½ past 12 o'clock this day.

NOV 1 Mon   Stranger. Mr F.Foster. *Far Away Where Angels Dwell.* Mrs Alfred Davis died this day in Glasgow. Aged 32.

3 Wed   No Benefit, but First Piece changed tonight to *Lady of Lyons.*

4 Thurs   First Piece – *Lady of Lyons.*

5 Fri   First Piece tonight *Far Away Where Angels Dwell.* Last Piece, *Guy Fawkes.*

6 Sat   First Piece tonight *Far Away Where Angels Dwell.* Mr F.Foster. *Guy Fawkes.* Enormous House.

8 Mon   Martin the Foundling (1st time for 22 years). Mr F.Foster. Miss Ruth Stanley (her 1st appearance).* *Guy Fawkes.* Grand Display of Fireworks . . . Rehearsal *Molly Sullivan* ½p.10. *Martin the Foundling* at 12. This last piece over by *12.20.* ΔL.I.E. till 12.40.

12 Fri   Rehearsal this morning *Mary Sullivan* 10.30. *Siamese Twins* ¼ before 12. *Katherine & Petruchio* ¼ past 12. First rehearsal over at 12.10. ΔL.I.E. from 12.10 to 12.47. i.e. 37 minutes.

13 Sat   Rehearsal *Mary Sullivan* 10-30. *Siamese Twins* ¼ before 12. *Italian*

---

*Edward Stirling** was a particularly prolific dramatist, who also wrote a history of Drury Lane Theatre. The play in question here was first performed at the Surrey Theatre on 24/6/1847. **William James Lucas's** version had first been performed at the Queen's Theatre on 28/6/1847.

*Ruth Stanley** was a serio-comic vocalist from the Theatre Royal, Bath.

Boy, ¼ past 12. First rehearsal over 3m. before 12. ∆L.I.E. from 3m before 12 to 25 m. p. 12 i.e. 28 min.

14 Sun Home all day about Bill of Pantomime.

15 Mon   Molly Sullivan tonight & tomorrow (Change on Wednesday for rest of week). Mr F.Foster (Girl of the Period). Miss Ruth Stanley. *Siamese Twins. Martin, the Foundling.*

16 Tues   Rehearsal *Pure as Driven Snow* – 10.30. ∆L.I.E. from 11 m. to 1 – to 1.27 = 38 minutes.

17 Wed W.H.Pitt's Benefit. *Pure as Driven Snow.* (1st night). F.Foster, Miss Ruth Stanley. *Katherine & Petruchio. Carlo Ferrari or, The Murder of the Italian Boy* (New Version by C.Pitt, 1st night). Very foggy day & night, no cessation . . . Rehearsal of *Pure as &c.* over at 12.25 ∆1st E.L.H. till 12.55 = 30 minutes. C.Pitt went in with me to lock up desk.

20 Sat Won a Cigar Holder in a RAFFLE at the Theatre tonight, 30 members at 4d. each – two throws with 3 Dice – Threw 33, which won. W.Newham, in the Treasury, today, told the Management he was too ill to undertake Pantaloon in this year's pantomime.

22 Mon   Pure as Driven Snow. Mr F.Foster. Miss Ruth Stanley. *Joan of Arc. Siamese Twins.* Wretched House – Rainy all day – never ceasing . . . Mr Bigwood '*drunk & incapable*' in the last piece.

29 Mon   Pure as Driven Snow. Mr F.Foster ('Girl of the Period', his last week). Mr C.Woodman (1st week after his accident). *Bride of Aldgate.*

30 Tues   Rehearsal *King's Death-Trap* 10.30. *Wife* 12. 1st Piece over at 12.20. ∆L.I.E. till 12.40 (i.e.) 20 mins. Very cold wind. So many draughts, obliged to have a screen round Prompt table to enable the candle to burn – useless – Everybody catching cold.

DEC 1 Wed No Benefit, but Performances changed to *The Wife*, Extras between & *Pure as Driven Snow*. Hard frost last night & today . . . Rehearsal, *King's Death Trap*, 10.30. *Wife* 11-30. 1st Piece over at 11.53. Very cold.

4 Sat 1st Rehearsal of Pantomime.

6 Mon   True as Steel (1st time). Mr J.G.Forde. Mr C.Woodman. *Pure as Driven Snow*. . . Gave Mrs S.Lane the copy of Bill for her Benefit. ∆L.I.E. from 12.55 to 1.12. Saville then came on the stage to announce dinner.

8 Wed Benefit of Mr_____(sic)* a member of the 'Loyal United Friends', (a decayed tradesman). Last stock piece changed to the *King's Death-Trap*, Mrs S.Lane thus playing in 2 Pieces.

10 Fri 1st Rehearsal of Comic Scenes. Clown (Jean Louis) not there. Celeste Stephan ill – not there. Only W.Buck as Pantaloon (Mr Newham having, from illness, given up the part, after playing it for (sic) years and Mr Carena, the

---

*Mr Burns** was the beneficaire on 8/12/1869.

new Harlequin . . . Gave Mrs S.Lane sketch of Puff for newspapers which she approved.

11 Sat △L.I.E. after 1st Rehearsal (*Death-Trap*) 40 minutes.

13 Mon The Death-Trap. N.A. Indian Tamburinist (10 Tambourines at once).* J.G.Forde. *True as Steel.* △L.I.E. at Rehearsal 42 minutes.

14 Tues Wretched House again.

15 Wed 1st Piece changed to *Othello* and *Death-Trap* played as a last Piece. Finished & gave up 20 long puffs (for newspapers) of Pantomime!!

20 Mon Last night of Season. Benefit of Mrs S.Lane. *Hop-Pickers & Gipsies.* Duett, Miss A.Downing & her husband (Mr G.Lewis). *Festival.* Great '*Fillis*'* Troupe of French Female Acrobats. Pas de Deux Madlle Annetta Galletti & Signor Cardella (all these Extras 1st time here). *Bob Lumley's Secret.* △L.I.E. after rehearsing *Hop-Pickers* from 33 p.12 to 3m. past 1 (30 minutes) during rehearsal of *Bob Lumley's Secret.*

21 Tues Given for Study to Principals. Rehearsed Supers in *Business* of Opening & choruses at 11 o'clock; then *Comic Scenes* with the Pantomimists. Saw & Gave out Supers' masks for the Opening (but not the Properties of the 'Opening'). Examined Properties for comic scenes & gave lists of the missing to Property Man. Home before 4 p.m.

22 Wed To the ALHAMBRA with Fred. Saw 2 Ballets *Coming of Age & The Spirit of the Deep.* E.W.Mackney.* Songs by Jonghmann*. Comic Ballet by the D'Aubans & Wardes. Band of 60 Performers in the Orchestra (splendid). Tableaux of *The Fratricide* by the 'Harry Boleno' Troupe*. Scenery, Dresses & Props of Ballets magnificant. Première Danseuse Madlle. Pitteri*.

24 Fri Night Rehearsal of Scenery (Artists, Thomas Rogers and W.Beaumont)* of Pantomime called at 7, began about 9, over ¼ past 1. Scenery very beautiful but much carpentering yet to do. *Only 1 comic scene yet marked.* Rehearsal at ½ past 10 of the Whole Pantomime. As usual number of Properties not produced. Property Man (W.Hart) ill. Not home till *about 4 P.M.* Treated by J.Pitt(!), W. Beaumont (scene painter) & W. Crauford.

25 Sat Went to the Theatre & marked the comic scenes left unmarked yesterday (the first time I was ever in a Theatre on Xmas day).

27 Mon BOXING DAY. (Morning Performance of Pantomime). *Giant of the Mountain, or The Savage, The Shipwrecked & the Belle of the Period.* 1st

*The Tamburinist was G.J.Ritz, from North America.

*The Fillis Troupe consisted of one tall man and four girls, all dressed as male acrobats, who performed balancing acts.

*E.W.Mackney was billed as 'the Negro Delineator' and is considered the music hall's first coon singer. F.Jonghmann was a 'Buffo Vocalist', song writer, and Morton's musical director at the New Canterbury and the Oxford. Harry Boleno, a popular Drury Lane clown, had appeared originally in ballets at the Grecian. Mme Pitteri, a popular music hall dancer, was also noted for her dyed 'golden' hair.

*W.Beaumont had just been engaged at the Britannia. He had also been a scene painter at the City of London Theatre.

night of Mr G.Lewis & of re-engagement of Miss A.Downing. Signor Cardella and Madlle Annetta Galletti (Italian Dancers). Mr A.Carena, 1st time, as Harlequin. Misses E.Parry* & Rose Nathan as Columbines. Madlle. C.Stephan as 'Harlequin á la Watteau'. Miss Charlotte Lauri* (1st time), with *Bob Lumley's Secret.*

1870

JAN 3 Mon Pantomime. Madlle Annetta Galletti & Signor Cardella, dancers from the Grand Opera, La Scala, Milan. Miss Charlotte Lauri (vocalist). Mr G.Lewis, Miss A.Downing. Mr A.Carena (Harlequin), Mr W.Buck (Pantaloon), with *Bob Lumley's Secret.*

6 Thurs Mr W.Beaumont (Scene Painter) gave me a small Oil Painting of a Cottage near Pangbourne.

8 Sat Crowded House at Britannia.

10 Mon Capital House.

13 Thurs With Amelia & Mrs James to see the Pantomime at the Standard Theatre* – very showy – dresses superb – doing great business. Sat in orchestra stalls on order for 3 from J.Douglas.

15 Sat Lalla Sawford died (24 years old). Subscription in Theatre tonight, to bury her . . . Mrs S.Lane gave £1.0.0. Crauford 5/0. Reynolds, Rogers, W.H.Pitt & Bigwood 2/6 each, self 2/0, Miss Henderson 1/6, Miss A.Ross & others 1/0 each, amounting to *2.16.6* which sum by this day week was raised to *4.13.0.* Miss L.Sawford died at 22 Ion Square, Hackney Road, of Consumption – which the doctor who attended her says was brought on by starvation!

20 Thurs Lalla Sawford buried today at Bow . . .Aged 24.

22 Sat Mr S.Lane
'In two brief rules he summed the ends of man
Keep all you have – & try for all you can'.
Bulwer Lytton in *King Arthur.*

25 Tues Annual Meeting of 'Sick Goose' Fund at Britannia, – 1 o'clock, P.M.

31 Mon 1st Rehearsal since Xmas, for new Piece to be brought out either next Saturday or Monday.

FEB 5 Sat First change of Performances since Xmas, Last Piece (*Bob Lumley's Secret*) changed to *The Hedge Carpenter*. First Night of the 'American Skaters'.*

---

*Emma Parry, daughter of Britannia actor John Parry, had been a ballet girl at the theatre since 1867. Charlotte Lauri, a serio-comic vocalist, had been engaged to sing one song in the pantomime.

*The Standard pantomime was *Harlequin, Jack the Giant Killer and the Seven Champions.*

*Moe and Goodrich, the American skaters, appeared in the fourth act of the pantomime, combining speedy and graceful evolutions of their patent drawing-room skates with laughter-provoking impersonations of skaters taking their first lessons on the ice and of the Swell and Girl of the Period, as yet unable to keep their balance.

10 Thurs Met Nelson Lee in Thomas Street – told me that Starmer* & Campbell (of the Dramatic College) were still alive but both bed-ridden.

12 Sat Wrote to Mr Nelson Lee (by Mrs S.Lane's desire in the Treasury) to say Mr S.Lane does not feel himself well enough to interfere in the matter of Morning Benefits for the Dramatic College & would rather not have anything to do with the matter[1].

14 Mon Received courteous answer from Nelson Lee.

18 Fri J.Martin told me Crauford had said the skaters got *£8.0.0.* per week, the Italian Dancers *£8.0.0.*, the Acrobats *£10.0.0.* and Clown *£10.0.0* and half a clear Benefit.

21 Mon *Turned Out to Starve* (1st night). Pantomime. 1st night of Misses (sic) (Dancers) (in place of the Italians, Signor Cardella & Mdlle. Annetta Galletti.)

22 Tues Miss E.Clayton* behind the scenes at night.

26 Sat Subscription in Theatre for the Widow of Mr Lacy (Harlequin of Astley's Theatre) who died suddenly from the rupture of a blood vessel, February. This subscription amounted to *£1.5.6*, Mrs S.Lane giving 5s/0d. Received A piteous note from Mrs Mary Howard (widow of Henry Howard the Actor who died 17 years ago) asking the '*loan*' of a '*trifle*' & saying she is in '*the deepest distress!*'*

28 Mon Capital House – Everybody saying the Pantomime is to be too soon withdrawn – being an unusual success.

MAR 1 Tues Benefit of J.Louis, Clown. *String of Pearls.* Fillis (one of the *soi-disant* French (Female!) Acrobats) between the Pieces, on 'The Magic Tub'. Pantomime last – Very good house in spite of the rain, which fell fast during the evening.

2 Wed ASH-WEDNESDAY. Grand Concert (Ash-Wednesday Festival (Carnival) as Maynard's* Bills call it).

3 Thurs Pieces changed to, Ballet *The Village Torment* (Fred Evans & Alhambra Palace Company). *Turned Out to Starve. Hop-Pickers & Gipsies.*

5 Sat Subscription at Britannia for Mrs M.Howard, widow of Henry Howard, the Leading actor, – amounted (with 5/0 from Mrs S.Lane & 5/0

---

*Richard Starmer** had performed as both singer and actor at the Bower and Apollo Saloons, the Britannia, the Surrey and Sadler's Wells. As a singer he had popularised 'Paddy's Wedding'; as an actor he specialised in playing old men.

*E.Clayton**, the 'heroine of the Domestic Drama', had been engaged for short periods at the Britannia since 1856.

*Henry Howard**, as well as stage-managing the Britannia for a short time, had been a great favourite at the Standard and City of London Theatres. Hanley (pp.36–37) remembers him as an excellent actor, 'a fine, tall, handsome man, with a good figure and a noble voice'. His health gave way, however, and he died aged 33.

*Ambrose Maynard**, one of the first music hall agents, had managed the Ash Wednesday Concert at the Britannia for the last ten years.

from S.May) to 30/0. Met her brother outside Theatre & not having yet collected the subscription, gave him 10/0 & gathered in the rest at night.

*7 Mon	The Pace that Kills* (1st time), preceded by comic Ballet of *The Village Torment* (which is nearly identical with the old Ballet of *The Barber & the Beadle*) – Fredk Evans & the Alhambra Company. After the Drama, El Chico Humel (Horizontal Bar Performer & Double Somersault Thrower (1st night)).

12 Sat	Capital House. Gave Mr F.Evans a week's notice of termination of engagement.

14 Mon	1st night of *Il Diavolo, the Terror of Naples* (Ballet) (Fredk Evans & Alhambra Company). *The Pace that Kills* (2nd Week). El Chico Humel (2nd week). *Turned out to Starve* (4th week).

*21 Mon	The Pace that Kills. The Mechanical Toy.* Miss Marion Taylor & Miss Ada Taylor* (their 1st Appearance). El Chico Humel. *Therése.* Shy House for a Monday.

23 Wed	Benefit 'Sons of Britannia'. Had no bills printed – but changed last piece to *Man of Red Mansion.* Capital House. Upwards of £60 of Tickets.

26 Sat	△L.I.E. 45 min. After rehearsing *The Two Gregories* which occurred from ½ past 10 till 11.00.

*28 Mon	Capitola,* 1st time. *Mechanical Toy.* El Humel. *The Pace that Kills.* Bad House. △L.I.E. 40 m. after *2 Gregories* – till Jacobs came.

29 Tues	△L.I.E. Again 40 m. exactly after rehearsing *Two Gregories* which ended at 12.28. The 40 m. ending at 8 m p.1. – Horrid Bad 'House' at Britannia Theatre tonight.

30 Wed	Mr Bigwood's Benefit. *John Felton, or The Man of the People. Two Gregories* (Mrs S.Lane). *The Mechanical Toy* (Miss Marian Taylor & Miss Ada Taylor). El Chico Humel. *Italy & Ireland, or, The Organ Boy's Monkey.* Excellent House, not *£80.*

APRIL 1 Fri	△L.I.E. 30 min. Reh. of *1 Blk Spot* ending at 33 m.p.12 △L.I.E. till 3 m.p.1 during which F.Charlton rehearsing scenes of *Pace that Kills* in which he plays W.H.Pitt's part tomorrow night.

2 Sat	△L.I.E. 15 m after rehearsing *One Black Spot.*

*4 Mon	One Black Spot* (1st Week). *Mechanical Toy* Miss Marian Taylor & Miss Ada Taylor. Duett Mr G.Lewis & Miss Downing. *Capitola.* Wretched 'House'.

5 Tues	Wretched House at Britannia tonight.

6 Wed	Last Piece changed to *Tom & Jerry* tonight & Saturday – very shy House.

9 Sat	Good, but not great 'House'. ACCIDENT. Mrs S.Lane, running out

---

*The Taylors were popular burlesque actresses, vocalists and dancers.

of Prompt Entrance quickly to take up a cue for entrance on stage, tripped over a protruding piece of scenery & fell heavily behind scenes – hurt her knee.

11 Mon   Lady of Lyons (James Anderson – Today, Tuesday & Saturday)[2]. *Mechanical Toy* (Misses Marian & Ada Taylor). *The Black Spot.* – Changed on Wednesday & Thursday to *Hamlet* (James Anderson; Ophelia, Marian Taylor) & *One Black Spot*. Mrs S.Lane laid up with injured knee through fall behind scenes Saturday night. Miss A.Downing played her part in last piece (not over till ½ past 12). Shy House.

12 Tues   James Anderson played Claude Melnotte . . . Note from Mrs S.Lane in these words 'My dear Mr Wilton, I am sorry to tell you my knee-cap is broken. Please see that my name is taken out of M.Faucquez's bill. yours &c., Sara Lane.'

13 Wed   James Anderson played Hamlet tonight. Miss Marian Taylor played Ophelia for the first time in her life. A very bad 'House'. Harriet & Jessie went to see the play but could not sit it out. They left at the end of the closet scene, denouncing James Anderson's Hamlet as insupportably *prosy* . . . *Richard Starmer* died Aged 85 at the Dramatic College, Maybury, Born 25th August 1785 – Debut, Tottenham Street Theatre 1810.*

15 Fri   (Good Friday) Haydn's Grand Oratorio, *The Creation*, played tonight at the Britannia (1st time). Singers Mdlle. Natalie Carola, Mr Vernon Rigby, Mr Lewis Thomas. Doors open ¼ before 7. Began ½ p.7. Over 3 min. past 10. Very good 'House' but said to be not so good as last Good Friday when the 'Messiah' was performed. Conductor Mr Kingsbury . . . W.Newham died at 3 p.m. of consumption, after a long illness. He had been many years the stock Pantaloon and 3rd Low comedian at the Britannia – has left a widow with 8 children.

16 Sat   Last Night of Thos Rogers, Scene Painter. James Anderson's last night. Subscription made in Theatre for Mr & Mrs Burton (actor & actress) only amounted to 10/0 in consequence of our actors receiving only 5 nights salary this week (& none of them knowing Mr & Mrs B).

18 Mon   Easter Monday. *Masked* (new piece by Travers) 1st night (Miss E.Clayton engaged for a month). *Tom & Jerry* – not a great 'House' for Easter Monday.

19 Tues   Charles Rice sent up *£1.1.0.* to the Subscription for Mrs Newham.

21 Thurs   Benefit of Hoxton Philanthropical Society. Last Piece changed to *Dark Cloud with Silver Lining*. Shy House. *£26* odd Cash. *£13* Tickets.

22 Fri   W.NEWHAM buried today in Abney Park Cemetery.

23 Sat   Subscription for Mrs Newham, behind the Scenes of the Theatre, amounted to £5.1s.6d. Paid Mrs Newham £4.1.0 in addition to 15/6 given her last Saturday.

---

*Starmer's 1st appearance, according to the *Era*, was at Eastbourne in 1793.

25 Mon   Masked. Darby & Joan (1st time these 17 years). *Volunteers.* Shy House.

26 Tues   Wretched House at Britannia. Rain came, at last tonight, & very cold after weeks of hot summer weather.

27 Wed   No Benefit, but last Piece changed to *Mutiny at Nore.* Wretched House.

Mem.   Awful bad bus. at Theatre all this week, except Saturday.

MAY 2 Mon   Marriage, not Divorce, or, The Love that Blooms for Ever (1st week). *Masked.* Good House, but not great.

3 Tues   Dr Lang said behind the scenes that Mrs S.Lane was going on very favorably, & he hoped in another month to be able to let her rise from her bed – but she would never be able to dance again.

4 Wed   Jacobs' Benefit. *Man in Cloak* (The Pantin Murders by Tropmann)* 1st time; *Irene, the Greek Girl* (Miss E.Clayton). *Alone in the Pirate's Lair.* Good House, weather having been very favorable, – (wet on Saturday & Monday) & cold ever since, £84 odd.

7 Sat   Good House at Britannia.

9 Mon   Marriage not Divorce (2nd week) – Duett, Elton, A.Downing. *Poor Girl's Temptations,* Miss E.Clayton, her last week of a month's engagement.

11 Wed   Miss E.Clayton's Benefit. *Idle Apprentice* (Miss E.Clayton's version of *Jack Sheppard*). 5th Act of *Richard 3rd* (Richard, 1st time, Miss M.Henderson; Richmond, Miss E.Clayton). Duett, Mr & Mrs G.Lewis. *Red Lamp* (Drama by Travers) 1st time here. £42 odd.

16 Mon   Fire-fly, 1st week. Miss Edith Sandford* & her Horse, 'Etna', & Mr Mervin – their 1st appearance here. *Marriage not Divorce.* House slack at the beginning of the evening but pulled up afterwards to *very good* if *not great.*

17 Tues   A falling off in the 'House'.

18 Wed   'House' shy.

19 Thurs   'House' still worse.

23 Mon   Shy House for a Monday. Fred to Cambridge Music Hall – Saw Edward Travers* who promised to send M.S.S. of *Red Barn* tomorrow.

30 Mon   Hagar (1st Appearance of Miss A.Ross after her confinement). *Fire-fly* 3 acts without the Prologue.

JUNE 2 Thurs   Mr F.Charlton's Benefit. *Rapier Jack* (1st time, a new Piece

---

*Jean Baptiste Tropmann** was a notorious, real-life French murderer, whose case had been much commented upon. The benefit referred to here is described in minute detail in *L'International,* 11 and 12/5/1870.

*Edith Sandford** was an equestrian performer in the style of Ada Isaacs Mencken.

*Edward Travers** seems not to have been the actor/dramatist William Travers.

written by F.Charlton). 2 last acts of *Fire-fly* (Miss E.Sandford & horse 'Etna'). *Ticket of Leave*. Bad House . . . Fine Weather.

3 Fri   Rehearsed *Flamma* for next Monday. Amelia & Fred to Britannia to see *Fire-fly*.

4 Sat   Mr Bigwood (who had to begin the 1st Piece, *Hagar*) did not arrive (by Mrs Borrow's watch) till 20 minutes past 7. The part of Fritz was necessarily cut out altogether, of course to the great detriment of the piece, as we had nobody to go on for it. Mr Bigwood, on being reproached by Mrs Borrow when he arrived, had gone away again directly, & Mr E.Elton had to play Mr B's part in *Fire-fly*.

6 Mon   Whit–Monday. *Flamma* (1st week). Miss Edith Sandford and horse 'Etna' – preceded by *Our Lot in Life* (1st time these 8 years). A *Great* but not an Immense House . . . Mr Bigwood . . . went to Mrs S.Lane at Tottenham & brought a letter from her to Mr Borrow saying he was to be re-instated. Mr Borrow opposed this, but on an earnest apology from Mr Bigwood, consented.

Mem.   Last Monday getting up such heavy pieces as *Our Lot in Life* & *Flamma* terribly harassing for the carpenters & exhausting to the actors on a/c of long rehearsals.

7 Tues   Capital 'House' tonight – better than last night.

9 Thurs   Benefit of Miss Edith Sandford. *Flamma, the Child of Fire*. 3rd Act of *Hagar & Firefly*. (Shy House). Miss E.Sandford announced to ride up the Burning Mountain without Saddle or Bridle!

11 Sat   Excellent House. Very windy weather. Mrs S.Lane came on the stage during rehearsal this morning 1st time, since her accident . . . looked very well – but walked slowly & cautiously, her leg appearing stiff (going off to Brighton tomorrow or Monday).

13 Mon   Our Lot in Life (1st time these 8 years). *Child of the Regiment* (Miss Carry Nelson,* her 1st week). Shy House for a Monday.

14 Tues   Cecil Pitt buried his son, 7½ years old.

15 Wed   Mr J.Reynolds's Benefit. *Old Rag Shop* (Piece of F.Marchant, 1st time). *Loan of a Lover* (Miss Carry Nelson). *Devil of Paris*. Intensely hot day. Only £45.8.4 in the house (Mrs Parry says £44.17.0. with £13 tickets.)

18 Sat   Good House tonight. Morris Abrahams in Mr Lane's Box. Mr Borrow says Mrs Lane has replied (to my request for F.Dewar to play Captain Crosstree for my Benefit) that she can't allow it – she had refused Mr W. Richardson* to let his wife play for *his* Benefit.

19 Sun   Home all day writing Bill for *Taking the Veil*. Wrote Miss Edith Sandford (*Firefly*) in reply to her enquiring for the parts of Maohiotee, and Mrs Skunk in *Flamma*.

***Carry Nelson** was a 'piquant actress' and pleasant singer, popular in burlesque and pantomime.

***W.Richardson** was an actor who had just joined the company.

20 Mon   Love & Duty. Midas (1st week) Miss Carry Nelson as Apollo. Last 2 Acts of *Our Lot in Life*. Hot day, shy House.

22 Wed   Mr R.Leslie's Benefit. Green Hills of the Far West. The Youth that never Saw a Woman (originally an old Cobourg Piece, right title *Fifteen Years of Labour Lost*, but called as above for this occasion) in which Miss Carry Nelson played the part of Lubin & sang two songs. Last Piece, *The Blind Beggar of Bethnal Green*. Intensely hot day. House not so good as Mr J.Reynolds's last week. *£35* odd.

*23 Thurs   1st Piece changed to *East Lynne* (for this night only), Master John Manley playing for an Engagement, his father, Mr John Manley, playing Sir Charles Levison in the same Piece. House better than the average of many stock nights previously & the child engaged for 5 nights next week in consequence.

*25 Sat   Decent House. Weather cold.

*26 Sun   Home all day preparing Burlesque of *Ganem* for Miss Carry Nelson's Benefit.

27 Mon   East Lynne (Master John Manley, the Australian child actor, 5 years of age) . . . *Midas*, Miss Carry Nelson, her 3rd week, & 2nd week of Apollo. *Love & Duty*, 2nd week.

29 Wed   Mr J.Parry's Benefit. Money & Misery, 1st time. *Midas* (Apollo Miss Carry Nelson – her 3rd week & 2nd week of *Midas*). *One o'Clock, or The Knights & the Wood-Demon*. Cleolyn, Miss Emma Parry. Weather very favourable since Friday last – rainy & cold on that day & on Saturday, cold on Tuesday & lowering. Receipts as stated by Mrs Parry *£47*. Tickets *£18*.

JULY 4 Mon   Spectre of the Sea. Youth that Never Saw a Woman (Miss Carry Nelson). *East Lynne* (Master John Manley). 2nd Piece changed on Wednesday to *Ganem* & played rest of week.

*5 Tues   Received note from Lacy (the Theatrical Bookseller) saying he had a 2 sheet Wood Cut of *The Child Stealer*. Pictures 3d each if I would like to have any.

6 Wed   Miss Carry Nelson's Benefit. Diogenes. Burlesque of *Ganem*. *Child of Regiment*. *£21.16.9*. . . Went to Lacy's about Wood Cuts – did not like them – & only bought one. Mr Borrow approved of it – and said 'Write for 50' – did so – telling Mr Lacey Jacobs should call for them tomorrow.

11 Mon   Ride to York. Jas Harwood (1st week). *East Lynne*, Master John Manley (5 years of age) 3rd week. *Spectre of the Sea*. House not great when the Curtain rose, but filled to a great house afterwards so that it appeared the child drew more than the *horse-rider*.

13 Wed   Own Benefit. Ride to York. Miss M.Henderson. *Child-Stealer* (1st time here). *Maria Martin* (Version written by Mr Edwd Travers) (*M.S.S.* lent by Mr Isaack Cohen).* Total Receipts *£45.7.0*. Tickets *£2.6.6*. Cash *£43.0.6*. Printing, Posting, May & Lacy *£9.3.6*. Hot Saturday, Sunday & Monday previous, Cool today & shadowy. One shower in the afternoon. Scarce anybody in the Stalls!!! so that the expectation of great numbers of girls to see Miss Henderson ride the horse was not fulfilled! It is very doubtful indeed if that incident *drew* at all. Capital half-price & Miss M.Henderson played the part of Dick Turpin capitally – to the admiration of everybody – but the horse a failure – condemned by audience – not docile.

16 Sat   An Immense Pit & Gallery at the Britannia tonight (£15 in the Gallery).

18 Mon   *Emerald Queen* (1st night). *Ride to York* (James Harwood). Very good House but not great.

20 Wed   Benefit of a Mr Rice (a Druggist & Truss-Maker, whose premises had been destroyed by fire, with all his Stock in Trade). *Work Girls of London*. *Ride to York*. Rifle Band. F.Foster ('Girl of the Period') who did not make his appearance at all but sent apology for illness. *Prairie Flower*. *£15* cash, Tickets out *£100*.

22 Fri   Benefit of Mr Jas Harwood. *Claude Duval*. *Emerald Queen* – a wretched 'house' – far the worse Benefit yet! – said to be only *£9.0.0*.

24 Sun   Home all day making out Super Plot for *Mazeppa*.

25 Mon   *Emerald Queen*. *Claude Duval* (James Harwood – re-engaged for 5 nights more). Wretched House. Hot, hot, hot! . . . Miss A.Downing absent from Theatre on account of illness, having had several fits (epileptic, it is supposed).

26 Tues   Miss M.Henderson disappointed of the horse she expected to play Mazeppa with for her Benefit tomorrow evening, telegraphing to several places in the country to Mr Edwin, the Proprietor of the horse which the late Miss Ada Isaacs Menken* rode for the same part, at length agreed to give Mr Edwin his terms £5 for that horse . . . Miss A.Downing again absent from Theatre tonight on a/c of illness.

27 Wed   Miss M.Henderson's Benefit. *Hunchback* & *Mazeppa*. Mazeppa (1st time), Miss M.Henderson. Receipts *£70.6.6*. Had Edwin's mare, the same formerly ridden by Ada Menken . . . Miss A.Downing absent from Theatre again tonight from illness.

AUG 1 Mon   *Taking the Veil* (produced last Saturday). *Emerald Queen*. Miss A.Downing unable to come to the Theatre tonight – ill again – & not likely, it is said, to be able to come for a week. Miss L.Rayner also absent – 'confined'!

3 Wed   Mr W.J.Richardson's Benefit. *Honest Labour* (new Piece, written by

*Isaac Cohen** was stage manager under Morris Abrahams at the East London Theatre (formerly the Effingham). Both were shortly to move to the Pavilion Theatre.

Ada Isaacs Menken, an American actress at one time married to J.C.Heenan, gained notoriety for the scanty attire she wore when bound to a galloping horse in *Mazeppa*.

F.Marchant). *Jim the Dodger* (formerly called *The Lawless Witness*). Mrs W.Richardson, wife of the Beneficiare, between the Pieces, 2 Songs & Dance. *Wild Boys of London* (C.Pitt's piece). Total Receipts *£43.16.0*. Tickets *£9 odd*.

4 Thurs   Miss A.Downing, actress of Chambermaids at Britannia Theatre died ¼ before 11 a.m. Paralysis of Brain – brought on by – (sic).

6 Sat   Change of Performances. *Lischen & Fritzchen* (Operetta by Offenbach) – Miss Constance Loseby & Mr Edward Perrini,* their 1st Appearance. *Taking the Veil & Mary Edmonstone*. Good Half Price, but not a great 'House'.

10 Wed   Miss A.Ross's Benefit. *Marie the Gambler. Plot & Passion* (Taylor's writing) Miss Constance Loseby singing 'Sally in our Alley'. *Lady of Lyons*, Miss Ross playing Claude Melnotte. Between *£48 & £49*. House bad at beginning . . . Amelia at Theatre – told by Mrs Borrow that Mrs S.Lane *will* go to church of a sunday!!!

15 Mon   *Sharps & Flats* (new Piece by F.Marchant, 1st time. Bad Piece – no interest in it). *Fortune's Frolic. Taking the Veil*. Indifferent House – but good Half Price.

17 Wed   W.H.Pitt's Benefit. *Striking the Hour* (Written by W.H.Pitt, but belonging to Morris Abrahams & lent by him for the occasion). *Mysteries of Paris* (called on this occasion *The Streets of Paris by Night & Day*) and *Marco Sciarro* (called on this occasion *War on the Frontier*). House – shy at commencement, but good Half-Price. *£54 odd*.

22 Mon   *Sharps & Flats* (2nd week). Champion Vaulters (1st week). *Taking the Veil*. Much Rain late in the afternoon. Indifferent House in consequence.

24 Wed   No Benefit, thank Heaven! 'For this relief much thanks'. Yet changed bill notwithstanding to *The Sea*. The Champion Vaulters. Grand Concert: Madame Pedley, Miss Pattie Goddard,* The sisters Lotto & Jessie*, Messrs Cobb & East* 'niggers' *Sharp & Flats*. Very middling House.

25 Thurs   Midnight – Wrote Mrs E.D.Davis telling her that the 'woman' sent for to *price* the Theatrical Dresses left by the late Mrs Alfred Davis, had depreciated every article – offering only £6 for the lot.

29 Mon   *Sons of the Forge* (my title) 1st time. Champion Vaulters. *Sharps & Flats*, on Monday, Tuesday & Saturday. *Taking the Veil* (my title) on Thursday & Friday.

31 Wed   G.Lewis's Benefit. *The Woman with the Gold Hair & The Man with the Iron Heart*. Champion Vaulters. *Turn Him Out. Nicholas Nickleby*. Total Receipts *£54 odd*.

SEPT 1 Thurs   Delivered Box and Baskets (containing Dresses of the late

---

*Constance Loseby** was the daughter of Madame Losebini. **Edward Perrini** was billed as from the Gaiety Theatre.

*Patti Goddard** was a serio-comic vocalist. **Lotto and Jessie** were clog hornpipe dancers. **Cobb and East** were billed as Negrophotists.

Mrs Alfred Davis) to Driver of Van from Gt Northern Railway, to be sent by Rail to Mrs E.D.Davis, & addressed to her at the Lyceum Theatre, Sunderland.

5 Mon *Sons of the Forge.* Champion Vaulters. Swiss Brothers Bale (Jugglers, Balancers &c). *Three Lives.*

7 Wed No Benefit, but change of Performance. *Ocean Monarch.* Champion Vaulters. Swiss Brothers Bale. Concert, Miss Amy Horton,* Victor Liston,* Messrs _____ (sic) & Lucette* (Niggers). *Sons of the Forge.*

12 Mon *He Would Be A Sailor.* Skaters. M.Elliot & Mdlle. Fredericka. Swiss Brothers. *Sons of the Forge* and *Ocean Monarch.*

14 Wed C.Pitt's & E.Harding's Benefit. *Deadly Nightshade.* Skaters. Swiss Brothers (Jugglers, Balancers &c). *Bells that Rang. Black Rollo.* Not a great House.

17 Sat Great House. Gave a week's notice to E.Harding & Skaters.

19 Mon *Zana, the Bride of the Alhambra.* Skaters & Brothers Bale. *Verdant Giles & He Would Be A Sailor.* Shy House . . . Letter from Miss Bessy Forde• – saying she has just arrived in London & asking a subscription to bury her husband whom she found dead on arriving from Sheffield.

24 Wed Benefit of Messrs Perry & Wade. *Was He the Man?* (New Piece by C.Pitt). Skaters & Brothers Bale. *Orlando the Outcast.* Various Bands & Musical Performers. *Bertha Grey.* Not a great House, about £63 . . . Met T.Drummond at the Bar of the Britannia.

26 Mon *Rich & Poor* (revived). Brothers Bale (Balancers, Jugglers &c). *Zana.* Mrs S.Lane came to the Theatre, 1st time after her return from the country; Mr S.Lane a little better – able to articulate several words, such as 'Hope', 'Wine', 'My Mother'.*

28 Wed Benefit of Messrs Summers & Light. *Damon & Pythias.* Hoxton Dyers Band. Brothers Bale (Jugglers, Balancers &c). *Last Appeal. Hand of Cards.* Capital House. Tickets said to be over £50.

29 Thurs Went to Lord Chamberlain's Office to get the *License* for Britannia Theatre with Mr Beckett & Mr Boyce as Securities – received under promise that Mr Lane should sign & send it back tomorrow. Paid fees at Lord Chamberlain's Office, 4 14 0. Did not get to bed till 3 o'clock.

Mem. Expenses incurred in getting License. Luncheon with Mr Beckett & Mr Boyce at Simpson's (Strand) 9s/3d. Waiter 6d. – Half-way House to

---

*Amy Horton** was a vocalist and impersonator. **Victor Liston**, an ex-legitimate actor, was a comic vocalist with a pathetic strain. His songs included 'Shabby Genteel'. **Lucette's** partner has not been identified. The playbill gives '. . rcourt'. They were American, black-face comedians, who played the banjo and violin and performed a 'Squash Plantation Dance'.

*Bessy Forde** may have been the wife of a Super named Forde employed at the Britannia from 1865–66.

*Lane** must have suffered a stroke during the summer of 1870; Crauford (p.302) confirms this, but dates the stroke a year later.

Greenwich – Bitter Ale 6d. W.Borrow (Cab-Driver) 1½d. Dinner at Trafalgar Hotel, Greenwich £2.2.9! W.Borrow – 2s.6d!

OCT 3 Mon   Tally Man. Swiss Brothers Bale. J.Hillier (comic singer).* *Rich & Poor.* 'House' middling.

5 Wed Mr W.Crauford's Benefit. *The 3 Temptations* (a new piece by F.Marchant), not over till long past 10, playing 2½ Hours. Pat Corré, Mr St. Aubyn & Mme. Harrie in an Operetta (name unknown). Arthur & Bertrand French Clowns (who could not wait & went away without performing at all). Mr J.Hillier (comic singer). The Swiss Brothers Bale, and Mr H.Lynn, mimic & comic singer.* *Eily O'Connor.* With Mrs S.Lane in the 1st Piece. Immense House. *£120.* Cash *£83.9.9.* Gallery filled at 6d each before the Doors were open. Not over till 20 minutes past 12.

6 Thurs Twice to East London Theatre to see Morris Abrahams (the Proprietor) about the Title of our new piece (*The Three Temptations*) which he claims. Could not find him at home. Meantime changed the Title to *The Three Perils.*

8 Sat Great House at Britannia & noisy.

10 Mon   Three Perils (title altered by request of Mr Morris Abrahams from the *Three Temptations*). Mr J.Hillier (comic singer). Price's Christy Minstrels.* *Eily O'Connor* (very badly acted – compared to the way in which it was acted when first produced).

12 Wed Benefit of 'Loyal United Friends'. No change of Pieces – but 'Banquet Scene' & Extra Incidentals. Immense House.

13 Thurs Went to see Mr Beaumont according to letter received yesterday stating his illness – could not see him on account of his being asleep.

14 Fri Mrs S.Lane told Amelia that Mr S.Lane had not been able to speak for a month. That she was afraid she would be obliged to give up acting for a time as Mr Lane required all her attention, – adding that they have to feed him every 10 minutes . . . Mr Beaumont (Artist) no better.

15 Sat Last Night of Miss A.Ross at the Britannia – going to Leeds – travels tomorrow – opens there on Monday night . . . Mr Beaumont (Artist) still the same.

17 Mon   Three Perils. Great Price 'Christy Minstrels'. *Mill of the Happy Valley.* Miss M.A.Bellair's* 1st Appearance . . . Mr Beaumont (Artist) stil confined to his bed, unable to lift his left arm. His family seem to avoid naming his disorder. Suspect Paralysis.

---

*James Hillier was a popular low comedian at the Surrey, the Grecian and the 'Vic'. His favourite song was 'Tickling in the Tunnel'.

*H.Lynn gave imitations of actors, including a number of Britannia favourites.

*Price's Christy Minstrels combined ballad singing, instrumental music, jokes, choruses and burlesque acting.

*Miss M.A.Bellair was to become a very popular actress of melodramatic heroines.

18 Tues   Told Miss M.Bellair to understudy Mrs S.Lane's Benefit . . . Mr Beaumont (Artist) said to be no better.

19 Wed   Benefit of a society. No change of Pieces – Indifferent House. Very heavy Rain & Rainy nearly all day. Mr S.Lane no better . . . Received letter from Mr E.D.Davis – going to play *Eily O'Connor* next Saturday & has a Company coming to play *Little Emily* very shortly. This in answer to my offer to him of Jessie's concoction of a version.

23 Sun   Home all day . . . making 'excerpts' for Pantomime Bill.

24 Mon   Performances same as last week. House middling. Jessie offered *M.S.S.* of *Uncle Peggotty's Darling* to Mrs S.Lane – declined.

25 Tues   Mr Beaumont, Scene Painter, still away from Theatre ill – supposed *Paralysis*.

26 Wed   Benefit 'Hand in Hand' Society, but no change of Pieces. Capital House. Received all three Comic Scenes from Mrs S.L.

27 Thurs   Gave out Plots of 1st Comic Scene . . . Much inconvenienced by Mr Majilton's non-arrival to rehearse. Many alterations & re-writing of Advertisements in consequence. Finally he arrived – late this evening.

28 Fri   Gave out Plots of 2nd Comic Scene.

29 Sat   Immense House. Rainy day.

30 Sun   Home all day. At work on Pantomime.

31 Mon   *Seven Years' Secret* 1st time. Majilton Family 'in a Ballet Extraordinaire' *Les Deux Diables* (1st week). Price 'Christy Minstrels'. *3 Perils*, Mrs S.Lane. Received Picture from Mr W.Beaumont. Gave out Property Plot of 3rd & last Comic Scene, having given out Scene Plot on Saturday.

NOV 2 Wed   Very bad House. Gave out Scene Plot of Opening of Pantomime.

3 Thurs   Very bad House.

4 Fri   Gave out Property Plot of Opening.

5 Sat   *Guy Fawkes* and *Fireworks* . . . Tremendous House at Britannia – crammed. *£107* . . . Gave out Wardrobe Plot of Pantomime.

6 Sun   Home all day (Super Plot – Pantomime).

7 Mon   *3 Perils*. Xty Minstrels (re-engaged). Majilton's Ballet, *Les Deux Diables*. *Guy Fawkes* & Fireworks (Monday, Wednesday & Saturday). *Seven Year's Secret* (Tuesday, Thursd & Sat). Capital House, but not equal to last Saturday. *£12.8.0* taken in Three-pences at Gallery.

9 Wed   Jessie saw Mr Morris Abrahams & left with him her version of *Little Em'ly* called *Uncle Pegotty's Darling, or, The Flight from the Ark*, which he promised to read next Sunday. Ergo he is not going a-fishing on that day.

*14 Mon	Magic Whisper* (1st week). Price's Christy Minstrels. Niblo* on the Trapeze. *Seven Years Secret.*

15 Tues	Went to the Grecian Theatre by desire of Mr Borrow to tell Mr Conquest that the Piece of the *Beggar's Petition* which is announced to be played there on Thursday night next for the Benefit of a Mr MacDermott,* is Mr S.Lane's Property – Mr Borrow showed me the Assignment of that Piece to Mr S.Lane by Mr R.Sheppard*, for the sum of £7 dated Jany 7th, 1849. Saw Mr B.O.Conquest and he showed me a note from Mr R.Sheppard giving Mr MacDermott permission to play the piece – and saying it was his property, & wherever it might be played, he should claim for it. Evidently he had forgotten that in the Assignment of the East London right to Mr S.Lane he had expressly undertaken that it should never be played at the *Grecian Theatre.* However, having Mr Borrow's instruction to do so, I told them that they might play it on Thursday as they had their bills out, on Mr Conquest's promising that it should not be played afterwards, which Mr Conquest readily promised.

*21 Mon	Magic Whisper.* Niblo, Trapezist. *Effie & Jeannie Deans.* W.H.Pitt's wife died this day of an Accident – The Balcony of a Window fell with her as she was cleaning a Window last Saturday.

26 Sat	Mrs S.Lane says the Doctor fears Mr S.Lane will have an Apoplectic Fit. That is what he is afraid of. Great House at the Britannia.

*28 Mon	In the Holly* (Piece written by W.H.Pitt) 1st week. Niblo. *The Magic Whisper.* Shy Monday night's House.

29 Tues	Jessy to the East London Theatre. Saw Mr Morris Abrahams, who agreed to accept her piece of *Uncle Peggotty's Darling or The Flight from the Ark* at his Theatre, to produce it after Xmas, & to pay her 5/0 per night for it.

*DEC 5 Mon	Formosa,* an Entertainment by W. & Mrs W.Randall. *Wealth Got & Lost* (Drama by Hazlewood), 1st time. *In the Holly.* Horrible Weather. Frost again last night.

6 Tues	Sent Mrs S.Lane's Benefit Bill to the Printers tonight (after Mr Beckett's shop was shut up). Row with Mr R.Leslie.

8 Thurs	Wretched Houses all this week. Fall of snow.

9 Fri	Mrs S.Lane's Benefit Bills printed and in the 'house' tonight.

10 Sat	Mr J.Martin told me of an Extraordinary Incident he had seen from the Flies – Prompt Side – where he had been to look for Mr H.Morgan

---

*Niblo (Thomas Clarke) had first appeared at the Canterbury two years earlier with 'a marvellous flight from the balcony to the back of the stage'. He is said to be the first man to throw a double somersault between bars.

*G.H.MacDermott began his theatrical career as a straight actor. He was later engaged at the Britannia. He gradually developed into a singer, achieving great success with songs like 'Dear Old Pals' and 'We Don't Want To Fight But By Jingo If We Do'. R.Shepherd had been manager of the Surrey Theatre from 1848–1869.

(Lime-light man) – and which, if '*all the world*' had told him they had seen, he would not have believed unless he had seen it, as he had done with his own eyes. He added that 'Fred Matthews had told him that he (F.Matthews) had seen the same *incident* several times'.

11 Sun   Wrote 20 long Descriptions of the Pantomime (by Manifold) for the Newspapers. Began about one P.M. – finished about 10 p.m. – having a rough M.S.S. copy previously written.

12 Mon   'Musical Olio' (Mr & Mrs W.Randall). *Wealth Got & Lost*, Mrs S.Lane. *In the Holly*. Wretched House . . . Mrs S.Lane told Mr C.Pitt that Mr S.Lane was affected, on Saturday, with blindness which lasted all Sunday, but that he got better Monday Dec 12th.

14 Wed   No Benefit, but changed last piece to *Beggar's Petition*. Very bad House. Gave up 16 Long Puffs of Pantomime for newspapers.

19 Mon   Mrs S.Lane's Benefit & Last Night of the Season. *Forger & his Victim* (Cecil Pitt's piece). *Dance* Miss Celeste (Celeste Stephan's daughter). A.F.Forrest (Clown & sons) Acrobatic Entertainment. (No *Fairy Fountain*, by H.Morgan, as announced, because water-pipes burst on trial this afternoon). Dances by Mdlles Lizzie & Lily Wright & the 3 Clog Hornpipe Sisters, Lottie, Jessie & Grace (called in the bills the *Three Fairy Dancers*!!!). *Loan of a Lover*, Miss Julia Summers* (her 1st Appearance here) & Miss M.Willis* (ditto). *The Deer Slayer* (new Piece by C & W.Pitt). With all these attractions no wonder there was a *good House* notwithstanding slight rain.

20 Tues   With Jessy to the Queen's Theatre to see *The Midsummer Night's Dream*; Phelps as Bottom;* Ryder as the Duke; Jemmy Howard; Egeus, H.Marston; Puck (best of all), Miss Tilly Wright*; Helena, Miss M.Henderson.

21 Wed   Rehearsed Super Bus. & Ballet of Pantomime. Wrote Advertisements.

22 Thurs   Rehearsed Super Bus. & Ballet of Pantomime. Marked Comic Scenes.

23 Fri   Night Rehearsal of Scenery, called to commence punctually at 6 o'clock, began at $\frac{1}{2}$ past 9. Mrs S.Lane not being at either rehearsal – having been to Brighton with Mr S.Lane since last Tuesday.

24 Sat   Rehearsed the whole Pantomime. Began at *10.30*, not over till nearly *5 o'clock*: (the Ballet taking more than an hour). Had called neither Scenes nor Properties of the Opening, but both Scenes & Properties for Comic Scenes – the Properties very imperfect.

26 Mon   BOXING-DAY. Morning Performance of Pantomime (the only one) at 12 o'clock. *The Man Loaded with Mischief, or, King Cricket & Polly-Put the Kettle On*. Followed, at night, by *The Deer Slayer*. Great House.

---

*Julia Summers, engaged to play soubrettes and chambermaids, later became the wife of J.B.Howe. Miss M.Willis was engaged to play the Fairy Queen in the pantomime.

*Samuel Phelps had first appeared at the Queen's as Bottom on 17/9/1870. Tilly Wright had been praised by the *Era*, 18/9/1870, for her bye-play and for the intelligent delivery of her lines as Puck.

1871

JAN 12 Thurs   Amelia to see the Pantomime at the Britannia.

18 Wed   Mr & Mrs Askew* here to tea – & afterwards to the Britannia with Fred & Harriet; then here again to supper – (fried fish) – stopped till near 1 o'clock a.m.

21 Sat   Tremendous 'House'. Thos. Rogers (artist) behind the scenes tonight (tipsy) said he was going to Paris in a fortnight – 'he had invented *a gun* which &c –'[1].

FEB 4 Sat   Great House at Britannia.

6 Mon   Mrs S.Lane unable to play – Quinsy. Miss J.Coveney played her part.

7 Tues   Meeting of Members of 'Sick Fund' at Britannia. Paid for last month – 1.0. Attended the setting of 3 Principal Scenes in *Wreck of Golden Mary*, on stage (1st act).

9 Thurs   Rehearsed *Some Bells that Rang.* (1st Rehearsal since Christmas).

13 Mon   Last Piece changed to *Some Bells that Rang.* 1st Change since Xmas. Mrs S.Lane still absent – Quinsy. Miss J.Coveney played her part in the Pantomime.

20 Mon   Pantomime & *Work-Girls of London.*

22 Wed   (Ash Wednesday) *Grand Concert.* Miss Constance Loseby, Miss Annie Tremaine,* Jas Hillier, D'Aubans & Wardes, Mdlle. Donti, Madame Colonna* (née Miss Newham) & Troupe. Le Petite Sylvia (the Baby Paganini). Geo Fredericks & Carry Julian.* Fred French* . . . Marvels of Peru.

25 Sat   W.Hart, late Property-Man of Britannia Theatre, died. 1st night of *Wreck of Golden Mary* (with entire new scenery). Mrs S.Lane re-appeared after 11 days' absence (ill of quinsy). Alfred Davis & son Exeter behind Scenes of Britannia Theatre.

27 Mon   *Wreck of Golden Mary* (1st week with new scenery). *Pantomime* (1st night as Last Piece). Miss J.Coveney absent; her part, in 1st Piece, played by Miss J.Rogers;* J.Parry absent, subpoena'd to Winchester, his part in 1st piece played by Mr G.Lewis; in Pantomime by Mr T.Hyde.* House bad at first piece but capital for Pantomime.

28 Tues   James Anderson behind scenes of Britannia Theatre tonight – had no opportunity of speaking to him – saw him at a distance only – His hair white; moustaches (which, it is said, he dyes) jet black . . .[2]

*Mr and Mrs Askew, of Victoria Park Farm, were friends of the Wilton family.

*Annie Tremaine was an actress and vocalist. Madame Colonna and her troupe of can-can dancers were fast gaining notoriety. Later in the year they appeared in *The Three Masked Men* at the Britannia Theatre. George Fredericks and Carry Julian were popular duettists of the period. Fred French was a comic singer.

*Jenny Rogers, a daughter of Johnathan Rogers, the theatre's trombonist, was engaged as a ballet girl. T.Hyde had recently been engaged as a supporting actor.

MAR 2 Thurs Jemmy Howard* died (comedian), many years of the Victoria Theatre. Died almost suddenly. Poor little Jemmy! and his 1st wife died suddenly too!

4 Sat Subscription to bury W.Hart (late 1st Property-man, Britannia Theatre) *230*. Misses Pearson, Beaver & Claremont, 3 Ballet Girls, received a week's notice of Discharge.

6 Mon *Wreck of Golden Mary*, revived last Monday, with entire new Scenery (and a dead failure) all last week. Pantomime (11th & Last Week) . . . Jane Coveney, absent from illness all last week, returned tonight to play her part in the 1st Piece – still very ill.

7 Tues Jane Coveney very ill still; worse tonight – fainting & in fits behind the Scenes. Great confusion on the stage in consequence of her not being able to go on – carried by carpenters down into her dressing-room – there lying on the floor in convulsions & being at last obliged to be taken home in a cab.

8 Wed Benefit of D.Jacobs & T.Fuller. *Kenilworth*. Entertainment (Drawing Room) by A.Forrest & Sons. Opening of Pantomime, *Polly Put the Kettle on*. Highland Fling by Miss R.Nathan. Pas de Deux, Mr A.Carena & Miss E.Parry. *Six Degrees of Crime*. Great House in spite of Rain falling about 6 P.M. Guessed at *£85*. Mr Jacobs says *£95* odd (Thursday). Tickets *£45* odd.

9 Thurs Answered note from Mr W.B.Donne, Examiner of Plays, assuring him there is nothing whatever objectionable in the songs of our new Burlesque (*King Lear* by Mr E.Elton) to be produced next Monday Week; no allusions to politics or the current topics of the day[3].

10 Fri Told *au secret* by John Martin that the yacht *Wanderer** has been sold – a few nights since. Two sailors tonight, the mate of the yacht & one of the crew, came to fetch some paper connected with the transaction.

11 Sat Last Night of the Pantomime of *Polly Put the Kettle On*, after an eleven weeks' run. Excellent House before the Comic Scenes commenced, but shockingly bad when Curtain rose for 1st Piece.

13 Mon *Kenilworth*. *Forger & his Victim*. *Wreck of Golden Mary*. House not *very* bad.

15 Wed Benefit of 'Sons of Britannia'. Decent House.

17 Fri 2 Seafaring men (yachtsmen looking) brought on stage tonight between pieces by Mr Borrow to enquire about spars of the *Wanderer* (yacht) recently sold, and John Martin dit (au secret) that the '*brougham* is bought'.

20 Mon *Kynge Lear* (new burlesque, 1st night, by E.Elton). *Kenilworth*. *Wreck of Golden Mary*.

21 Tues Very bad house.

---

*Jemmy Howard** had achieved a reputation as a comic performer in the London minor theatres and the provinces. He and his wife had been engaged at the City of London Theatre in 1841, when Wilton may also have been there.

*The Wanderer** was owned by Samuel Lane.

23 Thurs	Very bad house – very bad indeed.

25 Sat	Beautiful, fine day – very bad 'House' at Britannia tonight . . . Subscription for Little Dolphin* at the Theatre tonight.

*27 Mon	Jessie, the Mormon's Daughter.* Burlesque, *Kynge Lear* (written by Mr Elton). *String of Pearls.*

29 Wed	Mr Bigwood's Benefit. *Daughter of Night.* Burlesque, *Kynge Lear.* *Unlucky Bob* (written by C.Pitt for the occasion). House not so good as expected; the half-price piece proving the greatest attraction.

31 Fri	Harriet, Jessie & Fred to Britannia to see Burlesque – laughed excessively at Milton* as the Physician.

*APRIL 3 Mon	Daughter of Night.* Burlesque of *Kynge Lear.* Price Christy Minstrels.

7 Fri	(Good Friday) Concert of Sacred Music at Britannia under management of Mr Jennings. House not half full . . . Rose & Fred Dewar here after concert at Standard Theatre – Standard 'House' not having been great.

*10 Mon	Truth or The Spells of Love* (Oriental Spectacle written by W.H.Pitt) 1st night. *Don Juan.*

11 Tues	Petition sent in from J.Carter* for a Subscription to bury his Daughter.

12 Wed	Young, the copyist, called – hard up. Just come from the country, wanted 'trifle to get a bed for the night' – gave him a shilling.

13 Thurs	A man called himself 'Parenicon', 'the celebrated Harlequin, upwards of 70 years of age', sent into the Britannia Theatre a pencilled note asking a subscription – & though told we had two subscriptions then getting up in the Theatre from persons formerly members of the establishment & consequently having a claim on us, so that it was not in our power to assist him, got behind the Scenes & came into the Prompt Entrance – found him an accomplished beggar & having a powerful remembrance of Mr Prynne, was firm & got rid of him, tho' with great difficulty.

15 Sat	Wrote Week's Notice to Mr J.Gooderham, Scene Painter, by Desire of Mrs Lane. Changed Last Piece to *Robinson Crusoe.* Subscription in Theatre for John Carter, formerly Super & afterwards Door-keeper there. Gathered from performers *1 1 2 0.*

*17 Mon	Truth, or, The Spells of Love* (2nd W.) Price's Christy Minstrels. *Robinson Crusoe.*

22 Sat	Gave a Week's written Notice to Robert Rowe (Master Carpenter of

---

*Little Dolphin was John Dolphin, who played Clown in the Marylebone Theatre's pantomimes. He had been resident in Hoxton in the early 1860s.

*Milton was a Britannia Super from 1860–1874, often billed in small roles.

*J.Carter was a theatre check-taker.

the Britannia). Last Night of Mr J.Gooderham, Scene Painter of the Britannia.

23 Sun   *Sunday Times* of today contains Charles Mathews's speech (Farewell to Australia) – sent to me by George & by me forwarded to Mr Crane (one of the *Sunday Times'* Theatrical Reporters).

24 Mon   *Truth, or, The Spells of Love* (3rd week). C.Woodman. Leggett & Allen (comic singers).* Baptiste Delaine Japanese Juggler (or Chinese Illusionist). *Joan of Arc* (Joan, 1st time, Miss M.Bellair). Shy House. Gave Robert Rowe a Week's Notice by order of Mrs S.Lane.

29 Sat   Last Night of Robert Rowe master carpenter at the Britannia. Subscription for Mr E.Harding, late an actor in the Britannia Theatre.

MAY 1 Mon   *Heart of a Brother*, Melodrama in 2 Acts by C.Pitt (1st week). Messrs Leggett & Allen (comic singers). Mr C.Woodman (Double-voiced Singer & Instrumentalist) & Baptiste Delaine (alias Watkins – Japanese Juggler) – *Truth or, The Spells of Love*.

5 Fri   Mr Bolton, new stage carpenter, arrived to take place of Robert Rowe.

6 Sat   Mr G.Lewis (comedian) received a fortnight's notice – not from the stage manager – who knew nothing about it – till told at night by other parties.

8 Mon   *Forlorn Hope*, new drama by Hazlewood, 1st week. Extras as last week. Mr W.T.Critchfield* in addition, and Duett by Mr E.Elton & Miss J. Summers. *Heart of a Brother*.

10 Wed   Wretched Houses at Britannia all this week. Very cold weather, with Northerly winds.

11 Thurs   Still very cold – night & morning. Bad Houses at Britannia all this week.

12 Fri   Miss J.Rogers, actress at Britannia (daughter of Trombone Rogers) received Notice of termination of her engagement.

15 Mon   *Forlorn Hope*. Leggett & Allen (comic singers). C.Woodman (Double-voiced singer). Mr W.T.Critchfield (comic singer) *Mother Brownrigg*.

17 Wed   Bad Business all this week at Britannia. Wind E. & bitter cold at night.

19 Fri   Went to see Mr Morris Abrahams at the East London Theatre by desire of Mr Borrow, he (Mr M.A.) having written to say we were infringing his right by calling our piece of *Mary Clifford, Mother Brownrigg*. Showed him bills to prove that we had used the latter as a 2nd title for many years (perhaps 24 years). He said he was not aware of the latter fact, but his piece, written by F.Marchant, was licensed, & the title *registered*, & said he would be satisfied & feel obliged if we would omit the name of *Mother Brownrigg* from our title in future as it injured him & did no good to us.

*Leggett and Allen, 'Anglo-American Comic Duettists', performed a burlesque 'Driven from Home'.
*W.T.Critchfield was a comedian and comic singer, giving impersonations.

20 Sat Better 'house' at Britannia tonight – Had to play my old part in *Mary Clifford*, in consequence of Mr G.Lewis having left last night. Last Night of Leggett & Allen & C.Woodman. Gave a week's notice to Mr W.T.Critchfield, the most disagreeable part of my office as Stage Manager.

22 Mon   Lady Anne's Well, revived. Mr G.Harding, formerly low comedian of this Theatre, – now Comic Vocalist – & Don Espiro 'Female Impersonator'(!) singing a speaking Duett. *Forlorn Hope* (1st time as a Last Piece).

23 Tues Wretched bad 'House' at the Britannia. Fine, hot day – Wind S. by E.

24 Wed DERBY DAY. Hot, fine day – Wind, S. – Wretched House at Britannia – First Piece changed to *Othello*.
△L.I.E. Rehearsal of 2 last acts of *Happiness at Home*, new Piece for next Monday, over at (sic) – not out of Prompt Entrance till 35 minutes after.

26 Fri Mr E.Siddons's* last at the Britannia.

27 Sat C.Pitt played Mr E.Siddons's part in *The Forlorn Hope*.

29 Mon   Happiness at Home (1st time). Young America & La Patrie (juvenile velocipedists). E.Lauri & B.McCormack's Ballet Troupe* in their sensational Ballet *Ko Ko Ki Ki Oh Ki Key*. *3 Fingered Jack* (condensed into one act) . . Immense House at the Britannia.

30 Tues To the *Oxford* to see Mr Robert Syers (the Proprietor) by Desire of Mr Borrow; & to appeal to him respecting the *Writs* received, summoning Mr S.Lane to cause an *Appearance* to be put in for him in the Court of Queen's Bench, within 8 days. Assured him that Mr S.Lane had never been a party to the recent prosecutions of Mr R.Syers for acting Theatrical Plays at the Oxford without a License & said Mr Lane therefore hoped the action would not be proceeded with. Mr R.S. said he would not *then* make a promise as to who he would proceed against, or who not, but he would first consult his lawyer[4].

JUNE 3 Sat Miss M.Henderson told me that on her journey today, up from Stratford with her husband,* *Hail* fell on the gig! – Bitter cold at midnight – glad to cower over the fire for a long time on getting home after the Performances. Mr Morris Abrahams called respecting the Actions threatened by Mr Robert Syers . . . to ask if Mr S.Lane would agree to join the other Defendants in conjointly sharing the expences of the one proceeded against.

5 Mon   Happiness at Home. Young America & La Patrie – (infantine velocipedists – children of the *ci-devant* Mrs Shapcott, mother of the Infant Drummer Boy); E.Lauri & B.McCormack's Ballet called *Ki-Ki-Ko-Ko-Oh-Ki-Key*. *Ride to York* (J.Harwood as Dick Turpin) – Same cold, bright weather.

6 Tues Wretched Business at Britannia all this week till Saturday night.

*Ernest Siddons had joined the company as an actor in October 1870.
*E.Lauri and B.McCormack's Troupe was a knockabout acrobatic company.
*Miss Henderson's husband was a Mr Aubrey.

7 Wed   Mr F.Charlton's Benefit. *Macbeth* (all 5 acts) Extras as rest of week, and *Esmeralda* (called *Notre Dame*). Very good House. Weather cool & fine. Receipts *£64* odd.

10 Sat   Immense House at Britannia – like a Boxing Night.

11 Sun   Mr & Mrs Buchanan (née Sally Vivash) here to tea; recommended me to take *Octoroon* for Benefit.

12 Mon   Happiness at Home. Chantrell's Troupe of Acrobats with the Wondrous Karl. E.Lauri & B.McCormack. Ballet of *Ki Ki, Ko Ko, Oh, Ki Key. Eliza Fenning*.

14 Wed   Benefit of Miss J.Summers. The *Omadhaun*, 3 act piece (called in the bills *The Half-witted*). The 'Chantrell' Acrobats; E.Lauri & B.McCormack's Ballet *Ki Ki. The Female Detective*. Shy House.

19 Mon   The Bitter Reckoning (1st time). Chantrell's Family (acrobats) with Wondrous Karl. Mr & Miss D'Auban (comic vocalists). Young America & La Patrie (the Lilliputian Velocipedists) recovered from illness (measles). *Happiness at Home*.

21 Wed   Benefit of Mr J.Reynolds. *Richard 3rd* (Richard, 1st time, Mr J.Reynolds). Extras as rest of week. *Merchant & Mendicant*. Weather rainy & favourable. House said to be £65 . . . Sir Roger Tichborne, Bart. Wrote to Claimant asking his Name & Patronage to my Benefit (next July 5th) & sent him 2 newspapers – one *Bathurst Times*.

26 Mon   The 3 Masked Men (1st night). Mme. Colonna & Troupe. Extras same as last week. *Bitter Reckoning* (2nd Week). House shy at first, but pulled up . . . To W.H.Pitt's, 3 Union Place, Lambeth Rd, to learn address of Mr Walter Edwin owner of the horse *Gipsy*.

27 Tues   Went in search of Mr Edwin, equestrian, to engage his mare, *Gipsy*, for Miss M.Henderson to play *Mazeppa* with, for my own Benefit, next Wednesday. Found, after a long search at the West End of the town, that his name was Brown & that he was to be found at his father's Livery Stables, Cavendish St., Portland Square. Agreed to give him *£3.3.0* for the use of the Horse for the one night.

28 Wed   Mr J.Parry's Benefit. *Fall of the Leaf*. Extras same as rest of week (Peterson with his dogs instead of Young America and La Patrie, coming as substitutes tonight & last night). *The Three Thieves of Bucklesbury*. House shy at first – pulled up at Half-Price – Day fine – overcast in Evening – Cold N.W. wind at Midnight.

JULY 3 Mon   Last Night & Last Morning. Mme. Colonna (late Miss Newham) & Troupe. Young America & La Patrie (Velocipedists), two very handsome children. Harvey & Connolly, Eccentric Duettists. Mr & Mrs D'Auban. *The Three Masked Men*.

5 Wed   Own Benefit. *Mazeppa*, Miss M.Henderson as Mazeppa, Mr Edwin's Horse, *Gipsy*, for which I have agreed to pay £3.3.0. Extras as on Monday.

Octoroon (1st time at this Theatre). Weather very favourable i.e. rainy for some days past, & cool. Thunder-storm today & Hail as big as peas, – cleared up in afternoon. Cash *£50.13.3.* Tickets *£3.15.0.* Total *£52.8.3.* (sic). Expences *£14.8.11.* (Pd for Horse *£3.3.0* included in *14.8.11*).

10 Mon   Victim of Falsehood (1st time for many years). Mme. Colonna & Troupe (Cancan Dancers). F.Foster (Comic Singer 'Girl of the Period'). Mr & Miss D'Auban (Comic Duettists). Messrs Harvey & Connolly (comic Duettists). *Last Night & Last Morning* . . . To Newspaper Offices with Jacobs to rectify error in Advertisements announcing Double headed Nightingale* for this evening instead of next Monday and to Standard Theatre tonight to explain to J.Douglas – found Douglas senr gone to Margate, so explained to his son.

12 Wed   Rain all Monday night & then Tuesday. Miss M.Henderson's Benefit. *Hamlet* (Hamlet, Miss M.H.) Extras as rest of week. *Black Eyed Susan* (William, Miss M.H). A capital House – Immense Pit & Gallery – filling not only the Audience part of the house, but the passages as well – to the astonishment of all the actors & the management – who had very gloomy forebodings of the prospect for some days previous.

10 Mon   Victim of Falsehood. F.Foster, comic singer, called 'The Girl of the Period'. The Two Headed Nightingale (a monstrosity with 2 heads & 4 legs, with the faces of negresses, brown, not black, about 15 yrs of age). Captain Bates & Miss Anna Swan (American Giant & Giantess). *Black Eyed Susan* (Admiral, Mr J.Reynolds; William, Miss M.Bellair; Susan, Miss M.Henderson). No Admission under sixpence. House far from great.

19 Wed   W.H.Pitt's Benefit. *Hidden Crime* (new Piece by Cecil Pitt). *The Borderer's Son* (new Piece by Alfred Coates).* *Famished City* (Cecil Pitt's condensation of *Surrender of Calais*). The 2 Headed nightingale, Giant & Giantess. Immense House, after a fine, hot & bright Saturday, Sunday & Monday. *£88 odd.*

Mem.   Weather remarkably favourable this year for all the Benefits except Miss J.Summers's.

22 Sat   Tremendous House at the Britannia. George Taylor guessed it at *£120* or *£122.*

24 Mon   Hidden Crime . . . The Two Headed Nightingale. Captain Bates & Anna Swan (American Giant & Giantess) 2nd week. *Victim of Falsehood.* A Great House. Extra Prices taken off. *£20* more than last Monday.

25 Tues   An Immense House with the monstrosities.

26 Wed   Mr R.Leslie's Benefit. *Rory O More.* Extras as rest of week.

---

*'The Two-Headed Nightingale**, Millie Christine, was another distinguished visitor . . . There were two of her – negresses of a considerable intelligence, fair vocalists, joined as the Siamese Twins were. They were brought to this country by the son of a Cotton Planter, on whose estates they were born, and tended with much love and kindness . . .' H.G.Hibbert, *A Playgoer's Memories* (1920), p.212.

*Alfred Coates** was an East End dramatist, several of whose plays were performed at the Britannia; he also wrote for serial publications.

Hornpipe, Mr Leslie. *Carpenter of Rouen.* – Tremendous House. Obliged to stop the last Piece at end of 2nd Act to set for the 2 Headed nightingale & Giant & Giantess; & to resume the drama after they had appeared. This retarded the Performances so much, the stars not arriving for 30 minutes after, that it became necessary to cut the last 2 acts of the *Carpenter of Rouen.* In consequence 3rd Act played only 8 minutes & the 4th act 13 minutes. *£93.15.0* in the house. A night of terrible worry & anxiety.

27 Thurs   Rose Wilton, Fred Dewar & Wm Dewar* at Britannia to see 2 Headed Nightingale – all came on stage, in Prompt Entrance. 'House' not so good as last night by £30.

28 Fri   *A Miracle*
This morning received Note from Rose Wilton, saying she had lost her *brown check shawl*, last night on the stage at Britannia. – Enquired of everybody in Theatre about it tonight – in vain – till spoke to Mrs Borrow & found she had picked it up. (There were hundreds of strangers on the stage at the time!) . . . – 'House' not so good tonight as last night.

29 Sat   House shy at commencement but pulled up as the night proceeded, till just before the 2 Headed Nightingale appeared, when it was crowded to suffocation, though found to be not quite equal to last Saturday or to Wednesday of this week. This looks badly for the Theatre, as it proves the Performances are not attractive, but belies the Prophets, who foretold that the 2 Headed Engagement would be a failure as they had appeared the week before at the Standard.

31 Mon   Wednesday & Saturday. *Hidden Crime.* Mdlle Esther Austin & Ballet Troupe (Cancan Dancers). F.Foster (Comic Singer). Two Headed Nightingale. Capt Bates & Miss Anna Swan (Giant & Giantess); with *Carpenter of Rouen.* – On Tuesday, Thursday & Friday commencing with *The Forest Child*; Esther Austin & Troupe; F.Foster; A new '*Musical Originality*' introducing Emma Kerridge, Nina Anato & Sophie Burlette;* with *The Carpenter of Rouen. £67* in House.

AUG 2 Wed   Upwards of *£70* in the House – this being one of the Two-headed Nightingale's nights whom Alf Beckett* brought his mother on the stage & into the Prompt Entrance to see.

7 Mon   The Lost Wife (1st night). Mr H.White (Nigger).* Professor Holton* (King of the Cannon Ball) – These two all the week. S.Howard & A.Deulin* (Tuesday, Thursday & Friday only) Niggers. *Forest Child* or *Fairlop Oak* (all the week). *2* Headed nightingale. Giant & Giantess (Monday, Wednesday & Saturday only).

---

*William Dewar** was Fred Dewar's uncle.

*Emma Kerridge, Nina Anato, and Sophie Burlette** were performing *Fascination* by Charles Merion.

*Alf Beckett** was a son of the Britannia's printer.

*Harry White** was billed as the 'eccentric nigger'. He was a young performer, who wore huge boots and walked on stilts. **John Holtum** caught a cannon ball fired at him from a gun, a feat first exhibited this year at the Holborn Amphitheatre. He was billed as 'King of the Cannon Ball'. **S.Howard and A.Deulin** performed 'a popular nigger olio'.

9 Wed Attraction of the 2 Headed Nightingale, Giant & Giantess diminishing.

12 Sat 'House' with 2 Headed nightingale, a decided falling off.

13 Sun Home all Day – Plots of *Woman* (Drama by W.H.Pitt, written for Mrs S.Lane's return).

14 Mon Tuesday & Saturday. 2nd & 3rd acts of *Rob Roy*;* H.White (Nigger). – Thursday & Friday beginning with *Maid & Magpie* & H.White. After which, Every Evening, the 1st sc. of Act 4 of *King John*, Hubert Mr J.Manley, Arthur Master John Manley. *Rip Van Winkle*, Rip by Master John Manley . . . Gave Scene Plot of Mrs S.Lane's Piece to Scene Painter.

15 Tues Letter from W.B.Donne (reader of plays) prohibiting the performance of *The Devil's Pool* tomorrow night, because he had been treated with disrespect by the author – the author having written the word '*immediate*' on the *M.S.S.*, when he left it with the fee at the Examiner's office. I myself then wrote a long letter to Mr Donne explaining that the young man was a novice & had '*erred in ignorance – not in cunning*' – & received a very polite answer from Mr Donne, the Examiner, expressing himself satisfied & withdrawing the prohibition. The piece, which was in fact a very common-place piece of melodramatic fustian, was played – & '*went*' immensely.

16 Wed Mr F.Marchant's Benefit. *Devil's Pool* (new Drama by a Mr Pealling.* H.White (Nigger) & 2 or 3 strange names (Concert-Room Singers).* *Forsaken* (written by F.Marchant). The Deposit-money for this Benefit advanced by Mr Tom Pealling, author of the *Devil's Pool*, & who is said to have taken £35 worth of Tickets. Mr F.Marchant, indeed, said at the bar of the Britannia he would *answer* there should be *£35* worth of Tickets in the House, & consequently – notwithstanding the hot weather, everbody expected a tremendous 'house' – The result was but *£40*.

17 Thurs Amelia to Harriet's to tea . . . got caught in Rain at night coming home – brought me a little umbrella to Theatre – caught me in the bar! after Performance over.

19 Sat Last night of 2 Headed Nightingale, Giant & Giantess – Very good House – a rough lot – a hundred or two on the stage. This Party took Half the Receipts. Their Engagement has lasted 5 weeks – The last 3 of which they would only come 3 nights a week – because, as they said, the work was too much for them. Gave a week's Notice to Miss J.Summers & Miss L.Rayner – believing they approach confinements.

21 Mon *Cast on the Mercy of the World* (1st time these 9 years). H.White (Nigger). *Lost Wife*. Miss J.Summers ill (Inflammation of the heart) – husband brought doctor's certificate. Miss L.Rayner to play her part in 1st piece, Miss J.Coveney in the last, *The Lost Wife*. This night our large steam-ship in the last

---

*Rob Roy** was one amongst a spate of revivals during the centenary year of Scott's birth.

*Peally** is also given by Wilton. The strange names probably included **Scheffler**, the **Tyrolean Minstrels** and **Florence Sanger**, a serio-comic vocalist.

scene of *Cast on the Mercy* stuck against a Boat Truck on the stage midway & would not come down[5].

22 Tues This night our large steam-ship broke through the stage, & stuck fast mid-way.

23 Wed This night *our large steam-ship* broke through a plank at the back of the stage and would not come any further – much anger from Mr Borrow – & ultimately an order given to repair & strengthen the stage with new timber. This occurred tomorrow, Thursday, entered here by mistake – The incident mentioned above, as having taken place on Tuesday, occurred tonight – Wednesday & on Tuesday night, the wheels caught in the shaking waters & clogged & wouldn't come down (i.e. to the front of stage).

Mem. 1st Tangled Week. So many changes in the Pieces & Casts of Pieces & Rehearsals that the Performers have been worried out of their lives all this week.

25 Fri Our large steam-ship. Tonight it stuck *at the back of the stage* & would not come forward at all – at least for a very long time. A grand alteration had been made, placing two scenes of the 4th act at the end of the third, so as to leave only the steam-ship scene for the 4th act, that the scene-shifters might be able to lay down sheathing all over the stage under the water-cloth, to strengthen the stage. This was done; but the ship could not be got to mount the sheathing for a long time. At last it was persuaded with the assistance of Herculean exertion & performed the voyage to the front without further mishap.

26 Sat Our large steam-ship (see every night of the week for its doings). Tonight broke through the Vampire Trap!

27 Sun At 10 o'clock tonight, Miss L.Rayner sent 3 parts, saying too ill to play tomorrow evening.

28 Mon Cast on the Mercy. H.White (Nigger). *Romantic Tale* (a Piece of Absurdity) to introduce Mr J.A.Cave* (Manager of Victoria Theatre) & Miss Bella Moore.* Concluding with *Ding Dong Will.* (This announced for all the week, Tuesday excepted, which see). *The Romantic Tale* changed to *Mayor of Garret* – neither Miss Bella Moore nor Mr Cave appearing, – the former sending word late, during rehearsal, that she could not play because her brother had died & Mr Cave declining to play without her; sent on W.H.Pitt to make an apology for the change which the audience took very quietly.

29 Tues Benefit of R.Bell. *Happy Jack*, Grand Scena from *Lucia di Lammermoor* (by Mr *(sic) & Mdlle Rheinstein – This lady did not appear; consequently the scena was not done). *Ellen Harwood.* Miss J.Rogers, 1st night of re-engagement. House shy, very shy, at beginning, pulled up at Half Price. Telegram received from Mrs Lane saying Mr Cave must be allowed to play.

*J.A.Cave, a member of the Britannia's original company, had been manager of the Marylebone Theatre from 1858–68 and of the 'Vic' from 1867–71. He performed in a Lyrical Romance, *The Burgomaster's Daughter*, in which he played the Burgomaster and **Bella Moore** of the Adelphi played Ruddy Cheek.

*Mdlle. Rheinstein, billed as Lucia, was to have been partnered by **Mr C.Selwyn** as Edgardo.

30 Wed   In consequence of the Telegram received from Mrs Lane yesterday evening, Mr Cave played tonight in *The Burgomaster's Daughter*, Miss Jenny Rogers (daughter of Rogers, the Trombone player, in Britannia Orchestra) playing the part Miss Bella Moore was to have appeared in on Monday night. – And, though the part (a long one) was only given to her last night, she was wonderfully perfect.

Mem.   *2nd Tangled Week.* 'Confusion worse confounded!' An awful week of worry – partly owing to Miss J.Summers & Miss L.Rayner leaving the Theatre (on a/c of expected illness) & no one being engaged in their places; partly to Miss Bella Moore refusing to play because her brother (6 years of age) had died.

31 Thurs   During all the time I have been at the Britannia Theatre, never knew so worrying a week's business. (See however next Sunday, Monday & Tuesday).

SEPT 2 Sat   A Report that Walter Montgomery* blew his brains out last night. After the Performance tonight the Trapeze & Netting were fixed for Lu Lu* & she went up & examined it, tried the ropes & the fall from the Spring Board into the Netting, staying up about half an hour, or 3 quarters, but did nothing more. Her father said she had a weakness in the knees & he 'didn't know what the *hell* to do' – adding that she had been obliged to leave the *Amphitheatre, Holborn* for a fortnight's rest, a little while ago.

3 Sun   Went to theatre at 2 p.m. to see machinery tried for *Lu Lu* – learnt from her father that she was suffering from weakness in the knees and could not perform tomorrow . . . At 10 p.m. met Lu-Lu's father in Mr Borrow's room & drew out a bill to be printed and published tomorrow morning, announcing Lu Lu's inability to perform tomorrow, in consequence of having '*sprained her wrist.*'

4 Mon   *Dying Flower* (formerly the *Farm Servant* – W.Rogers's writing). W.J.Collins, the 'Black Storm', his 1st appearance. *Cast on the Mercy.* Lu Lu was to have appeared, but see yesterday . . . House crowded, & – 'spite' of the bills, hurriedly came & went away again on learning that Lu Lu could not perform. Much worry & anxiety for hours – neither Lu Lu nor 'Black Storm' arriving. At length the former (sic) came & was sent – keeping the stage for half an hour – still no Lu Lu, & the last piece began. Then a loud call for *Lu Lu* & she was promised the instant she came. The piece was then allowed, with some murmurs, to proceed. At last Lu Lu & her father did come, – I announced them, the Piece was stopped – & they went on – the father introduced *Lu Lu*, spoke a few words of apology, promised her for next Monday, & bowed himself & daughter off the stage. The Audience then allowed the piece to proceed.

---

*Walter Montgomery was a tragedian, whose notable roles included Hamlet. He had recently experienced managerial problems and had married only a few days before his suicide. Lu Lu was actually a boy, adopted by his manager Farini, who passed as a girl for many years. He made his debut in London this year at the Cremorne Gardens and the Holborn Amphitheatre with a leap from the stage to a trapeze bar 25 feet above, which was achieved with the aid of a concealed spring.

5 Tues *Lu Lu* did not perform, but appeared again with her father on the stage & apologised.

6 Wed The father of *Lu Lu* came to the Theatre tonight & said his daughter, he had no doubt, would be all right by Monday next. She had had a Mustard Plaster on her knee & the improvement was magical – she had had two or three hours practice – & had done her triple somersault &c. Agreed to leave the *decision* till tomorrow night, & to keep back the Advertisements till Friday morning. He to come again tomorrow night & say how she is then.

Mem. Gave out Scene Plot of Pantomime Opening (last Saturday).

7 Thurs Went to LuLu's lodgings, 2 Vernon Place, Bloomsbury, by desire of Mr Borrow & agreed with her father that she should come to the Theatre at night & go through her Feats, that we might venture to issue bills & advertisements of her appearance next Monday. She came accordingly & dressed, & after the Performances were over tried some of them, but not all – the ropes having relaxed in some places & tightened in others, & desired to have more light at the back of her Trapeze. – Home at 12.30 midnight.

8 Fri Gave Property Plot of Pantomime (last night) to J.Short,* for Mr Johnson* who was not in Property Room. Enquired tonight and found Mr Johnson had received it. (Scene Plot out last Saturday). Also gave the Lithographer, last night, the particulars for 4 Tableaux in *Cast Aside*, the Lithographer not having come before. On this occasion he promised to let us see a sketch of the Tableaux on Saturday night. This he agreed to with reluctance. NB. Had given the description on Thursday week last to Mr Charles.*

9 Sat Lu Lu practising today & yesterday & will do so tomorrow – her weakness in the knees much better.

10 Sun Engaged all day in finishing Super Plot & rough copy of bill of 'Opening of Pantomime!'

11 Mon *Dying Flower*. Troop of Vaulters (old Delavanti's) called in the bills, 'The Great Olympian Troop of Vaulters!' W.J.Collins, the 'Black Storm' (Nigger). Lu Lu. *Cast on the Mercy of the World*. Not a great 'House'.

15 Fri Annual Inspection of Theatre by Mr W.B.Donne (Examiner of Plays) & the Architect Mr_____ accompanied by a Major _____ (names unknown). Came ¾ an hour before their appointment – expressed themselves well satisfied.

16 Sat A tremendous 'House' – George Taylor says it was *£110*.

18 Mon *Snow Drift, or + on the Boot*. Musical Murray Family.* Lu Lu. Collins, the 'Black Storm' (his last week). *False Mother*. Received 2 Comic Scenes (Toy Shop &c & 'Turkish Baths') from Mr Borrow. A great 'House' again.

---

*J.Johnson** had been Property Man since 1870. **Joe Short** was his assistant. **W.Charles** had been a scenic artist at the theatre since 1870.

*The Musical Murray Family** were singing trios, duets, glees and ballads.

19 Tues   Sent 3 Comic Scenes (lent by Mr Borrow) to Alfred Davis (Those we played in Pant. last Xmas).

21 Thurs   A Subscription in the Britannia Theatre solicited by & for Mrs Atkinson this evening through the mediation of Mrs Borrow who put Mrs S.Lane's name down for _____ *5.0*.

23 Sat   Another immense 'house' at the Britannia drawn by Lu Lu. Gave out Propy Plot of 2 Comic Scenes & Wardrobe Plot . . . Gathered a Subscription for Mrs Atkinson in the Theatre _____ *1.15.6*.

25 Mon   Performances same as last week – (except *no Collins*). A capital 'house' in spite of rain.

27 Wed   Benefit of Messrs Summers & Light. *Winter's Tale* (1st time ever performed in this Theatre). Musical Murray Family. Mr _____ 's (sic)* Performing Dogs. *Ambrose Gwinnett*. (No Lu Lu tonight) but Great House (said to be *£94*) in spite of Heavy Rain nearly all day. △L.I.E. at Rehearsal from ½ p.11. when *Cast Aside* ended till ¼ past one at least (one hour & three quarters).

29 Fri   Went to *Lord Chamberlain's Office* to get next year's license for the Britannia Theatre with Mr Beckett & Mr Boyce as Securities. Received it under promise that Mr Lane should sign and send it back tomorrow or next day (same as last year). Paid Fees at Lord Chambn's *4.14.0*.

Mem.   Expenses incurred in getting License. Fees *£4.14.0*. Sherry – 3 Glasses at bottom of Haymarket 1/0. Dinner at Simpson's *£1.6.0* (including Port & Sherry & Ale. 2 dishes of mock Turtle Soup, 1 of Oxtail Soup. Fish, 2 Dishes of stewed eels & 1 fried sole. Roast Goose & 2 Partridges.) Total *£1.6.0*. Waiter 6d. W.Borrow (Cab-Driver) 2/0 to get his dinner. Coffee & Cigars in Swan 2/6. Total *£1.12.0* and lost 1/0 which I can't a/c for.

30 Sat   Great House again tonight.

OCT 2 Mon   *Avarice*. Lu Lu. Musical Murray Family. *Ivanhoe. Monster of the Deep* (Italian Pantomime) by W.Rowella's Ballet.* Great House . . . Leslie ill – did not play tonight. (Mr T.Hyde doubled Prince John with the Grand Master).*

4 Wed   W.Crauford's Benefit. Mrs S.Lane's 1st appearance for the Season. *Cast Aside, or, Loving Not Wisely But Too Well* (1st time). Lu Lu. Musical Murray Family. *Monster of the Deep*, (Ballet by W.Rowella's 'Star' Ballet Troupe). The Delevantis (Acrobats). Young Tom Sayers (comic singer, & son of the late Pugilist). *Box & Cox. Robert Le Grange*. Receipts said to be *£105*; Fine Day.

7 Sat   Another capital House at Britannia. Miss Henderson's last night.

---

*Professor Etherton's** Performing Dogs are billed for that night.

W.Rowella had previously been Clown at the Grecian Theatre. **Prince John** and the **Grand Master** are roles in *Ivanhoe*.

9 Mon   Cast Aside (Mrs S.Lane). Lu Lu. A.Walker (Comic Vocalist).* *Gondolier's Daughter* (Ballet by W.Rowella's Ballet Troupe). *Avarice.*

10 Tues   Last night Mr W.ROWELLA said that he considered that the Week's Notice of the termination of his Engagement next Saturday, given to him last Wednesday Evening by me, was not valid, as it was only *verbal* & he having a written Engagement was entitled to a written Notice, & would expect either another week's engagement or another week's salary with a written notice. Went to G.Lewis, Ely Place, Holborn, this day, Tuesday, & asked his opinion, which was that he did not think Rowella could claim it, but would look into it & send us word tomorrow.

Tuesday night   A letter from Lewis & Lewis, solicitors, with reference to the 'Rowella' business . . . as follows . . . Dear Sir, If the contract does not say, the notice is to be in writing, a verbal Notice is sufficient . . .

11 Wed   Benefit of 'Loyal United Friends'. Performances same as rest of week, except the last Piece changed to *Man of Red Mansion*, & on account of length of Performance, the Rowellas doing only a dance instead of a Ballet. Enormous House.

13 Fri   Gave W.Rowella a week's written Notice.

16 Mon   Cast Aside (Mrs S.Lane) 2nd Week. A.Walker (comic vocalist). Rowella's Ballet Troupe in the Ballet of the *Gondolier's Daughter* after the farce of *The Siamese Twins*. Lu Lu.

18 Wed   Benefit of the 'Hand in Hand' Society. Pieces not altered. House fair – neither good nor bad.

19 Thurs   Benefit of Mr Brown (Ex-Cat's-meat-man) of Whitechapel & Beer-shop Keeper. Very good House – Many (very many) of the Box Tickets 5/0 each. No change of pieces. All the scum of Whitechapel on the stage to see Lu-Lu.

23 Mon   Cast Aside. Lu Lu (last week but one). Mr Walker (comic singer). *Lady Audley's Secret* (1st Appearance of Mr W.Bailey as George Tallboys). Fine day, but shy house comparatively. Geo. Taylor ill, not at Theatre tonight . . . Mr Bigwood told me that Leslie had his discharge & was going to leave the Theatre next Saturday, adding that both Leslie & Mrs S.Lane had told him so.

24 Tues   Shy 'House' tonight – no audience on stage.

25 Wed   Benefit of a Society – very good House.

28 Sat   Gave Mr W.Bailey, our newly engaged Actor for the Walking Gentlemen, a week's notice . . . Miss M.A.Bellair came into Prompt Entrance tonight & told us that Mr R.Leslie had given in his Notice today to leave the Theatre. Mr C.Pitt had also just previously told me, Leslie had told *him* he was going to leave – and Mr Bigwood told me the same a week ago! that both

*Alf Walker caused amusement with his song 'Medicine Jack'.

Leslie & Mrs S.Lane had told him. Miss Pickerdite, Daughter of a Glass-blower somewhere in the City Road, la jeune demoiselle á cause de qui, on dit que M.R.Leslie vient de quitter Le Théatre Britannia.

30 Mon Maid & Magpie. Lu Lu. A.Walker (comic vocalist). *Cast Aside* . . . (& on Saturday *Cast Aside* as a first piece, concluding with *Guy Fawkes & Fireworks*). Mrs S.Lane gave me 2 Photos of herself – one to send to Lizzie – one to keep for myself. One of them contained also a likeness of little Hope Crauford (Mrs S.Lane's niece).

NOV 1 Wed Miss M.Bellair's Benefit. *Lady of Lyons* (Pauline, Miss M.Bellair). Lu Lu. A.Walker. *Corsican Brothers* (The Brothers – Miss M.Bellair) – House shy at first, but pulled up at half-price. Bets offered & taken that it would reach *£60*. – Miss M.Bellair says *£65*.

4 Sat Immense House – noisy as usual on Holiday nights.

6 Mon Monday, Tuesday, Friday & Saturday. *Maid & Magpie*. Lu Lu, Monday, Tuesday & Thursday (Her last 3 nights). Tuesday & Friday concluding with *Cast Aside*. Monday & Saturday, as a 2nd Piece, the 5th Act of *Richd 3rd*. Concluding on Monday & Saturday with *Guy Fawkes*. A.Walker (comic vocalist). See Wednesday & Thursday.

8 Wed Wade & Perry's Benefit. *Woman*, Mrs S.Lane (1st time). Several Brass Bands &c. *Oliver Twist*. House shy at first, but pulled up afterwards.

9 Thurs LU-LU's Benefit & Last Night. *Mutiny at the Nore*. Lots of Music Hall Singers & Acrobats. *Prairie Flower*. House not so good as expected.

10 Fri Wretched House.

11 Sat Last Night of R.Leslie in the Britannia Theatre!

13 Mon Woman, Her Rise or Fall in Life (Mrs S.Lane) produced, 1st time, last Wednesday. Mr Jas Hillier (comic singer). Mr A.Walker, ditto. Mr & Mrs J.F.Bryan. Adair, 'the modern Sampson'.* *Jessie, the Mormon's Daughter* (now called *Brigham Young, or, The Mormons of Salt Lake City*).

15 Wed Benefit of C.Pitt & Leather. *The Red Dwarf* (written by C.Pitt) 1st time. Adair. A.Walker. Mr & Mrs J.F.Bryan. Selection of Scenes from *Pizarro*. *Wild Boys of London*. – Shy House at first – rose afterwards to *£63* odd – but C.Pitt said he had been betting on *£90*. Believe, myself, that the Wood-cut of the Red Dwarf was repulsive. Showers of Rain (short) at intervals during the day.

17 Fri Received Poetical Address for the Festival at Xmas from C.Rice (not available).

20 Mon Woman. Adair (modern Sampson). F.Power (Irish Vocalist).* Mme Lennard Charles (double voiced singer) and J.F. Pastor (Alto Vocalist). *The Bottle*. Shy House.

*Adair was a 'classical athlete'.

*F.Power was also a comedian and vocalist.

22 Wed   Benefit of a Mr J.Blade, recently suffered by a Fire. *Rescue of the Orphans.* Extras as above. Messrs Harman & Elston, niggers* (who did not come, but sent an excuse of 'bad cold'). 3rd act of *Othello. Nat Graves* (Nat Graves, Mr F.Charlton). Bad House.

23 Thurs   Wretched 'House'.

27 Mon   Hamlet (with James Anderson[6]) on Monday & Tuesday. *Lady of Lyons* (with do. Wednesday & Friday) *Othello* (with do.) Thursday & Saturday. Adair (the modern Sampson). Mdlle Lennard (the double-voiced Phenomenon). J.F.Pastor (Alto-Vocalist) all the week, concluding with *Woman* (Mrs S.Lane) all the week.

29 Wed   Benefit of Widow & 6 Children of T.Hughes, a Gas Meter. *Lady of Lyons* with James Anderson. Adair. Military Band (the Gas Meters). *Woman.* Capital House.

DEC 4 Mon   Macbeth (Jas Anderson & Julia Seaman). Adair, the modern 'Sampson'. *Woman,* Mrs S.Lane. 1st night of Julia Seaman as a Star. Very shy house. Hard frost & a very slight attempt at snow . . . Julia Seaman did not arrive in London till 3 p.m. and had no rehearsal.

5 Tues   The Prince of Wales dangerously ill of Typhoid Fever. Bulletins frequently issued.

6 Wed   Hard frost. No Benefit, but 1st Piece altered tonight & Thursday to *Lady of Lyons.* – Wretched Houses, all the week. *Macbeth* every other night but today & tomorrow. *Mem.* Today (or it might be yesterday, or tomorrow) *Huline* the clown showed me his letter of engagement to prove that it entitled him to a fortnight's rehearsal before Xmas – which I told Mrs S.Lane, afterwards, & she admitted, after previously expressing a doubt on the subject. I saw that his terms were £18 per week for the family.

8 Fri   Rumours of the Prince of Wales being given over. Some persons (W.H.Pitt) believing that 'he died at 6 o'clock this evening'. A scene shifter in the Britannia Theatre brought in word that he had seen the Death of the Prince posted up at the Eastern Counties Railway Station. This report afterwards denied.

9 Sat   The Prince of Wales still alive but reported to be 'sinking fast'. About 11 a.m. Mr W.Crauford brought word on to the stage during rehearsal, that it was *all over.* A messenger sent to the Mansion House had just brought word that notice was posted up there that the Prince died at 10 o'clock this morning. At 4 p.m. J.Pitt went to the Mansion House & found that instead of 'Death', the Placard announced 'favourable symptoms'. Much concern in the Theatre & much sorrow among the actors, the sincerity of which need not be doubted – because if the Prince dies they will lose a night's salary, as the Theatre will be shut.

---

*Harman and El(s)ton were billed as having belonged to the original Christy Minstrels.

11 Mon   Leah, the Forsaken, Julia Seaman. Brothers Rizareli (Trapezists).*
Joe Brown* (comic singer). *Woman.*

12 Tues   G.Bigwood drunk at Theatre tonight.

13 Wed   Benefit of a Mr T.George (a decayed Publican). *Leah.* Brothers
Rizareli. Joe Brown (comic singer). Extra entertainments & *Molly Sullivan.*
Not so great a house, by any means, as was expected – the members of the
committee had boasted that thousands of tickets had been sold – actually paid
for.

14 Thurs   Julia Seaman's Benefit. Hamlet (Hamlet, J.Seaman). Joe Brown.
Brothers Rizareli (Trapezists). *Ivanhoe.* House very bad indeed, but with a
Benefit last night & Mrs S.Lane's Benefit coming next Monday, can it be
wondered at? . . . The Prince of Wales still alive! – Dr Wood said in the
Theatre tonight that if the Prince lives till after 3 o'clock tomorrow P.M. he
will recover.

18 Mon   Mrs S.Lane's Benefit and Last Night of the Season. *The Flirt.* Huline
(clown) family. Miss Louie Austin (Vocalist comic). Mdlle Ellena Spinola &
Kate Vaughan* (Dancers). *Festival*, and a new Drama by Hazlewood, called
The Artificial Flower Makers. Not a great House.

19 Tues   Went with Fred to Philarmonic Theatre, Lower Road, Islington.
Saw 4 extraordinary Frenchmen (Dancers) calling themselves '*Clodoches*'* –
never saw any grotesques made up so *outré.*

20 Wed   Home all the Evening, writing Advertisements for next week –
morning rehearsals being so long as to give no chance in the day-time.

21 Thurs   Precious wearisome rehearsals – lasting from ½ p.10 a.m. till 3.30
or 4 p.m. Then detained for an hour after to give & acquire information to &
from employers . . . At night with Fred to the Alhambra.

22 Fri   With Jessie to the Lyceum to see *The Bells* – & *Pickwick* – both
excellently well got up & acted . . . Scene Rehearsal of Pantomime put off till
tomorrow – not ready.

23 Sat   Long, heavy, tiresome rehearsals all this week. Received full week's
salary as did C.Pitt. Night Rehearsal of Scenery, called at 7 p.m., not ready
to begin till *11 p.m.*, & then far from perfect. Many Pieces intended to sink not
being fixed – obliged to be held up by men & worked off at the sides. This being
in the Transformation Scene which alone was shown. No attempt made to
show the Scenery of the Opening, which we must use on Boxing Day without
having seen it. Over at 12.30.

---

*The Brothers Rizareli, billed as from Spain, were early exponents of the flying trapeze act, including
flying from bar to bar blindfolded. Joe Brown was advertised as being from the original Royal Christy
Minstrels at the St. James's Hall.

*Kate Vaughan, who began her career as a dancer at the Grecian Theatre, was to become a popular singer
and dancer and member of the famous 'Gaiety Quartet'.

*The Clodoches, consisting of M.M.Clodoche, Flageolet, Le Comete and La Normandie, had visited
England before with great success. They performed their 'Danse Eccentrique' from Offenbach's opera
bouffe *Genevieve De Brabant.*

26 Tues   BOXING-DAY. New Pantomime. *The Old Man & the Ass or Robin Redbreast & his 11 Hungry Brothers.* Miss Louie Austin & Miss Emily Scott* engaged for the Opening. Mrs S.Lane & Miss J.Summers also in it. Clown. Pant. Har. & Sprite by the Huline Family. Mdlle C.Stephan as Harlequin á la Watteau did not appear. Misses R.Nathan & E.Parry as Columbines & *Artif. Flower Makers.* Celeste Stephan did not appear – Abscess in leg.

27 Wed   Mr S.Lane much worse – not expected to live the night out. Mrs S.Lane did not play in the Pantomime – her part performed by Miss L.Rayner, who had notice to be prepared yesterday morning. A great 'house' again tonight.

Mem.   *Houses* on Boxing Day guessed by G.Taylor at *£100* in the morning & *£180* at night.

28 Thurs   Mr S.Lane died this morning at 7 o'clock in his new House at West Green, Tottenham.

29 Fri   The Theatre, not closed last night, was closed tonight, much against the wishes of Mr & Mrs Borrow, by Order of Mrs S.Lane. Wrote to Mr W.B.Donne to inform him of the death of Mr S.Lane & to ask permission to carry on the Theatre for a few days as at present, till she can, with propriety, apply, in form, for the transfer of the License to her own name . . . To East London Theatre & Pavilion with Jessie.

30 Sat   Received tonight, answer to the above letter as follows: Decr 30th 1871 – Lord Chamberlain's Office, St. James's Palace, S.W. Sir, I enclose, by Mr Ponsonby's desire, a new bond for the Britannia Theatre. Will you be good enough to ask Mrs S.Lane to sign it and witness it yourself. This will save Mrs Lane the trouble of coming to this office – but the Sureties will have to attend here as soon as possible between the hours of 11 and 4. There will have to be 10/0 paid here for the stamp to the bond – but no fees will be charged to Mrs Lane. I beg to express to Mrs Lane my sympathy upon her great loss – and in which the other gentlemen of this office join most sincerely. I am, Sir, yours very faithfully, Fredk H.Jennings. (over) Please let me have the full christian names of Mrs Lane. Fredk Wilton Esq.

1872

JAN 1 Mon   Weather colder. House not so great – doubtless injured by Mr S.Lane's death. Wrote to Mrs S.Lane, The Elms, West Green, Tottenham, suggesting that Mr Beckett should be invited to attend the funeral. Also another letter to W.Green Esq. Head Constable, Tower Hamlets, to ask his assistance to procure the transfer of the License of the Britannia Tavern to Mrs S.Lane's name. Miss Rose Nathan (Columbine) absent from illness.

Tues 2   Answer from Mrs S.Lane. 'Yes – invite Mr Beckett to the Funeral'. Went twice to Central Bank, Shoreditch, to enquire if necessary for Mrs S.L.

---

*Emily Scott had previously performed at the Britannia from 1864–65.

to take any particular steps before appropriating Railway Dividends & Bank of England Dividends now due (about £400) her name being entered with Mr Lane's conjointly as owners. Saw Mr Wilson & Mr Reeve (the latter the Principal) will enquire & give information tomorrow. Ordered Mourning Cards at Mr Beckett's & Placards to post about Theatre announcing that the funeral cortége will start from Britannia Theatre at 11 a.m. for Kensal Green Cemetery . . . Mr Nelson Lee, many years the respected manager of the City & other Theatres died Jany 2nd 1872, buried in Abney Park Cemetery, Friday January 5th.

3 Wed Saw Mr Reeve, Principal at Central Bank, Shoreditch, who said that his opinion was that no forms were necessary . . . especially as she was left sole executrice . . . An alarming rumour in front of the bar at the Britannia tonight, after the performance was over, that Miss Rose Nathan died this afternoon! the rumour brought by the wife of Mr F.Perry the drummer – who says the husband of Miss R.Nathan informed a friend of hers from whom she heard the story.

Mem. In the Bond sent from Lord Chamberlain's office it is stated that Mrs S.Lane is to be bound for £300 & her two Sureties in £50 each.

4 Thurs Mr S.Lane buried this day in Kensal Green Cemetery . . . Scarves & Hatbands given to all the Followers viz. Messrs W.Crauford, W.Robinson, W.Borrow, Robt Borrow, Master Samuel Crauford,* Mr Beckett senr (Printer), Messrs J.Reynolds, G.Bigwood, C.Pitt & self, D.Jacobs (Theatre Messenger), Mr Boyce (Undertaker) & the officiating Clergyman . . . 84 yards of Silk cut up (said Mr Boyce, the undertaker) to make the Scarves & Hatbands . . . The Procession left the Theatre at 11 a.m. or 11.15. Hearse with 6 Horses & 2 Mourning coaches with 4 horses each. Recognised in the Chapel & in the Cemetery, or round the grave, Mr Morris Abrahams, I.Cohen, C.Morton* (actor), R.Bell (actor), J.Parry, F.Charlton, J.Pitt, W.Bailey, Bolton (carpenter), Mrs J.Parry, Mrs Newham, Miss J.Summers, Mr F.Perry, Burford* (& other Musicians), S.May, W.Clarkson, Weston.* A remarkably fine, sun-shiny day, but Rain & Wind at night . . . Read the Will, dated 1860, which left everything to Mrs S.Lane & named her sole Executrix. Afterwards read the list of Mr S.Lane's investments & of the whole of his Property, which amounted to £22,900 besides the Theatre . . . A great concourse of people in Hoxton about the Theatre to see the Procession start, & the pavements on each side lined with spectators, all up Hoxton Street. Number of people in the cemetery about 300 . . . About 25 cabs & Broughams followed the mourning coaches, Jacobs the Theatre Messenger & Bill Inspector, driving Mrs S.Lane's private Brougham . . . Saw in the cemetery, besides those mentioned – Mr Watson, father of Ellen (W.Crauford's 2nd wife). (Heard & believe that H.Pitt & Misses Bellair & Rayner & F.Marchant were there – but did not see them). Saw Mr Faucquez. J.Martin (Gas Engineer of the Theatre). Miss Claremont

---

*Samuel Crauford, son of W.H.Crauford, was later to become Landlord of the Britannia Tavern. Charles Morton had been a leading man at the Marylebone Theatre in the 1860s. C.Burford was Repetiteur in the orchestra. Weston was employed in the theatre wardrobe.

(formerly Ballet lady of the Theatre). Leather (check taker at the Stalls Door). Procession arrived at the cemetery at 1.15 p.m. & on returning reached the Theatre again at 3.40. Miss J.Coveney & Mr E.Elton, 2nd Low Comedian of the Theatre, did not attend the Funeral (said to be the only members of the copy. absent!) . . . Messrs J.Reynolds, G.B.Bigwood, C.Pitt & F.Wilton had each a new suit of mourning – paid for by the management – & were accompanied by Mr C.*Beckett* Senior in a Mourning Coach . . . Theatre closed & no performance tonight.

5 Fri   Miss Rose Nathan, Columbine at the Britannia, Died on Wednesday last – Rheumatism of the Heart – after 4 days' illness. The Doctor's certificate assigns *Rheumatism of the Heart*. She came to the Britannia Theatre last Saturday night with face swollen, but played in the Pantomime.

6 Sat   Went, yesterday, to the *Lord Chamberlain's* with Mr Beckett & Mr Boyce as Sureties, & got the License transferred to Mrs S.Lane – paid 10/0 for stamp – no fees. Went to Simpson's on the way back . . .

7 Sun   Mrs S.Lane & Mrs Borrow both went away to Hastings.

9 Tues   Mrs S.Lane attacked by ulcerated sore Throat!

10 Wed   Went with Mr Borrow to Mr Jas Lewis, the Lawyer, Ely Place, Holborn – took the lease of the Theatre to him to ask advice how to proceed. Mr Lewis asked if we kept any 'combustible matters' such as Gunpowder in the Theatre.

Observed that the Lease was for 46 years to Mrs S.Lane – only. That there was a convenant in the lease (which was made out in the single name of Mr Lane only, not in the joint names of Mr & Mrs Lane) – said *covenant* stipulating that Mr Lane should not assign the Theatre to anybody without the approval of the Lessor – And Mr Lewis thought that considering the money Mr Lane had laid out on the Theatre that clause should never have been inserted.

That it was necessary 1st to have an Appraisement of the Theatre taken including Scenery, Furniture, Plate & everything not standing in the joint names of Mr & Mrs Lane – which the Theatre, Plate &c. does not.

That when Mr Lewis had got the appraisement he could, in one day, establish Mrs S.Lane as sole Executrice & dispose of the Property & that on that occasion he must see her, but she need not come to town before.

That he thought Mr Boyce's charge for appraising (£20) very high, but perhaps he had better be allowed to do it.

That it was necessary to get a *Protection Order* till next Licensing Day for the Public House – he had asked his brother who is Clerk to the Licensing Magistrate.

Mr Lewis remarked that the lease was for 46 years & that it was necessary for Mrs S.Lane to show the Will & Probate at the Bank of England & Offices of Railways where investments were lying.

Mem.   Sat, Jan 6th. Miss Patti Goddard played Mrs S.Lane's part of *Robin* in the Pantomime for the 1st time, being engaged for that purpose. She had, once before, some months ago, sung in the Theatre as a Music Hall singer.

19 Fri Mem.   Mrs S.Lane & Mrs Borrow both still away (down at Hastings) all this week.

20 Sat   Immense House again! another Boxing Night. Business ever since the Pantomime produced much above the average of years . . . Paid Salaries of Extra Singers & Dancers in Pantomime.

22 Mon   Meeting at the Britannia of 'Sick Fund'.

24 Wed   Transformation Scene this year – said universally to be the best (i.e. the most brilliant) ever had at the Britannia – (This painted by Charles – the subject, Sea-Weeds under the sea – prevailing colour, pink).

31 Wed   Mrs Borrow very ill at Hastings with a bad cough. Mrs S.Lane with her (& better).

FEB 2 Fri   Went to Mr Lewis (Ely Place, Holborn), by desire of Mr Borrow, to say; Maynard, the Agent, had sent a note stating that many London Theatres were going to open with a Concert on Ash-Wednesday; & to ask Mr Lewis if he was still of opinion that it would be dangerous for *us* to open. Mr Lewis said, 'yes – our counsel say you must not – you would be liable to a penalty of £500 (five hundred pounds) – Both the Lord Chamberlain's License and a Public House Music License forbid it – and suppose the Lord Chamberlain were to take offence at your infringing the regulations & were to withdraw his license, where would you be then?' He added that he did not believe what Maynard said – that Drury Lane was going to open on Ash Wednesday – unless for an oratorio – or sacred music – which we should not be safe in doing[1].

   Saw also Mr Boyce, Auctioneer, by desire of Mr Borrow.

   Mr Borrow said that not opening on Ash Wednesday with a concert might make a difference of £40 to the Treasury – he sent a message to this effect to Mr J.Lewis the Attorney . . . by me.

   Mr Boyce, speaking of the valuation, necessary to be had – in consequence of Mr S.Lane's death — he (Mr Boyce) should put down the *Rent* of the Theatre at £400 per annum; and the stock of *Theatrical Properties* (including *scenery* & every adjunct necessary for working the stage Performances) at *£1000*. Then he should value the *Rent* of the *Public House* at *£60 a year* and the stock of *Liquors, Wines &c.* at *£280* 'because, don't you see, Mr S.Lane was a very peculiar man – don't you see?' Then he wanted to estimate the fittings for the public – accommodations &c & he wanted to 'see Mrs S.Lane, to have a talk with her about *that*, because Mr S.Lane was a very peculiar man, you see, – for instance there were none of those chandeliers – those Gas Fittings there in *his* time – don't you see, Mr Wilton, don't you see?' (Laughing) 'You let me alone. I know what I'm at'. I told Mr Borrow all this & wrote the figures down for him.

BRITANNIA THEATRE MEMS
Mrs S.Lane's Dress for the Pantomime called *The Old Man & His Ass* (1871) *15 15 0* (May's bill)
6 Fisherwoman's Dresses for comic scenes including legs of Pant. Clown &

Har. for Comic Scenes *14 0 0*

Theatre has held, on several occasions, *4,000 people.*

Britannia Saloon, 1st opened for Theatrical Performances, Easter Monday 1841.
The present Britannia Theatre was opened on the 8th of Novr 1858.
It cost £22,000 (Mr C.Pitt says Mr S.Lane told him so). Mr J.Martin says the Architect told *him* the same & moreover, he (J.Martin) saw the contract – the Gas Fittings were not included in this sum, nor the Chandeliers; but the timber used in constructing the stage & the Flies *was included* – though worked up by the Stage Carpenters – and see *The Builder* of – – –(sic).
The first Britannia Theatre closed with Miss C.Borrow's Benefit, June 23rd 1858 and the new Britannia Theatre . . . opened Novr 8th, 1858.
Britannia Sick Fund Established Septr 24th 1860.
Capacity of the Britannia Theatre
Boxes (Private and others) hold *895*. Pit *2,151*. Gallery *877* Total *3923*.
No stalls.
Ditto of *Standard Theatre*; Boxes *1000*; Pit *1,600*. Gallery *800*. Total *3,400*.
No stalls.
Ditto of *Pavilion Theatre*. Boxes *500*. Stalls *800*. Pit *1,000*. Gallery *1,200*.
Total *3,500*.
Taken from Report of Select Committee, House of Commons June 1866, Blue Book Page 295.
Weekly consumption of Gas about 100,000 feet, according to J.Martin, *Feby 7th 1872.*
Salary of Police Constable *1.12.8* per week, paid to commisioners of Police.

7 Wed   Wrote to Mr W.B.Donne saying Mrs S.Lane wished the Drama of *The Ribbon Men** (as Mr W.B.Donne desired its title should be altered) to be called *The Verdict of the World*, which is the last line of the Piece. (Jacobs to carry the note up to Mr W.B.Donne tomorrow.)

19 Mon   Mr Borrow said, the Management lost £70 one week & £50 another week, last year, by running the pantomime too long.

23 Fri   Accident, about 20 m. before 6 this evening, in Dressing Room of Ladies of Ballet. Annie Pitt (daughter of C.Pitt, Prompter), dressing for a *Folie* in the Pantomime Ballet, & having fixed her jute headdress with hair-pins to her own hair, the jute caught fire & she was much burnt about the face, neck & back, but, fortunately, Miss Neumann (Mrs Manning) had the presence of mind to throw a petticoat over her head, & extinguish the fire.

MAR 8 Fri   Went (by desire of Mrs S.Lane) to see Mr G.W.Harris* at North House, West Square, St George's Road, Southwark, who had written to say he had a 'Great Novelty' he wished to engage for at the Britannia. Saw Mr

---

***The Ribbon Men or the Wearing of the Green**, about a secret society dedicated to assassinate an unjust Irish landlord, was evidently too explicit a title.

***Mr and Mrs Harris** presented an entertainment with small puppets.

Harris & learnt that he & wife were duettists & gave a Drawing-Room Entertainment of Songs & Dialogues involving 25 characters & lasting 20 minutes, for which they asked £6 p.week. Wrote tonight by order of Mr Borrow & engaged them 6 nights, commencing Monday March 18th.

13 Wed One of the Acrobats (Rizarelis) had 2 falls tonight – in the 2nd one, on striking the end of the net, he rebounded & fell on the stage – hurting himself but not seriously. In consequence they did not finish the performance.

19 Tues Benefit of D.Jacobs & T.Fuller. *Idle Apprentice* (F.Marchant's piece – now called *Blueskin*) . . . *Wenloch of Wenloch* (now called *The Phantom of the Black Tower*) – 10 or a dozen Wood cuts issued – 7 or 8 of which depict incidents not in the piece! – Above £90 in the House. Usual charge for the House on Benefit nights £38.0.0. Paid for a Tuesday night by D.Jacobs & T.Fuller £40.0.0.

26 Tues Ely Pryce, Carpenter & Flyman, discharged for drunkeness.

MAY 1 Wed (M.Clevermann,* the Illusionist, with his Mystic Cabinet, a monstrous failure. Mrs S.Lane rang down the curtain in the midst of the performance!)

6 Wed Dispute between Mr J.Rawlinson & Mr W.Putnam (Harpist) of the Minstrels* – the latter asking me to observe that he was ready on the stage with his harp to perform, but was not permitted by the former. Mr J.Rawlinson also asking me to bear witness to the fact, & adding 'Mr Wilton, the Curtain must not rise till that man is cleared off the stage'. Mr Putnam then retired.

10 Fri Mrs S.Lane attacked by Quinsy, barely able, tonight, to go through her part in *The Wife's Evidence* (which Miss J.Summers is to play tomorrow night) . . .

11 Sat Mr J.Reynolds & Mr F.Charlton ivré during last piece (*Captain Firebrand*) & Mr J.Rawlinson, one of the *soi-disant* 'peerless tenors', hissed on the stage for the same offence.

18 Sat Messrs Reynolds, Charlton & Bigwood fined a night's salary each – for being *ivre* last Saturday night . . . Mr Ernest of the Xty Minstrels made a long speech to the audience (it being their last night here) – And after him Mr Sylvester, the *Bones* of the Company, made another speech, both thanking the audience for their kindness during the engagement. Mr Fred Foster, the 'Girl of the Period', did not appear tonight, but he sent a letter complaining of sore throat. Audience did not call for him – No Apology was made.

20 Mon WHITSUN WEEK. *House* not full, but no admission under 6d.

21 Tues A fuller 'House' than last night – Prices being as *usual* (last night no Admission under sixpence 'To prevent crowding at the Entrances!')

*M.Clevermann had taken over the management of the Robert Houdin Theatre in Paris in about 1864.
*The Minstrels were The Prince of Wales's Royal Christy Minstrels.

25 Sat   J.B.Howe behind the Scenes showing an engagement he had made (at Covent Garden) with Boucicault – to play 'leading character parts'.

28 Tues   The two skaters* (males) did not make their appearance at the Theatre tonight, but sent their two 'Ladies', whom we did not allow to 'go on'. The two ladies said the men were both ill – though one of them, the oldest, admitted they had performed at the Alhambra tonight. The audience did not call for them and no apology was made.

JUNE 1 Sat   Met Mrs Smith* (Julia's mother) in Hoxton, who told me R.Leslie to be married today. Mrs S.Lane still absent from the Theatre, her throat said to be worse, with a third Quinsy; her brother W.Borrow also very ill – almost hopelessly.

5 Wed   Robert Bell (actor) came into the Prompt Entrance with his right arm in splints & with a sling to support the arm across his breast, saying that by an accident in falling out of his Gig today when there was no horse in it he had broken his arm between the wrist & the elbow.

6 Thurs   W.Borrow died at 4 A.M. at Mrs S.Lane's house, West Green, Tottenham. Aged 43 . . . Reubin Leslie behind the Scenes! – came into the Prompt Entrance & spoke to me!

8 Sat   *Celeste Stephan*
Mr J.Martin (Gas-man) told Mr C.Pitt & myself this evening in the Prompt Entrance, as a secret, that a day or two before last Xmas, W.Borrow took home to his wife (Mdlle. C.Stephan) some provisions for their Xmas dinner – that the lady said 'no, William, I should like to have a sucking-pig for our Xmas dinner, I have made up my mind to have a sucking-pig' – that Mr Borrow went to Leadenhall Market & bought one – that, on his return home with it, at night, he found that Mdlle. C.Stephan, in the meanwhile, had been to the Treasury of the Theatre, drawn her half salary (i.e. for the rehearsals) and borrowed £8 for her Harlequin's dress – (and had never been seen since!')

10 Mon   A curious incident occurred during the last Piece. G.B.Bigwood (*ivré*) got giddy in a Dance with Miss J.Summers & reeled off the stage into the orchestra!

14 Fri   Mr Vivian* not favourably received.

15 Sat   This night (Saturday) there was some hissing during his songs, & he stopped & addressed the audience, who then applauded. Mr Borrow then sent Mr Jacobs round to desire me to give Mr Vivian a week's notice. I did so; but Mr Vivian replied he was entitled to & should claim a week's notice from next Saturday, as last night & tonight were '*nothing*' – adding that he would speak to Mr Borrow before he left the Theatre tonight.

*The Skaters** were the 'Guido' Troupe of Skaters.

*Mrs Smith** is not identified.

*Mr Vivian's** unfortunate experience here did not deter him from pursuing a theatrical career, and he was still appearing as a comic vocalist at Wilton's in 1876.

28 Fri   Paid M.Jullien* for himself & Mdlle B.Delgrange for 5 nights £5 & released them by their own desire, from their engagement to sing tomorrow night. Mr Borrow had sent round but £4 to pay them, as they had not sung on Monday night last – but they had declined to accept the sum, saying it was no fault of *theirs* that they had not sung on that night, as they were engaged to sing at half past eight, & waited in the Theatre till long after that time, on account of our new piece not being over, when they were obliged to leave to go to another engagement. Mrs S.Lane gave me another sovereign & paid it to them, making the sum £5.0.0.

29 Sat   Went with C.Pitt & J.Martin to Mrs S.Lane's lawyer (Mr Jas Lewis of Ely Place, Holborn) to receive *Subpoena* commanding us to appear in the *Court of Probate* as Witnesses in the case of *Challis v. Mrs S.Lane*, which Mrs S.Lane says is to be tried next week. Mr J.Parry also came in while we were there. Mr Lewis only enquired if we could take oath that we had never seen any symptoms of insanity in Mrs S.Lane & gave us *10/0* each[2].

JULY 1 Mon   Mr Superintendent Mott in the Theatre tonight – promised to appear as witness for Mrs S.Lane in her chancery suit, if she wished it. He had not heard of the action till I mentioned it to him.

3 Wed   Mr W.H.Pitt did not play tonight. His part read by Mr T.Hyde – No apology made. C.Pitt greatly agitated – said his brother was dying & could not go to him, not knowing where he lived.

4 Thurs   Every night this week, after Wednesday, C.Pitt voluntarily made an apology for his brother's absence.

10 Wed   Own Benefit. *Sledge Bells* . . . Mr Borrow received Letter from Messrs Vallance & Vallance (Solicitors to Mr H.L.Bateman, Lessee of Lyceum Theatre) complaining of title of his piece *The Bells* being used in my bill and desiring it might be obliterated. Went to the solicitors & apologised & had 50 slips printed to cover the word '*Bells*' . . . Mr Irving & Mr Grennel,* original actors in *The Bells*, in the Boxes tonight.

11 Thurs   Mrs S.Lane told me that a wet Sunday always adds £10.0.0 to the Receipts on the Wednesday following.

16 Tues   Rehearsal of a new Piece by G.H. MacDermott, called *The Fragment*, a Dramatic version of *The Mystery of Edwin Drood*; lasted 5 *hours*! from ½ *past 10* to ½ *past 3*!!!

23 Tues   Wrote, by desire of Mrs S.Lane (conveyed thro' Mr Borrow) a '*Character*' for Mr B.Bolton, our Master Carpenter, & gave it to him.

29 Mon   Mr Borrow Senr ill (Diarrhoea & Vomiting) kept his bed all day – unable to come down stairs tonight. *Mem.* W.H.Pitt told me that he had received a letter from Mr W.Borrow, telling him that, if he would accept a

---

*Monsieur Jullien and Mdlle B.Delgrange were French Opera Artistes.

*Mr Grennel was probably Herbert Crellin, who had played Christian at the Lyceum. Wilton must have misheard the name. Joseph Reynolds played Mathias in the Britannia version.

certain reduction of salary, his engagement might continue; if not, he must leave on Saturday. He expressed himself much hurt in feeling, but could not accept the reduction & as he must answer Mr Borrow to that effect, he feared the matter might result in his leaving on Saturday.

30 Tues   Received instructions from Mrs S.Lane verbally to give Mr MacDermott on Saturday next a fortnight's Notice & the Ballet a week's Notice . . . Saw Mr Borrow – in bed – his Tongue *fearfully* crusted with white! Mr Crauford telegraphed to Mrs S.Lane at Brighton – Mrs S.Lane & Mrs Borrow came up immediately. Mrs S.L. told by Doctor (her father's doctor) whom she had sent for this afternoon . . . that her father's disorder was *cholera*! (English, I presume).

AUG 3 Sat   Last night of Mr J.Plumpton; the audience *chaffing* & some *hissing* (as they have done several times during his engagement), he would only sing one song tonight.

6 Tues   Mr Borrow still lingering this morning. Mrs S.Lane, during rehearsal, sent a message down requesting that nobody would come up stairs to her on any account. At night Mr Jacobs told me that some time after the message, Mr F.Charlton had 'come up', wanting to borrow money to buy furniture, and some time after Mr Gregory (Mrs S.Lane's cousin, a super) had 'come up' & also wanted to borrow money!

7 Wed   Leaving the Theatre tonight, at midnight, after the Performance, horrified at seeing Mr Borrow's coffin taken from the undertaker's to the Theatre . . . Mr Borrow Senr died of English Cholera, Wednesday morning, 2 A.M., . . . Aged 74, after little more than a week of much suffering.

12 Mon Mem.   Mr Borrow's funeral . . . Hearse with 6 Horses, Two mourning coaches with 4 Horses each, starting from Britannia Theatre at 11.15 a.m. followed by 3 cabs and a wagonette . . . Went in a cab with Messrs Reynolds, Bigwood & C.Pitt, no members of the company having been invited to follow as mourners . . . Paid for cab *10/0* & gave driver *2/0* . . . Could only hear a few words of the Service which was over at 1.45. At end of the Service a very long pause in deep silence after which, first the clerk walked out alone – no *Bearers* having appeared – then, after another long pause, the clergyman walked out alone. Then Mr Robinson* walked out, then Mr Reynolds, – then several mourners & Followers and a general rise with looks ominous of '*something wrong*'; Mr Bigwood & self then rose & followed out & then we learnt that the grave had been made too small!!! One hour elapsed before this was rectified!!! Got home to Hoxton at 4 p.m. Had stopped our cab at a beer house, on returning, about a mile or two from the cemetery, for *refreshment*. The rest of the Party went on to Harry Brunton's Tavern.*

27 Tues   Mr G.H. MacDermott not at the Theatre tonight & Mr Robinson informed me his Salary was £6 per week.

William Robinson, Sarah Lane's brother-in-law, replaced William Borrow as the theatre's acting manager. **Harry Brunton**, a former pugilist, had been Tom Sayers's second in the fight against Heenan.

28 Wed   Mr G.H.MacDermott's Benefit. *A Bright Beam at Last.** . . . Good House, chiefly Brick-makers to see the first piece.

30 Fri   At 4.55 p.m. Mrs C.Reeve called & said her son, Mr C.Reeve,* would be unable to play tonight, in consequence of severe illness (Cramp in the stomach). He was very bad last night. Sent off Jo Pitt to Gt. Ormond Street, W.C., in a cab to bring Mr W.Bailey down to play Mr Reeve's parts – could not find his lodgings. J.Pitt had to go on for the part of 'Roy Lee' in the 1st piece, and Mr E.Newbound* for his part in the last piece. Mr W.Bailey playing Mr E.Newbound's part (W.Bailey having arrived in the interim). Had, myself, to play Mr Bailey's character (Counsel McQuin) in the last piece (*Verdict of the World*). After the play was over, got the part of Roy Lee from J.Pitt & gave it to Miss J.Summers to play tomorrow night & all next week if Mr C.Reeve should be unable.

SEPT 5 Thurs   Mr F.Charlton taken ill with English Cholera – unable to play tonight, Mr J.Reynolds played his part in *Naomi*. Mr G.B.Bigwood *ivre* tonight.

6 Fri   Mr G.B.Bigwood ivre again tonight. Miss M.Bellair unable to come to Theatre tonight, said to have had '*Une fausse couche*'. Miss J.Coveney played her part in *Naomi*.

7 Sat   Mr G.Bigwood fined 5/0 for being 2 nights *ivré* and warned that if it occurred again, he would be instantly *Discharged*.

13 Fri   Annual Inspection of Theatre. Mr W.B.Donne, Mr Ponsonby & Architect came – suggested 2 Hydrapulls in the Flies; the taking away of a little seat close to Door in Gallery R.H. and widening of the Door L.H. of ditto; cleansing of walls of Box Saloon (L.H. corner); the general whitewashing of bricks in passages (which Mr Ponsonby did not think necessary); & particularly the keeping of *Knives in the Flies* to cut down burning matter.

14 Sat   Mr Charlton half drunk tonight – perhaps *more* than half (not perceptible to Audience.)

19 Thurs   A row with Miss M.Bellair on account of her having been cast a very inferior part in the new piece for next Monday. Tears & threats of throwing up her engagement. Mr C.Reeve also refused to play the part cast him (Cropley Clarke) in the same piece. Thought of giving the part to T.Hyde but C.Pitt, at night, volunteered to play it.

21 Sat   Letter from Mr Ponsonby, enclosing a long, printed extract from the *Daily Telegraph*. The extract was a sensational letter to the Editor abusing the management of the Britannia Theatre for permitting Wainwratta to perform on the wire without a net under him, & pointing out the danger of a fall not only to Wainwratta himself but to the audience, or that portion of it, under

---

*A Bright Beam at Last featured a heroine who was a brick maker's daughter and one of the scenes in the play actually represented a brickfield.

*Charles Reeve had been an actor at the Britannia since April, 1872. Edgar Newbound joined the company as a leading actor in June 1872.

him. Mr Ponsonby saying the performance could not be permitted without the net[3]. Fortunately the '*Young England Brothers*',[*] who appear next week, had been fixing their net today & gave us permission to use it tonight – so we got over the difficulty.

23 Mon   Letter from the Lord Chamberlain demanding copies of all songs sung at the Britannia – saying he had been informed one had been sung inciting to 'strikes' & another on the 'Tichborne Case' which was also objectionable, & asking what steps had been taken to secure safety in Wainwratta's performance.

24 Tues   Went alone (by Mrs S.Lane's desire) in a cab (cost *4/0*) to see Mr W.B.Donne at his house (40 Weymouth Street.) to give explanations relative to the matter of yesterday. Carried a copy of Mr Laburnum's[**] song which had been complained of. Mr Donne read the song & said he could see 'nothing amiss in it' & suggested only the alteration of 1s.6d. to '*shillings two*' in it – & was quite satisfied on learning that we now had a net under Wainwratta.

27 Fri   J.Reynolds *ivré* tonight, was fined in the Treasury on Saturday *10/6* with warning that if it occurred again he would have to take a fortnight's holiday – & if he objected to that, he would have to take – *the other thing* – (meaning his discharge!) – This Mr Robinson told me.

30 Mon   . . . Lieut. Cole (ventriloquist)[*] instead of Walter Laburnum.

OCT 26 Sat   John Radford (Dayman) received a week's notice (Ivresse), from Mr Robinson. Fracas between *Charlton* (*ivré*) & *Reeve* (also 'slewed'?) in which Mr Reeve returning a blow (in the Dressing Room) hit Monsieur Charlton in the eye causing the optic to swell! – Mrs S.L. observing something wrong on the stage, came into the Prompt Entrance & said, 'Pretty goings on, I think – three of our actors, *ivrés*, at once on the stage!!!' She afterwards explained she meant W.Pitt, F.Charlton & Reynolds.

NOV 2 Sat   Mr Charlton fined a Guinea for being drunk & fighting in the Dressing-room last Saturday night – Mr C.Reeve fined a guinea for fighting with Mr Charlton on that occasion. Neither of these gentlemen played tonight – both having told Mr Robinson in the Treasury when the fine was exacted that unless it was returned, they should not appear – The result was Mr Reynolds played Mr Charlton's part in *Confidence*, Mr Bigwood played Mr Reynolds's part and Mr Crauford played Mr C.Reeve's part. In the last piece C.Pitt played Charlton's part, I played C.Pitt's part, and Elton played C.Reeve's part. NB. By all accounts, in the above fight, Charlton struck Reeve first – & Reeve did but return the blow.

4 Mon   A Mr Dallas (engaged by Mr Robinson) made his 1st Appearance,

---

[*]**The Young England Brothers** were subsequently billed as 'Children of the High Trapeze'.

[*]**Walter Laburnum's** songs on this occasion included 'Waiting for Nelly at the Temple Bar' and 'It's very Strange to me'.

[*]**Lt Walter Cole** had served in the Royal Navy before taking up professional ventriloquism, which he presented with great success with quite a 'family' of life-size dummies.

as Geoffrey in *Guy Fawkes*, & proved an utter novice, exciting such a roar of laughter in the audience that he is not to *go on again*.

8 Fri   Amelia received annuity from R.G.T.Fund. Saw Mrs Campbell (or Barry) and Mr N.T.Hicks,* the latter a wreck, perfectly nerveless & pitiable – Formerly a '*Star*' in the Minor Theatres – a fine, big, handsome man, distinguished for the high & fearless leaps he took off Rocks & into Ravines – &, whatever may be said, not a bad Melo-Dramatic actor.

9 Sat   Paid Mr Hope (Leader of the Orchestra) his last salary, £2.5.0, as he leaves tonight.

23 Sat   Heard tonight that Mrs Atkinson, formerly an actress at the Britannia Theatre, died on the same day as Mr Borrow Senr.

DEC 3 Tues   Gas-men struck at most of the London works. Very bad supply of light – scarcely able to see to write in afternoon – & very bad at Theatre – improved as night grew on – but not equal to usual supply.

5 Thurs   *Darkness Visible*
Strike at the Gas Works – Hurried the Performance on, upon a/c of very bad light on the stage and got all over by 20 minutes before 11. Theatres at the West End dismally lighted.

24 Tues   Call at 10 a.m. Rehearsal not over till 5.25 p.m. Another Rehearsal for Transformation Scene called at 6 p.m. Went about 7 & had to wait till about 12 at Midnight before it was ready to work – & then the rehearsal of it kept up till 2.12 in the morning.

28 Sat   Mr Robinson paid me one night's salary too much – forgetting to deduct for Xmas day. 3rd comic scene rehearsed again! the fact being that clown is a failure.*

1873

JAN 9 Thurs   *Narrow Escape*
This morning, a mass of fire which must have been smouldering all last night, was discovered under the back part of the Pit of the Britannia Theatre! supposed to have originated from some person smoking, and carelessly throwing down a lighted fuzee . . . Mrs S.Lane and Mrs Borrow here tonight, after the Opening of Pantomime was over, to play a game of cards. Fred & Harriet here to meet them . . . Louis Napoleon, Ex-Emperor of the French,*

---

*Newton Treen Hicks '(who memory writers of the present day treat with a ridicule quite undeserved) was a capital actor, possessing a fine figure and a sonorous voice . . . he was a great favourite and always "a draw"'. (Hanley, p.8.) Hicks' claim on the Royal General Theatrical Fund had commenced after an accident in 1864.

*The 1872/73 Pantomime was *Tommy and Harry, or, The Spelling Book, the Lion and the Mouse, and What Don't Care Came To.* The clown was C. Stilt.

*Napoleon III had lived in exile in England since the defeat of France in the Franco-Prussian War. A feature of his foreign policy, during the second Empire, had been his attempt to cultivate friendship with England.

died this day at Chislehurst, aetat 65. Verse sung on Thursday night . . . on the stage of the Britannia Theatre in the 6th Scene of the Opening of the Pantomime by Mr Fred Foster & Mrs S.Lane.
With feelings of great sadness//Allow me now to say
That friend of France & England//Napoleon died today.
A better, truer Monarch//No Frenchman ever knew
It's very sad! It's very sad!//But yet – alas! 'tis true.
By way of Symphony, at end of words, the orchestra played '*Partout pour La Syrie*', to which the actor and actress beat time & marched off the stage.

24 Fri   Received Letter from Sophie Miles, dated Jany 23rd, from Congleton, a town in Cheshire stating that Mr T.Drummond was lying dead at Shrewsbury,* that she was going there to perform her last duty, & requesting me to inform Messrs. C.Pitt, J.Reynolds, G.Bigwood and Mrs Newham.

FEB 6 Thurs   By Mrs S.Lane's desire, read 1st Act of a piece which she informed me, she had *herself* translated!! (The original French Title, she said, was *L'Aveugle*).

12 Wed   Wrote copy of letter for Mrs S.Lane to write to author of Novel on which *Mabel Lake** is founded – the author claiming £50 for permission to play the Drama – he having previously himself, as he says, dramatised the novel.

14 Fri   Mrs S.Lane said that she had received an answer to the letter I wrote for her . . . and that the Author agreed to accept her offer of *£1 per night*.

26 Wed   (Ash Wednesday) No Performance. With Amelia to Fred & Harriet's to meet Mrs S.Lane & Mrs Borrow, who came to tea at 5.30 & spent the evening playing cards – brought home by *Mrs S.Lane*, in her brougham!

MAR 3 Mon   Mrs S.Lane not at Theatre tonight, laid up with bad legs (rheumatic gout) . . . Told (by Mr Robinson) *must* be at Westminster Hall at 10.30 on Wednesday (for *Mrs S.Lane's Will Case*).

6 Thurs   Mrs S.Lane's law-suit *Lane v. Challis* decided in her favour at the Probate Court today. The only witnesses examined were a Mr Tupper (or Tapper) from Dawlish, Devonshire, Mrs S.Lane, Mr_____(sic) the Lawyer who drew up the Will, & Mr Green, his clerk, who sketched the drafts of it from Mr S.Lane's dictation[1].

22 Sat   First piece changed to *The Serpent on the Hearth* (*Frou-Frou** being a complete failure – unfit for a Britannia audience – '*all talkee-talkee*').

28 Fri   To Tower to ask permission for 24 soldiers, 2 sergeants, 2 Buglers, to '*assist*' in our new Military Spectacle on Easter Monday. Found the 2nd Battalion of Scots Fusiliers in garrison, Lord Abinger Commanding Officer,

---

*Drummond had joined Loraine's dramatic company, in which he had been playing roles such as Iago. He played Friar Laurence in *Romeo and Juliet* on 15 January and returned to his lodgings in his usual health. Early in the morning he was taken ill and, within 10 minutes of the doctor's arrival, he was dead.

*Mabel Lake was first performed on 8/2/1873.

*Frou-Frou was first performed at the Britannia on 17/3/1873 with Marian Lacey as Gilberte.

Captain Montgomery, Adjutant. Leave would have been granted readily, but as they quit the Tower on Easter Tuesday for Dublin it would have been useless. Tried the Artillery who are always stationed at the Tower, but found they were only 40 in number & could not spare as many as we wanted. Then tried at the Artillery Ground, City Road, where Sergt Halton promised to provide us with the number – all – Colour & Drill Sergeants.

APRIL 14 Mon   Napoleon, or the Story of a Flag, New Military Drama (1st time) supported by a Detachment of the Staff of Royal City Military (2 Segts, 2 Buglers, 24 men).

17 Thurs   Johnny Gideon* in Stage Box & Nelly Power* over the Prompt Box.

19 Sat   One of the worst Houses ever seen on a saturday night at the Britannia.

22 Tues   Johnny Gideon at the Britannia with the owner of the Horse, Mornington;* winner of the chief prize at the Epsom Races.

MAY 7 Wed   MRS W.CRAUFORD née Ellen Watson DIED, at Hampstead.

14 Wed   My dear Amelia died at about 5 m. p. 7 yesterday evening of 'Atony of Intestines'. 'There is one more angel in Heaven'.

26 Mon   Sir Roger Tichborne, the '*CLAIMANT*'[2] appearing at 8 o'clock on the stage & addressing the audience.

27 Tues   Johnny Gideon at Rehearsal, 1st time* . . . Not a great 'House' to see the 'Claimant'. Bad at first, pulled up afterwards – variously guessed at from £50 to £70 . . . '*Claimant*' did not impress with an idea of gentility. Thought there was more of the Butcher than the nobleman about him. His voice was not 'husky' as one of the witnesses said Arthur Orton's used to be. Saw no pock-marks nor signs of 'St. Vitus's Dance'. Fancied he was trying to keep his eyes wide open to avoid '*winking*' (as he had been said in court to do) or '*twitching his eyes*'. He spoke only a few words, but said his friend, Mr Whalley, M.P. for Peterborough, who accompanied him, would speak for him. Mr Whalley then spoke for 20 minutes. Finally, the Claimant again addressed the audience, hoping the public would not form an opinion, for or against him, till the trial was ended.

JUNE 5 Thurs   Mr Bigwood not playing all this week – seized with *Delerium Tremens*. . . . Mr Robinson tells me it is settled – he is certainly going to leave us on Saturday week.

10 Tues   Mrs Lane, Mrs Borrow (& Johnny Gideon) behind Scenes all this

*Johnny Gideon, a bookmaker, had been Tom Sayers's manager. He lived partly in Paris and exercised a strong influence on the Britannia's repertory for several years after Samuel Lane's death. He was 'a very clever, cheery, chatty man'. (Emily Soldene, pp.92–93). Nelly Power was a serio-comic vocalist and burlesque actress, a star of music hall and pantomime. An impersonator of swells, she was also known for a jockey song which she sang in costume and for 'The Boy I love is up in the Gallery'.

*Mornington was owned by a Mr Brayley.

*Gideon's play *Brewing a Bruin* (a piece of absurdity) was being rehearsed.

night, except the last act of last piece – & Mr Robinson going to leave us on saturday.

11 Wed   Mr Robinson told me tonight – the Difference between him & Mrs S.Lane is settled amicably – he stops – all the servants of the Theatre in ecstasies – shaking hands & laughing & greeting each other with 'Good news! good news!' –

16 Mon   Romah* of the Golden Wing (Trapezist) 1st week. Romah's apparatus not being ready (after very hard work by the Carpenters) he could not perform tonight. Apology made by W.H.Pitt – who took Romah on the stage & introduced him to the audience – who took all quietly. John Martin (Gas-man) met with an accident by which it is feared he will lose the sight of one eye. The end of a piece of wire, suddenly released from a strain, jerked up & struck his eye while he was helping to fix Romah's apparatus.

17 Tues   Got savage with Performers at rehearsal for being shamefully imperfect in *Wandering Jew* & turning it into ridicule – a piece which has given me most distressing anxiety to put it *en train* for performing tomorrow night . . . John Martin's eye better.

18 Wed   Benefit of Miss J.Summers. *Wandering Jew*. Romah. *Fireman of New York*. 'House', at opening, very bad indeed – 'pulled up afterwards'. *£34* Receipts. Performers serious – & trying to do their best with *The Wandering Jew*, which, in consequence, went well – all the Performers being 'called before the curtain' at the end of the piece.

28 Sat   Mr Robinson showed me Hazlewood's receipt for the 'entire London right of the drama of *Naomi*' proving that he sold it to Mrs S.Lane for *5.0.0*.

JULY 3 Thurs   Mrs S.Lane at Theatre tonight to see Model of the Transformation Scene for the next Xmas Pantomime.

4 Fri   Benefit of Mr Morgan Smith (Coloured Tragedian).* *Othello* . . .– very poor 'House' – only about *£20* cash. A soft, drizzly rain falling at intervals. Bigwood having to begin *Othello* as 'Roderigo' alarmed us by not arriving at the Theatre till time to ring in overture – half tipsy . . . Saw Mr W.Travers's Receipt for the entire London Right of *All But One £10*.*

8 Tues   Mr Robinson showed me a letter from Mr G.Bigwood, consenting to receive *£3* a week in future instead of *£4*, & to conform to the Rules and Regulations of the Theatre.

AUG 10 Sun   Mr F.Charlton* called making an abject apology for having insulted me, as he said, in the way he left the Theatre last Novr 2nd 1872!! *Mem.* This week 67,000 feet of gas burnt.

---

*Romah** was described as a Mexican athlete.

*Morgan Smith** was known as the 'African Roscius', a title he had taken over from Ira Aldridge. **£10**: Possibly *16* (Dairy entry was very indistinct).

*Charlton** was re-engaged from 11/8/1873.

16 Sat   Bill changed . . . concluding with A Ballet called *The Origin of Harlequin* by 'The Lupino Pantomimists'.*

22 Fri   Began to work on Opening of Pantomime . . . Narrow escape of Mr Robinson's youngest child from being crushed by the Act Drop, as it descended at the end of an act.

23 Sat   *Mr G.Bigwood*
Mr Bigwood, at night, during performance of *Phillis Mayburn*, distracted by family troubles, & either drunk, or seized with incipient *Delerium Tremens*, broke down utterly in the Piece of *Phillis Mayburn* – suddenly and without cause began abusing *Miss M.Bellair* on the stage, and when remonstrated with by Mr Robinson went up stairs into the Dressing Room, pulled his dress half off, & refused to finish the part. Cecil Pitt offered to 'go on' and do his best to get through the rest of the piece – but Mr Bigwood would not take off the remaining portion of his dress. Finally Mr Robinson prevailed on Mr Bigwood to dress again & finish the part – which he did in a wild & most incoherent manner. Not thinking it safe to trust him with the part of '*Qui-tain*' in the new Piece next Monday, wrote, by desire of Mr Robinson, to Mr Elton requesting *him* to study and play it – and sent him the *M.S.S.* – Much excitement among the actors during the affair.

SEPT 9 Tues   Miss Amy Ellis* sent to say she had been taken ill last night on her way to the Theatre & was obliged to return home, but would come tonight – & did come, apparently without anything the matter with her. Perhaps because Mr Robinson had written to the Agent threatening an action!.

16 Tues   Mr Bodham Donne . . . Mr Spencer Ponsonby & a Mr Robinson (an Architect) came from the Lord Chamberlain's office to make the *annual inspection of the Theatre* – seemed well pleased (as well they might) with everything – except one, – the Hydrant was not attached to the hose[3]!

OCT 18 Sat   Meerschaum Pipe given me by W.Crauford – a present from himself, not the result (like a former pipe) of a subscription. (This pipe, given today, before Mr Crauford's death, slipped off the stem while in my mouth & was shattered to fragments in the Curtain Road.)

21 Tues   Polly Robinson told me as an inviolable secret that Mrs S.Lane is to be married to Mr W.Crauford as soon as he is recovered from his present illness.

28 Tues   Mr W.Bailey refused Admission to the Theatre & discharged, Mr Robinson having learnt that Mr B. was playing at the Alexandra Theatre* & sent a person who saw him act there.

NOV 15 Sat   Mr Robinson told me that he had detected Mr Hoggins, our

---

*The Lupinos were one of the great families of pantomimists. Later in the century they were to appear regularly in Britannia pantomimes and one of Sarah Lane's nephews was to marry into the family.

*Amy Ellis, a concert room singer, was known as the 'Northern Star'. She had performed very successfully at a number of music halls.

*The Alexandra Theatre had opened recently in Camden Town.

new Master Carpenter, in getting liquors from the *Bar* to the amount of above three shillings, unauthorised, in the name of Mr Dickson, the 'Comet' Acrobat,* & would have discharged him instantly, but for the Pantomime. This matter was afterwards cleared up satisfactorily.

22 Sat Excitement in the Theatre in consequence of Notices to terminate their Engagements at Xmas being given to Messrs. R.Bell, T.Grahame,* E.Elton & Miss Lily MacDonald* – (Miss L.Rayner, Mrs H.Morgan, also leaves at Xmas to be 'confined'!)

DEC 7 Sun By working hard, from 12 noon to 9 p.m., succeeded in filling up Pantomime bill with names of Songs & Concerted Pieces, names of Scenery &c, as far as known, and sketched out a puff for Newspapers for Xmas Pantomime.

9 Mon Abominable Fog all day . . . Could not see across the road going to the Theatre to rehearsal. Could not draw breath. Expected to sink going up Huntingdon Street.

10 Wed 'Darkness which may be felt'. Same *Horrible Fog* all day & night . . . Impossible to see into the R.I.E. from Prompt Entrance. Much fog on stage – Actors must have been scarcely visible to audience.

17 Wed Benefit of Mrs S.Lane and Last Night of the Season . . . At end of Address, Mrs S.Lane fetched on Mr W.Crauford R.I.E. He looked very ill indeed but spoke to the Audience, said 'he had come from a sick bed to pay his respects to the audience & thank them for their past favours as he had always done on his *"dear sister's"* Benefit night. He had done so for 21 years – & he hoped with God's blessing, he should do so for 21 years more'.

20 Sat Rehearsal of Super Business in Opening of Pantomime; trying on animal dresses & rehearsing one Comic Scene from 10 till 3.

23 Tues Heavy Rehearsal of Opening & Comic Scenes, both in a frightfully imperfect state. No Properties shown today – though they were peremptorily called by Mrs S.Lane, as they also were yesterday when not half were ready.

24 Tues W.Huline (Pantaloon) ill – supposed of Rheumatic Fever. *Milton* (Super) who had *never* played Pantaloon, engaged by Mrs S.Lane (it being a case of dire necessity, it being so near Xmas) to supply Mr W.Huline's place. He proved a great failure. *Night Rehearsal of Scenery*, Transformation Scene only, not over till 3 a.m. though called at 7.

26 Fri BOXING-DAY Two immense 'Houses' morning & evening. Properties of Comic Scenes distressingly deficient. Transformation Scene very far from perfect.

27 Sat Scenery & Properties of Pantomime still lamentably deficient –

---

*The Dickson Family of Acrobats** appeared with M. & Mme. Boisset and children, the latter being billed as the Comets of 1873, throughout October and November.

*T.Grahame**, an actor from Boston, had been with the company since early in 1873. **Lily MacDonald**, previously an actress in Bath, had joined the company in December 1872.

though the plots were issued full a month earlier this year than ever they were before.

29 Mon   Pantomime. *Cocorico, & the Hen with the Golden Eggs*[4].

1874

JAN 1 Thurs   W.Crauford in Mrs S.Lane's Box tonight alone, but so altered that I could not recognise him, after gazing at him several times – but Mr C.Pitt & others spoke to him and proved that it *was* him.

16 Fri   James Anderson, the actor, and Lord Alfred Paget, Fred & Harriet at the Britannia tonight. The two first, after the Opening of the Pantomime, came round on to the stage, & into Mrs S.Lane's dressing-room, drinking champagne.

31 Sat   Immense 'House'. Mr Robinson says that 225 more people paid at the doors this evening than did last Boxing Night or on Boxing night last year! greatly owing, no doubt, to the Standard Theatre being closed for the death of John Douglas.*

FEB 12 Thurs   Received last night of Mr Robinson, the 1st act of a Drama called *Patrie* translated from the French by Mrs S.Lane (credat judens)!!! to prepare for Easter – made out Scenery Plot, Property Plot, Wardrobe Plot & Sketch for the Bill & returned it to Mr R. on Saturday night.

16 Mon   1st change of Performance since Xmas . . . A new comedietta by Mr J.Gideon (announced as E.Manuel Esq., in bills & advertisements) called *One for his Nob* . .

24 Tues   Benefit of Miss E.Parry, Columbine. *Eagle & Child*. Pantomime. Not a great House – guessed at about *£50* . . . C.Pitt, in Prompt Entrance, told me he *knew* that the Terms on which Miss E.Parry had her Benefit were – half after *£20* . . . Clown Huline's Salary, his engagement shown me by Mrs Robinson . . . per week *£9* and half a clear Benefit.

25 Wed   Benefit of J.Huline Clown (called in the bills 'The Great, Little Huline') . . . Last night of Comic Scenes; withdrawn after tonight – thus ending Clown's engagement – to his great mortification and feeling of injustice – he fancying he was engaged for the 'run' of the Pantomime, which he was not, for I saw his engagement, which was shown me by Mrs Robinson; he was engaged only for eight weeks. Receipts of House about *£43* . . . Mr Robinson told me that the salary which John Parry & Mrs Parry together received as their joint salary – *2.5.0*, Mrs Parry being a Check-taker . . . C.Pitt's dress for 'Columbine' on Clown's Benefit night (White muslin) cost *4.3*.

26 Thurs   Mrs S.Lane subpoena'd to the Court of Requests, Old Street, to show 'her books' & prove J.Parry's salary on a suit brought by J.Parry's

---

*John Douglass, who had acted at the Britannia in the early 1840s, had been manager of the Standard Theatre from 1848–1861 and from 1864 onwards.

Landlord against him. Mr Robinson took the books & appeared for Mrs S.Lane. J.Parry was ordered to pay *£2 per month*.

MAR 4 Wed   Told by Mr Robinson that the Elephant used in the Pantomime cost *15.0.0.*, which Mr W.Charles confirmed – & said he knew it originally cost *£30* when new – & that it was made for Covent Garden Theatre.

5 Thurs   W.Crauford 'tapped' today for Dropsy; nearly 4 gallons of water drawn from him.

13 Fri   Saw Thos. Rogers (Artist) at Theatre – come to ask Mrs S.Lane to give him a testimonial as to talent to aid him in an action at law against a defamer of his ability. *Poor W.Crauford* – has lost his sight! – and has been raving all night! is not expected to live till Sunday . . . W.Crauford died ¼ to 4 P.M. Aged 45.

31 Tues   The worse 'House' tonight ever seen at the Britannia! 'You bet your bottom dollar on it, old man'.

APRIL 2 Thurs   Mr Robinson told me that Mrs S.Lane had made him an advance of £1 a week on his salary & it was made in this naive way: 'You promised when I first engaged with you that if I suited, you would give me "a lift" but you haven't done so'. – 'You haven't asked me'. – 'Well then I ask you now'. – 'Well, take what you like'. – 'No, no that won't do, you must say'. – 'Well, then, will £1 a week do?' – 'Yes, that will do – if *you* are satisfied, *I* am'. – 'Well then that's settled'.

7 Tues   Mr Robinson said the Gas in the Britannia cost p. hour = *16.0.*

22 Wed   Little Celeste (daughter of Celeste Stephan & William Borrow, her husband) came into the Prompt Entrance to bid us 'good bye', saying she was going to France tomorrow to school, with her cousin, 'Hope Crauford', at a town called '*Guines*' – & that she was to stay there till Xmas. News that Mrs S.Lane has had '*another*' fit today.

23 Wed   With R.Bell to his pretty little house, 21 Kent Villas, Grange Road, E.Dalston – a very snug, cosy & well furnished dwelling.

27 Mon   Johnny Gideon at Theatre tonight – had a conference with Scene-Painters about his son's piece (*Les Deux Orphelines*) for Whitsuntide and wished to have a particular scene of it set next monday, that he might see it. Promised him it *should* be. Mr Robinson afterwards told me that he would not allow it unless Mrs S.Lane gave the order.

28 Tues   A letter from Mr Neville, Manager of the Olympic Theatre, claiming all rights to the English version of *Les Deux Orphelines* & wishing to see Mrs S.Lane about it.

JULY 18 Sat   Mr Robinson told me seriously as a fact that Mr MacDermott was engaged by Mrs S.Lane for the next Pantomime at a salary of *£16* per week! That Mr Forrester* was engaged last year at a salary of *£10* per week

---

*W.Forrester, a burlesque actor, had joined the company to play a 'reflective young gentleman' in the 1873/74 pantomime.

– and that the sum paid for *To the Green Isles Direct* was Two Guineas per night, and Mr and Mrs J.F.Brian at £8 per week.

19 Sun   Price paid to Mr Hazlewood the author some years ago for the *Hop-pickers* £5.0.0.

SEPT 29 Tues   To the Lord Chamberlain's Office with Mr Beckett Senr & Mr R.Boyce to get the License (in a cab). Mrs S.Lane had been there before us in her 'Brougham'. & paid for the Licence – which she had taken away with her – leaving me to give the usual '*douceur*' to the Attendants which I did, viz. *£1.0.0*. Went afterwards to the *Criterion* (Spiers & Pond's). Had Luncheon . . .[1]

OCT 5 Mon   John Parry robbed last saturday going home from the Theatre at midnight (about ½ past 12) just over the Kingsland Road Bridge. The Thieves (6 or 7 in number) used no violence beyond hustling him. Fortunately he had little money about him & they took from him only *1s.7d.* in cash, his great coat, an old one, & handkerchief, and a little gold swivel of small value – he had no watch.

NOV 3 Tues   To Westminster Hall on *subpoena* to give evidence in the cause of *Rogers v. Sloman*. Not necessary – was not put in the witness box – the case occupied some hours & was adjourned till tomorrow. Expenses 1s/6d[2].

7 Sat   Last Piece changed to *Guy Fawkes* & Fireworks.

9 Mon   4,630 people paid to go into the Britannia theatre last saturday evening.

10 Tues   Mr Robinson told me it was possible E.Newbound might leave us as he (Newbound) had received an offer of Engagement at a higher salary from a West End Theatre & asked *4.10.0* a week to remain with us which of course Mrs S.Lane would not give having already raised his salary some time since to £2.15.0.

20 Fri   Coming off the stage tonight, after singing a Duett & dancing an Irish Jig with Mr G.Lewis, Mrs S.Lane informed by Mr Robinson in the Prompt Entrance that her two nephews S. & A.Crauford were both gone to bed ill of fever. She burst out crying &, in the middle of her lamentations, had to dry her tears suddenly & go on the stage again *to take up an encore*. Mrs Robinson her sister also laid up with Pleurisy before recovery from her late confinement.

30 Mon   Mr Herbert Campbell (Topical Vocalist)*. . .

DEC 22 Tues   Rehearsal of Pantomime – lasted from ½ past 10 till ½ past 4 . . . The '*Gallinatial*' (Johnny Gideon's word) Procession of Toys being the curse and nuisance of the Rehearsal. Properties being in an awful state of unpreparedness.

---

*Herbert Campbell, described as 'the epitome of music-hall fat men', made a feature of parody songs like 'I don't want to fight, I'll be slaughtered if I do . . .' From 1883 he appeared as a pantomime dame in enormously successful partnerships over the next twenty years. His act at the Britannia included an ironic version of 'Britains Never Will Be Slaves'.

23 Wed   Rehearsal of Pantomime, *The Black Statue*, lasted from ½ past 10 till 7. Night Rehearsal of Transformation Scene called at 7 – went at 8.30 – did not commence till 10.45, all over at 11.50 midnight.

24 Thurs   Rehearsal of Pantomime at ½ past 10 for Supers & Ladies for Procession of Toys – very few came – did little with them. Rehearsal of Opening commenced at 12. Comic scenes after – did not get home till past 7 at night.

31 Thurs   Evident falling off in the 'House' at the Britannia. Fred & Harriet to see the Pantomime, very much dissatisfied – think it the worse they ever saw there[3].

1875

JAN 19 Tues   A man died in the Gallery of the Britannia Theatre this evening during the performance of the pantomime.

APRIL 14 Wed   To the Lord Chamberlain's Office, St James's Palace, to see the Reader of Plays, Mr Piggott,* by his desire, at 2 p.m. – relative to a new Drama we had sent to be licensed under the title of *Alsace and Lorraine*. Mr Piggott requested that the *Title, Date & Locality* of the piece might be altered as he feared the subject being political was too '*risky*' & might give offence. He suggested that we might lay the scene in Warsaw, 100 years ago[1].

15 Thurs   Received back, by Post from Mr Piggott . . . the M.S.S. of the drama called *Alsace and Lorraine* with a request that when reconstructed it might be returned to him, as in its present state he could not sign it.

27 Tues   Went to Lord Chamberlain's office to see Mr Piggott . . . by his own appointment, with altered copy of Drama *Alsace and Lorraine* for which he would make no charge. Paid him fee to license *Bras de Fer 1.1.0*.

MAY 8 Sat   Row with a Super, named Kelsey,* in the Theatre tonight. He had rushed into the Ladies' dressing room, drunk, & was, it was said, 'knocking his wife about'. Went down & had him taken out by other supers.

JUNE 5 Sat   Difference with Miss J.Hill,* who did not arrive until after arrangements had been made for the Majiltons to go on before her (supposing she would be late as on monday night last) – would not pay her her salary as she refused to '*go on*' after them. At length Mr Robinson persuaded her & she '*went on*'.

11 Fri   Row with Johnny Gideon who wanted to see Mr W.Small (Scene Painter) about catch scene of next Xmas Pantomime. Mr Robinson would not allow it & sent Mr W.Small away.

*Edward Piggott (1824–95) replaced Donne as Examiner of Plays on his retirement in August 1874.

*William Kelsey had been a Super at the Britannia since 1867.

*Jenny Hill was 24 years old at this time and in the early years of her successful career as one of the first female music-hall stars. She danced well, could do male impersonations, and could slip from comedy to pathos.

JULY 3 Sat   Gave Mr Robinson one month's notice of my intention to leave the Theatre.

10 Sat   Mr Robinson told me that he had arranged with Mr Newbound to succeed me after I leave as Stage Manager.

29 Thurs   Last night on entering the Theatre found a Notice in Mr Robinson's handwriting, calling all the company to be on the stage at 12 o'clock today . . . At that hour today I was called out of my dressing-room by C.Pitt, & to my astonishment, Mr Robinson presented me with a very handsome Silver Ink-stand, Gold Pencil Case, Mother O'Pearl Card Case, & a lot of Address Cards with my new address on them! These, he said, were a testimonial of respect from Mrs S.Lane and all the members of the company, on my quitting the theatre after a service of almost 30 years . . . Mr Worthington* & John* guess the value of the testimonial to be over £50.

31 Sat   Left the Britannia! after 29 years & 7 months engagement there, besides 9 months in the years 1842, 3 . . .
Inscription on the above Ink-stand
'To Frederick Wilton Esquire, from Mr and Mrs Lane & the Britannia Theatre Company as a tribute of profound respect on his retiring after nearly 30 years services as Stage Manager. *July 31st 1875*'.

*Mr Worthington was a friend of John Byron, Wilton's son-in-law, temporarily residing with Wilton.

Notes

1863

1.   The Lancashire Distress Fund had been set up to alleviate the hardship caused to the workers in the Lancashire cotton mills as a result of the short fall in cotton imports from the northern states of America during the American Civil War.

2.   In order to re-imburse the London theatres for opening free on the occasion of the Prince of Wales's marriage, the Lord Chamberlain's office had requested detailed estimates of each theatre's average takings for one night. Lane, whose terms are referred to in the diary entry, claimed £100, stating in a letter of 23/2/1863:

> at this time of the year, the pantomime just running its successful career and with the additional aid of T.Sayers the champion of England who appears in it being engaged with a large salary, my receipts since Christmas have been on average £100 per night. But on such a glorious occasion as the marriage of H.R.H. the Prince of Wales with H.R.H. Princess Alexandra of course the receipts I would expect would be nearly double, mine being the largest minor theatre in London and capable of holding a greater number of Persons than any other either minor or major . . *LCP*, LC1/127, 10/3/1863 and LC1/128, 23/2/1863, PRO.

3.   Professor Pepper's ghost effect had been first demonstrated at the Polytechnic in Regent Street in January 1863. Its use in *Faith, Hope and Charity* was its first appearance in a fully dramatised form. A sheet of glass was placed on the stage between the audience and where the ghost was made to appear; the representative of the ghost was placed at a level below the front of the stage and at an angle which caused his reflection in the glass to be visible to the audience, but not to the actors on stage. The principle was similar to that which caused the reflection of a lamp in a room to appear in the window of the room as if suspended in the street outside, and it depended upon the actor who played the ghost being brightly lit in comparison with the more subdued lighting on the stage. To achieve this he was sometimes lit by a Drummond oxy-hydrogen lamp. The ghost in *Faith, Hope and Charity* took the form of a widow who enters the chamber of the wicked Sir Gilbert, to warn him to desist from his evil courses. He attempts to strike the figure, but his sword meets only empty air. See George Speaight, 'Professor Pepper's Ghost' *Theatre Notebook*, XLIII, 1, pp. 16–24 and *Shoreditch Advertiser*, 22/8/1863.

4.   The Prompter's Whistle was used as a signal by the prompter to the back-stage staff to co-ordinate scene changes. It could also be presented to a prompter as a testimonial to his worth. In 1845, for instance, George Cressall Ellis was presented with a silver, ornamented whistle at Drury Lane by Emma Romer. See Charles H.Shattuck, 'A Victorian Stage Manager: George Cressall Ellis', *Theatre Notebook*, XXII, 3, pp. 102–112.

5.   *Reynold's Miscellany* had commenced serialising *Deeds of Darkness, or A Fight Against Fate* by Charles H.Ross, an adaptation of Taylor's play. The woodcut showed Robert Brierely protecting May Edwards.

6. 'The Lobby, added since the last Inspection to the centre entrance to the Pit, should be altered as the egress is too narrow – For the present single door, two doors should be substituted, each swinging both ways. In all other respects the Theatre is in its usual good condition'. Report on Annual Inspection, 1863, *LCP*, LC1/127, PRO.

7. William Seaman, previously house dramatist at the Britannia, had appeared on 22/8/1863 in an action against Copeland, proprietor of the Theatre Royal, Liverpool, under the dramatic copyright act. Copeland had played Boucicault's *Jessie Browne or The Relief of Lucknow*, which Seaman alleged was derived from a play he had written for the Britannia Theatre, where it was first performed on 1/2/1858. Boucicault's version was performed only 3 weeks later in America on 22/2/1858. Copeland, who had performed the Boucicault version during November–December, 1862, alleged that there was no piracy as both plays were based on a common source, an account by a lady, one of the rescued party, published in the *Times* (14/12/1857), and Seaman's piece had never been published. However, both plays had used a tableau in the last scene, similar to an illustration that had appeared in the *Illustrated London News*. Seaman, rather unconvincingly, denied knowledge of these publications, stating that he based the dialogue of the last scene, where piracy seemed most evident, on a song he had heard. The Jury found against him, dismissing his claim for 40s per night for the 24 performances of the play in Liverpool. The Judge claimed that the action was unnecessary and that it had been 'scandalous' to bring it. See, also, Edward Stirling, *Old Drury Lane* (London, 1881), I, 263–265.

8. The serial, in fact, appeared in *Bow Bells* (a periodical which provided the source for a number of Britannia melodramas) and was entitled *The Chimes, or The Broken Heart* by the author of *Leonard Leigh* etc. It commenced on 19/8/1863 through to 18/11/1863.

1864

1. The *Flowery Land* was a British cargo ship, scuttled and plundered of its cargo in 1863 by mutinous crew members. On 22 February, 1864, five of the mutineers were publicly executed at Newgate, the first time since 1828 that so many had been hung there at one time. A great crowd turned out to witness the execution.

2. Theatres and Saloons were licensed by the Lord Chamberlain on the understanding that an agreed price was charged for admission. The managers of the East and South London theatres and saloons, however, persisted in attempting to undercut each other. In December 1846 the managers of the Britannia, Standard, City of London, Albert, Bower, Queen's and Victoria were amongst those called into the Lord Chamberlain's office to account for their reductions in prices. Lane claimed he had been forced to do so after the Garrick, Pavilion, City of London, Standard and Victoria had reduced their prices. *LCP*, LC7/6, PRO.

3. The *Alabama*, attacking a federal steamer on Sunday 19 June, 1864, was overcome and started to sink. A number of men and officers were picked up by the *Deerhound*, an English yacht in the vicinity, and brought to England.

4. 'This House requires a thorough cleansing and lime-whitening. The nuts and bolts of water tank to be examined, as they are considerably oxyolised'. Report on Annual Inspection, 1864, *LCP*, LC1/141, PRO.

5. The trouble began when a barge carrying explosives exploded in the vicinity

of the powder mills the previous day. Bricks and machinery were thrown a distance of a mile, shop windows broken, houses destroyed, people killed and a part of the Thames Embankment shattered. Damage was caused within a 15 mile radius and the shock caused by the explosion was felt up to 40 miles away.

1865

1.   The injury to Ellen Geary elicited close scrutiny from the Lord Chamberlain's office. There had been questions in Parliament two years previously when a ballet girl at the Princess's Theatre had been burnt to death after her costume had been ignited by sparks from the fire boxes used in the pantomime. In 1864 a Columbine had been burnt to death at the Pavilion Theatre, Whitechapel. On 20/2/1864 W.B.Donne published an article in the *Saturday Review*, entitled 'Columbines and Casualties', in which he argued for greater vigilance, stating that 'Annual victims are a high price to pay for the most sumptuous transformation scene or the most picturesque of ballets'. The Lord Chamberlain's office was concerned that adequate safety precautions were being taken in all theatres under its jurisdiction: it was looking for cases of negligence to bring a prosecution for manslaughter, as a means of more strictly enforcing tighter safety regulations. After visits to the theatre and to the accident victim, W.B.Donne and Spencer Ponsonby drew up an extremely detailed report in which they conceded that no positive blame could be attached to the management or to anyone on the stage, especially as the ballet girl had mounted the ladder without waiting for the usual assistance. They concluded: 'The accident might no doubt have been prevented – *firstly* – had there been at the time a Wire Guard in front of the Gas burners – *secondly* – if she had waited for the Painter – and – *thirdly* – if the muslins had been steeped in solution; but, *firstly*, Wire Guards on these particular lights are not usual at the Theatres, and at the last inspection of the theatre . . . directions were not given to cover these lights, the glass shades upon them being thought sufficient. *Secondly*, it does not appear to be usual to give definite instructions to the Ladies of the Ballet, the Person in charge of them being considered a sufficient safeguard and – *thirdly* – that incombustible solution has been recommended by the Lord Chamberlain, but not ordered – the opposition to it by the Ladies of the Ballet themselves appearing to be insurmountable'. *Report. LCP*, LC1/154, PRO.

2.   The Lord Chamberlain's office circularised all theatres with a letter reminding managers of the advantages that would result if the ladies of their establishments were to wear uninflammable dresses, concluding that:

> The Lord Chamberlain must also earnestly impress upon the Managers that immediate necessity of screening with wire guards every light within reach of any of the performers in any part of the Theatre; he would warn them most solemnly that they will be held responsible for any accidents which may occur from a neglect of this instruction.

Circular Letter, LCP, LC1/154, PRO.

The reply, ostensibly from Sam Lane, stated that the Lord Chamberlain's suggestions were already being carried out and that fire-guards were even being placed in the performers' dressing-rooms. He added that Sarah Lane had visited Miss Geary that morning and that she appeared to be much better. Letter, 13/1/1865, *LCP*, LC1/153, PRO.

3.   Buck was the clown at Sadler's Wells Theatre. On his return from the theatre

on 27/12/1864 he found his wife burnt to death, still seated in her chair by the fire. In early February, at Croueste's Circus, Crosshall Street, Liverpool, the audience on one side of the 3-sided gallery (mainly children and young people) pressed forward to see what was going on on the other side of the stage. The Boarding gave way and about 50 people were precipitated 14–16 feet to the ground. In early January 20 people were killed when a rush down the steps for admittance to Springthorpe's Concert Hall in Dundee occurred. At the Catholic School in Westminster a large assembly had gathered to witness the drawing of a lottery when the floor collapsed beneath them and about 30 people were injured.

4.   On 6/3/1865 Wilton had written to the Lord Chamberlain's office, in the absence of Samuel Lane, to say that Mrs Geary was out of danger and convalescent:

> She is now able to walk about the ward, and her husband informed me, on Saturday night last, that he hoped she would be able to leave the hospital in about a month. I am happy to add that he also said she would have the free use of all her limbs, and that her face would not be in any way scarred or disfigured. Letter, *LCP*, LC1/153, PRO.

5.   The offending paragraph, entitled *Miss St.Casse in a New Part*, claimed to be a report of proceedings at the Westminster County Court. The article referred to a Miss Julia St.Casse, married to a commercial traveller named Stonor Petheridge, who discovered his wife was committing adultery with their lodger, an equestrian artiste engaged at the Agricultural Hall.

6.   Reference is made to a solicitor's letter stating no such case has been heard at the Westminster Court and that the 'statements are grossly libellous'. *Reynolds's Weekly Newspaper* claims the report was received from a reporter of good standing and that since the complainant is a Mr Graham, there must be some error, as he is the husband of quite a different Miss St.Casse from the one alluded to in the article. An action was brought after Reynolds printed an apology in small type, amongst notices to correspondents, rather than among the Law and Police Reports where everyone would see it. The defendant, who had already admitted liability and paid £10, was ordered to pay the plaintiffs a further £50. *Era*, 13/8/1865.

7.   An English version of *La Dame aux Camelias* had been suppressed by the Lord Chamberlain in 1853, although when Verdi's *La Traviata* was licensed in 1856, no scandal had ensued. In the same year a dramatised version *La Traviata, or The Blighted One* was licensed for performance at the Surrey Theatre. Donne, who had not been involved in granting the 1856 licenses, remained adamant that the play should not be staged in any shape or form. He was probably prepared, however, to turn a blind eye to a single Britannia performance, as he had done with a revival at Sadler's Wells in 1860, in order to avoid making too public an issue of it. See Stephens, pp. 81–84.

8.   *The Times* refers to a Henry Fleetwood, 44, of 216 City Road, describing himself as a writer, assaulting his wife Ellen. Witnesses claimed that he came out of his house, with a table knife in his hand, just as she had her right leg over the railing, seized hold of her leg with both of his hands and flung her back, head foremost, into the garden she wished to come from. They also contradicted his claims that she was drunk when the incident occurred. Presumably Wilton is referring to C.H.Hazlewood, the Britannia dramatist, although there is no other evidence that he also went under the name of Fleetwood.

9. In 1865 W.B.Donne particularly concerned himself about the conditions in the dressing-rooms of the theatres visited. Of the Britannia Theatre he wrote:

All gas-piping or tin-piping to be removed from the Dressing-Rooms as they are very dangerous from their material and their place. It is again (a third time) to be lamented that this excellently constructed and planned theatre should be in so dirty a condition. The Dressing Rooms, staircases and passages leading to them urgently demand cleaning and more ventilation, as they are very discreditable to the management and are *pestilential*.

It is understood by the Inspector that Estimates are taken for cleansing before Christmas next – as little time as possible should be lost in doing this most necessary and long-deferred work'.

In a pencilled note Donne added 'Mr Lane out of town – Mr Wilton (stage manager) attended in his place – I told him that the dirty state of the theatre was becoming serious – and that the Lord Chamberlain would order another inspection shortly to report on this'. A subsequent memo for 14/10/1865 states that 'Mr Lane called and shewed Mr Ponsonby a contract he had entered into for £800 for renovating and cleansing the theatre'. *LCP*, LC1/153, PRO.

1866

1. The article, entitled 'Calamity-mongering', quoted the bill for the evening's performance at the Britannia, asking how 'any honest heart could let pass the exhibition of shipwrecked men'? It considered that the heroic actions reported during the disaster were 'degraded' and 'dimmed' by the present exhibition and suggested that pit, boxes and gallery would doubtless enjoy 'a procession of real widows, real orphans and real bereaved relatives'. 'The advertisement *The Wrecked Men of London* presented on a London playbill', offered 'a dismal rebuke to those who are over-apt to boast of England's progress'. The same article went on to attack the Marylebone Theatre for casting 'Old Daddy', a genuine inmate of the Lambeth workhouse, in *The Casual Ward*. Other journals, including *Punch*, considered these exhibitions tasteless and the *Dramatic Telegram* (26/2/1866) referred to advertisements 'with flaming pictures of a ship in distress at every corner of Hoxton'.

2. 'This theatre has been cleansed, whitened and painted since the Inspection of 1865. But in consequence of its never closing much in the way of effective cleanliness is still required. In the Pit it is very desirable that there should be at the back of the orchestra an iron or zinc channel with down-pipe in centre to carry off water and in cleansing Pit floor a hose might be daily applied to wash down the floor'. (A pencil note is here appended that Mr Lane promises to attend to this.) 'The dressing rooms are still as in '65 dirty and in much need of better ventilation. In one of them, the Gentleman's, this may be obtained with the greatest ease by apertures made into the outer walls at certain intervals: in the rest by removing a board over each door-way. Great relief in all would be gained by taking out a pane of glass and substituting for it a wire panel. The naked lights also under the stage should be supplied with discs and chains instead of the present iron plates affixed to the woodwork (always a dangerous practice). A bonnet is also recommended strongly for the Gas lights in each wing'. Report on Annual Inspection, 1866, *LCP*, LC1/167, PRO.

1867

1.   H.Chance Newton recounted this elopement in a poem *Comedy and Tragedy* printed in *The Penny Showman and Other Poems* (London, 1886), pp.9–13. Clara Milverton (Sophie Miles) is married happily to George McFarley (George Fisher), low comedian, until Tom Beaville (T.G.Drummond) joins the company to play the lead:

> A rather clever actor, but unpleasant in his air –
> An overbearing fellow, with a disdainful air,
> At Mac's missus only was he ever seen to smile
> And it seems he wheedled round her in a very little while.
> In brief, she bolted off with him . . . .

Later Milverton and Beaville are engaged at the Roman (the Grecian): George goes to see them, has a fight with Tom after a row over the custody of Clara's children and eventually goes mad and dies.

2.   'The Britannia Theatre . . . can boast of what no other theatre can, a self supporting fund for sickness and distress'. Clipping, dated 24/1/1864, Theatre Cuttings, British Library. Wilton was the Fund's president, John Parry its secretary. As well as relief to personnel absent through sickness or to relatives of deceased personnel, the Fund also provided loans to its members.

3.   The architect was Mr Fincham from the Board of Works. Donne's report confirms the items listed by Wilton; he also notes that the Dressing Rooms have greatly improved since the 1866 Inspection. Report on Annual Inspection, 1867, *LCP*, LC1/185, PRO.

4.   The review stated that 'As good a pantomime as one would desire to see was first brought out at 12 o'clock noon yesterday, and received a hearty welcome from the holiday folks who filled the spacious precincts of the Britannia'.

1868

1.   The Britannia Theatre was the first theatre to be used for Sunday services in London. On 1/12/1859 the Lord Chamberlain's office received a request on behalf of the committee promoting special Sunday services for the working classes by the ministers of the various denominations of non-conformists to use the Britannia for Sunday afternoon and evening services. Admission would be free and no collection taken. Samuel Lane was willing the building should be used, if sanctioned by the Lord Chamberlain. A memo of 6/12/1859 states that the Lord Chamberlain is 'not in a position, under the terms of his powers, to sanction or prohibit Sunday services at the Britannia'. *LCP*, LC1/70, PRO.

2.   *Oliver Twist* had been linked since the 1840s with the 'Newgate' plays such as *Jack Sheppard*, which, it was thought, were likely to incite juvenile audiences to crime. From 1848 the Lord Chamberlain had refused to license any versions of *Oliver Twist*. In 1868 W.H.Liston sought a license to present a new version of *Oliver Twist* at the Queen's Theatre and demanded official evidence of its earlier ban. This was not forthcoming; consequently, Lord Bradford, the Lord Chamberlain, decided that, in future, versions of *Oliver Twist* might be licensed, subject to excisions, over-ruling W.B.Donne's objections to its revival. See: Stephens, pp.66–73.

3.   Boucicault claimed that he had written for a certain management a play, as yet unproduced, the title of which had been leaked into the London newspapers:

> 'Hereupon, a penny-a-scener gets wind of the subject, writes a something, dubs it with the title of my drama, and I find it advertised for performance at one of the principal suburban theatres. However, being a methodical person, I had registered my work at Stationer's Hall, so I sent a copy of the certificate to the manager, who immediately consented to withdraw both title and piece, ensuring me he had been greatly imposed upon'.

William Travers, author of the play in question, responded, asserting that he was a dramatist of 15 years standing and that he had never directly or indirectly infringed on the rights of a brother author or passed off the property of others as his own. He had written the play the previous February and the title had been suggested to him by an illustration in the *Tomahawk* entitled 'London By Night'. He sold the play immediately to the manager of the Britannia: not employing anyone to provide him with 'tips', he had no idea what was going on behind the scenes in the Princess's. If he had realised that Boucicault intended using the same title, he would have chosen an alternative – as it was, the 'obnoxious title' would be suppressed, but the play would not be withdrawn. The *Sunday Times* (24/5/1868), which reported this altercation, criticised Boucicault for being too extreme, especially since he was no stranger to plagiarism himself, and felt that if titles were appropriated by the East End Theatres, the managers were more often to blame than the playwrights. Boucicault's play was eventually produced at the Princess's Theatre under the title of *After Dark*.

4.   The coded entries, which are indicated by a △, seem to refer to the amorous activities of certain members of the company whilst rehearsals are in progress. Wilton is so discreet, however, that it is impossible to identify the personnel involved. L.I.E, which seems to have been a popular canoodling spot, is almost certainly 'Left first entrance'. See May 11 and October 1.

5.   'Martin said that he found ** kissing behind L.I.E. and George B'd said that he is embarrassed to, again, find himself running into everybody cuddling each other'.

6.   Butler had been the Liberal M.P. for Hackney for the past 16 years. Holms, also a Liberal, who beat Butler, had stood for Hackney before he realised Butler also intended standing again. A 'plumper' is a vote given by an elector entitled to vote for 2 candidates when he chooses to vote for only 1. When he does so, his second vote is thrown away.

1869

1.   Lost manuscripts could create problems, since it was important to protect new and unpublished plays from piracy. In 1862 Samuel Lane offered a £10 reward for the recovery of Hazlewood's *Mary Edmonstone*, stolen from the Prompter's Desk at the Britannia on 22/12/1862. Lane's notice added that the sole dramatic rights of the piece were vested in Samuel Lane and that it could not be played elsewhere.

2.   The review was, in fact, largely favourable, even praising the plot's pathetic interest without recourse to striking and sensational effects. The only critical comment referred to the introduction of too many 'clap-trap expressions', which could have been excised without detracting from the play's merit.

3.   The report for 1869 stated: 'No notes taken or needed. The long dressing-room greatly improved by the openings and windows made for ventilation. As the theatre is kept open all the year its condition is very creditable to the management'. Report on Annual Inspection 1869, *LCP*, LC1/221, PRO.

1870

1.   The Royal Dramatic College was in need of funds to maintain regular pensions to its pensioners, and to meet other expenses. The committee decided on a series of morning performances and other special events to help out. Various managers agreed to provide their theatres free of charge for these performances. *Era*, 6/3/1870.

2.   James Anderson states that in March, 1870, Sam Lane made him a handsome offer to play five nights in 'Passion Week'. 'As the work was not very heavy, and the remuneration satisfactory, I accepted . . . . On Monday, April 11th, I drove down to Hoxton in my brougham to rehearsal, taking my dresses for the week along with me. Mr and Mrs Lane were always most kind and attentive . . . . Mr Lane requested I would open in *The Lady of Lyons* . . . . The house was crammed as usual. I had a magnificent reception, and the play went off as freshly and triumphantly as ever. I never played Melnotte better, being called out every act, and receiving a perfect ovation at the end. Miss M.Henderson (a young and clever actress) played Pauline – a little too melodramatic perhaps for the West End, but well suited to please her patrons in the East. Mr Reynolds made an admirable Colonel Damas.

'Afterwards I played *Hamlet*. The tragedy was rather roughly handled by the actors, who, being used to performing in melodramas nearly all the year round, were somewhat too loud and demonstrative for Shakespeare. I was obliged to be doubly calm and impressive the first night, in order to throw out hints to mes *conferes* that we were not playing *The Bloody Brother of Bethnal Green*. They caught the idea, became subdued in tone, yet earnest in manner, and the play then went satisfactorily'. Anderson, pp.301–302.

1871

1.   The Franco-Prussian War was in its final stages; Paris was besieged and was being bombarded by Prussian forces; sorties against the Prussians were proving ineffective.

2.   Anderson was in the habit of visiting the Pantomimes when he was out of an engagement. He considered that, in 1870, both the Britannia and the Standard had provided better pantomimes than Covent Garden or Drury Lane. Anderson, p.300.

3.   However, the *Sunday Times* (26/3/1871) claimed that Miss Bellair as Foole 'was made to give vent to her feelings in remarks on the topics of the day, and from the sentiments she uttered and their enthusiastic reception, little doubt was left on the visitors' minds as to the amount of favouritism with which the French people are regarded by the Hoxtonians'. The *Era* (26/3/1871) refers to the Franco-Prussian War and the hardships of railway officials as topics on which the fool discoursed.

4.   Robert Syers, Chairman of the Music Hall Defence Association, had been summonsed in April by the Theatre Managers' Association, for keeping a place of public resort for the performance of stage plays without having a license from the Lord Chamberlain to do so. On 23/4/1871 Syers wrote to the *Era* complaining that the situation was unsatisfactory. In order to *force* a settlement he intended to seek penalties for offences against the law from some members of the society which had prosecuted him, in the hope that the Lord Chamberlain would intervene or new legislation be introduced. He pointed out that the theatres had successfully petitioned for spirits licenses in 1859, which had injured the music hall proprietors and licensed victuallers.

5.   *Cast on the Mercy of the World* concluded with a scene in which the heroine, trapped and abandoned on an ice flow by the villain, is saved by a passing steam boat. Crauford, p.280, states that 'the sensation scene depicted the Arctic regions. In this scene, persons in the play are shown in great danger owing to the ice breaking up, and at the crucial moment a steamship appears from the extreme back of the stage; it carries a complete crew and, forcing its way through the melting ice, rescues those in peril, and turns broadside to the audience as the curtain falls – an effect only possible in a theatre like the Britannia'.

6.   'Weary of being idle, I accepted another engagement for twelve nights at the Britannia Theatre Hoxton, in the autumn. The labour in store was not oppressive, being plays from my old list, selected by the management who, from former experience, was the best judge of what was most likely to prove attractive. I always had wonderful patronage at the Britannia, but this engagement was something extraordinary. The Hoxton audiences are not very refined, I am free to admit, but they are the most generous and enthusiastic in the East and it is a great treat to have a turn with them now and then'. Anderson, pp.311–312.

1872

1.   The theatres were not licensed to present plays on Ash Wednesday. To evade this restriction many theatres presented an Ash Wednesday concert, although the legality of this operation was somewhat ambiguous. In consequence of the theatre managers' zealous prosecution of any music hall manager who infringed the conditions of his license, the music hall proprietors were retaliating by urging the Lord Chamberlain's office to prosecute theatre managers for equivalent infringements. This placed the Britannia Theatre in a particularly vulnerable situation at this point in time.

2.   Challis v. Lane. Samuel Lane's sister, according to a report of the eventual court case in the *Hackney Gazette*, had brought an action contesting his will. Crauford, p.308, states that the case was brought by a cousin.

3.   The letter in the *Daily Telegraph* begged the Lord Chamberlain's intercession before Wainratta, who used no safety nets beneath the wire which extended from an elevation in the centre of the stage to a post in the middle of the dress circle, tumbled, killing not only himself but also members of the audience. The writer complained that 'it is one of Wainwratta's peculiarities to go through his most sickening feats directly over the murderously spiked partition between the stalls and the pit . . . . He puts his legs and body through a hoop; he takes off both his shoes and puts them on again; hanging on, as it appears, by one toe, and balanced on one foot, he sets himself and the wire swinging with frightful rapidity . . . . Last

night, when I saw this man swaying about on one leg, and *pretending* to stumble
and lose his balance, when I saw the men underneath him turning white, the
women hiding their eyes and the innocently-crowing babies alone unconcerned –
I felt the preliminary fever of a panic had already set in . . .'.

W.Robinson immediately replied to the Lord Chamberlain's office, stating that the
danger had been greatly exaggerated by the writer in the *Daily Telegraph*, but that
henceforth a net would be extended beneath Wainwratta's wire. *LCP*, LC1/263,
PRO.

1873

1.   Samuel Lane had, by his will dated in May 1870, bequeathed the whole of his
estate to the value of about £60,000 to his wife, Sarah Lane. The will was opposed
by Lane's sister, who alleged that Sarah had exercised undue influence over her
husband, but the plea was not substantiated. The court was informed that the
deceased was, by trade, a carpenter. He went to sea in one of HM's ships and
finally settled down in London. By great perseverance and industry he acquired
some little money and eventually married Sarah Lane, whose abilities had materi-
ally aided him in acquiring his large fortune. The will was prepared at Dawlish,
Devonshire, which place Lane often visited, and a short time afterwards he wrote
to his wife a letter, stating what he had done and adding that he had 'left the whole
of his property to her'. Edward Green, who drew up the document, said Lane had
been fully competent to make the will. Sarah Lane stated that she had always lived
upon the most affectionate terms with her husband and denied exercising any
undue influence over him or instructing that his sister should be refused an
interview with him. See: *Hackney Gazette*, 14/3/1873.

2.   Arthur Orton, a butcher from Wapping, had claimed to be Sir Roger Tichborne Bart, heir to the Tichborne estates, who had supposedly been drowned en
route for Australia. He was appearing at several theatres, the object being to
support his appeal for funds with which to conduct his defence, now that he was
charged with perjury, as a result of his claim being dismissed. Later in the evening
the claimant and Mr Whalley appeared at the Surrey Theatre.

3.   A particular concern of Donne, during the 1873 inspection of all theatres, was
the water supply and pressure available. *LCP*, LC1/275, PRO.

4.   The pantomime marked a new departure; instead of a nursery rhyme deriva-
tion, it was a version of a French spectacle *Le Poule aux Oeufs d'or*, which Sarah
Lane had witnessed in Paris and arranged to transfer to Hoxton, in a translation
by Hazlewood. Many of the songs in the pantomime were taken from the popular
French comic opera, *La Fille de Madame Angot*.

1874

1.   The annual inspection for 1874 made the following points:

   1.   Discs and chains and wire guards are required to gas lights in side gallery.
   2.   The Barrier to the stalls should be hung to open outwards.
   3.   The Gas in the cellar should be looked to, and guards and discs put to all
        gas lights.
   4.   The Gas lights in the property room should have guards and discs and

chains, without these they are very dangerous.

A copy of the report was sent to the manager. The theatre was considered generally to be in good order, but the report regretted it was so ill provided with regard to the dressing rooms. Report on Annual Inspection, 1874, *LCP*, LC1/286, PRO.

2.   Rogers had modelled a scene for Sloman's theatre at Manchester. The proprietor of the Alhambra was desirous of having a similar scene at his theatre, but according to Rogers, Sloman had said 'It's no use giving Rogers a scene like that – Who is he? He is known nowhere and it could be more than he could undertake'. Rogers had also been blamed for an accident to some scenery. All imputations were withdrawn by Sloman and each party ordered to pay their own costs. *Era*, 8/11/1874.

3.   The pantomime's cast included the Lupinos and G.H.MacDermott, the latter arousing the ire of an anonymous curate who wrote to the Lord Chamberlain complaining that MacDermott, in the part of a King, 'speaks of "taking a carrott"; that he is not fond of his "greens"; and of "rooting" a girl'. Even more objectionable were the words and attendant actions used to a lady 'who is supposed to be changed into a peripatetic telegraph office with a clock-face in front of her person – the allusion to her "machine" and having "a go at her apparatus", being frequent, and of an unmistakeable character . . .'. Letter, dated 14/1/1875, *LCP*, LC1/297, PRO. No action appears to have been taken.

1875

1.   The French had been forced to surrender Alsace and Lorraine during the Franco-Prussian war in 1871. Even in 1875, when France still had reason to fear Germany's intentions under Bismark, the title and subject-matter of the play was deemed too sensitive by the Lord Chamberlain's office. Consequently, the play was retitled *Banished From Home* and set in Warsaw in 1795.

Appendix 1

Wilton's Benefit Expenses 1863

Received for Tickets, Benefit August 19th 1863

Fred (3 Private Box Tickets)	6.0
Watchman at Pit Door	1.6
George Taylor	3.0
Lizzie (servant)	1.0
Bar of Britannia (see below)*	15.0
Payne (Firework man)	4.0
Fred (25th Aug)	1.0
Bar of Britannia (see above)*	1.0
Fred (Sept 4th)	2.0
Mr George Ransom, publisher of *Penny Newspaper*, of firm Ransom & Warren	6.0
Harriet	1.0
	2.2.6

Expenses of Benefit

Busses over to Victoria Theatre to get permission of Frampton and Fenton to have their M.S.S. of *The Detective* copied	6
My one third part of M.S.S. of *Detective* 'Ticket of Leave'	3. 4
Glass of Ale to copyist	2
Aug 12th: Busses to get Woodcuts, *Reynolds's Miscellany* & Ransom & Warren, Bouverie Street	1. 4
Aug 17th: Busses to return woodcuts 4d, 3d, 3d	10
Two Box Tickets given to Mr Cuthbert (Miss Lacey's husband)	2. 0
Ditto given to Fred	2. 0
1 Pit Ditto to Lizzy, servant	6
Printing 7.7.0 / May 1.0.0 / Bill Posting 12.0 / Joining 2.0 / Copying 14.0 } My ⅓ of these	3. 5. 0
Another glass of Ale to copyist (Mr Young)	1½
	3.14.11½
Treating Carpenters, Prompter & Martin	2. 6
	3.17. 5½

Extra Bill Posting   10. 0

4. 7. 5½

It is difficult to calculate the exact profits made by Wilton at his benefits. The normal charge made for the theatre on a benefit night was £30; however, this was only one of a number of possible arrangements that could be made with the management. Wilton often seems to take 25% of the cash receipts plus ticket receipts, regardless of the £30 levy. Publicity was his own responsibility; sometimes he shared the cost with the management, sometimes he seems to have shouldered it himself. The details he records vary from year to year. For instance, in 1873 he took home 6.7.11 in cash plus 1.11.0 in ticket sales. The benefit had made 31.0.3 in cash altogether and Wilton's share of expenses had been 3.1.6. The plays performed were *Death of Nelson* and *All But One*. In 1875 his benefit programme (*Dolores* and *Belinda Seagrave*) drew 45.8.0 cash and 2.5.6 in tickets. Wilton records 4.5.8½ as his share of the expenses, but does not state the amount he took home.

Appendix 2

Memoranda of Britannia Theatre

These entries, which commence in 1872 and occur as either appendices or weekly records of payments, are largely concerned with expenditure.

1872

Salary of G. Grimani, Assistant Artist, p.week		2.0.0
February 17th	Patti Goddard (*Serio-Comic Vocalist, replacing Mrs S.Lane in pantomime*)	3.10.0
	Louie Austin (*Comic Vocalist*)	3.10.0
	Ellena Spinola (*Principal Danseuse*)	4.0.0
	Kate Vaughan (*2nd Danseuse*)	3.10.0
February 24th	Rizarelis (*2 Spanish bros*) (*Flying Trapeze Act*)	22.10.0
March 16th	Ryley & Marie Barnum (*Comic Vocalists*)	6.0.0
	Beatrice Bermond	4.0.0
	Kate Garstone (*Serio-Comic Vocalist*)	4.0.0
	Leggett & Allen (*Comic Duettists*)	4.0.0
	Joe Brown (*Minstrel*)	4.0.0
23rd March	Mr & Mrs G.Harris (*Table Entertainment*)	6.0.0
30th March	Laura Fay (*Vocalist & Danseuse*)	4.0.0
	Edward Glover (*Comic Vocalist 'a mere boy'*)	2.1.8
	Harvey & Connolly	4.3.4
	Charles Lingwood (*'Celebrated mezzo-soprano vocalist'*)	2.18.4
	Brown and Newland *'the best and funniest niggers ever engaged at the Britannia'* (FCW 25/3/1872)	3.6.8
(*Salaries paid for 5 nights on account of Good Friday*)		
18th May	Miss L. MacDonald's salary (per week)	4.0.0
	Salaries of Ballet at Standard Theatre, p.week and 1/0 for each Morning Performance. All dresses & properties & washing also found them. Cotton tights left off on Saturday nights, brought clean on Monday morning for the girls.	7.0
June 8th	Praeger Family (*German Singers*)	20.0.0
June 22nd	Alf Vivian (*Vocalist*)	3.10.0
	Annie Anderson (*Comic Vocalist*)	3.10.0

	Ada Arnold (*Dancer*)	4.0.0
	M. Jullien & Mdlle. B.Delgrange (*French Opera Artists*) (*10/0 deducted on account of illness*)	4.10.0
July 6th	Florie Seaman (*Vocalist & Dancer*)	3.0.0
	Lizzie Herbert (*Serio-Comic Vocalist*) (*Her salary being 3.10.0 per week – deducting one night's absence, &* $\frac{1}{8}$ *Bar-Score for treating musicians*)	2.16.0
	Mrs J.F.Bryan (*Serio-Comic Vocalist*)	4.0.0
	W.West (*Stump Orator*) & Emma West	3.3.0
July 20th	J.Rowley (*Comic singer*)	4.0.0
	Nelly Maude (*Vocalist & slab skater*)	2.0.0
	J.Plumpton (*Vocalist*) (*This sum disputed; – said his salary was £3.0.0 p.week last time he was there.*)	2.10.0
August 3rd	Messrs Sidney & Jelline (*Double Globe Performers*)	4.0.0
	Mdlle. Riviere & her Ballet	12.0.0
August 17th	M.Garton (*Concertina Player 'very clever'*)	3.10.0
	Milly Howard (*Serio-Comic Vocalist – 'very dear at the price'*)	4.0.0
August 24th	Jolly Little Lewis (*Comic Vocalist*)	3.0.0
September 7th	Sailor Williams (*Vocalist*) '*deducting 10/0 he owed Mr Crauford*'	1.10.0
	Harman & Elston ('*niggers very good*')	3.10.0
	Fred Coyne (*Comic Vocalist*)	4.0.0
September 14th	Wainratta (*King of the Wire*)	6.0.0
	Mrs Ormond Collis (*Comic Vocalist*)	3.10.0
September 21st	Walter Laburnum (*Comic Vocalist*)	3.0.0
Dec	Told by Miss K.Percy (utility actress) her salary was	1.5.0

1873

March 17th	*Soldiers* for Easter Piece. All staff of the Royal London Regiment of Militia (Colonel Sir William Anderson Rose).			
	2 Sergeants, per week (one at £1, one at 15/0)	1	15	0
	2 Buglers (or *Drummers*) 10/0 each	1	0	0
	24 soldiers (8/0 p.week each)	9	12	0
	Total £	12	7	0
	Less Absentees at 1/4 each.			
May 26th	Geretti, Slack Rope Dancer, salary per week	6	0	0
	The Claimant to the Tichborne Estates, p.night	15	0	0
	Salary of Pryce, Master Carpenter	2	3	6
	Salary of another Master Carpenter to whom Mr Robinson has written.	2	5	0

July 16th	Miss L.Rayner's salary	1	1	0
August 8th	Salary of Choristers of H.M. Italian Opera (to find their own pianist) per week	12	0	0
	Salary of Levantine on his magic Barrel (i.e. Tub) p.week	6	0	0
	Salary of Nelly Moon (Concert Room Singer) p.week – Claimed £5 on Saturday but was shown agent's letter of engagement –	4	0	0
August 18th	W.H.Pitt's salary	2	10	0
September 27th	Salary of Property Man (Johnson)	1	11	6
	– & of Assistant (J.Short)		9	0
September 10th	Mr Robinson told me that Miss Louie Sherrington's salary was per week	5	0	0
November 15th	Receipts of House with *Guy Fawkes & Fireworks*	112	0	0
November	Forde, Artist, engaged to paint comic scenes, discharged for want of talent (utter incapacity) – Told by Mr Robinson his salary was to have been p.week	1	15	0

1874

March 5th	Salary of Algar's 'Grand Muscovian Ballet Troupe' p.week	14	0	0
March 7th	Salary of Manning (Dayman and Scene Shifter) p.week	1	6	6
	Supers per week, each =		9	0
October 10th	Salary of the 2 Mdlles Alberti (*Vocalists & Dancers*)	4	0	0

1875

Salary of the *Lupino* Family, Pantomimists in the Pantomime of the *Black Statue*, 1874–75 per week (including comic Policemen)	22	0	0
Salary of Macdermott (in *Black Statue*) per week	16	0	0
Salary of Miss Claremont (Mrs S.Lane's 'dresser' p.week)		5	0
Price paid for new Piece called *Alsace & Lorraine* (poor stuff)	5	0	0
Price of materials for State Bed in *Margot* besides salary of the Property Maker (Glenny) 'O, trumpery! O, Moses!'	9	0	0
Price of M.S.S. of *Bras de Fer*, including copy & Licensing, (& excluding 'Getting up'.)	50	15	0
Price of lithographs (coloured) for *Margot*	22	0	0
License of Drama called *Bras de Fer*	1	1	0
License of Drama called *Banished from Home*	2	2	0

Appendix 3

Performances of Shakespeare at The Britannia
1872–1875

12/6/72   *Othello* (F.Charlton's Bft; Othello, J.Reynolds; Iago, F.Charlton)

26/6/72   *Julius Caesar* (J.Reynolds' Bft; Brutus, T.Mead; Mark Antony, Alfred Rayner)

17/7/72   *Richard III* (W.H.Pitt's Bft; RIII, J.B.Howe)
            Othello (2nd Act – R.Bell)

31/7/72   *Hamlet* (3rd Act – Hamlet, Edwin Reynolds – Teacher of Elocution)

18/9/72   *Othello*

7/3/73   *Richard III*

10/3/73   *Othello* (J.B.Howe)

14/3/73   *Macbeth* (J.B.Howe)

13/8/73   *Hamlet* (omitting 2nd Act – Miss M.Bellair's Bft; Hamlet, Miss M.Bellair)

10/9/73   *Merchant of Venice* (T.Grahame's Bft; Shylock, T.Grahame)

25/2/74   *Merchant of Venice* (J.Huline's Bft; Trial Scene only)

17/3/74   *Richard III* (W.Forrester's Bft – with 5 Richards – Reynolds, Charlton, Bigwood, Bell & Forrester)

10/6/74   *Macbeth* (R.Bell's Bft; Macbeth, R.Bell)

17/6/74   *Othello* (F.Charlton's Bft)

24/6/74   *Romeo and Juliet* (Miss M.Bellair's Bft)

8/7/74   *Winter's Tale* (J.Parry's Bft)

16/6/75   *Hamlet* (F.Charlton's Bft; Hamlet, F.Charlton)

14/7/75   *Macbeth* (J.Reynolds' Bft)

Britannia Theatre Managerial Family Tree

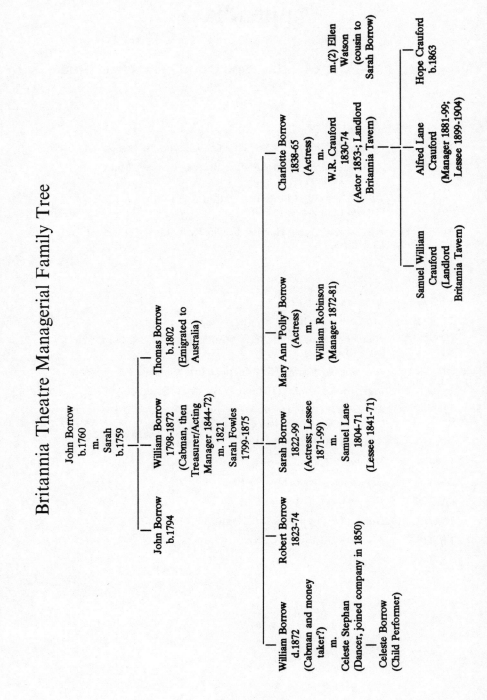

Select Bibliography

Anderson, James, *An Actor's Life*. London 1902.

Baker, H.Barton, *A History of the London Stage*. London 1904.

Barker, Clive, "The Audiences of the Britannia Theatre, Hoxton", *Theatre Quarterly*, 1979, IX, 34.

——"The Chartists, Theatre Reform and Research", *Theatre Quarterly*, 1971, I, 4.

——"A Theatre for the People", *Nineteenth Century British Theatre* ed., Kenneth Richards & Peter Thomson. London 1971.

Cave, J.A., *A Jubilee of Dramatic Life*. London, 1894.

Crauford, A.L., *Sam and Sallie*. London 1933.

Dickens, Charles, "The Amusements of the People", *Household Words*, 13 April, 1860.

——"Two Views of a Cheap Theatre", *All the Year Round*, 25 February, 1860.

East, John.M., *'Neath the Mask*. London 1967.

Erle, Thomas W., *Letters from a Theatrical Scene Painter*. London 1880.

Hanley, P., *Random Recollections of the Stage by an Old Playgoer*. London 1883.

Hibbert, H.G., *Fifty Years of a Londoner's Life*. London 1916.

Hollingshead, John, *My Lifetime*. London 1895.

——"Rule Britannia", *Entr'acte Annual*, 1885.

Howard, Diana, *London Theatres and Music Halls*. London 1970.

Howe, J.B., *A Cosmopolitan Actor*. London 1888.

Newton, H.Chance, *Cues and Curtain Calls*. London 1927.

——*Idols of the Halls*. London 1928.

——"Tales of the Old Brit", *Referee*, 27 January & 3 February, 1924.

Shaw, George Bernard, *Our Theatre in the Nineties*. 3 vols. London 1932.

Stephens, John Russell, *The Censorship of English Drama 1828–1901*. Cambridge 1980.

Trewin, Wendy, *The Royal General Theatrical Fund: A History 1838–1988*. STR 1989.

Wilson, A.E., *East End Entertainment*. London 1954.

Periodicals & Newspapers
Builder
Building News
Entr'acte
Era
Hackney Gazette
Illustrated Sporting and Dramatic News

The Players
Shoreditch Advertiser
Shoreditch Observer
Sunday Times
Weekly Dispatch

SPECIAL COLLECTIONS
BRITISH LIBRARY
Britannia & Provincial Playbills
Day Books indexing the Lord Chamberlain's Plays (1824–1903), 7 vols, Add. MSS. 53, 702–8.
Plays submitted to the Lord Chamberlain (1824–51), Add. MSS. 42, 984–7.

GREATER LONDON RECORD OFFICE
Middlesex Licensed Victuallers' Records (Music and Dancing Licenses)
Minutes of the Theatres and Music Halls Committee of the London County Council

GUILDHALL LIBRARY
Britannia Playbills

HACKNEY ARCHIVES, ROSE LIPMAN LIBRARY
Britannia Theatre Cuttings
Britannia Playbills

PUBLIC RECORD OFFICE
Lord Chamberlain's Papers – LC1/58–298
                              LC7/5–7

STATE LIBRARY OF NEW SOUTH WALES
(MITCHELL LIBRARY)
Diaries of F.C. Wilton, MS, 1181

THEATRE MUSEUM
Britannia Theatre Cuttings
Britannia Playbills

UNIVERSITY OF KENT AT CANTERBURY LIBRARY
The Frank Pettingell Collection of Plays

––––––––––

For further information on the Britannia Theatre consult P.P.Higley, *A Study of Some Social, Literary and Dramatic Aspects of the Victorian Popular Theatre as Illustrated by the Britannia Theatre, Hoxton, 1843–1870*. University of London, 1974–1975, unpublished doctoral thesis. Although Higley ignores the mass of primary material in the Public Record Office and sometimes relies too heavily on secondary sources, he provides a useful survey of the Britannia during his chosen period, with a detailed discussion of some of the plays performed there.

Apart from the playbill collections and periodicals cited above, the following books have been particularly useful in the identification of actors and of the "extra" music-hall type artistes who appeared at the Britannia:

Roy Busby, *British Music Hall: an illustrated Who's Who from 1850 to the present day*, 1976.
Sidney W.Clarke, *The Annals of Conjuring*, 1924 reprinted 1983. New York.
Frances Fleetwood, *Conquest: The Story of a Theatre Family*, 1953.
Thomas Frost, *Circus Life and Circus Celebrities*, 1875.
Peter Honri, *John Wilton's Music Hall: the handsomest room in town*, 1985. (This work covers the years 1854–1880 in considerable detail and records the appearances of many performers who also played at the Britannia.)
Malcolm Morley, *The Old Marylebone Theatre*, 1960.
——*The Royal West London Theatre*, 1962.
C.E.Pascoe, *The Dramatic List*, 1880.
Christopher Pulling, *They were Singing*, 1952.
Clement Scott, *The Drama of Yesterday and Today*, 1899.
Harold Scott, *The Early Doors*, 1946.
Emily Soldene, *My Theatrical and Musical Recollections*, 1897.
George Speaight, *A History of the Circus*, 1980.
C.D.Stuart & A.J.Park, *The Variety Stage*, 1895.
Valentine Vox, *I Can See your Lips Moving: the history and art of ventriloquism*, 1981.

General Index

Name Index

Play Index

Details of the plays listed below are taken from Wilton's *Diaries*; Allardyce Nicoll, *A History of English Drama 1600–1900* (Cambridge, 1955–59), Vols IV–VI; Harvester Microform, *The Popular Stage: Drama in Nineteenth Century England: The Frank Pettingell Collection of Plays in the Library of the University of Kent at Canterbury — An Inventory to Series One: Manuscript and Typescript Plays* (1987), 5 Parts; Britannia Playbills in the Hackney Archives and Theatre Museum Collections. It is often impossible to ascertain authorship with any certainty, as titles were duplicated from theatre to theatre and some plays (often pirated) might go under several different titles. In cases of doubt no authorship has been credited.